ENMITY AND FEUDING IN CLASSICAL ATHENS

ASHLEY AND PETER LARKIN SERIES IN
GREEK AND ROMAN CULTURE

ENMITY AND FEUDING IN CLASSICAL ATHENS

Andrew T. Alwine

 UNIVERSITY OF TEXAS PRESS, AUSTIN

Copyright © 2015 by the University of Texas Press
All rights reserved

First edition, 2015
First paperback edition, 2016

Requests for permission to reproduce material from this work should be sent to:
 Permissions
 University of Texas Press
 P.O. Box 7819
 Austin, TX 78713-7819
 http://utpress.utexas.edu/index.php/rp-form

♾ The paper used in this book meets the minimum requirements of ANSI/NISO Z39.48-1992 (R1997) (Permanence of Paper).

LIBRARY OF CONGRESS CATALOGING-IN-PUBLICATION DATA

Alwine, Andrew T., author.
 Enmity and feuding in Classical Athens / Andrew T. Alwine. — First edition.
  pages   cm — (Ashley and Peter Larkin Series in Greek and Roman culture)
 Includes bibliographical references and index.
 ISBN 978-1-4773-0248-4 (cloth : alk. paper) —
ISBN 978-1-4773-0802-8 (library e-book) —
ISBN 978-1-4773-0803-5 (non-library e-book)
 1. Hostility (Psychology)—Greece—Athens. 2. Vendetta—Greece—Athens.
3. Law, Greek. 4. Athens (Greece)—History.
5. Athens (Greece)—Social life and customs.
I. Title. II. Series: Ashley and Peter Larkin series in Greek and Roman culture.
 DF289.A46 2015
 938′.504—dc23
                    2015006777

doi:10.7560/302484
ISBN 978-1-4773-1216-2 (paperback)

Uxori dilectae et avae requisitae

CONTENTS

List of Abbreviations for Primary Sources ix

List of Abbreviations for Journals xiii

Acknowledgments xv

Introduction *1*

CHAPTER 1   The Social Dimensions of Enmity   *23*

CHAPTER 2   The Rhetoric of Enmity as a Legal Strategy   *55*

CHAPTER 3   The Flexibility of the Rhetoric of Enmity   *94*

CHAPTER 4   Enmity under the Law: The Limits to Vengeance   *117*

CONCLUSION   Personal Enmity and Public Policy   *153*

Notes 161

Works Cited 217

Index 231

Index Locorum 239

ABBREVIATIONS FOR PRIMARY SOURCES

The following abbreviations for ancient authors and works are used in this book:

Aesch.	Aeschylus
Supp.	*Suppliants*
Aeschin.	Aeschines
[Andoc.]	Pseudo-Andocides
Antiph.	Antiphon
Ar.	Aristophanes
Eccl.	*Ecclesiazusae* (*Women of the Assembly*)
Eq.	*Equites* (*Knights*)
Nub.	*Nubes* (*Clouds*)
Vesp.	*Vespae* (*Wasps*)
Arist.	Aristotle
Ath. Pol.	*Athenaiōn Politeia* (*Athenian Constitution*)
Eth. Nic.	*Ethica Nicomachea* (*Nicomachean Ethics*)
Pol.	*Politics*
Rh.	*Rhetoric*
[Arist.]	Pseudo-Aristotle (Anaximenes)
Rh. Al.	*Rhetoric to Alexander*
Audollent *Def. tab.*	A. Audollent, *Defixionum Tabellae*
Cic.	Cicero
Red. Pop.	*Post Reditum ad Populum* (*To the Citizens after His Return*)
Dem.	Demosthenes
[Dem.]	Pseudo-Demosthenes (Apollodorus)
Din.	Dinarchus
Dion. Hal.	Dionysius of Halicarnassus
Dem.	*De Demosthene* (*On Demosthenes*)
Lys.	*De Lysia* (*On Lysias*)

Eur.	Euripides
Bacch.	*Bacchae*
El.	*Electra*
Heracl.	*Heraclidae* (*Children of Heracles*)
HF	*Heracles Furens* (*Raging Heracles*)
Med.	*Medea*
Or.	*Orestes*
Supp.	*Suppliants*
Hdt.	Herodotus
Hes.	Hesiod
Hom.	Homer
Il.	*Iliad*
Od.	*Odyssey*
Hyp.	Hyperides
IG	*Inscriptiones Graecae*
Isae.	Isaeus
Isocr.	Isocrates
LSJ	*Greek-English Lexicon* (Henry George Liddell and Robert Scott; revised by Henry Stuart Jones)
Lycurg.	Lycurgus
Lys.	Lysias
Men.	Menander
Dys.	*Dyscolus*
Epitrep.	*Epitrepontes* (*Arbitrants*)
Peric.	*Perikeiromenē* (*The Girl with Her Hair Cut Short*)
Sam.	*Samia*
P. Oxy.	*Oxyrhynchus Papyri*
PCG	*Poetae Comici Graeci* (Rudolf Kassel and Colin Austin)
Pind.	Pindar
Pyth.	*Pythian Odes*
Pl.	Plato
Ap.	*Apology*
Chrm.	*Charmides*
Grg.	*Gorgias*
La.	*Laches*
Leg.	*Laws*
Ly.	*Lysis*
Men.	*Meno*
Phdr.	*Phaedrus*

Phlb.	*Philebus*
Resp.	*Republic*
Plut.	Plutarch
Alc.	*Life of Alcibiades*
Arist.	*Life of Aristides*
Nic.	*Life of Nicias*
Per.	*Life of Pericles*
Quint.	Quintilian
Inst.	*Institutio Oratoria*
SEG	*Supplementum Epigraphicum Graecum*
Soph.	Sophocles
Aj.	*Ajax*
Ant.	*Antigone*
El.	*Electra*
OR	*Oedipus Rex*
Theophr.	Theophrastus
Char.	*Characters*
Thuc.	Thucydides
TrGF	*Tragicorum Graecorum Fragmenta* (Bruno Snell, Richard Kannicht, and Stefan Radt)
	Vergil
Aen.	*Aeneid*
Wünsch *Def. tab.*	R. Wünsch, *Defixionum Tabellae* (= *IG* 3/3)
Xen.	Xenophon
Hell.	*Hellenika*
Hier.	*Hieron*
Lac.	*Respublica Lacedaemoniorum* (*Constitution of the Spartans*)
Mem.	*Memorabilia*
Oec.	*Oeconomicus*
[Xen.]	Pseudo-Xenophon ("The Old Oligarch")
Ath. Pol.	*Athenaiōn Politeia* (*Constitution of the Athenians*)

The works of the Attic orators (Aeschines, Andocides, Antiphon, Demosthenes, Dinarchus, Hyperides, Isaeus, Isocrates, Lycurgus, and Lysias) are cited according to the standard convention, whereby the first numeral indicates the speech number, and the second indicates the section number. For example, Dem. 18.121 refers to the Demosthenes, Speech 18 (*On the Crown*), Section (§) 121.

Unless otherwise noted, translations are by the author.

ABBREVIATIONS FOR JOURNALS

The following abbreviations for academic journals are used in the bibliography:

AHR	*American Historical Review*
AJAH	*American Journal of Ancient History*
AJP	*American Journal of Philology*
AncSoc	*Ancient Society*
BICS	*Bulletin of the Institute of Classical Studies*
C&M	*Classica et Mediaevalia*
CJ	*Classical Journal*
ClAnt	*Classical Antiquity*
CP	*Classical Philology*
CQ	*Classical Quarterly*
CR	*Classical Review*
CW	*Classical World*
EMC	*Échos du Monde Classique* (now = *Mouseion*)
G&R	*Greece and Rome*
GRBS	*Greek, Roman and Byzantine Studies*
HSCP	*Harvard Studies in Classical Philology*
ICS	*Illinois Classical Studies*
JHS	*Journal of Hellenic Studies*
PCPS	*Proceedings of the Cambridge Philological Society* (now = *Cambridge Classical Journal*)
Ph&Rh	*Philosophy and Rhetoric*
TAPA	*Transactions of the American Philological Association*
ZPE	*Zeitschrift für Papyrologie und Epigraphik*

ACKNOWLEDGMENTS

I would have wished that the honor due to many people for their good deeds were not to be jeopardized by a single individual who attempts to show his gratitude. Those acquainted with the long story of this book project know well that my debts cannot be repaid with mere words. Nevertheless, I offer here my heartfelt thanks to all who aided me along the way.

The genesis of this project was my work on a doctoral dissertation at the University of Florida, which I completed in 2010 under the direction of Andrew Wolpert. I was unaccountably fortunate in having Professor Wolpert and Konstantinos Kapparis, both distinguished scholars in Greek history, on my committee. Their guidance and leadership on this project were critical, and their good scholarship and sound approaches to research and writing were inspiring to me in this formative part of my career. I would also like to express my gratitude to Andrea Sterk and Robert Wagman for serving on my committee and helping me to advance and improve my work.

A two-year fellowship at Wake Forest University that carried with it a reduced teaching load was instrumental in taking the project to the next stage: expanding the scope of the study, deepening the research in both primary and secondary sources, and honing the rigor of the argumentation. I had the advantage of the support of excellent colleagues and the use of a fine library during this period. After the temporary position at Wake Forest, I completed this project at the College of Charleston. I must offer special thanks to the chair of my department, Timothy Johnson, who has proven a better mentor and friend than any junior faculty could hope for.

The debts I owe to those who read and provided feedback on my work are great in both number and weight. In chronological order, I begin by thanking two of my fellow graduate students at the University of Florida, Todd Bohlander and David Hoot, who read various parts of my doctoral work. I am also grateful to Edwin Carawan, who read a full draft of the manuscript at an early stage and provided important feedback that eventually led me to restructure and recast various arguments, with the result that the book was much improved. Similar thanks go to Jim Powell and Phyllis Jestice, who read the entire manuscript during the publication process and provided invaluable criticism and advice. I am also grateful to all those who offered me help and advice during the long process of publication and read parts of the manuscript in various stages of completion, including Andrew Wolpert, Robert Ulery, Mary Pendergraft, Timothy Johnson, Noelle Zeiner-Carmichael, and Jessica Rabun. Finally, I must comment on my happy luck in the peer-review process at the University of Texas. Jim Burr, the editor at the University of Texas Press with whom I corresponded, was a model of helpfulness and efficiency. The comments offered by David Mirhady and the other anonymous reader for the press pressed me on to making significant improvements in the shape of the book. This work is much better for their constructive criticism. I have been truly fortunate in receiving such excellent feedback at many different stages in the project.

I save the best for last. Any "thank you" I would offer my family would be not only pitifully inadequate but perfectly risible. My loving and most diligent wife, Megan, and my strong and supportive parents, Margaret and David, deserve more credit than I do for anything good that has come out of this project. Finally, I must mention the patient love shown to me by my children, Elizabeth, Charlotte, Mary Catherine, and Eleanor, who spent several years of their lives employing drafts of my manuscript for arguably the best purpose for which it was suited—as scratch paper.

ENMITY AND FEUDING IN CLASSICAL ATHENS

INTRODUCTION

It is unlikely that jurors in a modern court would hear a plaintiff introduce a case by airing his personal grievances against the defendant saying, "With your help I will try to retaliate against him both now and for the future."[1] It is equally unlikely that a plaintiff would say, "Everybody was coming to me in private and urging me to try to get back at him for what he had done to us. They were scolding me, saying I was no man if I didn't get justice for people who were so close to me."[2] Statements of this sort would probably not go over well. For the ancient Athenians, however, such a declaration of one's desire for vengeance was a conventional way to open a lawsuit,[3] and discussion of a longstanding enmity between the litigants was commonplace. Any reader of the Attic orators will be struck by the overtones of anger, hatred, and fear of humiliation. Lawsuits were high-stakes, personal affairs that encouraged the enthusiastic venting of all sorts of negative feelings and emotions.

Not only the Attic orators but all of Athenian literature is peppered with references to, discussions of, and arguments about enmity. The men (and probably women) of ancient Greece evidently spent a great deal of time thinking and talking about this subject, and so it is *a priori* plausible that they were much concerned with the dynamics of hostile relationships. A close scrutiny of the sources demonstrates that this was in fact the case. Everyone needed to know how enmity was contracted, pursued, aggravated, or avoided and to adjust his or her behavior toward others accordingly. Enmity could be ignored only at one's peril. For this reason, any historical model of Athenian society, legal practice, or politics that omits consideration of this fundamental fact of Greek political and social life will miss the full picture. The study of enmity is an important step toward understanding the Greeks.

The discussions of enmity in the ancient texts, especially those of oratory, provoke a series of questions. What exactly was enmity in the Athenian context, and how did it work? Why did the orators feel so comfortable talking about their hostile relationships? What was at stake when they deployed the rhetoric of enmity against their opponents? Did the Athenians recognize enmity as a problem, and, if so, what were they prepared to do about it? Broadly speaking, these questions may be differentiated into two separate though related lines of inquiry: (1) the question of how enmity fit within the broad context of Athenian politics and society and (2) the question of how enmity was used as a rhetorical strategy in the extant law court speeches. These two questions must be recognized as separate but at the same time must be considered together as they have implications one for the other.

The legal speeches composed by the Attic orators are our best sources for enmity in Athens, but using them to make historical claims about Athenian society and values is a tricky business. This problem must be encountered head-on by an analysis of the rhetorical function of enmity in the Attic orators. All the same, a basic understanding of the nature of enmity in Greek culture is necessary for analyzing the deployment of rhetorical strategies that rely on the audience's familiarity with the social dimensions of enmity. Accordingly, chapter 1 lays the basic groundwork for the study by providing a model for how enmity worked. After this, chapters 2 and 3 analyze the rhetorical use of enmity in the Attic orators. Finally, chapter 4 will advance broader arguments about how Athenian political, legal, and social practice put limits on enmity in the interests of the stability of the democratic regime.

A MODEL FOR ENMITY IN ATHENS

The citizens of the city-state of Athens accepted as fact that many people had enemies; this was an integral part of everyday life. They also believed that harming one's enemy was an acceptable practice and even the duty of every honorable citizen. Enmity was therefore more than mere emotional dislike of another person; it was a relationship that entailed responsibilities of those involved, including the expectation that enemies would engage in a cycle of repeated attacks and retaliations. Such acts of harm were the necessary building blocks of a relationship of enmity. Athens was full of competitive, honor-driven citizens who were seeking opportunities to score public victories against their rivals and were concomitantly on their guard against being shamed themselves. Enmity was a critical element in the power dynamics of these competitions for standing in the eyes of the community.

Obsession with the recognition of one's personal merit and insistence on respect and deference from others are familiar attributes of Homeric warriors and have sometimes been relegated to the preclassical past, but there is little reason to believe that this mentality met with significant challenge in classical Athens. The basic logic of the societal honor game between "agonistic" competitors remained more or less the same. Achilles' macho responses to threats to his honor are not qualitatively different from those of the fourth-century Athenian Conon, who, according to his opponent, humiliated his enemy by beating him senseless and then standing over him, flapping his arms like wings while imitating the crow of a victorious cock.[4] Conon's actions were over the top, but nevertheless the underlying system of values—defeating enemies, winning honor, shaming opponents—was still operating along roughly the same lines as it did in Homeric society. The pursuit of enemies even crossed over into the legal sphere, which is why many prosecutors open their speeches with bald declarations of aggression. Anything as public and antagonistic as a lawsuit was bound to have a profound impact on the negotiation of status and standing that was such a hallmark of social life.

Classical Athenian democracy led not to a radical questioning of the premises of such honor games but rather to a pragmatic concern with their implications. Enmity threatened the internal stability and harmony of the citizen body, and that threat could not be ignored. For example, several litigants point out that private animosities incited feuding citizens to ignore justice in single-minded pursuit of their enemies. Such overly aggressive law-court bullies pose a potential threat to modest citizens who are less experienced in court and have less rhetorical training and are thus less able to defend themselves. On the other hand, the honor games were there to stay; the entire system by which Greek men evaluated themselves was not likely to evaporate in a few generations. The resulting tension between the interests of democratic stability and the drives of the feuding ethos is an undercurrent in many episodes of Athenian history. The Athenians never attempted to stifle enmity outright, nor did they approve of it without qualification.[5] Enmity had to be channeled, not forbidden.

Given the limited nature of our sources, no comprehensive treatment of the various ways in which these opposing forces collided is possible. Consequently, a study of enmity in democratic Athens must focus on hotspots, the areas in which the competing values were most clearly at odds. Three such hotspots will form a major theme of the present work. The first was the potentially devastating impact of private enmities on public policy and everyday governance. If office holders were permitted to abuse their positions to pursue their own personal feuds, chaos could result. The Athenians' radically participatory system was designed to minimize the problematic role of personal relationships. Strict term limits and large administrative and deliberative bodies diffused the effect of personal likes and dislikes through the incredible number of citizens involved in the process.

The second was the intersection between enmity and the legal sphere of the courts. Although Athenian jurors were tasked with identifying whether a real breach of law had occurred and then voting based on justice and "without favor or enmity,"[6] litigants actively employed lawsuits in the service of their feuds to win honor for themselves and humiliate their enemies. Following the old feuding ethic, they cared more about defeating their opponents than they did about the broader issues at stake. The ideals of justice and fairness that the jurors were supposed to be upholding undoubtedly influenced litigants' strategies, but prosecutor and defendant were most concerned with winning.

The third hotspot was the public regulation of violence between citizens. The state had an obvious interest in preventing escalation of feuds that might lead to the murder of citizens or even to civil war (*stasis*). On the other hand, there was no logical endpoint to enmity other than complete defeat of one's opponent. As the Homeric proverb had it, "Foolish is the man who kills the father and spares the son."[7] Strong restrictions on homicide were already in place in Athens, and the absence of a special legal category that stipulated less severe penalties for declared enemies distinguishes Athens from other societies such as thirteenth-century France.[8] Yet, stronger regulations than homicide laws were needed to protect a poor Athenian from coercion by wealthy elites or gangs of thugs.

This study proposes that in these hotspots, when the conflict between enmity and the interests of the Athenian *polis* became clear, it was enmity that was forced to give way. While Athenians allowed their fellow citizens to engage in feuds and to pursue their personal enemies, they established parameters for enemies' conduct. Those parameters banned violence, which was a violation of the bodies of other citizens, and deceitful and vexatious abuse of the courts, which was a violation of the integrity of the legal sphere. Violence was unacceptable because it reduced a citizen to the status of a slave, who was liable on his body for his offenses and could therefore be whipped or tortured. Athenians saw the citizen's body as sacrosanct and brooked no violation of this space even by those involved in feuds. They were likewise concerned that excessive pursuit of vendettas not lead to abuse of public institutions, especially the courts. Enmity with one's opponent was no excuse for bringing a frivolous charge. Adversaries were expected to play by the rules, to put real offenses on trial, and to prove that their cases had not been fabricated.

These boundaries within which personal enmities were expected to be pursued were real. Athens did not sanction violence even in pursuit of feuds, nor did it look favorably on those who prosecuted their enemies in blind personal rage and without concern for truth and justice. These ideological expectations underlie many discussions of enmity in our sources.

Athens was thus a city with two seemingly contradictory aspects: it was in many ways a feuding society but not a violent or unstable one.[9] Athenians expected feuds, but they expected restrained feuds.

Athenians were concerned not to abolish the feuding ethic but to channel it so that it would not threaten the integrity of the city. The chief tenets of democratic ideology and practice were equality, freedom, and security for each individual citizen,[10] all of which aimed at allowing Athenian men to exercise their "shares" in the governing process without fear of coercion. Unrestrained feuding would threaten to undo the democracy by allowing the strong to oppress the weak by threat and force, and so enmity had to have limits. For Athenians to be able to "live as they please," as Pericles famously put it, they had to be able to serve as jurors and magistrates, vote in the Assembly, and generally order their daily political lives without fear. This commitment to freedom led to a curtailing of the privileges of the historic feuding culture. At the same time, citizens were also free to pursue their feuds so long as they observed the publicly sanctioned boundaries.

This understanding of the Athenians' attitude toward enmity differs markedly from several previously proposed models, including most notably the divergent models of David Cohen and Gabriel Herman. Cohen (1995), focusing on the extant law court speeches from fifth- and fourth-century Athens, argues that Athens was a "feuding society" in which litigants appealed to the rules of an all-encompassing societal honor game. Not only Athenian litigants but even the juries were uninterested in abstract ideas such as legality and justice (at least as we conceive of them) and more interested in "a social judgment of the parties,"[11] a referendum on the acceptability of the respective parties' behavior in carrying out their feud. Jurors approved of prosecutors who asserted that they were taking vengeance on their enemies so long as they were carrying out their feuds honorably. Moreover, it was perfectly honorable to engage in some casual violence. In fact, to bring one's enemy to court for assault was to risk appearing a weakling and coward. Ariston, who prosecuted Conon for nearly beating him to death, was in danger of being laughed out of court. A certain degree of violence was tolerated, and the use of the courts simply to continue a feud was perfectly acceptable and normal.

Against Cohen, Herman points to speeches in which prosecutors deny that enmity prompted them to lodge their suits, and downplay their personal incentives for revenge.[12] He argues that litigants presented themselves as moderate, restrained, and prone to underreact to the wrongs suffered at the hands of their arrogant, insulting opponents. The ability to make a convincing display of such behavior tied in directly to the outcome of the cases. Athenians were not supposed to seek personal, tit-for-tat vengeance in any context.

Others have endeavored to reconcile the divergent claims of Cohen and Herman by attempting to find a compromise position between the two. Matthew Christ takes a "middle ground" between Herman and Cohen: "While there is surely a gap between collective ideals of cooperation articulated in the courts and individual behavior outside of them, the courts and the peaceful values institutionalized within them in all likelihood had real and salutary effects on disputing behavior."[13] Similarly, Danielle Allen asserts that Cohen and Herman each emphasize only one of two values that were both at work in Athenian society.[14] Citizens were supposed to pursue their enemies in anger, as Cohen points out, but society also expected them to respect the honor of others, as Herman shows.[15] Other scholars have arrived at similar conclusions though disagreeing on which parts of the arguments of Cohen and Herman are sound and which are to be rejected.[16]

The problem is that the middle ground is too spacious. When two theses are as divergent as Cohen's and Herman's, simple concessions to both sides do not bring us much closer to a workable model. In an attempt to accommodate these competing viewpoints, scholars have occasionally resorted to vague ideas about two competing "codes," but such a nebulous compromise leaves unanswered many important and interesting questions, including how Athenians would have appealed to different codes, which code (if either) was dominant, and whether there were any consistent underlying principles. The middle ground may seem attractive, but it does not offer much help for our understanding of Athenian society. Perhaps because of the unsatisfactory nature of these compromise positions, the debate between the extremes has continued, as can be seen in Christ's critical review of Herman's book and Herman's heated response to Christ.[17] The model proposed above offers a different interpretation of the interplay between feuding and the state that is not obscured by an attempt to reconcile irreconcilable views. Instead, it clearly defines the parameters within which the pursuit of enmity was acceptable.

THE ATTIC ORATORS AS SOURCES FOR THE ATHENIAN WORLDVIEW

An important step in advancing this debate is to lay some methodological groundwork. Our concern is primarily with the speeches of the Attic orators since they are the major source of information about personal enmity in Athens. Every study that delves into questions about Athenian values or societal practice must at some point draw on the rich material in these speeches, but what is the method by which we may legitimately extract general principles from them? Will a litigant's statement about his own or his opponent's behavior provide information about Athenian values generally? How are we to discriminate between widespread beliefs and dissenting views about a controversial topic?

Because these texts are rhetorical, the rhetorical nature of arguments based on enmity must be understood before conclusions about other issues, such as the values of Athenian culture, can be drawn. Close attention to the intricacies of litigants' arguments is therefore an important prerequisite to appreciating how these texts can be useful to the historian.

Law court speakers desire first and foremost to win the case at hand and are generally willing to use any means that will further that end. Consequently, we must ask how these litigants' rhetorical presentations of enmity were thought to aid them in winning their cases. Although we can assume that everything in a speech will support the speaker's case, we cannot assume that everything in a speech is descriptive of a broad pattern in Athenian society or a common Athenian belief. The issue is slightly more thorny than that.

A starting point is to recognize that speakers portray themselves and their enemies in ways that allow them to support character and probability arguments about the legal points at issue.[18] Furthermore, they had many different strategies available to them depending on the particular features of their cases. For instance, a prosecutor in a case of physical assault may assert that the defendant had been his enemy for many years to establish a credible motive for the crime. Enemies are more likely than strangers or casual acquaintances to assault each other, and so a relationship of enmity would support the argument. On the other hand, a prosecutor in different circumstances may deny that his opponent is a personal enemy to prevent the jury from suspecting that he is an antagonistic and vexatious litigator who is likely to trump up frivolous charges to humiliate his opponent. Speakers must take every precaution to avoid the appearance of attempting to deceive the jury, and enmity can be an effective weapon with which defendants can batter their opponents' credibility. The flexibility inherent in the rhetoric of enmity allowed a litigant to choose from many different approaches and adapt his presentation of enmity to his own needs. Speakers employ rhetorical strategies involving enmity in ways that are closely related to their overall arguments about the truth or falsehood of their respective versions of events. They shape their discussions of enmity to make arguments about their legal claims.

Because the rhetoric of enmity is a flexible device, speakers' presentations of their behavior vis-à-vis their enemies cannot be taken, as they often have been, as straightforward appeals to a set of readily identifiable values about feuding. This observation about the specifically rhetorical nature of the orators' discussions of enmity reveals a problem with the traditional analytical approach. Recent scholarship has tended to cite litigants' descriptions of their own behavior as paradigms for Athenian morality. Such a method assumes that a litigant's discussion of his relationship with his opponent functions primarily to align him with dominant Athenian views about enmity. In other words, a speaker would portray himself as aggressive or restrained, honor-driven or reserved, depending on which ideal accorded most directly with the jury's moral principles. Hence, Cohen and others often take the orators' feuding narratives as exemplars that appeal directly to Athenian beliefs about how feuds should be carried out.[19] Even Herman, diametrically opposed to Cohen in most respects, is in essential agreement on the validity of this method, although he draws the opposite conclusion from it, arguing that "the more non-feuding characteristics a litigant managed to display, the better his chances of winning became."[20] The necessary premise behind such analysis is that speakers' presentations of their own and their opponents' actions constitute direct appeals to contemporary beliefs about acceptable behavior and therefore can serve as paradigms for Athenian ethical prescriptions.

This premise, however, is flawed. If litigants' chief concern in constructing their narratives of enmity had been simply to justify themselves by demonstrating their conformity to a particular code of behavior, certain commonalities in rhetorical strategies might be expected. If prosecutors, for instance, deemed it in their interests to present themselves as macho he-men, taking revenge on any who opposed them, then their speeches could be expected to explain that their prosecution was an act of retaliation against a long-standing enemy. On the other side, defendants would normally deny enmity to undercut the prosecution's claims. Likewise, if litigants thought it necessary to present as many nonfeuding characteristics as possible, prosecutors would have denied enmity as a motivation, while defendants would have accused their opponents of prosecuting out of hatred and malice. The evidence, however, does not fit either formula. A simple recipe that explains the Attic orators' use of enmity in terms of legitimizing or delegitimizing the court action does not exist. There is rather a wide variety of ways in which enmity can be approached. In view of the diversity of available rhetorical strategies, any attempt to extract Athenian values from these speeches by pointing to the frequency with which litigants portray themselves as either feuding or restrained is destined to fail. It would be imprudent to conclude from litigants' affirmations or denials of enmity that the average Athenian believed such relationships to be acceptable and legitimate on the one hand or morally reprehensible on the other. The multiplicity of available rhetorical strategies makes such a reading of these passages impossible.

Athenian litigants portray themselves and their opponents in ways that support their overall claims; they are not necessarily providing prescriptive moral commentary on general rules of conduct (how one should or should not pursue one's enemies). They are, on the contrary, employing enmity to make rhetorical arguments about their cases. When a prosecutor asserts that he has long been an enemy of his opponent or when a defendant tells a story about his restrained conduct in the face of a hubristic attacker, we cannot assume in the former case that Athenians would have approved of long-standing feuds nor in the latter that they would have disapproved of them. Other factors in their cases may have led these speakers to engage in such narratives.

The persistence in contemporary scholarship of radically different views about the nature of Athenian society is the result of this widespread misunderstanding of the purpose of narratives of enmity. When treated as paradigms for Athenian behavior, the speeches themselves express contradictory values. This problem is aggravated by two important biases inherent in this type of literature that have lent credence to nearly every position on the spectrum between the extremes of Cohen and Herman. On the one hand, the extant speeches concern only cases that could not be resolved in the preliminary arbitration phase and so actually came to trial. The corpus of Attic orators represents only the most virulent disagreements and fiercest hostilities. Cohen can draw upon stories narrated by litigants that follow a pattern of "feuding behavior" precisely because only the worst disputes are extant. On the other hand, all litigants are constrained by the legal setting of their cases. Invocations of an ideal of nonviolent restraint and adherence to a civic code of submitting to the ideology of the democracy are to be expected in such a body of literature.[21] Herman relies on litigants' use of this rhetoric of self-control to conclude that Athens "must be classed among the less violent societies of pre-industrial Europe."[22] Awareness that both of these tendencies are present has no doubt led to the many compromise positions between Cohen and Herman.

Another way to gain a firmer foothold in the sources must be found. The method advocated here is to view these passages primarily as descriptive rather than prescriptive. Litigants' narratives provide information about behavior believed to be typical of enemies, whether or not it was behavior believed to be right and honorable. They describe actions and attitudes that members of the jury would find plausible but not necessarily morally right. Because litigants discussed their relationships with their opponents to create probability arguments, they had to shape their narratives in ways that harmonized with the jury's view of society. The orators' rhetoric would be ineffective if their stories about their enemies did not resonate with what the jurors believed credible. An assertion that the speaker's opponent attempted to sabotage his efforts to provide a warship for the state, for example, would have no force if the jurors found this incredible and were likely to discount the entire scenario as an egregious fabrication. A crafty litigant would attempt to bolster his narrative with scenarios with which the jury was familiar and fit his opponent into a well-known character type. The more often a particular sequence of events recurs in the corpus of Attic oratory, the more likely it is that speechwriters were aware that the average juror would view such a scenario as plausible. Commonplaces are therefore of great importance because they bear witness to arguments that harmonized with Athenians' presuppositions.

This approach also obviates the difficult question of whether or not a speaker is lying. The orators are notorious for bending the truth in their own favor, but speakers in the courtroom nonetheless attempted to make their narrative believable by creating a facsimile of truth that the jurors would be willing to accept. A reconstruction of the way Athenians conceptualized the practice of enmity is possible without consideration of the truth or falsehood of individual stories.

When exploring the Athenian conceptualization of enmity, this study will draw attention not only to what Athenian litigants were actually saying about their relationships with their opponents but also to what they assumed about such relationships generally. These general patterns are instructive for recreating the Athenian worldview because they depend on underlying beliefs that appealed to a mass audience. The task of the following chapters is to show and explain the rhetorical nature of enmity in law court speeches and to uncover the implicit premises that governed speakers' presentations. These premises provide information about Athenians' conceptualization of how enmity worked in their society.

This is not to say that the Attic orators cannot be used as sources for Athenian values, only that they have often been misused. Such affirmations of enmity and denials of enmity do not speak directly to social mores; we should rather look for ethical norms that are universally assumed (and not argued). Chapter 4 identifies several such norms by demonstrating that all discussions of enmity in our sources, whether denials or affirmations, operate under implicit premises that are constantly reaffirmed no matter what rhetorical strategy a speaker adopts. These underlying harmonies, not the sordid details of the stories litigants tell, are the best means we have of understanding Athenian ideology.

ATHENIAN LAW

Any historical study that draws on Attic oratory must begin with a basic account of the uniquely Athenian process of law. Athens, the earliest democracy for which we have significant source material, had a legal system that complemented its political arrangement and was therefore distinct from other legal systems in history. The contrast with Roman law, which developed under an aristocratic republic and then a monarchy, is especially striking. The principles of representation and professionalism, bequeathed to civil and common-law institutions by the Romans, are directly contrary to the Athenian insistence on the direct participation of amateur jurors and litigants. A select group of highly trained specialists formed the backbone of the Roman legal system and its descendants. For instance, in modern European states, law is a preserve of those few who can afford to pursue an advanced degree and dedicate their lives to continued study and practice. Many others participate in the legal system, but their participation is mediated through this elite. In Athens ordinary citizens performed the roles normally reserved for professional judges and lawyers in civil and common-law systems so that Athenian law was directly connected to the values of the people and expressed popular beliefs and opinions.[23] The democracy's egalitarianism often took the form of an insistence that as many citizens as possible participate and that as little hindrance as possible be placed in the way of the average Athenian.[24]

The sheer number of citizens required for the Athenian system to operate is astounding, as was the time commitment required of those citizens. Out of a citizen body of approximately 30,000, each year 6,000 Athenians were selected by lot to serve as a pool of available jurors (called the "heliastic body"). Members from this pool were assigned, also by lot, to fill the daily juries, which ranged in size from 201 to 2,501 and judged all cases, both criminal and civil. The courts convened between 150 and 240 days each year, usually with four or more courts in operation each day.[25] The frequency with which the Athenians resorted to the court system, obvious even from a mere description of its practice, was recognized in antiquity. The tension of Aristophanes' play the *Wasps* centers around Philocleon's dangerous addiction to jury duty. A character in the *Clouds* shows a map to Strepsiades and points to Athens. "What?" Strepsiades replies, "I don't believe you! I don't see the jurors sitting."[26]

The huge numbers of citizens required for the legal system to function ensured that no small clique could control it, but the continued ideological dominance of the masses was ensured through other means as well. The swiftness and impersonality of the system is one example. Trials lasted only one day, and the jurors were selected only hours before the trial. Once the litigants had delivered their speeches, the jurors simply voted for or against by secret ballot, without guidance from professional judges and without deliberation. Elite litigants would have had a very difficult time bribing or threatening more than two hundred jurors in a single morning, while the secret ballot made recriminations after the fact impossible. Because the trial was over so quickly, there was no time for pressuring or coercion, and so the collective opinion of the jurors was sovereign.

This system of amateur jurors worked because Athens never developed a massive body of legal literature preventing the ordinary citizen from understanding and participating in the process. Although the orators occasionally cite the verdicts of previous cases as examples for the jurors to follow, no well-conceived doctrine of precedent bound them to investigate and submit to the decisions of previous courts. There was no need to engage in intricate legal reasoning based on a body of juristic literature that was viewed as a source for authoritative interpretations of the law. Again, Rome provides a useful contrast. Roman law developed by gradual accretions that eventually yielded a complex and cacophonous mass of writings so overwhelming that later jurists found it nearly impossible even to organize it. The famous law code of Justinian has many inconsistencies and repetitions.[27]

Preference for amateurs applied not only to jurors but to litigants as well. The Athenian system made no allowance for legal representation; there were no "lawyers" in the usual sense of the term. In private procedures, which were called *dikai* (singular: *dikē*), only the aggrieved party himself could appear in court, and he had to deliver a speech on his own behalf.[28] In public suits (*graphai*; singular: *graphē*) anyone who wished (*ho boulomenos*) was permitted to bring suit against the offender, but the person who lodged the suit had to deliver a speech at the trial; he could not simply hire a professional to speak for him.[29] Litigants could ask others to speak on their behalf, a practice called *synēgoria*, but these "advocates" (*synēgoroi*) usually offered a supplementary speech, not a substitute. The main prosecutor still had to speak. Furthermore, *synēgoroi* were expected to be close friends or family or persons who otherwise had a stake in the proceedings; they were not legal experts for hire.[30] The closest the Athenians came to legal professionalism was in the trade of the "logographers," speechwriters who offered their services for a fee. Nevertheless, the man who hired a logographer to compose a speech for him still had to memorize and deliver it himself.[31] Crime and punishment remained very personal affairs.

This emphasis on amateur participation was also supported by the Athenian method of publishing laws. Laws existed in physical space: they were published on plaques (stelai) scattered all over the city. To find the relevant statute, a prosecutor had only to locate the stele, read it, and copy it down. The medium of publication (stone) prevented these laws from running to extreme length or being constantly revised. One wonders if Alexander Hamilton had Athens in mind as a model when he warned his fellow Americans, "It will be of little avail to the people, that the laws are made by men of their own choice, if the laws be so voluminous that they cannot be read, or so incoherent that they cannot be understood: if they be repealed or revised before they are promulged, or undergo such incessant changes, that no man who knows what the law is to-day, can guess what it will be to-morrow."[32] Hamilton insisted on brevity, transparency, and stability for the law code. The first and third of these were accomplished at Athens by the publication of their laws in stone, and the second by their employment of standard Attic in the text of the laws; Athens knew no legalese.

As might be expected from a system that emphasized the participation of amateurs to such a degree, legal procedure was relatively straightforward and efficient. Most trials began with a summons (*proklēsis*) that the aggrieved person (or, in the case of public suits, the volunteer prosecutor) would issue to the accused in the presence of witnesses. Summonses specified a date for a pretrial meeting before the appropriate magistrate.[33] At this conference the magistrate would verify that the charge had been correctly lodged and set a day for a second hearing, the *anakrisis*, at which further preliminary matters were settled. For public suits (*graphai*), the *anakrisis* was the last step before the jury trial, while in *dikai* the disputants were required to attempt arbitration with a state-appointed mediator.[34] Only after failure at arbitration did they go to court.

The trial itself was also straightforward. The clerk read the prosecutor's charges and the defendant's response, and then both parties swore oaths to remain on topic. After this, they delivered their speeches, prosecutor first and then defendant. Using a "waterclock" (*klepsydra*), the clerk timed these speeches and ensured that both parties followed the limits appropriate to the procedure, which seem to have been a single speech of about three hours for *graphai* and two speeches in alternation of about forty minutes each for *dikai*.[35] In all trials each litigant was free to call as many cospeakers (*synēgoroi*) as he liked, but their speeches counted against the total allotted time. After both sides had finished making their cases, the jury voted without deliberation by secret ballot. In certain procedures, if a guilty verdict was returned, the trial moved to an assessment phase wherein the penalty was determined in another set of alternating speeches. (A famous example is the trial of Socrates.) Even cases prolonged in this way, however, were over by dusk of the day on which they had begun. The speed and efficiency of the process appear enviable to anyone accustomed to the plodding pace of justice in modern times.

Enforcement, however, was much more problematic. In the absence of a state apparatus for imposing the courts' decisions on unsuccessful litigants, the winner of the lawsuit had to ensure on his own that the dictates of the court were carried out. His opponent of course did not always comply willingly.[36] If his opponent proved belligerent, his only legal recourse was to return to the court under the suit of ejectment procedure (*dikē exoulēs*), which authorized the successful prosecutor to take the awarded amount by force and entailed an additional fine on the opponent equal to the penalty imposed by the original verdict and paid to the state treasury. Notably, even in a suit of ejectment, a verdict favorable to the plaintiff simply gave legal sanction to seize property to defray the opponent's debt and did not call upon impartial state officials to settle the dispute.[37]

Inevitably, the Athenian courts offered the potential for unscrupulous individuals to abuse the system by blackmailing innocent people and taking advantage of their speaking skills to sue on frivolous charges. Athenians had a specific word of insult for such a person: "sycophant" (*sykophantēs*). Debate continues as to the exact definition of "sycophancy," but it is quite clear that sycophants misused the court system for their own ends, often for monetary gain.[38] As will be seen below, these sycophants, together with enemies blinded by rage and without concern for the truth, constituted direct threats to the integrity of the court system. The prospect of being at the mercy of these two sets of ruthless individuals was terrifying: "When one divides up his life between his enemies and sycophants, this is the same as living no life at all."[39]

SOURCES FOR ATHENIAN LAW

Like the legal system itself, the sources for Athenian law differ markedly from the sources for other legal systems. In Athens the proceedings of trials were not formally recorded; magistrates did not write notes or commentaries as, for instance, Roman jurists did; and no handbooks on law survive.[40] Although laws in Athens were published on stone plaques and easily accessible to the public, the actual workings of the legal system were not embodied in a set of elaborate, codified rules but rather were constituted and reconstituted by the everyday practices of jurors and litigants.[41] Customs and norms were passed down informally and orally as jurors and litigants both learned about the system from what was happening in the courts and contributed to the process in their own ways. The historian must therefore look beyond the written laws and investigate the actual proceedings of the trials to understand how the Athenian system functioned. The speeches and actions of the litigants themselves are of paramount importance in this regard.

The forensic speeches in the corpus of the Attic orators, nearly one hundred orations composed between approximately 420 and 322 BC, represent our most important source for Athenian law. These texts occupy a special position not only because of the number of them that survive but also because they were intended for an audience of ordinary Athenian citizens. The elite bias of most other ancient sources did not control how the orators presented their cases, since speakers had to appeal to the ideology of the masses to win.[42] Thus, we can draw conclusions about the working of Athenian law and the ideology of Athenian citizens from a careful analysis of how litigants staged their arguments and attempted to sway the jury.[43] The study of rhetorical methods is therefore of prime importance for understanding Athenian law, politics, and society.[44]

Rhetorical practice undoubtedly developed and changed during the century with which we are concerned. At the same time, it would be an undertaking of the utmost difficulty to track such changes. The extant speeches are not evenly distributed over the period (c. 420–322 BC) but rather occur in clusters. Antiphon, Andocides, Isocrates, and Lysias all composed their speeches before c. 380 BC. The bulk of the remaining speeches by Demosthenes, Aeschines, Apollodorus, Lycurgus, Hyperides, Dinarchus, and Demades were written in the last two decades of the period.[45]

The possibly exceptional nature of the speeches that are preserved presents a further complication. Many of the transmitted orations doubtless owe their survival through the hazards of textual transmission at least in part to their peculiar and interesting features, such as the brutal attacks of aristocratic bullies in Dem. 54, the nearly comic adultery narrative of Lys. 1, and the competing interpretations of important historical events in Dem. 18 and Aeschin. 3. If such extraordinary cases are overrepresented, then many speeches do not necessarily provide an accurate representation of typical cases and disputes.

Complicating the matter still further, many orators seem to have specialized in certain types of cases. What may appear as differences in the presentation of traditionally used motifs over time may be more accurately attributed to differences in procedure. Demosthenes, whose corpus contains speeches of nearly every variety, is the exception; other orators had identifiable patterns in the types of cases they took on. Antiphon's corpus has only three judicial speeches, all composed for trials concerning homicide. The only other speech composed for the homicide courts was composed by Lysias. Isaeus composed six of his twelve extant speeches for the *diadikasia*, a procedure often employed for the inheritance cases in which Isaeus apparently specialized, while only three *diadikasia* speeches exist outside Isaeus' corpus.⁴⁶ Many procedures are attested in the works of only one or two orators. All *dikai emporikai* (mercantile cases) occur in Demosthenes' corpus.⁴⁷ Likewise, Lysias composed all extant speeches intended for delivery at a *dokimasia* (scrutiny of a candidate for a magistracy) except one, a speech by Aeschines.⁴⁸

In view of these limitations, a synchronic approach is the most logical way to evaluate the sources. It is possible to treat the period from c. 420 to 322 BC as a unit, since the constitution and the population remained essentially constant.⁴⁹ The formulaic nature of courtroom speech also exerted a normalizing force that would have kept rhetorical developments within certain bounds. Speeches from this time frame will be adduced as evidence for the rhetorical use of enmity in the Athenian courtroom without respect to chronological development. Despite the limitations in the nature of the evidence, the number of surviving speeches is more than sufficient to allow a synchronic approach to yield meaningful conclusions.

These speeches generally follow the four-fold structural division discussed in ancient theoretical sources (e.g., *Rhetoric to Alexander* §§29–37) although there are variations.⁵⁰ According to the conventional understanding, first came the *prooemium*, a brief statement of purpose and an attempt to gain the audience's goodwill, then the narrative of events (*diēgēsis*), then the formal arguments or "proofs" (*pisteis*), and finally the short closing plea (*epilogos*). In reality, proofs are often mixed into the narrative, and in any case the narrative invariably carries with it implicit argumentation (as will be demonstrated in chapter 2). The speaker typically tells the story from his own point of view in a way that encourages his listeners to sympathize with his points. Nevertheless, the formula of *prooemium*–narrative–proofs–*epilogos* was frequently used, probably because it aided both the speaker, by providing a framework within which the litigant could arrange his material, and the listener, who could formulate reasonable expectations about where the argument was headed.

The speeches make significant use of formulaic content and argumentative strategies as well. Repeated themes and motifs are to be expected in a form of literature that was disseminated orally, so it comes as no surprise that stock phrases and "commonplaces" (*topoi*) are quite common. Anyone who has read even a handful of the speeches of the Attic orators has probably come across speakers' complaints about their inexperience in legal matters. Another example is the frequent complaint that the opponent has declined a challenge to extract information from a slave by *basanos* (a sort of judicial torture).⁵¹ Because persuasiveness was prized over originality in the high-stakes game of the courtroom, the orators drew freely from a large stock of available themes and techniques in constructing their arguments.

The commonplaces that are repeated most often therefore represent some of the most persuasive, or at least those perceived to be the most persuasive, of the available methods for presenting a case.

Persuasion of the jurors through carefully articulated proofs was critical because trials tended to come down to a battle of words between the two litigants. Forensic science in the modern sense did not exist, and clear demonstration based on evidence that brought jurors to an obvious truth was difficult in the extreme. After the prosecutor and defendant delivered their speeches, the jury was left with the difficult task of discerning which of the two was representing the facts most accurately and was presenting the best interpretation of the relevant laws. Therefore, a successful speaker had to be able to integrate into his argument what little evidence was available and then produce a version of events that would seem more plausible than that of his opponent.

Aristotle makes a distinction between two types of "proofs"—the *atechnoi* and *entechnoi*, those that do not require *technē* ("art," "skill") and those that do. The *atechnoi* proofs are the raw materials, the givens of the case, such as witness testimonies, depositions, and laws. The *entechnoi* proofs are produced by the speaker himself and therefore require rhetorical skill. An example is the use of characterization: a speaker may carefully choose his words and plan his delivery so that he will appear to the jury as a reasonable man who should be trusted in these circumstances. A litigant may also make use of argumentative devices such as *eikos*, "plausibility," which appeals to the listeners' natural sense of what is inherently likely. For instance, a prosecutor who is suing for theft may point out that his opponent was in debt and that he had an easy opportunity to pilfer the goods in question. These assertions do not lead necessarily to the conclusion that the defendant in fact stole the goods, but if the audience accepts that it is likely that a man in such circumstances would steal if given the chance, then the prosecutor's case has been strengthened. Since the evidence was limited and was common to both litigants, the success of a speaker depended on his ability to bring the jurors over to his side by means of supplemental argumentation. The goal of legal rhetoric was persuasion, and a good speaker mobilized all available evidence, witnesses, and argumentative techniques to that end.

OTHER SOURCES FOR ATHENIAN POLITICAL AND SOCIAL PRACTICE

Because of their direct concern with enmity, the political sphere, and mass ideology, the Attic orators are easily our best source for enmity in

Athens. However, given the general paucity of source material for the ancient world, it would be unwise to neglect anything that may shed light on Athenian values. In fact, texts from several other genres provide limited but very useful supplementary evidence.

One such source is the corpus of fourth-century curse tablets discovered in Attica. These tablets usually consist of "binding spells" (*katadesmoi*), formulaic invocations of divine aid against one's adversaries,[52] that were etched into thin pieces of lead and deposited in various hiding places. It is of course likely that long-standing relationships of enmity were the context for such acts of spiritual aggression but in only some cases does this become clear from the text itself. For instance, the so-called legal curses refer to lost court cases or, more often, forthcoming ones, providing clear evidence for how personal and heated legal battles could become. If, as seems likely, these curse tablets were not inscribed as private religious petitions but rather represent the final product of an elaborate, formal, and public ceremony, each *katademos* provides a potential glimpse into a relationship of enmity, the rest of whose history is unrecoverable.[53]

The philosophical works of Plato and Aristotle provide some illuminating information about social practice and norms. The Platonic dialogues abound in examples drawn from everyday life in Attica that are introduced as clear-cut examples illustrating a more complex philosophical point. Many observations of this kind are useful for the historian because in such cases the philosopher had no reason to misrepresent common Athenian values and practice. (In fact, he had every reason not to; if he had, the point would have fallen flat.) These glimpses of everyday life, tangential to the main thrust of the discussion, can provide a window into contemporary reality.[54] Aristotle, whose works are treatises rather than dialogues with a dramatic setting, presents an entirely different set of difficulties, but much of what he says can be useful as well. This is especially true of the *Rhetoric*, in which Aristotle lists many types of argumentative techniques that can be employed to persuade an audience. When Aristotle says, "We get angry at those who rejoice or are generally happy at our misfortunes; for this is a mark of an enemy or one who belittles us,"[55] he is not attempting to arrive at abstract philosophical truths; this is his best attempt to summarize contemporary Athenian views.[56] Such information can be extremely valuable as a summary of unexpressed norms that we see operating in Attic oratory. There is, in fact, a lot of correspondence between Aristotle's ideas about enmity as expressed in the *Rhetoric* and the actual undergirding ideas in evidence in the law court speeches.

Another useful theoretical treatise from the fourth century BC is the

Rhetoric to Alexander, falsely attributed to Aristotle. This handbook on oratory is useful for many of the same purposes as Aristotle's *Rhetoric*, but the *Rhetoric to Alexander* is often a more valuable guide to rhetorical practice in Athens in that it describes many rhetorical strategies of which the Attic orators actually make use. Hence, chapters 2 and 3, which treat enmity as a rhetorical device, make heavy use of this treatise.

Finally, we have the dramatic works of Aeschylus, Sophocles, Euripides, and Aristophanes. The setting of Athenian tragedies was almost invariably a distant mythological past with larger-than-life characters, but nonetheless it was political drama and tended to reflect the values and contemporary issues of Athenian society. An obvious example of this is the famous passage from Euripides' *Suppliants*, in which Theseus argues with a Theban herald about the merits of oligarchy and democracy.[57] Theseus' statements that the ruling king of Athens is the people and that the city is therefore "free" have no place in the typical mythological events associated with the pre-Trojan War heroes. Rather, they are clear appeals to democratic ideology within the mythic framework of the play.

Another example is Sophocles' *Antigone*, which dramatizes the conflict between the unwritten and eternal laws of the gods and the positive law established by man. This is explicit commentary on current debates raised by Greek rationalist political thinkers who would become known as the "sophists." Likewise, mythological characters often conform more closely to contemporary Athenian norms than those of their Homeric predecessors. In Aeschylus' *Suppliants*, the king, Danaus, refuses to act without the people's consent.[58] Examples of this type could easily be multiplied, but these are sufficient to illustrate the point that Athenian tragedy is not a carnivalesque affair completely removed from contemporary realities. On the contrary, it often reflects Athenian values. The problem is telling whether a particular statement is summarizing the mainstream of Athenian thinking or is an archaizing, mythological convention of behavior. For this reason, it is best to use tragedy to corroborate evidence gleaned from other sources instead of attempting to establish a social practice on dramatic evidence alone.

The comic plays of Aristophanes, although their setting (contemporary Athens) is closer to home, are subject to at least as many problems as tragedy. They are highly satirical, make regular use of exaggeration and parody, and employ utterly fantastic characters and plots. Nevertheless, comedy, like tragedy, can be used in tandem with other sources to corroborate a thesis about Athenian society. These plays are filled with tantalizing references to Athenian social and political practices, but each passage must be handled with care and corroborated from other evidence.

PRÉCIS

A first and necessary step for this project is to establish what enmity was and how it worked in Athenian society. The decision to begin the book with this chapter rather than the study of the law court orations that commences with chapter 2 was a pragmatic one. Chapter 1 assumes the methodological premises that follow logically from the detailed rhetorical analysis of the speeches in chapters 2–3, but by the same token an understanding of how enmity works is necessary before the reader engages fully with the orators' rhetoric. The relationship between the historical question of the nature of enmity in Athenian society and the rhetorical use of enmity in the law court speeches is organic rather than linear. They have been separated for the sake of clarity and organization, but all of the chapters are interdependent.

Chapter 1 ("The Social Dimensions of Enmity") sets the stage by drawing attention to three important issues associated with enmity in classical Athens: (1) how hostile relationships were conceived in linguistic and social terms, (2) how they arose, and (3) how they propagated themselves. Athenians conceived of enmity as a communally recognized relationship, not simply an emotional state. The word *echthra* implied reciprocity: mutual acts of harming between enemies. For an enmity to exist, the participants both must be aware of the relationship and must actively attempt to dishonor each other. These relationships, furthermore, seem to have been quite common. Athenian literature presents a fairly cogent picture in which enmities were a part of everyday life. This resulted naturally from the relative ease with which one could make an enemy but also from the tendency of enmity to spread to include kinship and friendship groups. A hostile relationship, once started, caused a chain reaction, drawing in previously uninvolved third parties. Athens was thus an "enmity culture," a society whose people were frequently concerned with the problem of real, dangerous enemies.

The next two chapters (chapters 2–3) move on to consider enmity in the legal realm, concentrating on our most fertile source for enmity in Athens, the speeches composed for the law courts. These orations, being complex literary texts, require careful handling. Appreciation of their literary qualities should be prior to and preparatory for a study that exploits them as historical witnesses of Athenian culture. Most important for the present purposes is their inherently rhetorical nature. Speakers in court are not concerned to give a dispassionate description of Athenian values but rather to bring the jury around to their way of seeing things. The resulting manipulation of norms concerning enmity must be taken into account at all times. For this reason the study of enmity as a rhetorical device is a necessary step in employing the Attic orators as sources for Athenian thinking about feuding, violence, and other related practices.

The primary subject of inquiry in chapter 2 ("The Rhetoric of Enmity as a Legal Strategy") is the rhetorical approaches that litigants take when affirming or denying enmity. The speechwriters' commonest tactic is to include a narrative of a hostile relationship as part of an argumentative strategy supporting the speaker's legal contentions. Litigants often invoke their preexisting hostile relationships with their opponents to create a context for their version of events that will make their claims seem more plausible. Speakers thus exploit their narratives to make implicit arguments about the case and to speak to the relative credibility of the respective parties. For instance, a prosecutor in a case entailing financial reward may claim that the defendant has long been his enemy to preempt suspicions that he is motivated by desire for pecuniary gain. At the same time, he will attempt to downplay his own role in the feud so as not to fall into the opposite error of appearing to have trumped up a charge in pursuit of an enemy. He may also include information about his opponent's past that makes him appear to be the type of person that would commit the crime of which he is accused. His presentation of his relationship with his opponent must thus be carefully balanced to increase the credibility of his charges. This is an example from a prosecution speech, but defendants also employ the rhetoric of enmity in much the same manner. The strategies differ significantly from one litigant to another, but the basic principle of using enmity as a vehicle for probability and character arguments remains the same.

Chapter 3 ("The Flexibility of the Rhetoric of Enmity") works within the framework established by chapter 2 to show that the rhetoric of enmity was malleable and capable of adapting to a variety of rhetorical situations. The methods by which litigants shaped their rhetoric to fit their specific needs are diverse and sophisticated. Several recent attempts[59] have been made to discover a single determining factor for an orator's decision about affirming or denying enmity, but the strategies and the rationale behind them cannot be reduced to one or two criteria. Procedure, the type of dispute, the speaker's history with his opponent, the personae of the speaker and his opponent in the eyes of the public, and many other features of the case can all play a role. A holistic analysis of the use of enmity in these texts reveals that these presentations are not stand-alone pleas, the result of monolithic *topoi* that can be easily extracted from one speech and inserted in another. The orators mold the rhetoric of enmity to fit their own needs and integrate it fully into their overall argumentative strategies.

Chapter 4 ("Enmity under the Law: The Limits to Vengeance") shifts the focus from the rhetorical presentation of enmity to the ideology and practice of enmity. The exploration of the literary dimension of enmity in chapters 2–3 will have laid the necessary groundwork for such a study by challenging the methodology that assumes that we can extract Athenian values from litigants' narratives by treating them as paradigms of Athenian morality. In fact, the Attic orators' strategies are designed not to justify themselves so that the jury will vote for them based on their character and status and regardless of the facts of the case but rather to support the truth of their own interpretation of events. The rhetoric of enmity is not governed by a litigant's need to find extralegal justification but rather addresses legal concerns directly.

Using the framework established in chapters 1–3, chapter 4 investigates how Athenians conceived of the role of enmity in regard to the institutions of the *polis*. A "feuding society," as classically understood, is characterized by the privatization of vengeance as a legitimate way of pursuing an enemy. The state apparatus turns a blind eye to citizens who prefer to settle their disputes in their own ways, even sometimes by violent means. Athenian thinking was far removed from this sort of ethic. Although the exploitation of the courts to pursue private vendettas was not in itself problematic, Athenian ideology put important limits on feuding behavior. Litigants in court were expected to prosecute for real, identifiable offenses and to prove their cases. The jury did not make allowance for enemies who attempted to convict each other based merely on slander or falsifications. Speakers accordingly had to play to this expectation and attempt to prove that their versions of events were correct. Another important limitation on feuding was a strict prohibition on violence. Athenians viewed the citizen's body as inviolable and protected it with both institutional guarantees and informal injunctions to the citizenry at large to prevent escalation. Despite the strong presence of personal enmity as a pervasive force in societal relations, feuding behavior was firmly circumscribed by the rules of the game.

The Athenian attitude toward enmity was a product of its time. The agonistic impulse of the Greeks remained strong in Athens despite two centuries of democratic ideological hegemony, but, at the same time, this competitiveness was not permitted to wreak havoc on social order and threaten the basic tenets of the democracy. To protect the weaker citizen from abuse by the stronger, institutional and ideological safeguards had to be set in place to guarantee the security of each citizen's person. The result was a society with seemingly contradictory features. Athens allowed ample space for honor-driven citizens to pursue their enemies but also established checks that kept them from going too far.

1. THE SOCIAL DIMENSIONS OF ENMITY

Seeking redress when we feel wronged is a natural impulse. The principle of reciprocity has permeated human literature and art from the cry of Abel's blood to the latest revenge movie. The right to revenge is still invoked on a regular basis today, even if it is habitually softened with euphemisms such as "what goes around comes around" or "she'll get what's coming to her." For the ancient Greek, this is the language of gift exchange, a quid pro quo on the moral level. Perceived wrongs lead to retribution, which leads to further retribution, creating a potentially endless cycle of reciprocal acts.

The people of antiquity had good reason to be anxious about their personal enemies. Most readers of this book are probably accustomed to thinking of those whom they dislike as a nuisance, at worst perhaps a threat to their career, but in the ancient world an enemy posed a direct and real danger to one's livelihood, status in the community, and even life. If one man hated another man enough, he might sabotage his crops, slander him in the marketplace, or physically assault his family and slaves. Such attacks on person or property were difficult to prevent or remedy. There was very little if any coercive power of the state that the victim could bring to bear against the wrongdoer. Police forces were unknown, and forensic science was rudimentary at best. For most families in most societies, retaliation, or the threat thereof, provided the best guarantee against the aggression of hostile neighbors. A balance between friends and enemies was therefore crucial because one could become isolated and vulnerable if the latter group became too numerous and strong. The Psalmist's complaint that his friends had deserted him was a cry of deep despair, not paranoia: "Those who seek my life lay their snares; those who seek my hurt speak of ruin and meditate treachery all day long."[1] It was imprudent to ignore or fail to keep track of one's hostile relationships.

Athens was no exception. The literature is replete with references to enemies and Athenians' concerns about them. Turning the other cheek would have been a dangerous policy; Athenians had to plan their actions carefully to avoid being taken unawares by vindictive adversaries.[2] But the similarities between Athens and other societies do not necessarily indicate that they were similar in all regards. It seems *a priori* likely that Athens, being a rare example of democracy in the ancient world, would have differed from Sparta or Rome or the Near Eastern monarchies. What type of society was Athens, and how did it differ from other societies, if at all?

One way to answer these questions is to fit Athens into a known anthropological model. Cohen likened Athens to the "feuding societies" of the Mediterranean basin.[3] Anthropologists have long used this term for communities characterized by a widespread obsession with honor and shame and high levels of both casual and revenge-based violence. In many areas of the world, elaborate codes of honor provide scope for feuding among the members of the communities but at the same time limit such conflicts through widely recognized expectations about how feuds are to be carried out.[4] Rather than functioning to effect resolution and reconciliation, the legal system is incorporated into the overall feuding process. Enemies tend to take an instrumental view of the courts, using them for their own ends and retaliating against their opponents through lawsuits. Although such societies are often characterized by a high level of violence, disputes must still take place within certain parameters to be considered honorable and legitimate.[5] Despite the appearance of unchecked warfare, a feuding culture will thus establish boundaries for conflict that the community enforces, whether by informal norms and values, formal institutions, or both.[6]

Cohen argues that Athenians endorsed a feuding ethic similar to what we find in many communities of North Africa, the Near East, and the Mediterranean islands, although the courts mitigated the extreme, homicidal violence of "blood feud." As a result of Cohen's important work, the question of whether or not Athenian society can be called "feuding" has exercised the minds of many scholars. Cohen's use of modern comparative evidence has provided a useful starting point for the debate about hostile relationships in Athens.[7]

Such an approach can provide insights, but a model derived from societies separated from Athens by over two thousand years necessarily runs the risk of importing ideas and assumptions that do not apply. A label such as "feuding society" can be helpful as a device for describing overarching similarities between historical processes and events, but it can also prove limiting. Like any generalization, a model may simplify the picture at the expense of the more complicated reality. An example of such a problematic term in recent historical research is "feudalism," a label with which medievalists have become increasingly ill at ease. Many scholars object to grouping the very diverse societies of the High Middle Ages into a single category, as if the similarities far outweighed the differences. In a famous article published in 1974, Elizabeth Brown objected to the "tyranny" that this construct had imposed on historical inquiry and argued that it oversimplified medieval Europe, which was characterized by a variety of political and economic structures.[8] Labeling a particular set of societies as "feudal" tended to discourage scholars from asking more specific questions about how those societies worked. The term proved restrictive, constraining scholars' thought into categories that did not accurately capture the full picture.

Labeling Athens a "feuding society" is similarly problematic. Although there are many points of contact between Athens and the shame cultures Cohen discusses, the term "feuding" has semantic baggage that can cause confusion and misunderstanding. For example, the term "feuding society" implies a society in which the coercive power of centralized institutions is weak and maintenance of social order takes place at the private level. The implied contrast between feuding societies and modern states does not do justice to the Athenians' distinctive political arrangement. Communities governed primarily by an informal code of honor are commonly distinguished from those governed by formal institutions and the rule of law, and in some cases the development from one to the other can be clearly traced. An expanding centralized bureaucracy gradually arrogates more extensive powers to itself and eventually takes on the role of arbiter of disputes between its constituents. A dispute that in the past may have led to a feud and retaliation in accordance with an elaborate communal code of honor becomes subject to a publicly sanctioned apparatus (usually a court system) that mediates, hands down judgment to the parties involved, and compels them to abide by its decision.

This is what happened in many societies of medieval Europe in the tenth century, when individualistic feuding gave way to centralization as kings solidified their power. Over time, an offense against another person came to be viewed not as a mere private matter but as a challenge to the king's protection of his subjects and a breach of the "king's peace." The king and his deputies were therefore justified in subjecting feuding behavior to severe limitations and imposing the rule of law. To classify classical Athens with ninth-century England, much less other modern feuding societies in the Mediterranean, is misleading because Athens already had a centralized court system.[9] It is true that the Athenian system often relied on self-help (legally sanctioned retaliation by the victim of a crime) rather than official coercive institutions to enforce decisions, but the laws and institutions of Athens impinged on the dispute process at every step. Athens does not fit neatly onto the scheme of "feuding society" versus the rule of law.

Another problem with the label "feuding society" is its connotation of violence. It invokes the idea of blood feud, a series of tit-for-tat murders. Cohen's attempt to address this issue led to a broadening of the definition of "feuding society" that has devalued the descriptive force of the term. Cohen argued that a society may retain its feuding characteristics despite a centralization of power and concomitant limitation of violence, citing Stephen Wilson's work on feuding in nineteenth-century Corsica.[10] As the state bureaucracy expanded and the legal system became correspondingly stronger, Corsicans channeled their aggressive feelings through the courts, using lawsuits to pursue personal vendettas. Therefore, as Cohen would have it, a society with a strong vengeance ethic may be classified as feuding even if homicide levels are relatively low and centralized power is relatively strong. Certainly Cohen is correct to draw out the similarities in mentality between nineteenth-century Corsicans and participants in other feuding cultures, even very violent ones, but it should be noted how flexible the term "feuding" has become when used in this way. It would now refer merely to the ethic of revenge for personal dishonor with no specific connotations about how and where revenge should be sought. In the end, the term "feuding society" is objectionable not because it is inaccurate but rather because it is so broad and potentially misleading.

Focusing on whether or not classical Athens fits into the slippery category of feuding societies is therefore not a promising avenue. A better method is to begin with some more specific and limited questions about Athenian social dynamics. That is the aim of this chapter, which will provide a framework for understanding hostile relationships by posing and attempting to answer three basic questions: (1) how were enmities conceived in linguistic and social terms? (2) how did they arise? and (3) how did they propagate themselves?

Our concern here is with the Greek concept of *echthra* (commonly translated as "enmity"), not the English words "enmity" and "feud" themselves. These latter terms will be employed throughout this study as a matter of convenience, but *echthra* does not align perfectly with either term.[11] The term "feuding" as a descriptor of Athenian society, however, will be avoided because applying this term to Athens makes an implicit claim about the regulation (or lack of regulation) of personal enmities by public ideology and institutions, which is a topic that will be addressed in chapter 4.[12] A more limited claim will be advanced here, namely, that Athens was an "enmity culture," a society rife with hostile relationships that members of the community openly recognized and to which they attached considerable importance for evaluating individuals' honor and standing in the community.

Enmity was a relationship that entailed expectations of the participants, not simply an emotional state. It described not only how a person felt but how a person acted. If an Athenian referred to another person as an "enemy," he meant not only that he disliked him but that they both disliked each other and that at least one of them had taken steps to harm the other. A hostile act was required for an enmity to be consummated. Once this happened, it was assumed that enemies would be vigilant for opportunities to do injury to their rivals and would attempt to harm each other whenever possible. Just as friends were expected to help each other and to share in each other's victories, enemies were expected to seek each other's harm and to rejoice at each other's failures.

Enmity was a widespread problem. Numerous ancient sources assume that enmity was common and that it was natural for an Athenian to divide up his acquaintances into friends and enemies. The competitiveness of the ancient Greeks exacerbated the natural human desire for dominance over others and led to an agonistic society characterized by quarrels, bickering, lawsuits, slander, and the like. Athenians saw endemic personal enmity as a natural phenomenon and even took steps to adjust their political system to make full use of this social dynamic by playing enemies off each other.

The tendency of the ancient Greeks to divide themselves into networks of family and friends facilitated the spread of enmity from a dispute between two individuals to a complex web of hatreds and animosities. Once started, enmity seemed, like a virus, to have a life of its own. Not only could a single act engender enmity among former strangers, acquaintances, or even friends, it could also draw many third parties into the quarrel and breed additional related disputes. The citizens of classical Athens were aware of a multitude of scenarios in which conflict could ignite and spread. Enemies were simply a fact of life.

In Athens, the dichotomy between friends and enemies was of fundamental importance for how social life was organized. Enmity was, as it were, "the electricity of that social machine."[13] Individuals were honor-driven and concerned with gaining respect and avoiding loss of face. More important than one's self-image was the regard with which one was held by the rest of the community: "Goodness divorced from a reputation for goodness was of limited interest."[14] Friends tended to form informal associations of protection, power blocs that pursued the same interests, while enemies actively sought to harm each other and each other's associates.

MORE THAN EMOTION: ENMITY AS RELATIONSHIP

The Greek words *echthros* and *echthra* are just close enough in semantic range to English "enemy" and "enmity" (respectively) to mislead. "Enmity" shares *echthra*'s connotation of a dispute between individuals rather than a dispute between states or larger groups, but the word "enemy" introduces problems. "Enemy" in English can describe two disparate categories between which Greek makes a distinction. Although *echthros* can refer to all categories of hostile peoples or people groups, its typical referent is a personal relationship. Greek has another word for an enemy of the state: *polemios*.[15] Demosthenes would have considered Aeschines, a rival Athenian orator, his *echthros* and Philip, a king at war with Athens, a *polemios*.[16] A passage from Lysias illustrates the differences in the semantic fields of these two words: "As I am taking vengeance on Alcibiades, my enemy (*echthros*), I beg you to vote justly. You should have the same opinion and vote as when you thought that you were about to be in danger because of your enemies (*polemioi*)."[17] The English word "enemy" overlaps the categories of *echthros* and *polemios*. This study will be concerned primarily with words of the root *echthr-* rather than *polem-* since it addresses personal enemies within the Athenian citizen body rather than external threats. When a translation is provided of an Athenian text, the Greek word translated as "enemy" refers more specifically to private and personal enemies than the English word implies.

Enmity must be distinguished from anger (*orgē*), hatred (*misos*), and other such terms, which primarily describe emotions.[18] Enmity implies a matrix of three closely related concepts: emotion, action, and relationship. When *echthra* or similar words[19] appear in our sources, it suggests all three: two people dislike each other (emotion), are actively seeking to harm each other (action), and believe that their emotions and actions verify their status as "enemies" (relationship). This is why the English word "feud" is a useful term for describing the matrix of ideas implicit in *echthra*. In contrast to "enmity," feud implies a long-standing relationship rather than mere emotion and so is closer to *echthra* in this respect. Unfortunately, as Cohen himself recognized, it can invoke the image of blood feuds, which entail repeated acts of violence. He therefore distinguished "blood feud" from "feud," the latter of which he termed "an enduring long-term relationship of conflict following a retaliatory logic"[20] that does not necessarily imply homicidal violence. In this study "feud" will assume this meaning that Cohen outlines. Despite the problem of its linguistic kinship to the phrase "feuding society," the simple term "feud" itself is indispensable. The former must be rejected, while the latter is retained.[21]

Enmity (*echthra*) is parallel to its counterpart, friendship (*philia*).[22] Greeks tended to think in terms of polarities, and the polarity "friends versus enemies" was a natural and convenient way to conceive of social life.[23] Friendship and enmity were relationships, mutual bonds between two people who openly recognized each other as friends or enemies.[24] As Aristotle states in his discussion of friendship in the *Rhetoric*, "a friend is one who loves and is loved in return; those who think that they feel this way about each other consider themselves friends."[25] Aristotle assumes that the relationship must be reciprocal and that it must be known to be reciprocal. A friend must know that the other person also believes them to be friends. This principle applies *mutandis mutatis* to enemies.[26]

In many statements about enemies in our sources, a recognized, reciprocal relationship is simply assumed as a premise. For example, in Aristotle's list of the types of people likely to commit acts of injustice, he includes men "who have many enemies" because they suppose that they "escape notice because it seems unlikely that they would try anything against those who are on their guard."[27] These enemies can only be "on their guard" if they know against whom they need to protect themselves. The statement assumes that enmity is a mutual relationship, recognized by both parties. The Greeks lived their lives in the open, on display for the judgment of their community, and it should come as no surprise that enmities were carried out in the open as well.

The most secure basis upon which two people could know that they were *philoi* or *echthroi* was not their emotions but their actions. Hence, the Greek motto was "help friends, harm enemies," not "love friends, hate enemies."[28] Emotion was taken for granted; only active support or active injury could verify these relationships as genuine.[29] Friendship required acts of *charis* ("grace, favor") in an exchange of favors that ideally developed into an endless series of debts and repayments by which *philoi* continually reaffirmed and strengthened their bond.[30] This reciprocal gift-giving ethos applied equally to enmity, which required acts of revenge (*timōria*), the ugly side of *charis*. Like an act of helping, an act of harming called for repayment in kind. As Aristotle says, "It is noble to take vengeance on one's enemies and not to reconcile with them because payback is just."[31] The Greeks employed the same language of debt-and-repayment for both friendship/*charis* and enmity/*timōria*.[32] Helping friends and harming enemies were two sides of the same coin.

Because friendship and enmity were based on actions, not just attitudes, they could be verified with evidence. For this reason, if a litigant in court wanted to assert that he and his opponent were at enmity with each other, he was obliged to prove it. When Demosthenes calls Meidias his enemy, he does not mean merely that he dislikes the man. Several long narrative passages in the speech are dedicated to proving that they have for some time been involved in mutual acts of harming and revenge. Likewise, when Andocides complains that he is being attacked by his enemies, he demonstrates that they are worthy of the name by providing the jurors with a lengthy explanation of the previous disputes that brought him into enmity with his opponents.[33] Another litigant straightforwardly offers "proofs" (*sēmeia*) of an enmity and even asserts that he can provide witnesses who will testify to hostile acts between the two.[34]

Litigants who desired to counter an argument for enmity accordingly had only to establish the absence of evidence for such a relationship. In Lysias 1 (*On the Murder of Eratosthenes*), Euphiletus denies that he was an enemy of Eratosthenes and immediately follows up on his claim by denying any hostile actions (such as lawsuits, blackmail, fights, or other quarrels) between the two.[35] There is no question whether or not Euphiletus hated Eratosthenes (the man had cuckolded him in his own house), but Euphiletus' mere feelings are not important to the case. Rather he must deny *echthra*, the mutual bond that is verified by a history of hostile actions. The absence of such hostile acts indicates that there was no *echthra*.

When an Athenian spoke of his "enemies," he was not referring to a vague category of people whom he generally disliked; he was talking about specific people with whom he was involved in a hostile relationship. He could even have identified them by name, as we can see from an incidental reference in Plato's *Charmides*. In this dialogue Socrates discovers that one of his associates is enamored with a young boy, the title character Charmides, and so brings the two of them into a conversation on the topic of prudence (*sōphrosynē*). Charmides proposes to define prudence as "minding one's own business" (*to ta hautou prattein*), but Socrates takes issue. In his exchange with the youth, he employs an image that Charmides would be able to understand, one drawn from the life of a schoolboy: "Do you think that the scribe [who educated you] read and wrote only his own name and taught you boys to do so, or did you practice writing the names of your enemies no less than your own names and your friends' names?"[36] What is important here is not the significance of this rhetorical question for Socrates' argument about prudence but, rather, the implication that by the time they were learning to read and write, Athenian boys would be able to identify certain persons as their enemies (probably as a result of enmity passed down from their fathers or other members of their households). Socrates takes for granted that Charmides knew people whom he could identify by name as enemies, even when he was just learning the alphabet.

Curse tablets also indicate that Athenians did not have to struggle to come up with a list of the names of their enemies. Many of these *katadesmoi* ("binding" spells) simply record the name of the person to be cursed, but many more list a series of names.[37] Oftentimes a catch-all such as "and as many people as act as enemies toward me" concludes the curse, but in Wünsch *Def. tab.* 35, for instance, this ending phrase comes only after twelve people have been identified by name.

Athenians knew who their enemies were, and if they wanted to end an enmity, they literally had to do something about it. Because enmity was defined by visible acts of hostility, it did not simply fizzle out as passions receded and calmer thoughts prevailed. Such a contractual notion of enmity is rare in modern western societies, but journalist Laura Blumenfeld, on a quest for revenge on the man who shot her father, discovered a principle with which Athenians probably would have agreed: "Even when the hate burns out, revenge is a commitment. Like a marriage, after the love is gone."[38] The series of reciprocal acts of vengeance that were an expected aspect of enmity were self-perpetuating, regardless of emotion. Ending hostility required an act that interrupted the cycle and started the parties on a new path, an act that transferred the relationship from enmity to friendship. This act the Greeks called "reconciliation" (*diallagē, dialusis*). The speaker of Antiphon 6 (*On the Chorus Boy*) describes the end of his enmity with Philocrates as occurring at an identifiable time and place.

> My friends persuaded me to agree, and we were reconciled during the Dipolieia in front of witnesses at the temple of Athena. Afterwards we spent time together and talked in shrines, in the Agora, at my house, at their house, and everywhere else. To top it all off, by Zeus and all the gods, in the Council-house in front of the Council Philocrates here joined me on the podium, and with his hand on my arm he talked with me, calling me by name, and I did the same.[39]

This agreement put an abrupt end to one type of relationship and just as suddenly started another. The speaker and his enemy immediately stopped harming each other and began spending time together, even supporting each other at public events. A ceremony and exchanging of oaths decisively changed their relationship.

A successful reconciliation could be called simply an "end of the enmity"[40] because its purpose was to release two enemies from their quarrel and fulfill the apparent need for an authoritative and ceremonial act. In fact, the process of reconciliation may even have been designed with this end in mind, a function that distinguished it from the other type of out-of-court settlement, arbitration (*diaita*).[41] Reconciliation and arbitration differed primarily in that the former represented an agreement that the disputants themselves affirmed, while the latter was a mechanism for reaching a resolution by handing over the decision to mediators who imposed a settlement. Arbitration would have been an attractive option for enemies who desired to resolve some point of contention but could find no common ground on which to negotiate and did not necessarily wish to put an end to hostilities. In lieu of sorting out their differences themselves, they could agree to select arbitrators and swear to abide by their verdict.[42]

The ostensible purpose of an arbitration was to end a dispute, but only the most naïve would assume that parties who submitted themselves to arbitrators must therefore have been seeking real understanding and closure with their opponents. When quarreling persons seek the intervention of a higher authority, they are often seeking not to resolve their differences but to win justification for their actions and to be vindicated (as any parent who has refereed disagreements between two children well understands). Many arbitrants desired recognition of their rectitude and rehabilitation of their honor before witnesses from the community, which probably accounts for the practice of holding arbitrations in public places.[43] They therefore risked simply expanding rather than ending their feud. Potential arbitrators understood how dangerous it was to step into the middle of a dispute. Wrangling was inherent in the process, and some refused to act as mediators because they feared making an enemy of either party.[44] The process could be risky for all involved.[45]

While arbitration could easily devolve into posturing and recriminations, reconciliation represented a more honest attempt to find common ground and often aimed at ending the hostile relationship altogether. The parties tried to find a solution to their problem without resorting to a verdict handed down by a third party. Arbitrators in this case acted as intercessors and peacemakers. Reconciliation thus functioned as a ceremonial means for ending a hostile relationship.

Reconciliation agreements testify to the Athenians' penchant for defining enmity and friendship in terms of visible acts and rituals rather than emotions. Belief in the efficacy of this process was strong enough to allow litigants to cite such agreements and base legal arguments about their cases on them. The speaker of Lysias 4 (*On a Premeditated Wounding*) assumes that he can prove that the defendant is lying about being his enemy if he can show that a reconciliation took place.[46] As Stephen Todd points out, the speaker does not even entertain the possibility that he remained hostile after going through a reconciliation agreement, or that the reconciliation was only halfhearted.[47] This is because feelings were not what counted. If they were, the commonly included requirement that the two former enemies now treat each other as friends would not make sense. Several reconciliations contain an "amnesia clause," stipulating that the two parties involved "bear no grudge" (*mē mnēsikakein*) about past events.[48] The arbitrator could bid the reconciled men "to treat each other well in the future" and require them to take an oath that they would do so.[49] Acts of kindness serving as tangible signs of the covenant were expected to follow immediately.[50] The famous injunction of the Athenian political amnesty of 401 BC "not to dredge up grudges" (*mē mnēsikakein*)[51] was a typical feature of personal reconciliation agreements.[52] Reconciliation functioned not only to end a dispute but to end a relationship based on acts of vengeance and begin a new one based on acts of *charis*.

Reconciliations were so important that if two people who had been enemies became friends, a reconciliation could simply be assumed to have taken place. The speaker of Lysias 4 laments that his opponent, who apparently argued that they were enemies, was not on the board of judges for the Dionysia since he would assuredly have voted for the speaker's tribe and thus proven that they had been reconciled. The opponent's kindly actions would prove that enmity had ceased and therefore that a *diallagē* had taken place.[53] He speaks of reconciliation and of evidences of friendship as if they were equivalent, conflating the sign (the ceremony) and the thing signified (the relationship). By the terms of his argument, the speaker's friendship with his opponent had an identifiable starting point that could be proven if the results of a reconciliation could be shown to have taken place.[54]

Conversely, if two people who were previously known to be enemies had not engaged in reconciliation, it could be assumed that they were still enemies. The inheritance cases of Isaeus, which frequently include arguments about the relationship between a speaker's opponent and the deceased man who has left a will that is in dispute, illustrate this point. A litigant sometimes attempts to prove that his opponents had been enemies of the testator whose property is under adjudication to make it seem unlikely that the testator would have left his property to them. To support this claim, the speaker may specifically deny that the testator had reconciled with his opponent before his death and assume that this is evidence that they had still been at odds with each other.[55] By this rationale, either these men are still enemies or they had reconciled and become friends; there is no middle-ground option. Reconciliation was a necessary step to ending an enmity.

This formal and ritual procedure to end an enmity illustrates another important point about friendship and enmity in Athens: their public context. Once an agreement was reached, the parties solemnized their change of relationship through a ceremony attended by friends and family members who acted as witnesses.[56] Paul Hyams' observation about reconciliation agreements in medieval England is applicable to classical Athens: "Durable peace, like good justice, must be made manifest. The exchange of very visible symbols through ritual acts engaged the local community as spectators and witnesses. Peer pressure remained an important incentive for the keeping of promises."[57] Community participation in the restructuring of relationships was important to these agreements, as was the invocation of divinities to protect the newly formed covenant. Such formal ceremonies allowed the participants to hedge their bets. Divine oversight would bind them together, but sanctions from the human community were an important backup. The result was a visible symbol of the newly forged commitment.

Although enmities probably started as disputes between two individuals, in practice they must have only rarely remained personal affairs. More often, they involved the larger community, which was stitched together in a complex web of friends and enemies. An enmity had the potential to create a serious problem for other members of the community, who were not expected to stay neutral in the dispute. When Aristotle points out that friends generally have the same friends and the same enemies, he implies the need for friends to align themselves with each other's relationships.[58] In other words, Athenians tended to be drawn into the conflicts of their close associates. The mark of a true *philos* was a willingness to consider another's enemies one's own. Conversely, Xenophon's Socrates warns against associating with a "quarrelsome" person who will "provide his friends with many enemies."[59]

Because friends shared the same enemies, in a relatively small community such as a deme, an enmity created a problem of alignment for everyone involved in the complex, crosscutting network of friendships. An Athenian who discovered that two of his friends were each other's enemies had three options: (1) attempt to remain a friend of both (which went against the ideology of friendship), (2) take sides, remaining a friend of one at the expense of enmity with the other, or (3) attempt to end the enmity. Reconciliation proceedings represent a decision to pursue the third course. Reconciliation was a public and communal process because enmity was a public and communal concern.

How were these enmities made known to the larger community? One way to publish an enmity was to curse one's enemies publicly. The curse tablets represent only the end product of a process that likely included an elaborate series of "invocations, purifications, fumigations, prayers, instruments, rituals, and more"[60] and so were not private religious petitions but rather aggressive declarations of hostility. The author of a curse might even choose to leave the binding spell where an enemy was likely to find it. Plato mentions three typical locations for depositing curses, all of which were anything but good hiding places: doorways, intersections of roads, and tombs of ancestors.[61] Perhaps part of the effectiveness of these spells lay in intimidation and a sort of psychological warfare: those who had been "bound" would know that they had been cursed.[62]

Cursing ceremonies may well have been enmity's complement to friendship's shared sacrifices, but not all enemies would have gone to the trouble of commissioning a specialist to inscribe a curse tablet. Most news about new enmities probably spread through the normal channels: rumor and gossip. When Socrates in the *Apology* complains about a long-standing, concerted campaign of slander against him, he invokes a trope that appears many places in Attic oratory.[63] Slander was typical of enemies.[64] Gossip may have functioned as a form of social control by forcing conformity to communal norms,[65] but it could also be employed in the service of enmities. It is not difficult to imagine an aggrieved Athenian taking every opportunity to disparage his enemy in social settings. Lysias 8 (*Against the Members of a* Sunousia) provides a vivid depiction of how such slander operated. The speaker alleges that his opponents had acted as if they were his friends but were in fact slandering him behind his back. This behavior was outrageous because it confused the categories of friendship and enmity: friends were supposed to slander their enemies in front of their friends, but these men have slandered everybody without making the appropriate distinctions. They declare enmity with A in front of B and with B in front of A. The speaker chastises these men for inconsistency, claiming that the logical conclusion of this is self-defeating: "You will turn against each other and one-by-one everyone will become an enemy of everyone else, and finally the one who is left alone will slander himself."[66] The normal way for gossip and criticism to operate is for enemies to spread rumors about each other in the company of their friends (such acts being tantamount to declarations of enmity). By taking part in the same slander of the same enemies, friends reinforce their bond of friendship. They are joined as much by their common enemies as by their common bond of amity.

The most effective way to make public one's enmity with another citizen was opposition in a public forum, especially through the courts. The pretrial procedures necessarily introduced many new witnesses to the dispute (the very first action was the summons, which required witnesses), but the final appearance of prosecutor and defendant before a body of at least two hundred of their fellow citizens, along with friends, family, and other interested parties as a passive audience, was a public declaration of enmity. Even if the two parties had not been enemies when the prosecutor initiated the legal procedure, they became enemies through it.[67] The simple act of delivering speeches against each other was bound to create enmity, but more importantly, one of the litigants would have to win and one would have to lose, humiliated and shamed before a public audience. This created an imbalance of honor. The losing party would feel obliged to return harm for harm.[68]

Personal enmity was a state of declared war. Athenians could make comparisons between personal enemies (*echthroi*) and the state's enemies (*polemioi*) with relative ease. In Xenophon's *Memorabilia* (3.4) Socrates sets out to convince his interlocutor that a man who has flourished in the competitive arena of dramatic productions will have acquired the skills necessary for acting as a general. Both chorus producers and generals necessarily acquire enemies in the course of their activities and must defeat them to be successful, and so the skill set required by both occupations is essentially the same. Socrates' point of comparison between military officers and private citizens rests on assumed similarity between *echthroi* and *polemioi*.

As Peter Hunt has pointed out, the Greeks seem to have transferred their private morality to the interstate sector with ease.[69] The private friendship/enmity ideology finds a close analogy in interstate politics among Greek cities of the era. Like individuals, cities tended to divide all other cities into the dual categories of friends/allies and enemies. Friendly relationships were consecrated by ceremonial pronouncements (treaties) and formal expectations of aid. The similarities between reconciliations of private individuals and peace treaties between states are made clear in a passage of Isocrates 18 (*Against Callimachus*). As he impresses on the jurors the importance of observing contracts (*sunthēkai*), the speaker reminds them that on this basis "we put an end both to private (*idias*) enmities and public (*koinous*) wars."[70] A ritual, formal act, embodied in a *sunthēkē*, was essential for ending hostility, whether between *poleis* or individual citizens.[71]

None of the foregoing should be taken to imply that enmity was monolithic, that either two people were enemies or not, and that was all there was to it. Enmities could be more or less virulent, more or less public, more or less important to the people involved. Furthermore, enmities could be at different stages of development. The hostile relationship between Demosthenes and Meidias was full-grown, but other disputes that we hear about from the orators may have been at the beginning stages, when the enmity had yet to be recognized fully.[72] The point made here is that when Athenians talked about "enmity" and "enemies," they usually envisioned a communally recognized relationship based on both emotion and action. Dislike and avoidance of the object of loathing were not enough; enemies had to behave like enemies for the relationship to be considered a real *echthra*.

A PREVALENT SOCIAL PROBLEM

Speaking of his contemporary readers, Kenneth Dover pointed out, "Few of us expect to be involved for long in a relationship deserving the name of enmity, and a man who spoke of 'my enemies' could fairly be suspected of paranoia. Athenians took enmity much more for granted."[73] Richard Nixon's "enemies list," which was made public during the proceedings of the Senate Watergate Committee, was scandalous, but no one in

Athens would have been surprised if an "enemies list" belonging to Pericles or Demosthenes had come to light. It was not at all uncommon for Athenians to have enemies, and possibly lists of them as well.

Enemies are a ubiquitous concern in Athenian literature. That citizens would have people who hated them and wished them harm is an implicit assumption that often functions as a premise in the structure of other assertions. In the *Charmides* passage discussed above,[74] Socrates simply assumes that Charmides (or any other Athenian boy) would have enemies whose names he could use for writing exercises. In a speech against his enemy Meidias (Dem. 21), Demosthenes appeals to the jurors' awareness that each of them has enemies in the city who want to do them harm and are waiting for an opportunity to pounce. Stressing the importance of punishing criminals to deter future crimes of a similar nature, he argues that any time a man who has been physically assaulted (as he has) fails to obtain justice from his attacker through the courts, everyone else in the city must expect that he will be the next victim. In other words, if the Athenian juries stop punishing wrongdoers like Meidias for assault, then the jurors' own enemies will recognize their weakness and come after them.

The force of Demosthenes' argument depends on the assumption that the members of the audience all have enemies about whom they should be worried: "Perhaps Meidias hates me, but there is someone else who hates each one of you. Would you then allow this man, whoever it is who hates you, to have the power to do to each one of you the very things this man did to me? I do not think so."[75] Demosthenes takes the jurors' presumed fears about their own enemies and amplifies them by positing the specter of a city in which men could attack each other with impunity. Demosthenes' rhetorical appeal to the jurors' self-interest assumes that everybody needs protection from their enemies and that without laws everyone would be in danger. The indispensable foundation for this argument is an assumption that the audience was willing to envision enmity as a prevalent phenomenon. Demosthenes' argument would fall flat if this threat applied to only very few of the jurors.

Enmity was a fact of life, and a man's ability to overcome his enemies could be considered part of the definition of living well. A rhetorical question from the chorus in Euripides' *Bacchae* embodies the mentality well: "What better gift do mortals receive from the gods than to hold one's hand over the head of one's enemies?"[76] There was nothing wrong with laughing at your enemy's misfortune.[77] The title character of Xenophon's *Hiero* likewise asserts, "I think that the most pleasant thing of all is to take things from enemies against their will."[78] A character in Euripides' *Heraclidae* states that an enemy who has fallen out of prosperity into hard times is "the most pleasant sight."[79] Tragedy is an especially fertile source for such malevolent pleasure.[80] Even rage itself could be pleasurable, as a Homeric proverb expresses forcefully: "Anger makes even a wise man enraged and rises up in men's chests like smoke, sweeter by far than dripping honey."[81] But the thrill of victory brought the ultimate satisfaction. The author of a rhetorical handbook, while discussing intrinsically plausible motivations for action that would have been obvious to the audience because "everyone" has the same thoughts, can blithely include the wish that one's "enemies would suffer misfortune."[82]

It followed naturally that those who were involved in enmities could become paranoid about the possibility that their enemies were laughing at them. The Homeric-style characters of tragedy often calculate their actions just as much to avoid their enemies' ridicule as to win their friends' praise.[83] In fact, when laughter is mentioned in Greek tragedy, it is usually the feared or anticipated laughter of enemies.[84] On a grassroots level, this distress at the thought of being made a laughingstock manifests itself in many curse tablets, whose authors try to preempt the mocking of their enemies through divine aid.[85] Of course, the authors of these curses probably did not have any qualms about *Schadenfreude* as a concept; they merely wanted to arrogate it for themselves.

Enmity was a fundamental part of the fabric of Athenian society, and the legitimacy of seeking revenge on one's enemies was simply assumed. Not even the philosophers rise above this us-versus-them view of society. When Socrates proposes in the *Gorgias* that it is better not to retaliate against enemies, he never questions the legitimacy of desiring to see them harmed.[86] As he clarifies his rationale, he reveals that he is recommending a course of action that will result in maximum injury to the adversary. If one's enemies are permitted to do wrong without punishment or penalty, they suffer much more terrible consequences than if they were punished because their souls rather than their bodies are harmed. Socrates' prescription against retaliation does not overthrow the principle of harming enemies but rather reorients the way in which the just man should seek to do his adversaries harm. Socrates in no way challenges the natural division of one's acquaintances into friends and enemies.

Competitive Context

Athenian concerns about enemies are understandable in the context of the culture of competitiveness and honor-seeking that prevailed in Athens and in ancient Greece in general. This ethic is reflected in the earliest Greek literature. The entire plot of the *Iliad* centers on an insult paid to Achilles when Agamemnon takes his prize of war, the woman Briseis. This affront is in turn merely a response to another perceived slight. Agamemnon had been forced to give up his spoils of war, another slave woman, at Achilles' instigation and so took his frustration out on Achilles by attempting to lower his standing in the eyes of the rest of the Greeks. Achilles retaliates by refusing to fight, providing the main source of tension for the development of the story. The *Iliad*'s main subject, the "wrath" of Achilles, is a response to an insult that was in its turn a response to another insult. The rest of the epic chronicles the resultant drawn-out battle for honor. The Achilles-Agamemnon dispute exemplifies how Homeric heroes may be fighting for the same side but are at the same time in fierce competition with each other.[87] For men of this stamp, almost any interaction has the potential to create rancor and rivalry.[88] Greek epic is replete with examples of this constant struggle for standing.[89]

The Greeks' predilection for competition is also reflected in their passion for athletics.[90] The most revered athletic festival in the Greek world, the Olympic games, may well have owed its popularity to the extremity with which it represented the zero-sum game of honor. The Olympics had no team sports and no second-place prizes and included only events that had objective criteria for victory (that is, no music, dancing, or similar events).[91] In each event there was one and only one winner, and the standard by which he would gain victory would be clear to all: the man who threw his javelin the farthest, who ran past the finish line first, who threw his opponent to the ground. The Olympics reflected the Greek enthusiasm for activities that resulted in clear-cut victory and defeat in a battle for honor and standing. With justice did Montesquieu suggest that we regard the Greeks as "une société d'athletes et de combattants."[92]

The esteem in which such competitions were held gave rise to an important form of poetry, the celebration of athletic victories, a genre well known from the odes of Simonides, Pindar, and Bacchylides. The mere existence of this type of literature as a respected art form indicates how much the Greeks enjoyed competition, but these authors also provide evidence for how keen the desire for victory and how heavy the disgrace of failure could be. In one of his odes, Pindar sings of young boys who lost a competition and therefore "did not receive a happy homecoming," even from their mothers. Theirs was a bleak existence: "Staying clear of their enemies, they shrink down alleyways, bitten by failure."[93] The extreme depression of these teenagers is probably exaggerated, but the scene poignantly illustrates the dreadful consequences of loss of face, an inevitable companion to agonistic values. To avoid such dishonor, many athletes took solace in appeals to a higher power and authored or purchased curses against their competitors.[94] The Greeks pursued victory and shunned defeat with remarkable zeal.

On a deeper level, competition permeated everyday life. Activities of every sort were subject to judgment about who had performed the best or the most honorably or in a way consistent with some other criteria of evaluation. The excellence of one person constituted a natural challenge to those around him because when a community honored one person it necessarily withheld the honor from others.[95] In Greek culture, public esteem and standing in the community were of enormous importance, and both were constantly being negotiated and renegotiated through competitive displays of bravado and superiority. Athenians may not, like their Homeric predecessors, have sated themselves with violent reprisals, but they shared many characteristics with those honor-driven men, often revealing signs of their distinct "touchiness," a readiness to respond to any perceived slight to their honor or lack of the deference that they believed was due them.[96]

Far from attempting to stifle this competitive spirit, the Athenian constitution harnessed it for its own ends, encouraging citizens to contend for status in the eyes of the community with spirited displays of patriotism.[97] The Assembly granted recognized benefactors certain privileges such as exemption from taxation or an honorary crown.[98] This was a quid pro quo exchange: the city received support from the elite, while the elite received a boost in standing and an edge against their competitors in the struggle for public approbation. The many honorary decrees that archaeologists have unearthed demonstrate how active the Athenian Assembly was in granting favors in return for services rendered. That Athenians consciously encouraged this type of rivalry is clear from several law court speeches, including Aeschines 3 (*Against Ctesiphon*), in which Aeschines exhorts his audience to be more sparing in the prizes awarded to their benefactors so that the honors will have more value and the "good" citizens will be more ready to compete for them.[99]

By rewarding "competitive outlay," as David Whitehead terms it, the city harnessed the Greek competitive spirit for the good of the state,[100] but it also raised the stakes for ongoing rivalries among the elites. Thomas Hobbes, well schooled in classical politics, saw this as a permanent defect of deliberative government, "to see his opinion whom we scorne, preferr'd before ours; to have our wisedome undervalued before our own faces [. . .] to undergoe most certaine enmities (for this cannot be avoided, whether we have the better, or the worse)."[101] Politics, then as now, led to rancor that became personal, as Dinarchus pointed out: "Enmities and disputes that come from public matters become the causes of private disputes."[102] The system of state-sanctioned honors and incentives worked to the benefit of the community but also created an arena of institutionalized fighting that was bound to spill over into other areas of life.[103]

Competition for favor and status was also perhaps the most important motivating factor behind the elite citizens' performance of liturgies, specific responsibilities delegated by the Athenian government to members of the wealthiest class of citizens.[104] The richest men in Athens were selected to carry out certain duties such as the production of a dramatic play at a festival (*chorēgia*), support of an athletic team (*gymnasiarchia*), or equipping and command of a warship for the fleet (trierarchy).[105] Because all of these activities took place in the public limelight, wealthy citizens could take advantage of this institution to gain status and reputation in the city with their conspicuous expenditure.[106] Liturgies put a considerable financial burden on even a wealthy Athenian's estate, but they also provided opportunities for unabashed self-promotion.[107]

Although rival citizens would already be engaged in a continuous battle for status in the community, those who performed liturgies were often pitted against each other more directly. Anyone who organized a chorus for a play at one of Athens' festivals was engaged ipso facto in a battle against others who had been selected for the same duty. The outcome of the competitions, which were conducted at public gatherings before thousands of Athenians, would have ramifications on the relative status of the various chorus producers.[108] Indeed, a poor performance in a *chorēgia* was not necessarily a mere personal disappointment; it could entail loss of face in front of the entire polis.[109] The same could be said for the trierarchy. Athens' habit of constantly being at war with some city or other meant public interest would always attach to the activities of its warship commanders. Where the community cast its critical gaze, there the struggle for honor was keenest.

The state actively encouraged rivalry among liturgists by offering prizes for exemplary performance of duty. A formal competitive element was always present for *chorēgoi*, who contended for first prize at the festival at which they staged their dramatic productions, but in the case of trierarchs, when the city had a pressing need for the services of its warships, a decree was sometimes passed that awarded a crown to the person who most quickly completed the preparations for his trireme.[110] Additionally, Liddel suggests that the accounts of the naval *epimeletai*, which recorded the names of ships and numbers and types of equipment handed over from one trierarch to the next, may also have had an honorific function in that they provided a tangible public testament to the liturgists' benefactions.[111] Such formal recognition of one citizen's superiority heightened the participants' already considerable agonistic drive.

Formation of Enmities

That the Athenians' competitive and combative spirit caused friction between honor-driven individuals is hardly surprising. In such an environment, enmity naturally erupts. Enmity forms an integral part of the social and political machinery of agonistic societies. To identify the ways in which enmities could be made, attention must be given both to evidence for particular relationships of enmity and to evidence for societal and political practices or institutions that fostered competition and therefore created the conditions under which relationships of enmity were likely to result. Fortunately, a significant body of evidence about Athenian enmities allows us a glimpse into the many ways in which enemies could be made. The data on any ancient society are insufficient for drawing conclusions about how many relationships of enmity were operative at a given time, or about how often particular types of disputes resulted in enmities, but a glance at various circumstances under which Athenians could become enemies will give some idea of how pervasive enmity could be. When we see that enmity could arise in almost any context, we can understand why Athenians accepted enmity as a fact of life.

Before an examination of the various ways in which an Athenian could make an enemy, however, a pertinent methodological question presents itself: How can a relationship of enmity be recognized as such in our sources? The appearances of certain keywords such as *echthros* or *echthra* are clear indicators of relationships of enmity, but a purely lexical approach to the subject will fail to account for all the available data. Any mention of reciprocated acts of harm between two individuals (especially public acts) may be treated as a sign that a relationship of enmity either already existed or was in the offing. Therefore, the mere existence of a lawsuit between two Athenians implies enmity, whether that enmity has already been recognized to exist or would only have been truly consummated after the court's verdict. The same may be said about curse tablets, which probably represent the product of a public ceremony. In an honor culture, a man will not feel comfortable speaking about his anger against another man if he is not willing to consider him an enemy.

A convenient starting point for considering enmities in public and private life in Athens is the friction created by the operation of the Athenian political system, which depended on enmity as a catalyst for public action and therefore encouraged enmity between citizens. When Aeschines said that "private enmities very often correct public matters,"[112] he was referring to the democracy's reliance on volunteer prosecutors, many of whom brought suit more out of animosity for the defendant than concern for the public good. Enmity had a policing function: enemies could be relied on to provide a check on each other's behavior through the threat of prosecution. Unfortunately, this functionalist view of enmity had the effect of encouraging it by providing avenues for enemies to attack each other. The same dynamic is at work in the *dokimasia* and *euthynai* procedures, the entry and exit examinations for magistrates. After the candidate answered a series of questions about his formal qualifications for the post (citizenship, age, previous criminal convictions), any citizen could come forward to argue that he was an unsuitable candidate. These were open invitations for enemies to slander and potentially embarrass each other.[113]

The liturgical system is another example of how Athenian political practice both assumed the existence of enmities and created an environment in which they could flourish. In the two best-known liturgies, the *chorēgia* and trierarchy, the straightforward competition with other liturgists created a forum for conflict so charged that no one would be surprised to find multiple relationships of hostility taking root. The whole system was designed to encourage *philotimia* among the members of the upper class and thereby prompt each liturgist to perform to the best of his ability,[114] but in practice the distinction between the good and the bad Eris ("Strife") was difficult to maintain. Rivalry between trierarchs brought hostile relationships in tow, and conflict at the theater continued offstage. The *philotimia* system both depended on and encouraged rivalries between those who performed service to the state.[115]

Politicking and strife over liturgies began before the actual performance of them. Despite some uncertainty about the procedure for appointment of liturgists, it seems clear that the process allowed leeway (whether legal or not) for men of authority to influence the selection.[116] In a passage in Aristophanes' *Knights*, Cleon threatens the Sausage Seller, "I will see to it that you become a trierarch and spend all your money on an old ship."[117] Apparently, generals had the ability to manipulate the process, and a citizen with enough influence might force unprofitable trierarchies on his enemies to punish them.[118] Law court speakers' complaints that their enemies engineered their appointment to the *chorēgia* or other liturgies corroborate Aristophanes' witness.[119] At the same time, others may actually have sought out trierarchies, which in certain circumstances could apparently be quite lucrative.[120] The powerful and wealthy might promise trierarchies to their associates or dependents as a token of friendship. The profits available to someone who had one of the elite war vessels of the era at his disposal could have had their source in a number of avenues, but privateering and networking with business partners are aptly identified by Vincent Gabrielsen as two of the most likely.[121] Whether they were avoiding trierarchies or seeking them, Athenian elites did not see the selection process as random. Exactly how men of influence manipulated the proceedings is not certain, but it is clear that they did.

The negotiations behind liturgy selection brings to light another avenue for competition, disputes, and enmity. As is typical of the Athenian system, no impartial, state-provided officers oversaw the selection and performance of liturgists to ensure that everyone played by the rules. The participants had to police each other. For instance, the process for ensuring that only those most able to afford liturgical service were called upon was left up to individual citizens. Anyone who had been allotted a liturgy could avoid it only by suggesting someone else and challenging that man to a rather bizarre procedure called an *antidosis*.[122] The challenged individual had two options: he could take on the liturgy in the place of his challenger or he could agree to exchange property. If complications arose, the dispute went to court under the *diadikasia* procedure. Gabrielsen may be right to call the *antidosis* "a sophisticated mechanism designed by the state,"[123] but privatized policing of fellow liturgists meant that citizens, instead of dealing with the impersonal arm of the state, were in direct conflict with each other.[124] Any dispute over other liturgists' conduct was liable to end up in court and therefore in enmity.[125] The apparatus of the entire liturgical system, from appointment to performance to policing abuses, created a natural arena for elites to squabble over the various details.

Involvement in the political life of the city tended to foster the development of long-standing animosities.[126] Deliberation over foreign policy in the Assembly created factions among the "orators" (i.e., the elite politicians) that frequently took on a personal dimension.[127] Demosthenes' deliberative speeches (Dem. 1–17), addressed to the Assembly, illustrate how such enmity could arise. He does not draw a distinction between his opponents' political stances and their private lives but rather attacks them indiscriminately with *ad hominem* arguments.[128] It is not surprising, then, to find the orators continuing their political battles in the courts (most famously in the case of Demosthenes and Aeschines). Roberts points out that the prosecutions of public officials can often be traced back to factional strife and personal vendettas.[129] Many of the famous trials of classical Greece (e.g., Cimon's in 463/2, Pericles' in 430, or Demosthenes' in 330) have roots in the politics of personal enmity.[130]

An anecdote from Xenophon's *Memorabilia* corroborates this overlap between political debates and private enmities. Socrates asks Aristippus about the education of two hypothetical youths, one of whom will be educated to be a strong leader and the other who will learn to be obsequious. As Socrates and Aristippus discuss the various skills that each boy will require for their future careers, Socrates asks, "To which of the two does it seem right to impart the necessary knowledge for overcoming one's rivals?" Aristippus replies, "He who is being educated to lead, of course, since there would be no use for all the rest of these lessons without this one."[131] A successful politician could expect to make many enemies among his fellow citizens as a matter of course and therefore had to develop the skills necessary to master them. Otherwise, all the political skill in the world counted for naught.

Although liturgists and "orators" were members of the wealthy elite, the competitions in which they participated were not necessarily limited to the upper classes. First of all, many nonelites participated in the enmities formed in arenas that have been commonly considered the orators' exclusive preserve. The *chorēgoi* and playwrights may have been the visible faces for dramatic contests, but the competitive feeling trickled down to the rest of the group. Two curse tablets, one binding directors and assistant directors (*didaskaloi, hypodidaskaloi*), another binding an actor, demonstrate that more people became personally invested in these events than just the wealthy elites.[132] Although scholars have long considered the political battles in the Assembly and courts the domain of the super-rich, Rubinstein has plausibly argued that citizens of more moderate means participated in less conspicuous roles. For instance, the practice of *synēgoria* allowed the talented but underprivileged to attach themselves to important public figures through networks of patronage and, eventually, to ascend the political ladder in their own right.[133] Political factions could have constituents among the up-and-coming, so that even if only the top members of a partisan bloc actually spoke in the Assembly, personal enmity would affect a wider base as it spread through the ranks.[134]

Minor political characters could also be involved in public competitive enterprises at the local level. Demes put on liturgies, which invited competitive expenditure just as the city's liturgies did.[135] The rewards were also similar. Honorary decrees from the demes employed the same language of benefactor-recipient gratitude characteristic of the decrees issued by the Athenian Assembly and Council.[136] In the same vein as these latter institutions, local politics would no doubt have given birth to raucous meetings, passionate competition, and heated words. There were quarrels to be had, decrees to be debated, political wrangling to be waged. Demosthenes 57 (*Against Eubulides*) paints a vivid picture of what such wrangling could look like.[137] The deme reflected the city's governmental apparatus and, as a microcosm of Athens, provided many more opportunities for relationships of enmity to arise. The liturgical system and the oratorical debates of the city put citizens in constant conflict, and there is no reason to suppose that this was any different at the deme level or that the competitive atmosphere was any less charged. In a culture in which politics and personal honor are deeply intertwined, enmities are the price of radically participatory government.[138]

For all its importance as a source of quarrels and disagreements, public life was not the only area susceptible to the influence of enmity. Regular participation in nearly any activity could foster rivalry and hostility even when honor and prestige were not so obviously in focus. Financial disputes[139] and competition between businesses[140] were well-known culprits. That the rivalries of "workshops" (*ergastēria*) led to more than mere mercantile competition is shown by the many "commercial" curse tablets,[141] which often call down curses on their targets' "workshop" (*ergastērion*), "profits" (*kerdē*), "art" (*technē*), or more generally "doings" (*ergasia*).[142] The elite bias of our sources, deeply influenced by the ideology that gentlemen should not engage in manual labor, shields these lower-class occupations from our view, but many Athenians would have been involved in such commercial pursuits on a daily basis. The curse tablets provide a window into a world wherein shopkeepers and merchants fought against each other in a daily struggle, sometimes making enemies.[143]

The sources make abundantly clear that disputes over inheritance were capable of causing even the close-knit *oikos* to be riven by enmity among its members.[144] The complexity and proverbial opacity[145] of Athenian testamentary law[146] aggravated already sensitive disputes by allowing much leeway for intricate and often convoluted interpretations of the relevant statutes or elaborate claims about the circumstances surrounding a will.[147] One particular law that invalidated a will made under the influence of insanity, old age, drugs, or a woman was recognized in antiquity as being particularly responsible for such wrangling because it opened up virtually any inheritance arrangement to dispute.[148] No matter how well prepared the testament was, complete with hard documents and plenty of witnesses,[149] it would always be subject to dispute if another claimant could find, or invent, a plausible reason for its invalidation based on the testator's mental health, his true last wishes, or simply the rightful path for the property to follow.[150]

The Athenian propensity for competition meant that those who were in proximity to each other and knew each other's affairs were especially likely to have problems maintaining good relations. Neighbors quarreled over all sorts of things and were consequently employed as witnesses against each other.[151] Jones identifies disputes over property lines as a frequent source of quarrels for rural Athenians.[152] If the purview of the board of *horistai* at the Piraeus included, as their name suggests, oversight of boundary stones (*horoi*),[153] the mere existence of these officials points to an awareness that disputes over borderlines were a serious problem that needed an institutional remedy. Plato at least would agree. The Athenian stranger of the *Laws* provides a long list of disputes that can arise between neighbors and should be eliminated in his theoretical utopia. His concern to find a way to alleviate these sources of tension indicates the gravity of the problem: "Many small injuries occur between neighbors and, because they occur so often, engender a huge amount of enmity, making neighborly relations difficult and exceedingly bitter."[154] Plato's critical attitude toward the democracy probably led to an exaggeration of the problems of private wealth and land, but his viewpoint is still a product of the general Athenian milieu. Moreover, it harmonizes with the evidence drawn from the orators that reveals a basic assumption that enmities could arise from such problems. Neither orator nor philosopher needed to argue the point. In both cases a simple assertion or description of the problem was sufficient to tap into a general presupposition.

An Athenian was not necessarily safe from the danger of making an enemy even while he was at leisure.[155] Perhaps it should be no surprise that the evidence points primarily to activities involving sex and alcohol, both of which were recognized as stimuli to irrational acts.[156] Disputes over prostitutes find frequent mention,[157] and rivalries and even homicides resulting from competition over free women are also attested.[158] The curse tablets against rival lovers suggest that such a defeat in a lovers' game did not necessarily lead to mere sulking and self-pity; it could encourage active aggression against the perceived offenders. One rather lengthy curse discovered in the Athenian agora prays that Leosthenes and Peios, two rivals for the affections of a certain Juliana, would cease visiting her and would "not be able to speak or walk with one another, nor sit in Juliana's place of business."[159] These curses, which were formal (and possibly public)[160] acts of hostility against other persons, bear witness to the tendency of quarrels to devolve into open hostility.

An Athenian was in danger of making an enemy at virtually any time he was around other human beings. Even trivial disputes, flippant criticism, and gossip could spark conflict and engender animosity. In one of his philosophical works, Isocrates warns the young Demonicus to watch carefully how he speaks to others because, while praise for one's acquaintances can begin a friendship, censure can just as easily cause enmity.[161] Criticism by a friend or acquaintance could be a serious blow to one's honor and standing and therefore demand an appropriate response. The Athenians, it seems, were not particularly willing to put up with their friends talking behind their backs. The speaker of Lysias 8 accuses his so-called "friends" of having done exactly that, and so he willingly resigns their friendship.

"Turn the other cheek" was not a mainstream value. Consequently, Aristotle (*Rh.* 2.4) asserts that friends will likely be those who are not critical (*tous mē oneidistas*) or apt to slander others (*tous mē kakologous*) since such behavior could easily terminate a friendship. One had to be careful how one interacted with one's friends. Even the failure to return a friendly greeting or the nagging reminder of one's benefactions could be interpreted as an insult, causing ill will and turning a friend into an enemy.[162]

The vast array of ways in which hostile relationships could take shape makes understandable the Athenian assumption that enmity was a fact of life. Athenians could make enemies in any aspect of daily life that admitted of competition (which, for the Greeks, meant all aspects). The orators' casual admissions of long-standing feuds with other citizens make sense within this context. Yet, in spite of the great many avenues for making enemies on one's own merits, enmity created in these ways is only half, perhaps less than half, the story. Once established, enmity had the potential to spread like a virus.

AN INFECTIOUS DISEASE

Enmity was tenacious and infectious. Hostile relationships tended to expand—often dramatically—traveling through and disrupting affinity groups and social networks. Most enmities began with two individuals, but they seldom ended with them. A typical Athenian could come into conflict with another citizen in his own daily activities, but his friends and family could also provide them for him.

Spreading through Social Networks

The tendency of Athenians to group themselves into identifiable social networks and "circles" facilitated the spread of hostile relationships. *Philoi* (which included both friends and family) were expected to share each other's likes and dislikes, friends and enemies. Sharing the same enemies was a prerequisite for friendship.[163] Therefore, a newly formed relationship of enmity could cause a chain reaction among groups of *philoi* with far-ranging consequences.

The first level to which enmity expanded was the household (*oikos*), which was a fundamental unit of identity.[164] When the heads of two *oikoi* became enemies, they drew all members of their households into the relationship. Many of these would have been women and slaves, who, because of their marginalized status, could not make a significant contribution to the furtherance of hostilities, but sons of the *oikonomos* could perpetuate the feud into another generation.¹⁶⁵ As offspring were strongly identified with the head of the household and were expected to share the same interests,¹⁶⁶ a son was obliged to help his father's friends and take vengeance on his father's enemies even after the father died. Both defendants and prosecutors in court sometimes trace the origins of their trial to a feud inherited from the previous generation.¹⁶⁷ Indeed, young Athenians might reasonably expect that they would inherit a set of enemies at an early age. Even orphans had reason to fear an "ancestral enemy" (*patrikos echthros*) bequeathed by their father.¹⁶⁸ Transgenerational friendship and enmity were natural enough concepts to serve as a metaphor for viewing individuals' relationships to the *polis*.¹⁶⁹ This makes sense within the Athenian worldview, wherein an *oikos* rather than simply an individual contracted relationships with others.

The close connection between father and son was reflected in Athenian law, which provided that the son inherit his father's entire estate, including debts.¹⁷⁰ The enemies that his father had made in his business transactions would transfer readily to the son since the son could sue or be sued based on the activities of his father. A number of such cases survive.¹⁷¹ Sometimes a son was obliged to carry through a lawsuit on a dispute that had begun with his father. At other times he was compelled to stand trial for his father's offenses or debts. The heir had no way out of his liabilities because the bequeathing of debts was automatic. In fact, Athenian men were prohibited from making a will if they had legitimate sons in their household.¹⁷² The estate, including liabilities, passed on to the sons automatically (even in intestacy). The law of inheritance reflected the belief that sons were heirs to all of their fathers' debts and assets, whether what was "owed" was money, a favor, or an act of hostility.¹⁷³

The son's duty to settle his father's scores comes strikingly before our eyes in the story of a man named Dionysodorus, who on his deathbed identified his murderer and requested vengeance from all of his family members, including notably his unborn son.¹⁷⁴ This child would presumably have been taught that his eventual duty was to avenge his father. Several passages from Athenian tragedies further corroborate this ideology, sometimes even assuming that sons' duty to pay back their fathers' enemies was a prime motivator behind a man's desire to have children. In the *Antigone* Creon rebukes his son for failing to support him against his rivals: "For this reason men pray that they may have obedient children and keep them in their houses, so that they might repay their father's enemy with evils."¹⁷⁵ Creon probably does not mean that this is the only reason to have children, but he does imply that this is an important duty for a son to discharge, failure in which was liable to strong censure. Correspondingly, a father's hope for his children's success could be expressed in terms of their ability to overcome their hereditary foes. Jason addresses his children in Euripides' *Medea*, "How I wish I could see you being raised well and come into manhood, victorious over my enemies!"[176] Anyone who wished to harm his enemy had to take into account the potential of his rival's *oikos* to retaliate. As the proverb went, "Foolish is the man who kills the father and spares the son,"[177] and the man who kills neither must be ready to contend with both.[178]

The connection between father and son seems to have been a particularly important one, but a relationship of enmity had the potential to draw in any number of relatives. The Dionysodorus mentioned above asks for vengeance not only from his unborn son but also from his brother, brother-in-law, and all his friends.[179] His brother-in-law (or cousin) was in fact the one who lodged the suit with the support of Dionysodorus' brother, Dionysius, who probably served as a co-speaker.[180] Even in cases less extreme than murder, it was commonplace for *philoi* to support each other in disputes, especially once a formal court action took place, and thereby enter into a relationship of enmity.[181] The ideal of *oikos* solidarity prescribed this sort of behavior: kinsmen were expected to help each other, while failure to do so could be a mark of cowardice.[182] An attack on one was an attack on all. When the extended families, including brothers-in-law and second cousins are taken into account, it is not difficult to imagine how one relationship of enmity could have a large ripple effect throughout the group. Enmity with a *kurios* ("head of a household") meant enmity with the whole household but also with many other family members. The close family ties between even relatively distant relations in antiquity meant that any newly formed enmity had significant potential for claiming fresh victims.

The injunction to share enemies did not stop with blood ties; it was an important part of the Athenian conception of friendship in general. The bonds that held relative and relative also held friend and friend,[183] and so a man could appeal to his friend to be "wronged together" with him.[184] If there was truth in the Greek proverb that "friends share all things in common," they shared enemies as well.[185] This was the mark of a true *philos*. Friends tended to acquire each other's enemies as their own, so that social groups were apt to organize along the lines of friendship and enmity.[186]

An Athenian's request for his friend to become actively involved in his enmity could take on many different forms. It is not difficult to imagine chance encounters at festivals and deme meetings turning into shouting matches or scuffles, but we can only speculate on the manifold ways in which enmities played out on a practical level in everyday life. Our available sources compel us to concentrate on disputes that took legal form, but we should not forget that many other less visible ways of perpetuating hostile relationships have not left such a heavy mark in literature. The courtroom was not the only place that enmity could spread, although for us it is the most visible.

Spreading through Team Litigation

There were three ways in which an Athenian could formally include another person in his legal proceedings against his enemies: through third-party litigation, the use of co-speakers, and the use of witnesses. The first method virtually guaranteed a spreading of hostilities since it directly pitted a friend or family member against the enemy. Third-party litigation seems to have been a realistic option, especially for those with enough wealth or influence to "persuade" someone else to do their dirty work for them. Although such solicitation was frowned upon, there is much evidence for it.[187] For those who could not afford a hireling, an attractive alternative would have been to ask friends or family members to bring suit *pro bono*.[188]

Even when an Athenian prosecuted his enemy himself, friends and family could play supporting roles. Litigation was a team sport. Formally, a lawsuit was a simple contest between two adult citizen males who spoke on their own behalf and could not hide behind lawyers or representatives, but Rubinstein (2000) has pointed out that this "simple *agōn* model" is misleading. Litigants often brought teams of witnesses and advocates to court, so that litigation became "team-based." We should therefore envision two "teams" pitted against each other in an intensely personal and confrontational affair.[189] When one citizen took another to court, the battle between two individuals transformed into a battle between two competing power blocs, and the opportunity for the expansion of enmity correspondingly increased.[190]

The second way friends could get involved in each other's court cases was the practice of *synēgoria*, speaking as an advocate on another's behalf. This was quite common: approximately one-third of the extant speeches belong to a *synēgoros*, and even hostile sources do not condemn relatives who support each other in this role.[191] Direct involvement in the events leading to the trial was not necessary; many co-speakers saw their friendship with the main litigator as a sufficient excuse for appearing before the jury on his behalf.[192] It seems that an Athenian could expect to draw on his circle of family and friends to support him in court whether or not they had immediate personal interest in the outcome of the trial.

The third way to include a friend in one's trial was to call him as a witness. Because it was considered their duty to support each other in such circumstances, a litigant's witnesses often came from his known and trusted associates.[193] The loss of a friend could be equated with the loss of potential advocates or witnesses in future court cases.[194] So strong was the pressure exerted by the ideal of solidarity that the orators express many times the concern that friends and family members would be willing even to lie as witnesses on each other's behalf.[195]

The participation of *philoi* in the trial as advocates and witnesses widened the scope for new relationships of enmity because a litigant would believe that everyone on his opponent's side was performing a hostile act against him.[196] Members of the opposite team were fair game, and speakers had no reservations about verbally abusing their opponents' *synēgoroi* during the trial.[197] Those who were attacked in this fashion could be expected to carry a grudge. Demosthenes, in his attack on Aristogiton, reveals by his caution how easy it was to make enemies of an opponent's associates. In introducing his character assassination of Aristogiton's acquaintances, he recognizes that he embarks on a "very dangerous" task and expresses his desire to "limit the reproach to as few as possible."[198] Demosthenes does in fact restrict his attack to one person (Philocrates), but his belabored assertions about his own restraint reveal that he might typically expect to make many more enemies. If someone asked a friend to appear as an advocate on his behalf, he was asking that person to risk enmity with the opposing litigant.[199] A *synēgoros* would know that he was likely getting into a relationship of enmity.

Although less visible than co-speakers, witnesses also risked new hostile relationships. In *Against Demosthenes* Dinarchus attacks the opposing witnesses, warning the jury that those who dare to speak on Demosthenes' behalf must be "hostile to the constitution" and "common enemies of the laws and the whole city."[200] If the simple act of appearing in court against each other was not enough, insulting language of this sort would inevitably lead to the expansion of the feud.[201] Such verbal assaults on the opposing team are common in oratory, and the *Rhetoric to Alexander* (a rhetorical handbook from the fourth century BC) considered it imperative to attack the character of the opponent's witnesses.[202] Moreover, an unsuccessful litigant could use his opponent's witness as a scapegoat by suing him for giving false information (*dikē pseudomartyriōn*) in order to have the original verdict nullified.[203] Because witnesses were often drawn from affinity groups, such suits were often tit-for-tat prosecutions of the opponent's friends or family.[204]

Verbal assault on the opponent's *philoi* did not necessarily end with the formal members of the legal "team." Litigants also attacked each other's relatives indiscriminately. In one trial Demosthenes anticipated that Aeschines' brothers would speak on his behalf and so did not spare them from his abuse, insulting their occupations as clerks and calling them "loudmouthed and shameless."[205] Aeschines employed similar tactics against Demosthenes several years later, denigrating Demosthenes' mother, father, grandfather, grandmother, and aunt in his speech against Ctesiphon.[206] That Aeschines is making enemies by expanding his attacks to include Demosthenes' relatives is made clear by his reticence to insult the husband of Demosthenes' aunt. Demosthenes' mother, who was, Aeschines asserts, a barbarian of Scythian descent, was married off to Demosthenes' father, while her sister was married to a man whom Aeschines refuses to name since he wants "to avoid becoming an enemy of many people."[207] Aeschines may have intended this statement to be humorous; it is hard to see how his assertion that this man's wife was descended from barbarian Scythians could have been anything but an insult to his honor. Still, it reveals that Aeschines is well aware that his attacks on Demosthenes' family have enlarged the feud and the hatred that fuels it, cementing the hostile relationship between their kinship groups.[208]

Curse tablets[209] confirm that Athenian litigants took it personally when someone appeared against them in court, even merely as part of the supporting cast. The authors of several tablets include their opponents' fellow litigants (*syndikoi*) in their imprecations.[210] Wünsch *Def. tab.* 39 is representative of the pattern.

> Ariphrades, Cleophon, Archedamus, Polyxenus, Anticrates, Antiphanes, Zacorus, Antichares, Satura, Mika, Simon, the mother of Satira, Theodora . . . Antamis, Eucoline, Ameinias, and all of their fellow litigants (*syndikoi*) and friends.[211]

Several other tablets curse their opponents' *synēgoroi* and witnesses specifically.[212] Wünsch *Def. tab.* 38 provides an illustrative example.

> Philippides, Euthycritus, Cleagorus, Menetimus, and everybody else, whoever spoke as advocates (*synēgoroi*) for them.[213]

The common formulae on these tablets that curse an opponent's associates in trial confirm that Athenian litigants saw the opposition's entire supporting cast as hostile to them. The *katadesmoi* provide a window into the views of the common Athenian citizen. The blanket curses of all the friends and family of an opponent, along with the provision "and anyone else who . . ." that covers possible omissions, illustrate how quickly and how far a feud could spread. These *katadesmoi* demonstrate how infectious enmity could be.[214]

CONCLUSION

Athens' culture of honor, competition, and enmity was fundamental to Athenians' lives. Anyone who ignored the competitive atmosphere that Athenians breathed did so at his own peril. Aristotle observes that those most likely to suffer at the hands of others are those who "have been wronged by many but have never prosecuted."[215] Failure to respond to an enemy's attacks only encouraged predators. Those who turned the other cheek were easy targets, or "Mysian booty," as the Greek proverb would have it.[216] The frequent deployment of the language of "conspiracism" reflected a latent fear that groups of enemies would combine to defeat and marginalize their common foe.[217] The speaker of Demosthenes 57 (*Against Eubulides*) bases his whole rhetorical strategy on this fear. He portrays his opponents as a hostile power bloc that seeks his demise and claims that this coalition is attempting to *katastasiazein* ("overpower by forming a counter party") him.[218] Such gangs, or "workshops" (*ergastēria*), of villains were perceived to be a real threat,[219] as is apparent from the curse tablets that include blanket curses on the target's *philoi* or collaborators (*sunprattontes, vel sim.*).[220] Other tablets strike an even more paranoid note by attempting to preempt "anything that he is doing or plotting against me."[221] Enmity was a problem that could not be ignored.[222]

Athens deserves the appellation of a culture of enmity because of the importance of hostile relationships in the way society was organized. Enmity, which was communally recognized, was conceived of as a prevalent social force that created significant problems for individual Athenians. Enmities could be contracted with relative ease, and once started they created problems for the networks of friends and family involved. The Athenian ideology of friendship demanded that enmity spread among *philoi*, but even more complex problems were involved if two new enemies shared any *philoi*. This created a problem of alignment, to which the friends had to respond by taking sides or attempting to end the dispute through reconciliation. In either case, enmity quickly became a communal concern.

2. THE RHETORIC OF ENMITY AS A LEGAL STRATEGY

The courtroom rhetoric of the Attic orators occupies a privileged position in a study of enmity in classical Athens. Our heavy dependence on texts of this type is, however, by no means a hindrance; it is rather a stroke of luck. At the heart of the debate about feuding is the intersection between private vengeance and public power, which is precisely the matter at issue in legal orations. These speeches afford a glimpse into Athenian society from exactly the angle we want: private individuals coming to terms with public ideological prescriptions. Nonetheless, the nature of the evidence imposes certain limitations, and the reader should always be aware of the problems and biases of this particular type of literature. To engage successfully with our source material, the rhetorical methods that speakers use to present enmity in court must be made clear.

As litigants crafted their speeches, the desire to secure a favorable verdict from the jury determined how they presented their arguments.[1] Speechwriters in classical Athens were compelled to meet the specific expectations of the legal setting and to subordinate all other desires to the attempt to win the case.[2] They were prepared to employ every means that their craft made available to them to advance their arguments. In some situations the speaker might even be willing to cast himself in a negative light if he believed that such a self-characterization would predispose the jury to accept his claims. For instance, a defendant in a trial concerning justifiable homicide named Euphiletus portrays himself as naïve and even effete, anything but the model macho Athenian citizen. The reasons for this legal strategy are clear: he must avoid appearing as a clever, careful, and vindictive pursuer of personal honor and vengeance.[3] Euphiletus, admitting that he killed Eratosthenes after catching him in bed with his wife, claimed that the homicide was justifiable under the Athenian law that allowed a man to execute an adulterer caught in the act, but Euphiletus' opponents had apparently raised the suspicion that he had engineered the whole affair and concocted the adultery scenario as a cover story. To prevent the charge of entrapment from sticking, he emphasizes that he had no ulterior motives for wanting Eratosthenes dead (44–46). He presents himself as a simpleton, the type of person least likely to engage in elaborate plots to settle a grudge.

As portrayed in his narrative, Euphiletus' credulity and obtuseness are almost unbelievable. With heavy irony he outlines for the jury how much trust he had in his wife and her positive qualities as a housekeeper while he describes how she cleverly cuckolded him and thus laid the ground for his public disgrace.[4] Euphiletus even recounts how he slept through one of the adulterer's visits to his house (11–14), a detail that an Athenian citizen would no doubt happily omit in a setting other than the courtroom. This is bad enough, but the pièce de résistance comes when Euphiletus recounts how his wife, as she left her marital bed for her nocturnal rendezvous with Eratosthenes, had the nerve to chastise Euphiletus for trying to get her out of the room so that he could sleep with a slave girl (12). Her playful (and feigned) reluctance to leave Euphiletus has a dreadful irony to it. Euphiletus has been made to look the fool, at least according to Euphiletus.[5]

The orators' use of enmity as a rhetorical strategy is no exception to the maxim that litigants aimed first and foremost at winning the dispute at hand, even when the resulting portrait of the speaker is not entirely favorable. The various strategies employed in the extant speeches can be differentiated and categorized, but they share the common goal of making a litigant's legal argument seem more plausible. For instance, a prosecutor often claims that his enmity with his opponent prompted him to lodge suit because he wants to deflect the jurors' attention from other possible motivations, such as greed. Many procedures in Athens entailed a financial reward for the successful prosecutor, and so the jurors were naturally suspicious of unscrupulous tricksters who trumped up false charges in order to cash in on the reward. If the origins of the lawsuit could be traced to enmity, greed was not needed as an explanation. On the other hand, a defendant often claims that his opponent is an enemy so that he can paint the prosecutor as bringing a false charge in pursuit of a vendetta. The rhetoric of enmity could cut both ways. Yet another litigant may include a narrative of enmity so that he can describe specific incidents in an ongoing hostile relationship and thereby portray his opponent as a liar, sycophant, or monstrous villain. These brief examples give an idea of the general pattern but do not exhaust the many ways in which the rhetoric of enmity can function. In each individual case, the rhetorical exigencies, the particular problems that each speaker must confront, influence litigants' decisions about the best method for presenting their relationships with their opponents. The rhetoric of enmity is grounded in the confines of the legal sphere and limited by the constraints of the rhetorical situation.[6]

The subject of this chapter is the rhetorical manipulation of enmity, which is distinct from enmity as a social phenomenon. We are not concerned here with whether or not a particular relationship qualifies as a relationship of enmity but rather with the orators' argumentative strategies that are based on enmity. Attention will continually be drawn to whether or not a litigant "affirms" or "denies" enmity, not to whether or not a litigant and his opponents were real enemies. In all probability, the court case itself made all of these prosecutor-defendant pairs enemies,[7] but the rhetoric of enmity is based not on the hostile feelings aroused at the court itself but on a history of enmity that can be exploited for arguments about the facts of the case. Hence, Euphiletus in Lysias 1 denies not that Eratosthenes was an enemy (which, as a man who had cuckolded Euphiletus, he certainly was) but that there had been any enmity "except this."[8] The point at issue is whether the two had a history of animosity prior to the adulterous affair. The law court speeches are concerned with affirming or denying preexisting enmity, not enmity as such. For the orators, enmity had to serve as a rhetorical construct.

The individual features of each lawsuit are crucial to an understanding of how each litigant shapes his discussion of enmity to create arguments. Analysis of the extant orations, however, requires more detailed explanation of the *eikos* ("plausibility"/"probability") argument in its various manifestations, especially in regard to its function within litigants' narratives. Once the first section ("Plausibility Arguments, Narrative, and Characterization") has provided a framework for how we should read these narratives, the most prominent rhetorical strategies can receive consideration. The natural starting point is prosecution speeches ("Enmity in Prosecution Speeches") since prosecutors spoke first in trials at Athens and accordingly set the tone for the debate as a whole and for the rhetoric of enmity in particular. The following section ("Defense Tactics") will investigate the methods by which defendants respond to their opponents, employing enmity in ways that correspond to prosecutorial tactics but also oppose them. As will be seen, both prosecutors and defendants alternatively affirm or deny enmity depending on what suits their interests. Despite these apparent differences in tactics, both affirmations and denials support the same sorts of arguments; they both aim ultimately at arguments about the charges themselves.

Close attention to the devices that speakers employ for their arguments will enable a fuller understanding and appreciation of our oratorical texts and the authors' aims. Additionally, as the argument of the chapter progresses, it will become clear that the currently prevailing methodology for constructing models of Athenian belief and practice rests on a misunderstanding of the purposes behind the rhetoric of enmity and so is in need of serious reconsideration.

PLAUSIBILITY ARGUMENTS, NARRATIVE, AND CHARACTERIZATION

The Attic orators carefully planned every detail of their speeches to strengthen their cases by making their version of events seem more plausible. A careful reading of any of these texts reveals how meticulous the speechwriters were in crafting their narratives, emphasizing strong arguments and glossing over weaknesses. With painstaking detective work, scholars have uncovered what appear to be some very weak cases, but the original audience would not have had the luxury of scrutinizing the speeches in this way. An anecdote about the logographer Lysias, circulated in antiquity and recorded by Plutarch, humorously drives this point home. A litigant for whom Lysias had composed a speech complained that when he read the text the first time the speech seemed wonderful, but on the second and third read it seemed dull and hackneyed. Lysias laughed and asked, "Don't you intend to read it to the jurors once?"[9] Lysias, like other speechwriters, was fastidious in designing his speeches to have maximal persuasive force on their initial audiences.

The rhetorical techniques in the orators' arsenal were many and varied. The *Rhetoric to Alexander*, a handbook from the fourth century transmitted in Aristotle's corpus but probably to be attributed to Anaximenes of Lampsacus, bears witness to the manifold devices that litigants in democratic Athens consciously employed. These vary in complexity. Some are simple syllogisms, presented straightforwardly to the listener, while others are more subtle and indirect. All of them, however, depend on the speaker's ability to harmonize his argumentation with his audience's presuppositions.

A useful starting point to clarify how legal argumentation in Athenian courts worked is the *eikos* ("probability"/"plausibility") argument, which has the advantage of being relatively simple. A prominent feature of the extant Athenian law court speeches, this argumentative device received critical treatment from the two major rhetorical handbooks that survive from classical Athens: Aristotle's *Rhetoric* and Anaximenes' *Rhetoric to Alexander*. Aristotle describes *eikos* as "that which happens usually, not absolutely, as some define it, but in regard to things that are able to be otherwise."[10] In other words, an *eikos* argument is designed to persuade on matters that admit of some uncertainty; it is not a scientific demonstration. Aristotle regards the *eikos* argument as essentially a syllogism[11] in which the "probable" functions as the major premise.[12]

The simplest such syllogism consists of a major premise, a minor premise, and a conclusion. Take this example: "I never had a quarrel with the prosecutor. Why would I punch him as he alleges?" Here, the minor (stated) premise is that the speaker was not an enemy of the plaintiff. The major (unstated) premise is that people who are not enemies have no reason to harm each other. Combination of the stated assertion and the unstated presupposition leads to the conclusion that the speaker did not punch the prosecutor. Aristotle defines the major unstated premise, the lynchpin of the entire argument, as "the probable" (*eikos*). If the audience will not accept as a likelihood that people who are not enemies do not typically seek each other's harm, the whole argument falls apart. The reasoning process must be firmly based in the common belief of the audience.

The *Rhetoric to Alexander*, a more practical guide to rhetorical practice than Aristotle's philosophically oriented treatise, hits at the heart of the matter. Anaximenes ties the *eikos* argument directly to the audience's presuppositions, emphasizing that a speaker must be in tune with his listeners.

> There is *plausibility* [*eikos*] in what is being said when the audience has examples in their thoughts. I mean, for example, if someone were to say that he wanted his homeland to be great, his friends to do well, his enemies to have misfortune, and similar things, such things would, taken together, appear plausible [*eikota*]. Everyone in the audience agrees that he himself has such desires about these and similar things. So we must always take care in speeches that we grasp whether the audience agrees with us about the matter about which we are speaking. It is plausible [*eikos*] that they really believe these things.[13]

An effective argument from probability must take into account the expectations and assumptions of the audience.

Aristotle's *Rhetoric* and Anaximenes' *Rhetoric to Alexander* are both fourth-century works, but the Greeks had understood and employed probability arguments long before the time of those two authors. The *eikos* argument is in full flower in the works of the earliest of the Attic orators, Antiphon. As Gagarin points out, the four speeches of Antiphon's *First Tetralogy* (composed probably in the 430s BC), in which hypothetical litigants, prosecutor and defendant, make two speeches apiece concerning an imagined accusation, consist essentially of a series of probability arguments.[14] By this time, Greek orators had already developed a sophisticated use of *eikos* that they employed to great effect in the courtroom. This type of argument, however, predated even Antiphon and may have traced its lineage to the developers of the art of rhetoric themselves.[15] The ancient Greeks told anecdotes about two Sicilians named Tisias and Corax who supposedly pioneered arguments from probability in the middle of the fifth century.[16] Whether or not these are historical figures,[17] that this type of reasoning was known in Athens can be seen not only from Antiphon but also from a speech in Sophocles' *Oedipus Rex* (composed in the 420s BC).[18] Creon employs an implicit probability argument about his supposed motivations for usurping Oedipus' throne: why would he want to become king when he now has all the benefits of kingship and none of the disadvantages?[19] Greek authors employed such *eikos* constructions at least by the mid fifth century.[20]

The Greeks were aware of the problems that could arise from persuasion by probability. The study of rhetoric had the potential to allow an orator to misrepresent the truth and persuade his audience of falsehoods through a series of appeals to plausibility. Plato's dialogues are perhaps the most famous propagators of the criticism of this method of manipulation,[21] but the pioneers of rhetorical tactics, known as "sophists," had already come into suspicion in the fifth century, as Aristophanes' *Clouds* attests. Rhetoric allowed its devotees to make weak arguments seem strong and thereby deceive.

The Attic orators, the best-attested practitioners of probability arguments, do in fact make use of some rather convoluted tactics. One litigant on trial for his citizenship attempts to defeat the accusation that both of his parents were foreigners by arguing that if they had been noncitizens, he would never have claimed them but would have looked for others who would pose as his parents.[22] The very fact that he acknowledges his parents is supposed to prove that they must be citizens. This argument could be used by anyone and so does not shed much light on the credibility of the speaker's case, but it does show how a clever speechwriter could twist almost anything into a means of persuasion. In the absence of hard evidence to shore up such specious arguments, Athenian jurors may have often found themselves in the same quandary as Mr. Heaslop in *A Passage to India*, who had to "work hard in the court trying to decide which of two untrue accounts was the less untrue."

Arguments based on *eikos* can be much more complex than the relatively simple syllogisms discussed above. The *Rhetoric to Alexander* divides plausibility arguments into three categories: those based on natural emotional responses, those based on the habits of particular persons, and those based on the desire for profit.[23] The first and the third are straightforward: the audience will find it plausible if we say that our opponent did such-and-such because he wanted to see his enemy harmed (a natural emotional response) or because he stood to make money from his actions (desire for profit). The second type of argumentation requires more work. Before a speaker shows that his opponent is likely to have done such-and-such, he needs to fit him into a character type with which the jury will be familiar. This rhetorical strategy, which the *Rhetoric to Alexander* terms "taking a plausibility argument from the opponents themselves,"[24] requires that the speaker characterize his opponent before he can present his argument.[25]

The Attic orators make use of this stratagem in precisely the manner that Anaximenes recommends, to derive an argument from the opponents themselves. Demosthenes 37 (*Against Pantaenetus*) provides an example.[26] The speaker, Nicobulus, lodged a *paragraphē*, a barring action that would invalidate the original prosecution by Pantaenetus.[27] This speech contains a complex and confusing narrative, but only one aspect of it need be of concern here: Nicobulus' character assassination against his opponent. He relates how Pantaenetus used every conceivable tactic for manipulating the legal system and, when all else failed, employed a gang of thugs to intimidate innocent people. He accuses Pantaenetus of sycophancy multiple times and supports the accusation by listing his dishonest prosecutions.[28] This portrait of Pantaenetus' character supports Nicobulus' argument that he is lying: "Do you think that the man who misled those jurors will hesitate to mislead you?"[29] This statement makes an explicit connection between the narrative of Pantaenetus' wicked behavior in the past and the speaker's argument about the offense that is on trial. Indeed, the purpose of this narrative is "to show you that now too there's no impudence or lying that he won't resort to."[30] Demosthenes engages in character assassination against Pantaenetus to convince them that this prosecution is the latest in a long series of vexatious lawsuits.

The rhetorical question quoted above takes the normal form of a traditional *eikos* argument: the minor premise is that Pantaenetus has often lied in the past; the major premise, that people who are liars are likely to lie again; the conclusion, that Pantaenetus is probably lying in the present trial. What makes this form of *eikos* more complex is that the minor premise needs to be proven. The mere assertion that one's opponent was the sort of person to commit a certain offense could not go very far in convincing the jury. The speaker in court had to prove his point with reasoning that the jury would accept as plausible; he had to offer evidence. To bring his opponent's character vividly before the eyes of the audience, a speaker had to describe actions, to point to specific examples of what his opponent had done. This is where narrative becomes all important. It provides an opportunity for constructing a persuasive account of the events that led up to the trial and a forum in which arguments from character can gradually emerge. In *Against Pantaenetus* Demosthenes has deployed the rhetorical strategy that Anaximenes explicitly recommended: "Show that the defendant has done this many times before, and if not, things like it."[31]

Such arguments based on character could also be implicit rather than explicit.³² The Attic orators were well acquainted with such rhetorical strategies and were capable of employing sophisticated and subtle techniques for appealing to the mind of the listener. A broad theme or repeated allusions to certain aspects of the case could create in the jurors' minds a certain idea, a premise that leads naturally to a conclusion that the speaker intends for them to draw. For instance, in a case of physical assault, a prosecutor may make references to past examples of his opponent's reckless conduct to create an impression of his character that will tacitly support the accusation. The implied argument, even if it is never expressly stated, would be, "if my opponent characteristically acts in such-and-such a way, do you not think it likely that, given the opportunity and necessary motivation, he would punch me?" The subtlety of this type of argument has the potential to be even more effective on an audience than an explicitly formulated *eikos* argument because the jurors may not be aware of how they are being conditioned to accept the speaker's claims.

The hypothetical argument in the preceding paragraph is not an example of an *eikos* argument in the traditional sense, but it shares a similar logical structure, even if the premises and conclusion are implicit rather than explicit. Indeed, it is quite possible to make a compelling argument on the basis solely of narrative, as Jacqueline de Romilly showed so clearly in her study of Thucydides. Thucydides did not need to state his interpretations of the events he described because his views were clear from a close reading of the work. An especially illuminating example is the arrival of Gylippus in Syracuse at the beginning of Book 7, which is clearly the turning point in the Sicilian Expedition. As Romilly points out, Plutarch says that Thucydides gives all the credit to Gylippus, although Thucydides says not a word about the centrality of Gylippus' successful entry into the city.³³ He did not need to. The careful arrangement of the narrative before and after Gylippus' arrival makes it clear that this was the pivotal moment in the campaign. The narrative itself provided the author's interpretation without the need for explicitly formulated proofs and argumentation.³⁴

In similar fashion, the orators attempt to persuade their audience not only with detailed, reasoned "proofs" (*pisteis*) but also with their narratives, which are often more closely connected with the speaker's overall legal claims than may at first be clear. Unlike historical writers, however, litigants in court were not usually concerned with broad social movements or impersonal forces; they were involved with individual personalities. It is for this reason that characterization of one's opponent is such a common device in Attic oratory. Depictions of someone's character (*ēthos*) supported implicit claims that he or she would or would not act in a certain way under a certain set of circumstances.³⁵

The orators were well aware of the effectiveness of such tactics and made frequent use of them. Christopher Carey has demonstrated how Lysias allows such characterization to function as "an implied argument from probability"[36] in several of his defense speeches.[37] The speakers in these trials attempt to portray themselves in such a way that the jury will not believe that they have acted in the manner that their opponents allege. As Anaximenes advises, "Those who make defense pleas must especially show that neither they nor any of their friends have ever done any of the things of which they are accused or anything like those acts."[38] The defendant had to show that he was not the sort of person to commit any crime similar to that for which he was on trial in order to make the argument that he was not likely to have committed the specific offense in question. Prosecutors, of course, had to do the opposite.

Modern readers sometimes have difficulty understanding how these arguments from character work because our view of character itself does not always align with the ancients'. The Greeks took a more holistic approach to determining an individual's moral capacities than most inheritors of the western legal tradition. Anaximenes advises the orator to draw parallels from what many today would consider distinct areas in a person's life: "It is likely that whoever loves his friends also reveres his parents, and whoever reveres his parents will want to do well also to his fatherland."[39] A man's personal life informed all his other capacities.[40] The following gnomic statements voice common opinions:

> A bad father who hates his children could never be a good public leader; and a man who does not love his nearest and dearest will never feel concern for outsiders like yourselves; and a man who is worthless at home can never have been a man of honor as envoy in Macedonia—he changed his position [*topos*], not his disposition [*tropos*].[41]

Compare Demosthenes' harangue against Aristogiton: "I would really like to know who, after seeing this man betray his parents, could believe that he has the goodwill toward the people that he promises."[42] This tendency to conceive of individuals' behavior as an integrated whole meant that Athenian speakers could exploit many different aspects of their own or their opponents' lives to demonstrate to the jury what types of people they were.

The Greeks also saw an individual's character as relatively static and unlikely to change.[43] Hence, a number of preset character types were available for the orator's use, a few of which Aristotle outlines in the *Rhetoric*.[44] Young men were likely to be hot tempered and prone to act on impulse, while old men tended to be malicious and suspicious. Men with noble lineage were expected to be arrogant and to scorn those whom they considered their inferiors. Although individuality and rational choice were by no means foreign concepts, they were in the Greek conception always balanced against certain aspects of one's "nature" (*physis*) that compelled him or her toward certain types of behavior.[45] Dover has fleshed out many of these "determinants of moral capacity," which included national origins, gender, age, wealth, and citizenship status.[46] Law court speakers could employ these character types to their advantage by fitting themselves or their opponents into a recognizable pattern.[47] In Demosthenes 54 (*Against Conon*) the plaintiff makes good use of the aristocratic-youth motif, asserting that Conon's sons and their blue-blooded companions assaulted him and nearly beat him to death with very little provocation. In the hands of a speechwriter who knew how to use them, these typecast models could prove effective means of predisposing the jurors to accept the speaker's version of events.

The connection between a narrative that establishes an opponent's past behavior and an argument about the offense that is on trial is usually straightforward even if it does not necessarily jibe with modern ideas. In Demosthenes 24 (*Against Timocrates*) the speaker, Diodorus, includes a lengthy history of the former misdeeds of Timocrates to prepare the way for his assertion that Timocrates cares nothing for the laws and justice and can therefore be expected to engage in illegal conduct as a matter of habit.[48] Timocrates allegedly sold his services as a proposer of legislation and then drafted a law that manifestly contradicted another law that he himself had previously proposed.[49] Diodorus' narrative implies that if Timocrates was caught previously engaging in this sort of activity, the jury ought to find it easy to believe that he is doing it again.[50] Diodorus indicted Timocrates by *graphē paranomōn* for proposing a law that, Diodorus claims, is clearly contrary to the principles of the Athenian legal system.[51] As Diodorus would have it, Timocrates is attempting to introduce oligarchic features into the city's law code for his own benefit, just as he abused the legal system in the past for personal gain. The narration of the broader background of the dispute, including Timocrates' oligarchic and anti-Athenian actions,[52] supports the speaker's claim that Timocrates is now introducing a law that is contrary to the democracy and the interests of ordinary citizens.[53]

A broad-ranging assault on an opponent's character could also be used to support *a fortiori* arguments about more limited claims. If a prosecutor spoke at length about the defendant's long history of wicked behavior, the jury would find it easier to believe that he would commit more petty crimes without compunction. Speakers were not merely indulging in their hatred and reveling in slandering their enemies but rather were anchoring their audience's preconceptions. Even if the jurors did not believe a speaker's assertions that his opponent despised the democracy and its laws, the extremity of his accusations could make his other claims seem all the more reasonable. Ariston's narrative of the violent attack of Conon and his sons paved the way for later arguments about the opponents' willingness to subvert the legal system. Conon and his sons were exactly the sort of people who would attempt such illicit tactics.

> Do you suppose that men who break into houses and who beat people they encounter would hesitate to give false testimony for each other on a scrap of paper, these partners in viciousness, wickedness, shamelessness, and brutality so foul and extreme?[54]

Ariston derives this argument about his opponents' deceit from his earlier narrative about their moral turpitude and hubristic brazenness. Once a speaker accused his opponent of outrageous offenses against his fellow man, all other accusations became easier to make.

Another interesting feature of the character argument in this speech is the way in which Ariston lumps all of his opponents into a single category, assuming that they are all men of the same stamp. This illustrates the connection in Greek thought between a person's character and the character of all those with whom he associated. The assumed premise for many of the orators' attacks on a litigant's friends and family is expressed in a Euripidean fragment: "One's character resembles those whose company he enjoys."[55] The principle, based on the Greek ideology of friendship, was "guilt by association."[56] The many attacks on an opponent's co-speakers are not simply verbal fireworks; they support a negative evaluation of the opponent himself. Hence Anaximenes recommends that in addition to arguments drawn from the opposing litigant, a speaker should criticize his opponent's companions since it will seem credible that the opponent himself shares their character traits.[57]

Athenians were ready to believe that people associated with those who were similar in habits, morals, and natural disposition.[58] If you spend time with people who can be shown to be malicious and conniving, you are probably malicious and conniving yourself. Family members were especially susceptible to being cited as evidence.[59] Certain acquired characteristics, such as wickedness or pettiness, could be transmitted genetically from parent to child.[60] The Greeks debated whether nature or nurture was the deciding factor,[61] but most would likely have agreed that family members tended to share certain characteristics and patterns of behavior.

Characterization was important for predicting not only what a particular litigant was likely to do but also whether he was likely to lie. The issue of the credibility of a speaker was especially prominent in Athenian courts because the trials were primarily battles of words. In the absence of scientific evidence and professional investigators, the trial revolved around the alternating speeches. The outcome depended primarily on "words" (*logoi*) rather than "facts" (*erga*). The Athenians were quite aware that clever speakers could use their talents to deceive credulous jurors, and so litigants were often at pains to demonstrate their good faith and avoid being suspected of craftily skirting the true facts.[62] To convince the jury of his credibility, a speaker needed to cite particular *erga* that supported his position.[63] By exploiting the latitude granted by the court to choose one's own material and introduce arguments about character based on past actions, a litigant could appeal to the secure knowledge of how he or his opponent had acted in the past. The history of one's conduct could serve as a point of reference for the rest of the case. In this way, persuasion depended not just on the forcefulness of one's arguments but on the credibility of one's character: "A speaker's character (*tropos*) is what persuades people, not his speech (*logos*)."[64] In the midst of so many *logoi*, litigants' *tropoi* were important guides for discovering whether the *logoi* were true.[65]

This connection between character and truth was more important for the ancient Athenians than it usually is today. By the modern Cartesian perspective, we arrive at truth by weighing evidence until we can form correct conclusions. For the Greeks, the question of who possessed the truth was bound up intimately with the totality of one's moral character. As Michel Foucault put it, for the Greeks, "when someone has certain moral qualities, then that is the proof that he has access to the truth."[66] A man's actions in virtually any sphere of life could serve as indicators of his trustworthiness, provided that they revealed something about his moral disposition. There was a connection between acts of uprightness and honesty on the one hand and acts of moral turpitude and deceit on the other. To attack an opponent's immoral disposition as shown by his past actions was to attack his trustworthiness and so implicitly his claims about the case. Many of the prolonged invectives about seemingly irrelevant issues operate implicitly under the premise stated explicitly in a fragment of Lysias: "Lying is easiest for those who have sinned many times."[67] Compare also the comment in the *Rhetoric to Alexander* that "people who act wickedly also don't care about committing perjury."[68] Actions reveal moral qualities that affect trustworthiness.

The narrative section of a speech can thus function to create arguments even when they are not explicitly spelled out in syllogistic format. This is why the dividing line between the "narration" section of a speech and the "proofs" is often not clear; both narrative and formal proofs are designed with similar purposes in mind and usually work in tandem. A litigant's account of the events leading up to the trial can function as much more than simple storytelling; it is a method for forming arguments. Their methods may not be obvious at first glance, but the narratives of the Attic orators are oriented toward proving or disproving the legal claims. Dionysius of Halicarnassus recognized this strategy, viewing this type of tactic as a key attribute of Lysias' skill: "It seems to me that he made arguments of proof from character in a manner very much worthy of mention."[69] Indeed, the orators seem to have been quite consciously making such "proofs" from the narrative section where "character" was developed.

Inevitably, the focal point for such narratives was relationships, where character is most clearly revealed. We should expect that relationships (in court, of course, usually hostile relationships) would be the primary vehicles for engaging in characterization. In other words, the aspects of a litigant's character relevant to a lawsuit were usually revealed most clearly in his actions toward different groups of people, such as friends and family, enemies, and the public. Generalities about character could be important in a litigant's argument, but they had limited persuasive force if used in isolation as stand-alone rhetorical commonplaces. To assert that someone is capable of terrible crimes begs substantiating proof, such as a narrative of how that person had lied to juries, abandoned his family, defrauded government officials, or contracted alliances with enemies of the community. For this reason both prosecutors and defendants provided many details about their past relationships with their opponents, or their own or their opponents' relationships with others. The history of conflict between two persons or a person and the community at large provided an effective and readily available avenue for bringing out the personalities of the various people involved in a trial. Actions that demonstrated moral character had to be set forth in terms of relationships. Descriptions of relationships are accordingly very common in Attic oratory. Discussion of enmity is a familiar rhetorical maneuver because it provides an obvious opportunity to discuss the broader background of the case.

ENMITY IN PROSECUTION SPEECHES

A common goal of the Attic orators' discussions of enmity was to create character arguments that aimed at implicit arguments about the facts of the case and their rightful interpretation. A litigant could include a narrative of his hostile relationship with his opponent or deny that such a relationship existed, but in either case he attempted to portray both parties in a way that supported his overall claims. The following analysis will take into account the two polar opposite strategies available to a prosecutor (affirming or denying) to show that both aim ultimately at similar types of implicit argumentation.

A prosecutor often uses enmity as an offensive weapon, to attack the credibility of his opponents and, more importantly, to make it seem plausible that the defendant would commit the crime in question. On the other hand, enmity often has a defensive purpose in that it can be employed to protect the credibility of the speaker himself. This use of characterization lends credibility to the rest of the speech and is consequently of great importance. These two purposes behind the rhetoric of enmity blend and overlap and are often too tightly intertwined to be distinguished one from the other, but as a heuristic aid it will be helpful to draw attention to the separate ways in which enmity functions in these speeches.

One strategy that prosecutors employ is to admit a long-standing conflict with the defendant and provide the audience with a detailed background of the feud. This tactic can be employed to speak to the character of both the opponent and the speaker and thus can have both an offensive and a defensive purpose. As an offensive weapon, a narrative of enmity creates a forum for discussing an opponent's previous behavior and hence his character, allowing the prosecutor simultaneously to attack his credibility and to show that he is the type of person to commit the offense in question. In many cases this tactic takes the form of a balancing act for the prosecutor because he must recognize that his admission of enmity, the very device that provides an opportunity for attacking his opponent's character, could undercut his argument when not handled in the proper fashion. If a speaker focuses on his own role in pursuing a feud, he could weaken his claims about his opponent's wrongful behavior by admitting that he had done his part in provoking him. More importantly, a prosecutor who portrays himself as a vigilant pursuer of his enemies opens himself up to the criticism of having trumped up a false charge to take vengeance on a rival. An effective character argument must portray only the opponent as aggressive. Therefore, prosecutors who affirm enmity with their opponents stop short of admitting that they themselves had been actively encouraging the feud. The speaker must show that enmity exists but also that he himself neither started it nor pursued it.

If the prosecutor is able to maintain this balance, a narrative of enmity provides an effective way to suggest an opponent's guilt by deriving an argument "from the opponents themselves." Character assassination grounded in a discussion of past animosities can support the plausibility of the charges. Demosthenes employed just such a tactic against Aristogiton, indulging in lengthy digressions on Aristogiton's aberrant behavior in order to attack his credibility.⁷⁰ Acting only as a supporting speaker (*synēgoros*) in this trial, Demosthenes does not feel compelled to present the entire case against Aristogiton and is therefore free to focus on an argument about Aristogiton's character.⁷¹ As so often in Attic oratory, illustrative stories from the opponent's past serve as proofs against his credibility.⁷² For instance, near the midpoint of the oration Demosthenes inserts a brief digression on the history of his relationship with Aristogiton to show his audience that their long-standing enmity has afforded him personal knowledge about Aristogiton's character.⁷³ Aristogiton lodged *graphai* against Demosthenes seven times, accused him at his *euthynai* twice, and attacked and blackmailed countless other innocents. These acts bear witness to Aristogiton's nature, revealing the "sort of man he is" (*toioutos*), a person "full of many terrible crimes."⁷⁴ In these and other aspects of his habitual conduct, Aristogiton has revealed himself as a monster that needs to be exterminated.⁷⁵

Demosthenes shows his hand by admitting that he and Aristogiton have been on opposite ends of multiple court actions, but he does not allow his audience to draw the natural conclusion that malice and spite have driven him to settle a score with his enemy. The conspicuous omission of any reference to Demosthenes' initiation of a lawsuit against Aristogiton accords with his portrait of himself as an unwilling speaker at the present trial. Supposedly, the members of the Assembly coerced him to act as one of the prosecutors in this case, although Demosthenes was hesitant to participate.⁷⁶ Demosthenes knew that his enmity with Aristogiton would come out in the trial (or may have already been well known) and accordingly preempted the jurors' potential suspicion that his only stake in the whole affair was to make his enemy look the fool. Demosthenes is careful to leave the impression that he is not that sort of person; Aristogiton was the one who initiated and pursued a vendetta without provocation. Because Demosthenes never prosecuted Aristogiton and was unwilling to undertake the present trial as a co-speaker, Aristogiton's vexatious activities come before the jury's eyes in stark contrast to Demosthenes' restraint.

This character portrait is intended to convince the jurors that Aristogiton must be punished, but it also provides the foundation for an implicit *eikos* argument about the charges themselves. The prosecution's main allegation is that Aristogiton is a defaulting state debtor who illicitly exercises the rights of a citizen by speaking in the Assembly and the law courts. These are serious offenses. He allegedly incurred sanctions from the state for proposing an illegal law and for "sycophancy," shirked paying them, and brazenly ignored the laws concerning state debtors.⁷⁷ It is not difficult to see how the prosecution's case would be strengthened if Aristogiton could be made to look reckless and out of control, the sort of person who has utter disregard for the laws. Demosthenes portrays Aristogiton in just such a way, using his own personal history with the defendant to that end. The exploitation of the opponent's previous conduct for a character argument was by no means irrelevant, since it provided information about the charges at hand. If Aristogiton characteristically acted this way in the past, it was quite credible that he committed the offense for which he was on trial.

A prosecutor could mold his discussion of his relationship with the accused to cast his own character in a positive light at the same time that he attacked his opponent, thus using enmity both defensively and offensively. By asserting a personal interest in the case, a prosecutor could avoid the jury's other potential suspicions, such as that he was a "busybody" (*polupragmōn*) or was seeking financial gain.[78] Both of these were characteristics of the "sycophant," the boogeyman of Athenian legal thought.[79] Whether they were out for money, influence, or just the thrill of taking down another Athenian,[80] these law court crooks were feared and hated. The financial aspect of sycophancy is an especially prominent concern in the speeches. According to common belief, certain citizens were in the habit of blackmailing unsuspecting innocents, especially wealthy men with little experience in the courts, by threatening them with prosecution and accepting payment to withdraw the action. Alternatively, sycophants could bring their victims to trial by a procedure that entailed a financial reward. Aware of the damage even the suspicion of sycophancy could do to his credibility, a prudent plaintiff would offer other motivations as an explanation for his appearance in court. When a prosecutor admitted to having a personal stake in the lawsuit, he usually had a very good reason for doing so, often because he knew that even suspicions about other motivations could constitute a damaging blow to his credibility.

At the same time, admitting excessive hostility toward the defendant was also dangerous because personal animosities could lead to trumped-up charges and vexatious lawsuits. The prosecutor could find himself portrayed as a malicious attacker who was pursuing a private enemy out of spite and envy. Affirmation of enmity was not an escape from the problem of motivation; it gave rise to its own problems and merely recast the issue in a new light. Just as the prosecutor must avoid the charge of having no personal stake in the action, so must he avoid the charge of having too much personal stake. There was, however, a way to address both problems. The same balancing act that supports plausibility arguments about the defendant's criminal character could be used to protect the credibility and trustworthiness of the speaker. The prosecutor could affirm enmity to dispel the jury's fears about his sycophancy while avoiding the appearance that he initiated the feud so that he would not be suspected of malicious pursuit of an enemy. This defensive purpose behind the balancing act, to protect the speaker's credibility, harmonizes nicely with the offensive use of the same balancing act to attack the opponent's character. Two orations by Apollodorus ([Dem.] 59 and 53) illustrate these dynamics at work in narratives of enmity.[81] These speeches also provide a convenient opportunity for showing how previous scholarly discussions of enmity in the orators have often misunderstood their rhetorical goals.

Theomnestus, the main prosecutor in the lawsuit for which Apollodorus composed [Demosthenes] 59 (*Against Neaera*), discusses the history of the enmity between his family and the defendant to speak to the character of both parties in the trial.[82] Theomnestus must, however, put a slight twist on the conventional discussion of enmity by focusing on the relationship between his co-speaker, Apollodorus, and the defendant's putative husband, Stephanus, rather than the relationship between himself and the defendant, Neaera. The legal issue is Theomnestus' accusation that Neaera is falsely claiming to be an Athenian citizen,[83] but neither Theomnestus nor Neaera is the most important personality in the trial, which is part of a larger feud between Apollodorus and Stephanus.[84] The speech begins with a short address by Theomnestus, which serves primarily to introduce his father-in-law Apollodorus, who delivers the bulk of the argument as a *synēgoros*.[85] On the side of the defense, Neaera could not have spoken because women were prohibited from addressing an Athenian court, so Stephanus probably delivered the primary defense speech. In his introductory oration, Theomnestus therefore turns his rhetoric to the relationship between the two main antagonists in the trial rather than the principal prosecutor and defendant.

The prosecutor attempts to demonstrate that his opponent, Stephanus, has a history of harassing both Apollodorus and him. This rhetorical strategy fits the needs of this particular type of case, a *graphē* that awarded one-third of the proceeds of the trial to the successful volunteer prosecutor. According to the law transmitted in §16, if the plaintiffs secure a conviction, Neaera will be sold into slavery, while her husband will be forced to pay a fine of one thousand drachmas.[86] As a reward for bringing suit as a volunteer, Theomnestus will be entitled to one-third of the proceeds from the sale of Neaera.[87] Such monetary rewards were thought to be a strong incentive for unscrupulous men to engage in frivolous lawsuits to profit at the defendant's expense, and so prosecutors in these *graphai* are often especially concerned to deny that such base motivations are at the core of the prosecution. On the other hand, a simple declaration of private enmity as the primary reason for the lawsuit would not prove useful either. Because private enemies are likely to trump up charges to harm each other, the jury may be mistrustful of a speaker who presents himself as relentlessly pursuing a vendetta.[88] Theomnestus must achieve a balance between these two dangerous extremes. His short speech is dominated by the question of the speaker's motives, functioning almost as an apology for the court action. The first section provides a template for how Theomnestus will present the history of animosity between his family and Stephanus'.

> Many things have spurred me on to bring this action against Neaera and come before you in court. You see, Stephanus has done us—my brother-in-law, myself, my sister, my wife—great harm, and it is because of him that we came into extreme danger. Therefore, I am not taking the initiative in bringing this case, but am seeking retribution. In fact, I am acting in self-defense: he was the one who started the quarrel, though he had not had any trouble from our side—not in words, not in action. I want to start by telling you what he has done to us and how we have fallen into the great risk of exile and disenfranchisement.[89]

In this preamble the two themes of affirming enmity but denying responsibility for it are immediately visible. Although Theomnestus admits hostility toward Stephanus, he argues that the blame is not his. As will be stressed in the following narrative section of the speech, Stephanus started and has persistently aggravated the feud.

Although the suit was a public one, in which the jury would typically believe that their interests were at stake,[90] Theomnestus does not shy away from outlining his interest in the trial, even going so far as to assert boldly that he is prosecuting Stephanus for personal grievances for which he intends to take vengeance. He expounds upon the length and intensity of the "enmity" (*echthra*) between his own circle of friends and Stephanus' by pointing to several quarrels that have exacerbated the hostile relationship. At the same time, Theomnestus carefully presents Stephanus as the aggressor on each occasion.

First, he relates how Stephanus brought a malicious indictment (*graphē paranomōn*) against Apollodorus for proposing a decree concerning the appropriation of public funds, although Apollodorus was of course acting with the purest of motives.[91] Everyone would later recognize that Apollodorus was in the right on this issue, but in the trial, Stephanus succeeded in deceiving the jurors and securing a conviction by digressing on irrelevant subjects and offering witnesses who provided false testimony. Apollodorus and his friends were willing to overlook this malicious prosecution but were annoyed at Stephanus' unwillingness to make concessions on the assessment of the penalty. He attempted to impose a severe punishment that would effectively disfranchise Apollodorus and his family. Failing to achieve this goal but desiring to make good on his threats, Stephanus subsequently accused Apollodorus of homicide and made a proclamation at the Palladion, hoping to have him expelled from Attica.[92] The charge was clearly groundless, Theomnestus asserts, since it later became evident that Stephanus was in the paid service of two of Apollodorus' enemies. Yet this had not stopped Stephanus from daring to perjure himself by calling down an oath that invoked destruction on himself and his family, swearing to something he knew to be false.

In contrast to Stephanus' unwarranted attacks on Apollodorus and his family, Theomnestus emphasizes the restraint that he and Apollodorus exhibited. Stephanus started the whole affair, although he had received no injury from Theomnestus or his family. Theomnestus was quite reluctant to involve himself in the quarrel, even requiring prodding from friends and family before he made the decision to seek revenge.

> Everybody was coming to me in private and urging me to try to get back at him for what he had done to us. They were scolding me, saying I was no man if I didn't get justice for people who were so close to me—my sister, and brother-in-law, and nieces, and my own wife.[93]

As he introduces Apollodorus at the end of the speech, Theomnestus emphasizes again that Stephanus was "the one who started it." Neither Theomnestus nor his family bears responsibility for how hostilities have escalated. The blame may be laid squarely on Stephanus and his friends.

The character evidence developed in this narrative first of all affects the prosecutors' credibility as accusers. By presenting the relationship between Apollodorus, Theomnestus, and Stephanus in this way, Theomnestus addresses the jury's questions about possible pecuniary motivation. The trial has arisen not from lust for the reward of a third of the proceeds but rather from the pressure Theomnestus' friends and family put on him to punish Stephanus for his bad behavior. At the same time, his affirmation of hatred for the defendants obliges him to guard against the suspicion that he is maliciously harassing Stephanus and his family to settle a private score.[94] Theomnestus addresses this problem by asserting that his family suffered many other wrongs at Stephanus' hands and has shown restraint in responding to these injustices.

The narration of the background of the dispute also serves as a forum for providing evidence about Stephanus' character. At each point the rhetoric is calculated to speak to the credibility of the opposing litigants' versions of events. In his indictment of Apollodorus by *graphē paranomōn*, Stephanus deceived the jury by producing false witnesses. Later he brought a "false charge" against Apollodorus and was caught doing so. He was also convicted of lying under oath. Theomnestus, on the other hand, has demonstrated a calm fortitude worthy of a philosopher and now asks the jury to vote "according to the truth itself."[95] Theomnestus and Apollodorus may be trusted, but Stephanus has proved himself an unscrupulous liar on many occasions.

Theomnestus' implicit argument based on his narrative of enmity, then, takes at least three forms: one offensive argument and two defensive ones. (1) Because Stephanus has shown himself a deceiver, manipulator, and perjurer, it would be foolhardy to trust him. (2) Since Apollodorus and I are prosecuting Stephanus as an enemy, there is no reason to suspect that the prosecutor's reward is what we are really seeking. (3) Since Apollodorus and I have overlooked so many of Stephanus' offenses in the past out of personal restraint and a general unwillingness to appear in court, it is highly unlikely that we would invent a pretext to prosecute him. The history of the relationship between Stephanus and Apollodorus creates these implicit arguments of plausibility in the audience's minds and supports the overall attempt to prove the prosecution's case and discredit the opponent's.

A litigant would take virtually any opportunity to attack his opponent's credibility, but the legal framework of *Against Neaera* offered a particularly strong incentive toward this type of rhetorical assault. The charge against Stephanus and Neaera was essentially one of lying, of willfully deceiving the state by pretending that Neaera and her offspring were citizens. Stephanus' record of deceit in court and his previous use of false witnesses made this charge more credible. This character portrait was important for the prosecutors' attempt to show both that Stephanus was lying about Neaera's citizenship status and that he was brazen enough to defend his falsehoods in court. The argument formulated explicitly in Demosthenes 37 ("Do you think that the man who deceived those jurors would hesitate to deceive you?")[96] is implicit here. Theomnestus and Apollodorus must establish Stephanus as an unscrupulous manipulator of *polis* institutions. This is precisely what Theomnestus' narrative of his conduct accomplishes. Like any other litigant, Theomnestus desires first and foremost to convince the jury that his case represents the correct version and interpretation of events. He crafts a narrative that makes his charge seem more likely to be true, affirming enmity with his opponent to deny sycophantic motivations while also guarding against the charge of malicious prosecution based exclusively on personal animosity. At the same time, Theomnestus engages in character assassination against Stephanus, painting him as a consummate liar, while he asserts that his own claims are based on the facts.

Taking full account of the rhetorical purposes of this speech makes it easier to avoid the pitfall of assuming that the speakers' narrative of their own conduct was normative for all Athenians. The stories and anecdotes provided by Theomnestus and Apollodorus aim at implicit probabilities about the personalities involved in the trial and not merely at proving that they are morally superior to Stephanus by virtue of the way they have carried on the feud. Certainly the speech contains moral judgments and posturing, but the narrative does not necessarily provide an absolute ideal of behavior to which all Athenians would have ascribed. Herman cites this oration as an example of Athenian litigants' desire not to appear eager to seek revenge: "By the speech's concluding paragraph the idea of private vengeance has vanished altogether. . . . The speakers are at pains to point out that they have brought this case only as a last resort."[97] These observations are correct, but they do not support Herman's larger argument that Athenians believed that restraint in the face of grievous wrongs was a moral imperative. Theomnestus represents Apollodorus and himself as restrained because this particular character portrait supports his other arguments, not because that is how all Athenians would expect them to act. Herman's conclusions about the speakers' attempts to downplay personal vengeance fail to take into account how they reinforce the overall legal argument. This speech cannot be used to establish that Athenians would have approved of Theomnestus' restrained behavior as the only acceptable way to respond to Stephanus' attacks. Apollodorus' rhetoric is not calculated to provide a moral commentary on how to respond to one's enemies but rather to support the character portrayal of Stephanus as a hubristic and unprovoked attacker.[98]

Another way to attack the character of an opposing litigant was to attack the character of his friends. The Greek ideology of friendship implied that the morals of a man's associates were a relatively reliable indicator of his own morals.[99] A prosecutor was therefore free to look for the weakest links in his opponent's co-speakers and witnesses and direct his attention accordingly. If he could show that the defendant's friends and family were of a certain character and had acted in a certain way in the past, the jury would be more likely to believe the same of the defendant. When Apollodorus prosecuted a man named Arethusius, he focused most of his narrative energy against Arethusius' brother, Nicostratus, with whom he had been more intimately acquainted in the past. The speech ([Dem.] 53) reveals that this trial is in fact part of a larger dispute between Apollodorus and Nicostratus, into which family members and other parties have been drawn (whence the title *Against Nicostratus*, not *Against Arethusius*). The narrative of Nicostratus' dishonest and spiteful behavior functions to attack the credibility of the opposition as a whole and support the reliability of Apollodorus' own version of the facts, even if the target of the narrative is not the principal defendant. As in *Against Neaera*, Apollodorus asserts that he and his opponents are long-standing enemies, but he is careful to point out that Nicostratus and not he has consistently been the aggressor.

Apollodorus composed *Against Nicostratus*, like *Against Neaera*, for a procedure that entailed a monetary reward to the successful prosecutor. This procedure was an *apographē*, by which a volunteer prosecutor submits an "inventory" (*apographē*) of items that are to be confiscated and handed over to the state to defray the owner's alleged debt to the public.[100] Should the plaintiff gain a conviction, he would be entitled to one-third of the proceeds from the sale of the property by the *poletai* (the state's official sellers). In the inventory submitted for this trial are two slaves who, Apollodorus asserts, belong to Arethusius, Nicostratus' brother, and are liable to confiscation because of Arethusius' debt to the public treasury.[101] To counter the suspicion that he merely covets the proceeds from one-third of the value of the slaves, Apollodorus starts his speech by addressing this directly.

> Let the size of the *apographē* and the fact that I have brought action in my own name serve as powerful proof in your eyes, gentlemen of the jury, that I am doing this not as a [sycophant] but because I was wronged and roughly treated by these men, and because I think I should seek revenge.[102]

In a string of four causal participles, Apollodorus asserts both the grounds for the prosecution and the impetus behind it. His motivation is not malice or greed but rather revenge, based on wrongs and insults that he has suffered at the hands of the defendant. He ties his motivation for prosecuting to the reality of the offenses committed.[103] His desire for revenge demonstrates that his charges are true since there must have been a real offense that has caused him to seek vengeance.[104]

The jury may know, Apollodorus argues, that he is not falsifying the charges because he has brought the suit himself instead of enlisting another person to prosecute for him. He risks a fine of one thousand drachmas in a suit over slaves valued at only two and a half minae, one-fourth as much, and hazards being barred from acting as a volunteer prosecutor in the future.[105] His appearance in court over such a measly sum at great personal risk proves both that his motivation for revenge is legitimate and that he has been wronged.

I think the most terrible thing of all is to be wronged myself, yet put someone else's name forward on my behalf when I am the one who was wronged; and this would serve my opponents as proof that I am lying when I say that my hatred for them is the reason for my bringing the *apographē*.[106]

Apollodorus' presence in court demonstrates that he is telling the truth about his hatred for Nicostratus and his associates. If he had not appeared as the prosecutor, the jury would know that he had no personal stake in the matter and would be running no risk in the trial.[107] Apollodorus' explanation of his actions shows that behind them lies a basis in fact. In other words, motivation is an important concern because it proves that Apollodorus' claims are true. He asserts unreservedly that he is Nicostratus' enemy but constantly emphasizes that the reason for the ill will between them is Nicostratus' wrongdoing.

While Apollodorus asserts that his enmity with Nicostratus led him to prosecute, he is aware that an excessive display of hostility could leave him open to the charge of prosecuting out of sheer spite.[108] To preempt such an allegation, he narrates a litany of Nicostratus' unprovoked and outrageous abuses to show that Nicostratus was at fault for starting and continuing the hostility.[109] Nicostratus assisted Apollodorus' enemies in court, hired a third party to prosecute him, stole his furniture, and vandalized his property. He attempted to trick Apollodorus into assaulting an Athenian citizen so that he could be prosecuted for *hubris*[110] and, finally, ambushed him on the road between the Piraeus and Athens. Apollodorus, on the other hand, retaliated only rarely and, when he did, he sought redress through the courts.

This account, if the jury finds it credible, removes suspicions that Apollodorus has attacked the family of Nicostratus to settle a score. If he has put up with so many wrongs, why would he fabricate such a minor charge as one concerning slaves worth two and a half minae?[111] Likewise, if Nicostratus, Arethusius, and their associates have committed so many crimes with no thought to the interests of other citizens or the state, the jury may find it probable that they would collude in deceiving the state as Apollodorus charges. Apollodorus' focus on his own restraint and Nicostratus' aggravation supports the veracity of the charges by making Apollodorus seem trustworthy and Nicostratus a liar, the sort of scoundrel who would attempt to weasel out of a debt to the treasury.

Apollodorus includes character arguments to support his charges, not simply to prove that he is a good person and his opponent is a rascal. He does not say, "Vote for me because I am a decent person and do not worry overmuch about whether or not my legal case against Arethusius is sound." Characterization is not to be disentangled from the legal point at issue. The narrative of the enmity between Apollodorus and Nicostratus functions to draw consistent depictions of their characters so that the jury will find Apollodorus' accusations credible.[112]

This distinction between the use of character as part of a framework for the legal argumentation and its supposed use for extralegal legitimation has not always been carefully maintained. Cohen summarizes Apollodorus' narrative thus, "It is such abuse of legal process that Apollodorus uses to qualify Nicostratus as a sycophant, while portraying himself as legitimately resorting to the courts to obtain protection and revenge for these grievous wrongs."[113] The statement is accurate, except for what apparently is meant by "legitimately." For Cohen, a litigant who demonstrates that his motivation for prosecuting is a good one is making an appeal that he is a "legitimate" prosecutor, worthy of votes based on the intrinsic worth of his character. Cohen uses *Against Nicostratus* to support his argument that the opposing litigants' entire lives (that is, their character) are on trial, rather than their specific offenses. It is maintained here, however, that Apollodorus does not advance character arguments about who "deserves" to win based on past behavior but rather to support an argument from probability about who is telling the truth about the offense on trial. It is not character evidence per se that is vital to the case but character evidence as it affects the litigants' credibility and their claims. Apollodorus' narrative does in fact give him legitimacy, but this legitimacy arises from the probability argument about who is more likely to lie, not from his character in itself.

The problematic ambiguity of the word "legitimate" applies also to "justify" and "acceptable," which are subject to the same objections. Cohen cites the second section of *Against Nicostratus* to assert that "this presupposes that pursuit of revenge justifies litigating."[114] However, Apollodorus' character and motivation do not justify his prosecution *on their own merits* so that the jury feels obliged to vote for him because of his qualities as a person. Rather, they provide an implicit argument from probability that he is telling the truth.[115] Similarly to Cohen, Nicolas Fisher in his commentary on Aeschines 1 (*Against Timarchus*) observes that to avoid being labeled a sycophant, many prosecutors "emphasize the much more acceptable motives of personal revenge and the punishment of those who were wronging the city."[116] It is important to specify that these expressions of private motivations are "acceptable" insofar as they lead the jury to the conclusion that the speaker is more likely to be telling the truth than lying, rather than having persuasive force simply on their own merits.

Affirmations of enmity were common strategies but were not the only rhetorical options available to prosecutors. If the prosecutor felt that it was to his advantage, he could deny enmity to preempt any suspicion of personal involvement. This tactic was popular for those who brought suits with no financial reward. Freed from the fear that the jury would believe they were merely greedy, prosecutors had less incentive to attempt the precarious balancing act between affirming enmity and denying culpability. Those who brought prosecutions in these trials of special interest to the state probably chose to deny enmity because they felt that there was more danger in appearing to be pursuing a private vendetta than in looking like a sycophant.[117] Such speakers eschewed personal motivation and freed themselves to concentrate on the merits of their accusations, employing their disinterested stance to support an argument that their claims were credible since they had no reason to lie. By this strategy, litigants preempted suspicions of excessive pursuit of personal interest, and they also provided themselves with an opportunity for the high rhetoric of patriotism and pursuit of the city's interests.[118] The handful of speakers who attempted this strategy frequently highlight their own sense of civic duty, portraying themselves as having the best interests of the state at heart in purging it of a malefactor.[119]

Lycurgus employs this tactic in his prosecution of Leocrates on a charge of treason.[120] He denies enmity with the accused and tells the jury that he wishes to focus on the truth of his accusations since he has no ulterior motives. He even prays to the gods that if Leocrates is guilty, he would be duly convicted but that if Leocrates is innocent, he would be acquitted.[121]

> Men of Athens, I brought this impeachment because I know that Leocrates has fled from the trials of the fatherland, has forsaken his fellow citizens, has entirely disregarded your power, and is guilty of the offenses with which he has been charged. I did not undertake this trial because of any personal enmity or ambition or anything else but because I thought it shameful to watch this man enter the marketplace and share in public sacrifices while he has become an affront to both the fatherland and all of you.[122]

The legal action is grounded in Leocrates' offenses, he argues, not in the personal aims of the prosecutor.[123] Lycurgus expands on this argument to draw general principles.

> It is the duty of the just citizen not to indulge personal enmities by bringing people who have done no wrong against the city to public trials but to deem those who have transgressed the laws of the fatherland one's own enemies and to believe that their public offenses offer public reasons for a quarrel with them.[124]

Once again Lycurgus focuses on the truth of the accusation as the most important consideration in a trial. The truly civic-minded public servant does not attack personal enemies on frivolous charges but rather views those who harm the city as harming himself. Lycurgus employs a common motif for prosecutors denying personal acquaintance with the accused: shifting the focus away from the question of enmity between the defendant and himself and to the question of enmity between the defendant and the state.[125] As Lycurgus recounts Leocrates' misdeeds, he does in fact shape a narrative of enmity, but it is a narrative of the animosity between Leocrates and Athens.[126]

Several reasons could be posited for Lycurgus' desire to deny enmity in this trial. First, Lycurgus charged Leocrates with desertion from Athens in a time of crisis and thus placed patriotism at the very center of the case. If Lycurgus had voiced strong personal motivations, he would have undermined his emphasis on civic interests. Second, an assertion of enmity would not leave much room for Lycurgus to emphasize his restraint and moderation since Leocrates had been out of Athens for eight years and only recently returned. If Lycurgus had claimed to be an enemy of Leocrates, he would appear malicious and litigious, waiting until the very moment his enemy returned to pounce on him. Leocrates would then have had ample opportunity to portray himself as the victim of a feuding and hubristic elite politician who abused his powers to attack his enemies on trumped-up charges.

Speakers in court had to attempt to meet the exigencies imposed by the legal sphere and therefore do not provide evidence that feuding was viewed as always good or always bad, just as Aristotle in the *Rhetoric* does not imply that being young or being old was always good or always bad. Aristotle exhorts the orator to exploit the common characteristics of different age groups to make the jury believe certain things about his opponent, just as the orators use character portraits of feuding individuals to support their arguments about the offense with which the accused is charged. Character argument does not entail mere "justification" of the speaker as prosecutor; it aims at probability arguments about the case. When a prosecutor uses enmity to attack his opponent's character and defend his motivations for bringing suit, he makes legal arguments about the important issues in the trial.

DEFENSE TACTICS

The defendant was free to develop his arguments in whatever way he saw fit but at the same time was under certain constraints because of his position as second speaker. The prosecutor chose the procedure and spoke first at the trial, setting the tone for the debate and forcing the defendant to address the arguments presented in his speech. For this reason, some defendants complained to the jury that the prosecutor had an advantage.[127] Litigants were allowed only one or two speeches apiece (one in public speeches, two in most *dikai*) so that the order of speaking was of special importance. The prosecutor anchored the debate by providing the frame of reference around which the rest of the case revolved. To the defendant was left the task of attacking the prosecutor's points individually and opposing his argument as a whole. He was compelled either to challenge specific assumptions, facts, and interpretations in his opponent's account of events and establish his own version of the story or to reject entirely the notion that there was a story worth telling.[128] In either case, the defendant had to respond to the prosecutor.

In accordance with this general principle, defendants employ the rhetoric of enmity in ways that correspond to its use in prosecution speeches. Affirmations and denials of long-standing relationships of hostility typically function as part of a plausibility argument, based on characterization of both the defendant himself and his opponents. While prosecutors often narrate their feuds with defendants to establish that defendants are likely to commit the crimes of which they are accused, a defendant will use enmity to attack the credibility of his opponent and imply that he is not worthy of trust. By charging him with pursuing a long-standing hostility, the defendant can engender suspicion in the jury that the prosecutor is likely bringing trumped-up charges. Likewise, if the defendant can demonstrate that his opponent has already brought suit on false grounds and been caught doing so, he can cast doubt on his credibility. This strategy works as a counter to a prosecutor's attempt to portray himself as motivated by concern for the truth.

Prosecutors frequently attempted to find a middle ground between appearing to be motivated either by desire for financial gain or by private hatred. The former would leave them open to accusations of sycophancy, while the latter would leave them open to suspicion of trumping up a charge out of belligerent antagonism. If a defendant heard his opponent attempt such a balancing act, which seems to have been quite common, he would naturally try to push the prosecutor toward one or the other of the extremes. He might affirm enmity and depict the prosecutor as a malicious attacker driven by envy and spite, or he might deny enmity with the prosecutor and thus portray him as a sycophant. No matter which way they chose to present their opponents, defendants consistently used the rhetoric of enmity to undercut the credibility of the opposition and to lend authority to their own claims. Each litigant aimed at convincing the jury of the truth or falsehood of competing versions of events, and discussion of enmity ultimately sought this end.

Most of the extant defense speeches that address enmity at all affirm it.[129] Speakers in these cases used similar strategies to emphasize the malice and spitefulness of the person who brought the prosecution. An aggressive attack on the motivations of the plaintiff appears to have been a natural response to an opponent's attempt to deploy the rhetoric of enmity against the defendant. When prosecutors attempted the balancing act of affirming enmity while avoiding portraying themselves as excessively eager litigants, the defense could respond by knocking the prosecutor off balance. A defendant who affirmed enmity was attempting to push his opponent toward the extreme, claiming that his opponent was motivated entirely by desire for private revenge and consequently was distorting the facts to obtain his own ends.

The speaker of Lysias 9 (*For the Soldier*),[130] an Athenian hoplite named Polyaenus, employs this strategy, affirming enmity and focusing on it throughout in an attempt to show that his prosecutors are attacking him on false charges to punish him, their enemy. According to Polyaenus, the accusation of his opponents (several Athenian generals[131] who alleged that Polyaenus slandered them, an offense punishable in Athens by a fine) is utterly frivolous, a result only of the generals' malice and envy. Notably, he does not mention the reward of a third of the proceeds that would go to the prosecutors in a successful *apographē* but rather focuses entirely on his opponents' desire to pursue their feud.[132] The fine was undoubtedly small, and so probably it seemed disingenuous to attack the prosecutors for seeking financial gain.[133]

With his first sentence, Polyaenus reveals his shock at his prosecutors' brazen attempts to ignore the legal point at issue (the *pragma*) and engage in a malicious character attack. In the rest of the *prooemium* he emphasizes that they made the decision to lodge this suit against him because of their personal desire to slander him.[134] These men have utterly ignored the substance of the charge and have made the entire case a mudslinging campaign.[135] This tactic, Polyaenus assures the jury, is completely out of order because the trial concerns a legal charge (*enklēma*) and not his character or manner of living (*tropos*).

Polyaenus' insinuation that his opponents have engaged in an extended attack on his *tropos* simply to vent their personal feelings of animosity toward him makes one wonder what exactly those prosecutors had said. Had they employed narratives of enmity to create character arguments in a way similar to many of the extant prosecution speeches? The question is unanswerable, since the prosecutors' speeches have not been preserved, but Polyaenus' defense would be an effective counter to such a strategy. He eschews completely any legitimate use of character evidence for situating the charges in context and sets the attacks on his *tropos* in direct opposition to the matter at issue. The plaintiffs' tactics arise from their personal hatred, not concern with the truth. His opponents may have wanted to respond that they were attempting to illuminate the issue by framing Polyaenus' offense with examples of his similarly belligerent and insulting behavior in the past, but they would not get that chance. The defendant has the stage, and he will leave the jury with the impression that the prosecution was attempting to distract them from the facts of the case with irrelevant and untrue statements about his character.

His complaints about his opponents' attacks notwithstanding, Polyaenus employs very similar tactics himself. An important thread of argument throughout the speech is the representation of his opponents as liars driven by personal enmity. A short narrative (4–7) following the *prooemium* both details how the speaker committed no crime and at the same time attacks the prosecutors' motivations by innuendo. Shortly after returning to Athens from abroad, Polyaenus had learned that he had been called up to enroll in the army. He had immediate suspicions that it was "for no good reason," probably because he could already see the hand of his enemies working behind the scenes. In a series of incidents, the generals rejected his protest in an insulting manner, threatened to have him imprisoned, and invented a pretext to impose a fine on him for slander. Although he has thus already drawn a character portrait of his opponents to show how abusive and aggressive they are, Polyaenus cleverly delays any mention of a word from the *echthr-* root. The narrative ends when the matter of the fine reverts to the office of the clerks of the treasury (*tamiai*),[136] who immediately recognized the whole affair for what it was, a trumped-up charge arising from enmity.[137] Citing the generals' illegitimate abuse of their power, they declared Polyaenus innocent. The declaration that *echthra* was the motive force behind the fine caps the foregoing narrative with an appropriate climax: objective third parties who had no stake in the matter declared the baselessness of the charge and reprimanded the speaker's persecutors for attempting to punish an enemy on false pretenses.

After interrupting his attack on his opponents to consider the specifics of the law in question and argue that he did not commit an offense according to the definition of slander in the decree,[138] Polyaenus returns to the question of his accusers' motivation. He moves from innuendo to an explicit account of their behavior and the reasons behind it: "Now you need to learn not only the reason for the charge but also the pretext for their enmity."[139] The word for "pretext" that Lysias uses is *prophasis*, a provocative term because it could imply either legitimate grounds or specious excuse. The latter is in view here, since in his discussion of the prosecutors' character Polyaenus asserts that his opponents had no legitimate reason for the enmity.[140] He dismisses the idea that he had incurred odium because of his friendship with Sostratus (an individual otherwise unknown). Probably his opponents had traced the history of the feud back to his involvement with this man, who had presumably already been at odds with them. Polyaenus asserts that he was exceptionally moderate in his position of influence and specifically denies that he injured any of his accusers so that he may assert that in fact there was no good reason for their hatred.

By the end of the speech, Polyaenus has made a case that his enemies are utterly reckless and enjoy causing mischief for its own sake. In spite of the oath that they had sworn not to recruit men who had already served in the army, they perjured themselves and enlisted the defendant, knowing that he had already performed his duty. They attacked the speaker to "benefit themselves" and are therefore "eager" to see Polyaenus convicted.[141] Indeed, integrity and truthfulness were the furthest things from their minds. Consumed with hatred, "they treated justice with contempt, making every effort to hurt me."[142]

For the Soldier shows how a speaker could employ the motivations of the prosecution as part of an effective defense tactic for casting doubt on the veracity of the charges. Because the rhetoric of enmity aimed primarily at these claims, not mere posturing for the moral high ground, caution is needed for drawing conclusions about Athenians' normative expectations for everyday life. Facile readings of the text for statements about morality lead to faulty inferences. For instance, the speaker's assertion that he did not take vengeance on his enemies while he served in public office should not be cited as grounds for calling into question the importance of the "helping friends and harming enemies" dictum for the ancient Greeks.[143] Polyaenus presents himself as moderate and restrained to make his prosecutors appear malicious and deceitful, not to demonstrate to the jury that he is in the right because he does not respond when wronged. This statement is part of an implicit character argument and is not a commentary on contemporary morals. The enmity narrative works into the overall argument by providing a plausible explanation for the prosecutors' vexatious behavior.

Lysias' tack of trivializing the opponents' motivations by emphasizing their venality was not limited to relatively insignificant trials such as *For the Soldier*. Virtually any plaintiff was open to the charge of private spite and hatred, even (or perhaps especially) in cases of great importance to the state. On such occasions a prosecutor had to present himself as pursuing the state's best interests and so was vulnerable if the defendant could demonstrate that private enmity was the real motive for the lawsuit. Such was the case in the famous trial for which Demosthenes composed *On the Crown* (Dem. 18). The procedure (*graphē paranomōn*, an indictment for proposing an illegal law) and the well-known competition between Demosthenes and Aeschines for leadership in the Assembly assured public interest in the proceedings, as did the broader political dimensions of the trial. The actual legal proceedings concerned a decree in honor of Demosthenes proposed in 330 BC that Aeschines claimed was illegal,[144] but much of the speech (and the extant prosecution speech, Aeschines 3) centers on a debate about Demosthenes' management of the wars with Philip of Macedonia, which had ended with Athens' decisive defeat at the Battle of Chaeronea in 338. Demosthenes and Aeschines dispute whether Demosthenes' policy was true to the Athenians' historical devotion to freedom for the Greeks or was simply a misguided failure. Thus, among the issues at stake was how the Athenians desired to remember their past and whether they would believe that they had suffered the results of a wrongheaded policy or that they had been defeated gloriously while upholding their centuries-old commitment to freedom.[145] Demosthenes accordingly emphasizes the public dimension of the suit and at the same time underscores Aeschines' willingness to abuse the legal system to attack his personal enemies on the pretext of public interest.

The premise under which Demosthenes attacks the prosecution's motivations is made clear near the end of the speech: "No worthy, upstanding citizen should ask a court convened on a matter of public concern to endorse his anger or hatred or any other such feeling, nor should he come before you with that intent."[146] This principle is implicit throughout. Demosthenes emphasizes Aeschines' personal motivations in lodging the *graphē* and contrasts him with the ideal of the disinterested public prosecutor with which we are familiar from speeches such as Lycurgus 1.[147] Although Aeschines professes to arraign a malefactor for his injustices to the state, his actual goal is to abuse his enemy out of envy and spite. As evidence, Demosthenes cites Aeschines' decision to prosecute Ctesiphon, one of Demosthenes' political adherents, rather than Demosthenes himself. (Although the real competition was between Aeschines and Demosthenes as political antagonists, the parties in the trial were technically Aeschines and Ctesiphon because the latter was the person who proposed that an honorary crown be awarded Demosthenes in return for his service to the state. Aeschines therefore indicted Ctesiphon for illegal decree.) Demosthenes asserts that it is inappropriate for Aeschines to attempt to disfranchise Ctesiphon and at the same time make his feud with Demosthenes his foremost concern.[148] The attack on Aeschines' behavior concludes with the statement that "from this one can see that all the charges he has brought are likewise unfair and have no foundation in truth."[149] Demosthenes makes clear the connection between his negative portrayal of Aeschines' character and his argumentative framework. Because of Aeschines' previous behavior and his present motivation ("from these things"), the jurors should be suspicious of everything that he has to say.

Although Demosthenes attacks Aeschines on this front throughout the speech, one particular passage near the end merits special attention. Aeschines initiated the entire process of litigation incorrectly, Demosthenes asserts, because he brought a "suit of envy" (*dikē phthonou*). This wordplay based on typical Athenian legal language—the various procedures were called "suits" of something (theft, murder, or some other offense)—implies that the real basis for the lawsuit was envy. But it is wrong to pursue one's hatred without discovering a real crime to prosecute (123). Aeschines' penchant for using his rhetorical skill for private ends is wholly unfitting and contrasts nicely with Demosthenes' own habits.

> Even if I do have some [rhetorical] experience of this kind, you will all find that I always use it in the public domain to advance your interests and never to oppose them or in pursuit of private ends. He, on the other hand, uses his experience in speaking not only to help our enemies but also to harm anyone who has ever annoyed or crossed him.[150]

The likelihood that Aeschines would fabricate an accusation out of personal enmity and spitefulness follows naturally from his previous unscrupulous behavior. He does not want to help the state by prosecuting actual criminals; he wants to gratify his desire for revenge.

This passage, which is intended to support Demosthenes' character assassination of Aeschines and the concomitant implicit argument from probability, is another example of how close attention to the rhetorical purposes of the speech can prevent incorrect inferences about the function of enmity in the argument. Cohen cites Demosthenes 18.278–279 as evidence for an honor game that Demosthenes and Aeschines are playing out in the courts.[151] He asserts that Demosthenes attempts "to deny Aeschines that equal standing as a rival and, hence, man of honor." This may be true, but there is no reason to suppose that the primary purpose of Demosthenes' attack was to elicit a vote from the jury based on the relative social standing of the disputants. As shown above, Demosthenes employs the rhetoric of enmity to create probability and character arguments that reveal Aeschines' motivation. It is not necessary to infer that passages such as §§278–279 are intended primarily to speak to Demosthenes' or Aeschines' worthiness as persons, apart from the legal merits of the case. Demosthenes' use of enmity clearly functions as a part of the structure of his overall argument for the justice of his claims and the hollowness of Aeschines' vexatious attack.

Nor should *On the Crown*'s attack on Aeschines' motivations be taken as an indication of "a deep suspicion of enmity as a motive for litigation."[152] Demosthenes' statements do not prove that Athenians believed it wrong to prosecute out of enmity. Jurors were suspicious about a prosecutor motivated by enmity because of the possibility that he might be lying, not because enmity in itself was illegitimate. Demosthenes asserts that Aeschines had attempted a similar attack on his motivation when he prosecuted Aeschines for his role in the embassy to Philip thirteen years earlier: "[You asserted that] I brought a false, trumped-up charge against you because of private enmity."[153] The existence or absence of enmity in itself is not the point but rather the existence or absence of enmity as it sheds light on the truth of the matter. Private enmity has direct implications for credibility.

Rarely among the extant orations, the counterpart to *On the Crown* has survived. The speech for the prosecution, Aeschines 3 (*Against Ctesiphon*), provides useful insight into Demosthenes' tactics in *On the Crown* by allowing an examination of the arguments to which Demosthenes responds. Although Aeschines neither spares Demosthenes personal abuse nor denies that Demosthenes is his personal enemy (which he could hardly do), the conventional rhetoric of enmity is notably absent from his verbal attacks.[154] Other than a few scattered references to the personal dimension of their feud,[155] Aeschines keeps the focus on the public and legal dimensions of the trial. Only once does he introduce the theme of their personal animosity for any length of time[156] and even then only to counter an anticipated argument that Aeschines should have prosecuted him for these offenses long ago. *Against Ctesiphon* lacks *On the Crown*'s focus on the private dimension of the feud probably because Aeschines saw that he had much less to gain in emphasizing his hostility toward Demosthenes. As Demosthenes himself knew very well, if the jurors believed that Aeschines was pursuing his own private interests at all costs, they would be suspicious of his motives. Aeschines downplays enmity; Demosthenes emphasizes it. The issue, however, is not whether or not it is right to pursue enemies in court. Their strategies for presenting hostile relationships address their claims about the charges.

In a few instances, criticism of an opponent's motivations progressed from accusations of malicious spite into full-blown conspiracy theory. In *On the Mysteries* (Andocides 1), Andocides launches into a diatribe that borders on paranoia, accusing his enemies of sending their lackeys against him and orchestrating a concerted campaign to secure his exile from the state. The case concerns an accusation that Andocides had been one of those wealthy aristocrats who had celebrated the Eleusinian Mysteries in their private homes in 415, mocking one of the most revered religious festivals in Athens.[157] Andocides' later participation in the (real) Eleusinian Mysteries would therefore have been illegal because of his alleged act of impiety. As he states at the outset, his opponents have been planning this for a long time and have many ulterior motives, though he saves the sordid details of his prosecutors' personal motivations for his finale.[158] The speech turns to the narrative of enmity at §117, where our analysis will begin. These closing passages bolster Andocides' claims by providing a rationale for his opponents' false accusations.

First, the audience learns the history of Andocides' quarrel with Callias, a bitter enemy who, although not appearing in court himself, is backing the prosecution team.[159] Andocides and Callias have been in a long-standing dispute over an heiress whom Andocides claimed for himself and Callias claimed for his son.[160] While they were involved in a lawsuit over this woman, Callias bribed some sycophants to prosecute Andocides in the present trial so that he would not be able to pursue his rights to the heiress. He even informed some of Andocides' friends that he would have the suit dropped if Andocides would relinquish his claim. Clearly Callias does not have a stake in the truth of the accusation; he is merely using this prosecution as a screen so that he can pursue other ends.

Andocides then turns to the *de jure* prosecutors, focusing especially on a certain Agyrrhius, a man who suffered from an advanced case of moral myopia. Having run a tax-collecting cartel for several years, Agyrrhius and his co-conspirators abused their positions to extort obscene profits from those who were liable to the tax.[161] At one of the annual auctions for the tax farming, however, Andocides outbid them.[162] When he undertook the job, he performed his duties much more moderately.[163] Not to be outdone, Agyrrhius and his company of "those who met under the poplar" (evidently a well-known club) joined in the prosecution of Andocides to regain their monopoly on the collection of this tax. As in the case of Callias, Andocides highlights Agyrrhius' ulterior motives to call the trustworthiness of the prosecutors into question. His accusers are cheats and finaglers; how could they possibly be believed? With these vivid stories, Andocides attempts to establish private motivations for each of the prosecutors involved in the trial and thereby deny the justice and even the sincerity of their charges.

On the Mysteries is another of the relatively few orations with a surviving counterpart. A *synēgoria* for the prosecution in the corpus of Lysias affords an opportunity to compare the rhetorical strategies of two opposing parties. While Andocides 1 puts the private motivation of the prosecutors in the spotlight, the speaker of [Lysias] 6 (*Against Andocides*) virtually ignores the question of motivation, instead highlighting the negative effects that Andocides' impiety will have on the city if the religious pollution is not purged by punishing him.[164] The focus is entirely on the offense itself in *Against Andocides*, as it should be in a trial of so much interest to the state. The speaker, probably in anticipation of what Andocides would argue, specifically denies that the trial is merely the product of personal grievances: "What would break the settlement is not Andocides now paying the penalty for his offenses, but if a person is somehow punished as an individual because of public disasters."[165] The speech's solemn and public-spirited tone is exactly what was required in a high-profile religious trial and is exactly what Andocides needed to subvert. His emphasis on the private motivations of his accusers was the answer.

When defendants chose to affirm enmity with their opponents, they opened up an array of possible tactics for attacking the prosecutors' motivations and character. Like prosecutors, they employed narratives that allowed them to characterize their opponents in a certain light and to make arguments pertaining to the offense with which they had been charged. When the history of an opponent's actions came into focus, applicability to the present was always in view. Defendants attacked prosecutors' character to call into question the degree to which their accusations merited trust.

Compared to defendants' affirmations of enmity, denials are relatively rare. Yet denials of enmity, when they do occur, fulfill similar purposes. For instance, the speaker of Lysias 1 (*On the Murder of Eratosthenes*), Euphiletus, denies enmity with his opponent to create an explicitly framed probability argument. The rhetorical situation is somewhat unusual in that Euphiletus admits that he killed Eratosthenes and merely claims that his actions were legal under the law for justifiable homicide, which allowed a husband to kill an adulterer caught in the act.[166] Euphiletus apparently was worried that the prosecution would accuse him of luring Eratosthenes into a trap to kill him for reasons that Euphiletus of course does not state himself.[167] His concern was to prevent the jury from believing that he had ulterior motives. He is therefore careful to avoid admitting that he knew Eratosthenes beforehand and argues that he had no reason at all to hate Eratosthenes or want to see him dead.[168] That Euphiletus felt the pressing need to deny enmity is made clear by his decision to do so even though he apparently had to skew the truth to make his denial seem plausible. Todd points to some incidental remarks that indicate that Euphiletus and Eratosthenes were members of the same deme, although Euphiletus carefully disguises this fact.[169] Euphiletus' claims that he did not know Eratosthenes may therefore have been quite specious. Nevertheless, he pointedly denies enmity with Eratosthenes near the end of the speech: "Examine the affair in your own minds as follows. Ask yourselves if there had ever been any enmity between Eratosthenes and myself except for this. You will not find any."[170] Euphiletus immediately uses this denial of enmity to make an explicit argument from probability. He assumes that the jury would want to know whether or not Eratosthenes and he had acted with hostility toward each other.

> He had not maliciously brought a public prosecution against me, he had not tried to expel me from the city, he had not brought a private prosecution, and he did not know of any offense of mine that I would kill him for, out of fear that it would become public knowledge. And if I had succeeded, I had no hope of receiving any money (some people do admittedly plot the deaths of others for this purpose).[171]

He provides a list of circumstances that could drive someone to homicide and then rejects all of them as inapplicable to his own situation. Most importantly, to maintain that his act of homicide was justifiable and not based on a premeditated plan to punish an enemy, Euphiletus denies that he was in a feud with Eratosthenes. The speaker in fact had no ulterior motives to rouse the jurors' suspicions.

Euphiletus' insistence on his lack of personal interaction with Eratosthenes not only counters his opponents' version of events (the entrapment thesis) but also supports his own. If Euphiletus had never met Eratosthenes before, then he must have had another, very strong reason for killing him. This reason is, Euphiletus argues, the act of adultery against his household: "I had never seen this man before that night. What was I hoping for, then, by running so great a risk—if I had not in reality suffered the most terrible of injuries at his hands?"[172] Euphiletus' denial of enmity serves his stated purpose of supporting the credibility of his version of events.[173]

CONCLUSION

The reasons that speakers employed enmity as they did are tied to the exigencies of the individual cases and the strategies that they wished to employ. The need to support their credibility as speakers, to attack that of the opposition, or to create some other plausibility argument about the case drove litigants to discuss their relationships with their opponents in ways that integrated with their overall claims. The speeches analyzed in this chapter anticipate in substance Quintilian's statement that *narratio* is designed not just to inform the judge of the facts but also to convince him to assent to the speaker's interpretation.[174] These litigants develop a story about the dispute in such a way that subsequent claims about the character of the personalities involved and their likely actions and reactions will seem credible. Scholars have previously recognized the orators' use of past relationships for arguments about character but have not generally taken note of the rational manner in which they influence arguments about the legal merits of the case.[175]

Scholars have also drawn attention to the Athenian court system's apparent tolerance for argumentative techniques that would be considered irrelevant by modern standards, and rightfully so. The digressive discussions of hostile relationships do not fit neatly into the Western legal tradition's emphasis on technical criteria for assessing guilt and innocence. It is going too far, however, to assume that the construction of character based on such narratives was intended primarily to win points with the jury in some sort of sociological battle external to the legal arguments on trial. Despite the obvious and striking differences between the juridical practice of classical Athens and modern Western systems, jurors and judges in both systems share an interest in discovering whether a specific punishable offense had actually been committed. Athenians favored arguments based on the wider context of the offense and the nature of the personalities involved much more than modern legal systems, which tend to turn a skeptical eye on such subtleties, but the goals are often the same: to persuade the jury that the offense really did or did not occur. Enmity is not an argumentative technique whereby litigants appeal to social norms merely to win the jury over to a positive evaluation of their character. On the contrary, the function of enmity in these orations is grounded in legal arguments about the credibility of each speaker's version of the facts.

Within the framework of the Athenian legal system, in which the burden of the speaker was not just to argue for a particular point but to construct an entire scenario that made his claims seem plausible, the extensive use of character evidence in the Attic orators makes sense. The techniques of the orators often seem odd to modern readers precisely because of their willingness to widen the scope of what was considered information pertinent to the case. In the absence of modern civil law's rigorous evidentiary rules and insistence on strict application of the "facts" to the relevant statutes, the Athenians naturally turned to the method of argumentation that makes a claim truly convincing to the hearer, the narration of the broader framework that puts the actions of all parties in context. That this is normally the best means of persuading a listener is shown by several trials in the United States that have become famous (or notorious, depending on one's perspective). These cases share the common feature that the public, or large segments thereof, have remained convinced of the guilt of the defendant despite his or her acquittal by jury trial. Perhaps most famous is the (first) O. J. Simpson trial, but more recent is the trial of Casey Anthony.[176] Most followers of this case did not read the evidence presented by the prosecution, but they did hear the story of Anthony's previous behavior as a mother, her comments about her child, and her incongruous explanations of events and almost nonsensical accusations against other people. Whatever the evidence is and the laws say, it is the narrative, which provides glimpses of her character, that convicts her in the eyes of so many. Unless they are trained and instructed otherwise, humans tend to view questions of truth in this way, within the larger context that makes sense of the whole story.[177]

These stories, moreover, speak for themselves and do not require explicit commentary to draw out their importance for the situation at hand. Humans are well equipped to interpret narrative without aid from the narrator, and so it is no surprise that when the orators employ narratives to support their claims, their arguments usually remain implicit rather than stated. A prosecutor could assert candidly that his claim about the defendant makes sense because the defendant has already engaged in similarly degenerate behavior. He could have shown how the defendant aggravated him time and again without provoking a response and then argued explicitly that his appearance in court is a testament to the truth of his claims because he was so reluctant to engage in litigation in the past. But usually the speaker allowed the stories to speak for themselves. A well-crafted narrative does not offer a handful of propositions but rather constructs a consistent picture and makes all the actions and responses of all the parties believable and realistic. The connection between these techniques and rational argumentation is no weaker for being less obvious.

When a litigant regaled his audience with tales of his opponent's depravity or of his own uprightness, he was often sticking more closely to the point than we may at first realize.[178] Because these character arguments in the orators aimed at proving or disproving the respective versions of the events on trial, there is no need to assume that the discussion of character excluded the consideration of the merits of each party's version of events. The "otherness" of Greek law has occasioned considerable interest during recent years, but in this respect it may not be as "other" as is commonly thought. Athenian jurors were concerned as much as modern judges with the plausibility of the legal charges, even if they were willing to use the information drawn from the litigants' backgrounds to assess credibility. It may be true, for instance, that in Athenian courts the construction of character types often seems to have been more important than questions of fact,[179] but this is because the construction of character types directly addressed the establishment of fact. The focus on characterization does not mean that jurors simply ceased to care about the facts. It is the offense itself that was important;[180] characterization was designed to inform the credibility of the charge. Far from being uninterested in the individual facts at issue, speakers consistently insist that that is exactly what they are providing for the jury.[181]

The implications of these findings for modern attempts to extract Athenian values from courtroom narratives are significant. When character arguments are understood as vehicles for rational arguments, the nature of the debate about the role of enmity in the Athenian courtroom must change. The assumption that the orators intended statements about the actions of their opponents and themselves to speak to the overall moral worth of the respective litigants lies at the heart of the methodological premises shared by Cohen, Herman, and many others. If this theory about the use of character arguments were correct, we could assume that the orators' narratives provide us with paradigms of moral rectitude on the one hand and of decadent debauchery on the other, but in fact the purposes behind these rhetorical strategies are more complex. When a speaker attempts to paint himself or his opponent in a certain light, he does not necessarily ask the jurors to vote for whomever they find more acceptable as a person. He uses character portraits to create implicit arguments from probability about the key claims of the case.

This is not to say that the orators in no way craft their rhetoric to appeal to contemporary norms and values. Decisions involving morality are generally so complex that an attempt to boil down rhetorical strategies to a single driving factor would surely prove vain.[182] In this case, however, it would be a mistake to assume that an appeal to the jury's views on social mores was the only or even the primary reason behind the rhetoric of enmity in the courtroom. More immediate legal concerns are discoverable. Litigants do not treat their presentation of enmity as an end in itself, justifying their cases objectively, but rather as a means by which they can construct arguments about the case. In other words, speakers do not believe that the mere assertion or denial of a hostile relationship with their opponent can win favor simply by meeting the jury members' social expectations. Enmity functions within the context of the speaker's legal claims. The methodological premises upon which many other arguments about enmity in Athens are founded are consequently problematic; a new study based on the appreciation of the orators' use of enmity to support their rhetorical and legal goals is needed.

3. THE FLEXIBILITY OF THE RHETORIC OF ENMITY

While the goal of the rhetoric of enmity was straightforward, to make the overall argument seem more plausible, the methods by which this goal could be achieved were many and varied. Litigants adapted their presentations of enmity to a variety of different situations, and their consequent rhetorical choices had repercussions on how they presented their arguments. Despite enmity being a well-established rhetorical device that could be invoked in formulaic and often predictable ways, it was malleable enough to admit of many different variations. In the orators, we see not hackneyed and slavish reproductions of familiar set pieces but rather clever innovations on a well-known theme. Many factors influenced litigants' decisions on how to approach the topic of enmity, and the strategies that they devised were correspondingly sophisticated. The orators' rhetorical methods and the rationale behind them cannot be boiled down to one or two criteria; they were predicated upon a host of factors, including procedure, the type of dispute, the speaker's history with his opponent, and the personae of the speaker and his opponent in the eyes of the public.

The first section ("The Influence of Procedure and Other Factors") frames the discussion of enmity as a rhetorical device by demonstrating how flexible it could be across different types of cases. Contrary to certain recent theories,[1] the procedural choice of the prosecutor, although it influenced each speaker's rhetorical decisions, did not determine whether the speaker would affirm or deny enmity. Similarities and differences can be charted across procedural bounds. Each litigant's rhetorical decisions were dependent on multiple individual factors particular to his case.

The second section ("The Complexity of the Rhetoric of Enmity: Beyond the Affirm/Deny Pattern") further demonstrates that it is far from easy to categorize rhetorical strategies into a simple pattern of affirmation versus denial. The nuanced ways by which litigants shape their rhetoric make arranging their tactics into identifiable patterns a precarious undertaking. There were more options than the extremes of merely "affirming" and "denying," and within even broad groupings of strategies we find individualized techniques particular to each litigant and each trial.

The final section ("Interplay between Enmity and Other Argumentative Strategies") will draw attention to the methods by which speakers integrate the rhetoric of enmity with other commonplaces. Enmity and other rhetorical devices work together to fill in potentially vulnerable points in a case by covering argumentative gaps. When the particular details of the case impose limitations on the ways in which a speaker can develop his argument, he may substitute other types of argumentation to cover the holes. This close integration of the rhetoric of enmity with the entirety of a litigant's argument and its interplay with other rhetorical considerations are a testament to the complexity of the speeches of Attic oratory.

THE INFLUENCE OF PROCEDURE AND OTHER FACTORS

To understand why a particular litigant has affirmed or denied enmity, careful attention must be paid to the varied concerns facing the speaker. An analysis of these texts that fails to consider these disparate forces risks missing important evidence regarding the author's aims. The tendency to concentrate on the influence of a single factor on rhetorical decisions should be resisted. For instance, scholars have increasingly recognized the role of procedure in determining certain aspects of litigants' rhetorical strategies. While identifying such patterns is sometimes a fruitful endeavor,[2] it often gets only part of the picture. It is true that the plaintiff's choice of procedure limited his rhetorical options and that rhetorical strategies often changed based on whether the court action was public or private,[3] but procedure alone did not determine how a litigant employed enmity.

No readily discernible pattern may be detected even in the most basic distinction in Athenian procedural options, the dichotomy between public and private suits. Despite some recent efforts,[4] any attempt to make a straightforward correspondence between public/private and affirm/deny is bound to fail because litigants shaped their presentation of enmity according to their specific needs and not with an eye only to procedure. An example of the problems inherent in an analysis along these lines may be found in an article by Kurihara, which asserts that Athenians had "the normative expectation that public suits should not be motivated by private enmity."[5] It is clearly incorrect to say that public prosecutors normally deny enmity, as can be seen in the striking number of exceptions that Kurihara himself notes. Of the nineteen public prosecution speeches with references to enmity that Kurihara cites at the beginning of the article, eleven of them turn out not to follow the pattern (i.e., they do not deny enmity as expected).[6]

He carefully explains each exception in reference to particular attributes of individual trials, but this analysis only reinforces the idea that more factors were involved here than the type of procedure.

Moreover, Kurihara's explanations of the "exceptions" are themselves problematic, again because he attempts to reduce the decision to affirm or deny enmity to two or three criteria, such as the speaker's public persona (or lack thereof) or whether the speaker was an advocate or main prosecutor. Consequently, he has to argue contradictorily that speakers who were very well known to the public could admit enmity because it was manifest, while speakers unknown to the public were relatively free from the normative requirement to deny enmity.[7] Such an argument suggests simply that any speaker could admit enmity if he chose. To account for other exceptions, Kurihara posits that *synēgoroi* could take advantage of their position as co-speaker to admit enmity, but in the only extant set of speeches for a public prosecutor and his *synēgoros*, it is the prosecutor himself, not the *synēgoros*, who admits enmity with the defendant.[8] The problems in this analysis illustrate the necessity of considering as many different factors as possible instead of fixating on a small set of criteria to the exclusion of other rhetorical considerations.[9]

The temptation to look for a guiding principle in the orators' invocations of enmity that is tied to procedure stems from a few apparently obvious patterns that correspond roughly to procedural choices. In private prosecution speeches that primarily concern disputes about ownership, speakers usually affirm enmity.[10] In speeches composed for public trials of special interest to the state, prosecutors often deny enmity.[11] Several speakers in such cases deny that they even knew their opponent before the trial. There appear to be patterns, but unfortunately they are not consistent. Despite the frequent denials of enmity in public suits, the most candid assertions of enmity with the lengthiest narratives and most emotionally charged language also tend to come in public cases. What are we to make of these disparate phenomena?

First of all, these patterns are the result of tendencies and not prescriptive norms. Although prosecutors in a particular type of procedure tend to affirm enmity, this does not prove that they were expected to do so. If normative expectations for litigants' relationships with their opponents had existed, the patterns would be much more uniform and would not be riddled with exceptions. Second, procedure is a red herring: procedure is not the cause of the similarities in rhetorical strategies. The most important reason for similarity in rhetoric is similarity in the nature of litigants' argumentative goals. Cases involving inheritance will tend to have similar rhetorical strategies regardless of the procedure, as will, for instance, cases involving accusations of violent assault or allegations of illicit behavior in regard to liturgies. Similarities in the argumentative goals of different litigants often result in similar argumentative strategies and hence similar uses of enmity.[12] Thus, for example, in matters that are directly related to public interests and especially public policy, prosecutors often deny or at least downplay enmity with their opponents and choose to focus instead on their opponents' hatred for the city itself.[13] Such cases also tend to result in the use of public procedures.[14] Athenian juries did not, however, discourage affirmations of enmity in such cases, as is obvious from the number of litigants in public suits who parade their enmities before their audiences. Rather, the speaker's argumentative goals influence both the procedure and the rhetoric. The connection between procedure and the rhetoric is incidental because procedure and litigants' rhetorical decisions are both symptoms of one cause—the argumentative goals.[15]

The type of legal claims each litigant attempts to make may therefore seem a more promising avenue for discovering clear patterns in the rhetoric of enmity. Indeed, analysis along these lines is capable of uncovering general themes, but at the same time we should always expect exceptions and shades of difference even between very similar speeches because of the orators' attempts to fit each presentation to its individual case. In this regard it is instructive to consider trials involving accusations of a violent attack. This type of case has been selected both because it tends to cross procedural bounds and because it is particularly well attested.[16] The analysis offered here will illustrate both continuity and dissonance. On the one hand, broad similarities in the rhetoric of enmity are detectable in speeches that make similar accusations even when the procedures differ. On the other hand, the particular attributes of one case as opposed to another often force altered tactics, with the result that there is considerable variation even within this category.

The survival of trials involving acts of violence in significant numbers is undoubtedly due at least partially to the interest that their sensational and shocking details aroused. Still, the bizarre elements of these speeches notwithstanding, the rhetorical use of enmity is logical and intuitive to the observer. A litigant will describe the relationship between victim and accused in a way that will make the latter's motivation (or lack of motivation) for committing the crime seem compelling. In what follows we will consider first this strategy in prosecution speeches ("taking a plausibility argument from the opponents themselves") and then the corresponding strategy in defense speeches (countering such arguments).

Prosecutors who accuse their opponents of assault often attempt the balancing act of affirming enmity and denying culpability for starting or continuing it. The plaintiff can hardly avoid asserting that his opponent is his enemy since an assault on the body presupposes anger and hatred. To make it believable that the defendant attacked him, the prosecutor must provide a motive.[17] On the other hand, he must also avoid portraying himself as aggressive and vindictive or risk giving the defendant an opportunity to argue that he was equally at fault, having traded blow for blow as two combatants in a general melee. The prosecutor must affirm enmity to provide a rationale for his opponent's physical assault and, at the same time, prove that his opponent was the one responsible for escalating hostilities.

This rhetorical tactic can accommodate itself to a range of procedures with only slight modification. Homicide and assault were liable to prosecution through many avenues, but the rhetorical situation in these cases is always basically similar: the plaintiff must show that his opponent, given the opportunity, would likely have committed the crime in question. On the other hand, within this general pattern of employing enmity as a means of addressing the motive of the attacker, considerable variation in detail occurs from speech to speech. Most litigants in these cases employ essentially the same overall strategy, but they hone it for their own particular needs.

Demosthenes 21 (*Against Meidias*), Demosthenes 54 (*Against Conon*), and Antiphon 1 (*Against the Stepmother*) all take this approach to enmity, although none of them was composed for the same procedure: respectively, a public suit for misconduct at a festival, a private suit for battery, and a *dikē* for murder that would have appeared before a special homicide court. First, in *Against Meidias*, Demosthenes speaks on his own behalf in a case composed for an exceptional public procedure, a two-stage type of litigation called *probolē*. The only evidence for the *probolē* comes from this prosecution of Meidias and the other *probolai* that Demosthenes enumerates in §§175–180. The *probolē* gave an Athenian citizen the right to notify the *prytaneis* (the members of the Council responsible for arranging the meetings) that he intended to accuse someone of committing an injustice concerning a festival. The *prytaneis* then placed the action on the agenda of the Assembly for the day after the festival. In the first stage of the procedure, the prosecutor and the defendant each gave a speech before the Assembly. The Assembly then cast a preliminary vote for or against the defendant. It was up to the prosecutor to bring the suit to trial in the dicastic court.[18] As Demosthenes reports, he had already obtained a favorable verdict from the Assembly, and so he composed *Against Meidias* for the second phase of the procedure, the jury court trial.[19]

The procedural background is not as important as Demosthenes' desire to make full use of the rhetoric of motivation to paint Meidias as the sort of person to commit the offense of which he is accused. Because motive and character are crucial to Demosthenes' allegations, the history of the bad blood between Demosthenes and Meidias receives a lengthy narrative. The feud permeates the entire speech, which is punctuated by various digressions about Meidias' behavior. The audience learns that two years previously, Meidias hatched a plot to thwart Demosthenes' efforts to produce a play for his tribe (14–18). He opposed the release of members of Demosthenes' team from their military duties and attempted to destroy the sacred clothing intended for use at the festival. He even bribed Demosthenes' chorus leader to throw the competition and then tried to buy off the archon (the state official responsible for organizing the Dionysia, the festival at which these actions allegedly took place). He finally abandoned intrigue and adopted more forceful methods, sabotaging the props for the production.

Yet the history of hatred between these two goes farther back than that, as the audience learns in a later narrative section. The feud originated when Meidias incited Thrasylochus to break into Demosthenes' house during a protracted legal dispute.[20] Although Demosthenes won a conviction for slander against him, Meidias never paid the fee the arbitrator imposed and even thwarted Demosthenes' attempts to employ a suit of ejectment (*dikē exoulēs*). Meidias later responded by hiring a known sycophant, Euctemon, to prosecute Demosthenes for desertion from the army, voicing abroad that he had murdered a certain Aristarchus (102–110). Meidias then attacked him viciously at his *dokimasia*. This veritable fiend desired to harm Demosthenes at all costs, caring nothing for the validity of his claims and willing to say anything "whether it be true or false."[21] Meidias was out of control.

Demosthenes' narration of the dispute leaves the audience sympathetic to the idea that Meidias would have punched Demosthenes with hubristic intent and in total disregard of the laws and justice, even while Demosthenes was acting in his official capacity as chorus producer. In other words, Demosthenes' narrative of the feud, far from being mere slander, is designed to support his allegations of fact. To this end, Demosthenes admits enmity but at the same time emphasizes Meidias' aggression and his own restraint so that he may develop a persuasive character portrait of the two litigants. Meidias has proved on multiple occasions throughout his life that he is the sort of person who would assault an enemy at any opportunity and would attempt to inflict the maximum possible dishonor. In the context of this character portrait of Meidias, Demosthenes' charges seem perfectly plausible.

A similar charge of violent assault with hubristic intent is the subject of another well-known speech, Demosthenes 54 (*Against Conon*), which Demosthenes composed for a man named Ariston in a private suit for battery (*dikē aikeias*). Despite the procedural difference (*probolē* vs. *dikē*), the general strategy of Demosthenes' rhetoric of enmity is essentially the same. The narrative of *Against Conon*, which many critics regard as one of Demosthenes' best, tells a story of outrageous conduct that has fascinated many readers throughout the years with its shocking details.[22] The climax of Ariston's history of the enmity comes with the offense that is on trial (7–9). When Conon and his friends happen upon Ariston as he is out on a stroll, they take advantage of this seemingly random encounter to assault Ariston and, while several of them pin down his companion Phanostratus, beat Ariston mercilessly. They strip him of his cloak, push him down into the mud, and punch him. As a final insult, Conon crows like a victorious fighting cock and beats his elbows against his sides like wings.

Ariston's character assassination against Conon clearly has strong similarities to Demosthenes' against Meidias. Conon's actions are testaments to his ferocity and combativeness and therefore evidence in favor of Ariston's very negative evaluation of his intentions in the assault. At the same time, differences between the occasions for the two speeches called for slightly altered tactics. First, on simply pragmatic grounds, the time allotted for speeches in private suits was much shorter than for public cases like the *probolē*, so Demosthenes does not have the leisure to go into all the lurid details about the feud with Conon as he did with his feud with Meidias.

Nonetheless, the difference in social standing of the parties involved in the trial opened up for Demosthenes an additional rhetorical option in *Against Conon* that was not available in his case against Meidias. In the latter trial, Demosthenes speaks on his own behalf against another wealthy elite orator, but in *Against Conon* he composed a speech as a logographer for a young and inexperienced man named Ariston. Not bound by a formidable reputation, Ariston could go beyond the typical motif of portraying his opponent as the aggressor and paint himself as an entirely passive victim.[23] He does not even mention that he or Phanostratus offered any resistance.

> In the mêlée one of them, a man I didn't know, rushed Phanostratus and pinned him down, and Conon here and his son and the son of Andromenes fell on me. First they pulled off my cloak, then tripped me and threw me down on the mud, jumped on me and hit me so hard they split my lip and made my eyes swell shut.[24]

All of the verbal forms in this passage are active, with Conon, his son, and the son of Andromenes as subjects and Ariston and his companion as the objects. While recapitulating the same events later in the speech, Ariston again makes himself the passive recipient of Conon's abuse: "I did suffer at Conon's hands the insults of which I accuse him. I was dealt those blows, and my lip was split so badly that it needed to be stitched, and for this abuse I am suing him."[25] Ariston denies that he provoked Conon in any way and omits reference even to an attempt at self-defense.[26]

In fact, the speech's narrative up to this point very much downplays Ariston's role in the feud. The event that precipitated the offense on trial occurred while Ariston was on military duty at Panactum, where he had the misfortune of finding himself stationed in a campsite adjacent to Conon's sons. These men made sport of harassing other citizens, eventually pestering Ariston and his comrades enough that they complained to the generals. Ariston stresses both that Conon's sons were not singling him out for abuse[27] and that many other citizens complained to the generals en masse, "all of us messmates going to him as a group, not I apart from the others."[28] He specifically avoids portraying the incident as the genesis of a private feud with either Conon or his sons. This could hardly be called the beginning of a genuine relationship of enmity since Ariston, who was simply one of many who complained about Conon's sons, resolved to ignore the whole business once they left the camp.

Ariston may well be attempting to put his own spin on this incident because he was worried that his opponent would argue that the feud had its roots in this first confrontation.[29] Conon could have contended that the fight for which he had been brought to trial was merely the latest in a series of attacks and counterattacks in a long-standing relationship of enmity and the only difference between this episode and all the other skirmishes was that Ariston had lost very badly.[30] Ariston avoids portraying their relationship as a bona fide enmity and simply uses this incident to set the background for the heinous act of *hubris* that he intends to relate. He must of course admit enmity with the defendant because of the nature of the accusation, but he carefully portrays the "enmity" as a very one-sided affair. He does not provide the wealth of background information that Demosthenes does in *Against Meidias*, but he succeeds in portraying his opponent as an utterly hubristic and despicable bully by emphasizing his own passivity to a degree that Demosthenes could not in his dispute with Meidias.

Like the speakers of *Against Meidias* and *Against Conon*, litigants in homicide trials employed enmity rhetorically for implicit arguments about motivation, although the death of the victim meant that the procedural options changed and the rhetorical situation shifted slightly.[31] Homicide cases often came before the Areopagus Court, which specialized in trials of religious significance such as those for murder.[32] Also, the victim's relatives (rather than the victim) had to lodge the prosecution and consequently address the issue of enmity not between themselves and the opponents, since this was not relevant to motive, but between the defendant and the deceased. Despite these formal differences between homicide trials and other cases for assault, however, the strategy of using enmity as a means of positing a credible motive for the crime remains the most common. For example, the prosecutor in Antiphon 1 (*Against the Stepmother*), who claims that his stepmother intentionally murdered his father, asserts that she had expressed a grievance over her husband's wrongs toward her (15) in order to provide a reasonable motive for her alleged act. The stepmother is even given the epithet "Clytemnestra" (17), the famous mythological husband-murderer. The speaker draws on imagery and language from tragedy to make her appear angry and vindictive so that the jury will accept that she intentionally poisoned her spouse.[33]

Yet despite the broad similarity to the two speeches of Demosthenes considered above, the details of the speaker's presentation of enmity in *Against the Stepmother* differ considerably. In contrast to *Against Meidias* and *Against Conon*, the accused in this speech is a woman. The hostility between her husband and her would not have been a true relationship of enmity, openly recognized by their acquaintances, but rather a private affair between husband and wife, the most intimate details of which the speaker could not reasonably be expected to know. The speaker does not (and probably could not) go into a lengthy description of the hostility between his father and his stepmother. He contents himself with a brief appeal to a character type with which jurors were familiar, the jealous and vindictive wife who desires to be rid of her burdensome husband. The speaker understands that a relationship of hatred between murderer and murdered supports his argument and so carefully provides one, but he does not offer a list of his stepmother's grievances.

Defense speeches in cases of assault or murder confirm the pattern established, that the rhetoric of enmity in these trials tends to focus on the motivations of the accused. In contrast to their prosecutorial counterparts, defendants in these cases usually deny enmity. Lysias 1 (*On the Murder of Eratosthenes*) is a good example of this, even though it is somewhat unusual in that the speaker, Euphiletus, actually admits that he killed Eratosthenes. Euphiletus is careful to deny any preexisting hostility in order to counter the idea that he had an ulterior motive for killing him, an allegation about which Euphiletus is apparently quite worried. A similar denial of enmity that supports such arguments about motivation may also be found in Lysias 4 and Antiphon 5.[34]

Motivation and character were thus issues of primary importance in cases alleging physical assault regardless of the procedural details. Even in these emotionally charged trials, speakers employ histories of and allusions to previous hostile relationships to create arguments that, resting on implicit probabilities, support or undermine the accusation of a violent crime. Viewed in this light, the similarities in strategies across procedures are unsurprising, as are the corresponding tactics of prosecutor and defendant. Slight differences in speakers' methods of argumentation that account for changes in rhetorical needs and rhetorical options are also to be expected. Overall, we can detect a broad pattern based on similarities in argumentative goals that can accommodate nuances in particular strategies as the rhetorical situation demands.

Yet even this broad pattern has exceptions. In Antiphon 6 (*On the Chorus Boy*), the speaker, accused of murder, makes full use of the rhetoric of enmity, but not in the way typical of other cases of assault and homicide. In fact, he says nothing of the relationship between himself and the victim at all. Because the allegation is one of "unintentional" murder (essentially accidental homicide), motive was not a concern, and so the speaker does not waste time denying that the deceased boy was his enemy, although he probably could have pointed this out quite easily. Instead, he actually affirms enmity, but it is enmity between himself and his prosecutors. According to the speaker, his attackers have no faith in the truth of their accusations and have lodged the suit merely as a piece of strategic litigation.[35] A group of men whom the speaker intended to prosecute for embezzlement persuaded the relatives of the deceased boy to lodge a suit against him and prevent him from bringing his own case to trial. Hence, the rhetoric of enmity serves to attack the credibility of the prosecution and does not address the issue of motivation at all.

The speaker of Lysias 3 (*Against Simon*), a defendant on a charge of "wounding with intent" (*trauma ek pronoias*, essentially, attempted murder), similarly affirms enmity with the prosecutor (Simon). The tactic that one might expect from a defendant on such a charge would have been to deny enmity and hence any reason for committing the crime, but perhaps Simon had too much information about their dispute for this to have been a workable strategy.[36] Whatever his reasons, the speaker not only affirms enmity but provides a lengthy narrative of his dispute with Simon. The virulent hatred between the two provides an opportunity for him to emphasize the inordinate length of time that had passed between the alleged offense and Simon's prosecution.[37] In other words, this speech's presentation of enmity employs the *topos* of delay to question Simon's credibility.[38] The rhetoric of enmity simply functions differently than in the speeches discussed previously.

These affirmations of enmity by defendants in assault and homicide cases do not follow the pattern of prosecutors affirming and defendants denying enmity in such trials. Despite these exceptions, however, the general tendency is for speakers in such cases to cite enmity as a motivation for the offense or deny such enmity and hence motive. The speakers of *On the Chorus Boy* and *Against Simon* use enmity to an entirely different purpose, and their corresponding strategies are fundamentally dissimilar to, for instance, that of Euphiletus in *On the Murder of Eratosthenes*. To attempt to find one driving norm that dictated how enmity must be discussed in cases of physical assault would be to obscure important differences in technique and rhetorical goals and misunderstand the nature of the speeches. The litigant in court had only one governing imperative: to win the case.

THE COMPLEXITY OF THE RHETORIC OF ENMITY: BEYOND THE AFFIRM/DENY PATTERN

In this chapter and the previous one, attention has been drawn to whether or not a particular litigant "affirms" or "denies" enmity. This language is convenient for differentiating two divergent types of rhetorical strategies, but it can also easily mislead the reader into envisioning two basic categories into one of which any speech's rhetorical use of enmity can be placed. This section will attempt to forestall such an idea. A template or chart based on the criteria of affirm/deny simply will not suffice because Athenian litigants had more options available to them than outright admission or disavowal of a hostile relationship.

Affirmations and denials of enmity were not necessarily exclusive. A speaker could differentiate between two groups of his opponents and present his relationships with them in different ways. The speaker of Lysias 7 (*On the Olive Stump*) makes a distinction between his prosecutor, Nicomachus, and his personal enemies who hired Nicomachus to lodge the suit.[39] The speech gives the impression that Nicomachus was not a long-standing enemy of the defendant because the speaker prefers to concentrate on Nicomachus' sycophancy,[40] emphasizing that he is merely a hired agent of more powerful men who wish to harm him. Nicomachus' accusations are totally frivolous, and he is in fact simply inventing charges as he goes, probably because he never intended to bring the case to court in the first place but rather hoped to settle with the defendant before the trial.[41] The speaker points out that Nicomachus should have prosecuted him when the offense actually occurred, rather than wait four years. No one would delay the gratification of punishing his enemy for so long.[42]

At the same time that the speaker eschews considering Nicomachus an enemy, he explicitly draws attention to the reckless hatred of the men behind the scenes who have "persuaded" (that is, hired) Nicomachus to prosecute. In stark contrast to the motivations of the *de jure* prosecutor, these men are genuine enemies.[43] *On the Olive Stump* thus includes both a denial and an affirmation of enmity, defying easy categorization.

Denials and affirmations of enmity could also vary in intensity. Not all affirmations or denials are equal. There was a broad range of options, from *Against Meidias*' dogged emphasis on the hostility of the two litigants to much briefer admissions of enmity that do not impinge on the rest of the argument. We have already encountered straightforward assertions of enmity and straightforward denials, but a litigant could also choose a middle ground between the two. When a plaintiff had no desire to dwell on the commonplaces that narratives of enmity make possible but at the same time felt that he could not plausibly deny enmity, he could admit enmity with the opponent but downplay it. Several speakers do precisely this, beginning their speeches with an assertion of enmity but quickly pushing all private motivation into the background.

When the narrative of the offense itself presupposed a hostile relationship or when the personalities involved in the trial were well known to the public as outspoken enemies, speakers found it impossible to deny enmity. A prosecutor could not simply lie about his history with the defendant if he knew that the defendant could easily expose him, but he could obscure and suppress the details of their relationship and put other issues at the center of the debate. The privilege of speaking first in the trial lent to the plaintiff an enviable opportunity to set the tone for the dispute and force the defendant to respond to his points. Several prosecutors exploit this structural advantage to sideline the issue of their personal enmities.[44]

When Lysias accused Eratosthenes of murdering his brother, he could not credibly deny private motivation for lodging the suit. A juryman would have been puzzled at the suggestion that such a heinous act against one of Lysias' family members somehow failed to elicit hostility from him. At the same time, however, Lysias had good reason for wanting to avoid putting his personal feelings at the center of the trial. At the time of the alleged crime, Eratosthenes was a member of The Thirty, whom Athenians later came to view as public enemies, scapegoats for the disastrous aftermath of Athens' defeat in the Peloponnesian War. The citizen body therefore had an interest in how The Thirty were remembered and depicted.[45] Lysias would have been disingenuous to portray his suit as merely a private affair. After affirming his hatred for the defendant in the prologue, Lysias quickly shifts the focus from his private motivation to public concerns, asserting that he is prosecuting "because we all have many reasons to be angry on personal or public grounds."[46] This clause is a turning point in the oration's focus, from Lysias' personal concerns to the public dimension of the trial.[47] All private motivation gradually disappears.[48]

In this speech of Lysias', enmity was manifest from the speaker's kinship with the victim. In other cases, a denial of enmity was impossible because of the high-profile nature of the trial and the personalities involved in it. In Aeschines 1 (*Against Timarchus*), Aeschines must admit that enmity played a role in his lawsuit because of the visibility of his conflict with Timarchus and Demosthenes over the negotiations with Philip of Macedonia. Timarchus, one of Demosthenes' colleagues, had prosecuted Aeschines for misconduct at his exit examination (*euthynai*) following his role in the second embassy to Philip in 346, to which Aeschines responded by prosecuting Timarchus preemptively by *dokimasia tōn rhētorōn*, the present trial.[49] Although Aeschines admits all of this, he conspicuously shuffles his private motivations into the background, confessing that his opponents are his enemies but also strongly maintaining that the prosecution he is bringing benefits the state.[50]

> Never before, men of Athens, have I brought an indictment (*graphē*) against any man or persecuted him at his final audit; no, I have in my opinion shown restraint in all such matters. But since I could see that the city was suffering serious damage from this man Timarchus, who addresses the Assembly illegally, and since I am personally the victim of his malicious prosecution (just how, I shall explain later in my speech), I concluded that it would be utterly disgraceful not to intervene in defense of the city as a whole, the laws, you, and myself. And in the knowledge that he is guilty of the charges that you heard the clerk read out just now, I declared this formal scrutiny against him. It seems, men of Athens, that the claims usually made in public cases are not untrue: private enmities very often do put right public wrongs.[51]

Aeschines boldly states that he has appeared in court in response to Timarchus' previous prosecution of him.[52] At the same time, he carefully ties his own interests to those of the public. He supposedly saw Timarchus harming the state by speaking contrary to the laws and "knows that he is guilty" of the charges laid, namely, that Timarchus prostituted himself while he was a youth and squandered his inheritance, two offenses that would disqualify him from participating in the democracy as an Athenian citizen.[53] Thus, Aeschines can claim that he is protecting simultaneously "the whole city, the laws, you, and myself." In the concluding proverbial statement, "private enmities often correct public matters," Aeschines again attempts to make the connection between his prosecution and the public good. His use of this aphorism implies that Aeschines' personal motivation is subservient to his concern for the welfare of Athens. Even though he is indicting a private enemy, he wants to make his own reasons for prosecuting appear secondary to the cause of justice.⁵⁴ Aeschines portrays himself as a civic-minded citizen concerned for the interests of the state, which happen to coincide with his own interests in this case. He emphasizes that he is not the type of person to pursue a private vendetta or invent baseless charges.⁵⁵

Like affirmations of enmity, denials of enmity also admitted of different levels of intensity. Sometimes the denial of previous hostility between prosecutor and accused is quite explicit, as in Lycurgus 1 (*Against Leocrates*): "I did not undertake this trial because of any personal enmity."⁵⁶ At other times it is more subtle. The prosecutor in Demosthenes 41 (*Against Spudias*) never explicitly addresses the topic, but he exploits his kinship with his opponent to build arguments off an implicit denial of enmity. He carefully avoids portraying himself as a long-standing enemy of the defendant so that he can point to Spudias' intransigence and pettiness as responsible for forcing the issue to trial. The speaker harps on Spudias' unreasonable refusal to submit the matter to arbitration, and so he implies that they had previously been on good terms and had mutual friends who were available to arbitrate between them. The speaker builds arguments upon the assumed absence of enmity.⁵⁷

The rhetoric of enmity was multifaceted and capable of undergoing many permutations to fit the needs of particular trials. Even after a litigant decided to affirm or to deny enmity, he still faced a spectrum of possibilities as to what to do next. Would he affirm enmity and allow the rhetoric of anger and hatred to permeate his speech or limit his admission to a handful of remarks and omit a narrative? Would he address his relationship with the *de jure* prosecutor, his enemies "behind the scenes," or a victim of an alleged offense? Would he use his admission or denial to attack the speaker's credibility, support his own, or support some other argument about the case? These are but a few of the many questions that faced a potential speaker in court. The possibilities of the rhetoric of enmity were many, and the accompanying strategies were correspondingly sophisticated.

INTERPLAY BETWEEN ENMITY AND OTHER ARGUMENTATIVE STRATEGIES

Each litigant had certain aims, arguments, or ideas he wished to impress upon the audience and also multiple avenues for achieving them.⁵⁸ He might use one line of reasoning to flesh out one part of his case and another type of reasoning for another. The rhetoric of enmity might address the defendant's motivations for committing the alleged crime, while a different stylistic device might attack the opponent's credibility. The many rhetorical techniques available to Athenian litigants, of which enmity was only one, could overlap in their rhetorical purposes, be substituted according to the needs of the speaker, or cover gaps in the speaker's argument. The orators had available to them a large stock of motifs on which they could draw for their own particular purposes. Enmity worked within speakers' strategies and integrated with other rhetorical motifs to support their argumentative goals.

Because of its ubiquity in the Attic orators and its flexibility for developing a number of types of arguments, enmity often impinges on multiple aspects of the case and is accordingly molded to harmonize with the rest of the speaker's rhetoric. This theme is therefore a useful starting point for investigating the interplay between the commonplaces of Athenian rhetoric in general. In the following discussion, we will view the argumentative strategies of law court speeches through the lens of the rhetoric of enmity, investigating how enmity interacts with other commonplaces, including additional probability arguments, the speaker's public persona, appeals to "rumor" (*phēmē*), the language of sycophancy, and the "delay" *topos*. This analysis will make clear that enmity in Attic oratory is invariably incorporated into the overall legal strategy.

Because enmity often supported implicit plausibilities, other types of plausibility arguments could substitute in its place. The speaker of Lysias 3 (*Against Simon*) does not deny enmity like most defendants in cases of physical assault because he has opted for another method of addressing the issue of motive. Instead of asserting that he is not involved in a hostile relationship with Simon and therefore had no reason to want to kill him, he fully admits enmity and makes extensive arguments about motive drawn from the particular circumstances of the alleged offense. This line of reasoning appears to have been quite sufficient, in the speaker's estimation, to expose the absurdity of Simon's charges.[59] He points out that he would have been extremely foolish to attack Simon in the manner alleged. The speaker is supposed to have confronted Simon in broad daylight and with no one else to aid him while Simon was in his house with many companions. A more inopportune moment for an assault on Simon could hardly have been found. Furthermore, because the speaker had gotten the worst of his previous encounters with Simon, it would be ridiculous to envision him single-handedly taking on Simon's entire gang by entering his house.[60] The speaker thus points out that he not only lacked reasonable motivation for approaching Simon in this way but even had every reason to want to avoid Simon entirely. Since his arguments all have their basis in the particular attributes of the case and have little to do with the presence or absence of a relationship of enmity with Simon, the speaker does not have a pressing need to deny such a relationship. He has already found a way to problematize his opponent's accusation by pointing to his lack of motivation for committing this crime in the manner alleged.[61] He is therefore free to use enmity to other purposes.[62]

Another factor that could change a speaker's approach to the rhetoric of enmity was his status as a public figure. Lycurgus, for instance, could be more single-minded in his denial of enmity than most other public prosecutors because his visibility as a benefactor to the state allowed him to avoid the problems usually associated with this tactic. In many cases, speakers in Lycurgus' situation would strike a balance between affirming enmity and denying culpability to ward off suspicions of illegitimate private motivation. They do not want the jury to believe that either personal malice or the desire for profit drove them to prosecute. Lycurgus, on the other hand, denies enmity outright, which protects him against suspicions of hatred-based prosecution but does nothing to dispel the charge of sycophancy. A certain degree of danger accompanies emphasis on public-spiritedness since, as Mogens Hansen points out, it "tends to make ordinary folk even more suspicious,"[63] but Lycurgus had another means of defending himself against the accusation that he lodged the suit as a vexatious and litigious busybody: his political clout. His status as a well-known public figure (in Roman terms, his *auctoritas*)[64] made possible his counterargument about the importance of disinterested public prosecutors who bring wrongdoers to account.[65] His special position in Athens as *de facto* leader of the state would have made his appeals to patriotism and loyalty to the public especially plausible in the eyes of the jury.[66] As "treasurer," he had been responsible for the "Lycurgan building program" of 338–326 and so had built up a considerable amount of popular prestige.[67] For Lycurgus, an affirmation of enmity was unnecessary because he could support his credibility in other ways.[68]

A denial of enmity, in addition to compelling the speaker to find another way to protect himself against suspicions of sycophancy, also deprived him of an especially convenient forum for exploring an opponent's past behavior and bringing his character vividly into the audience's mind. Without a narrative of enmity, a litigant often must discover a comparable way of maligning his opponents. An argumentative technique frequently employed to fill this gap was appeal to common knowledge and rumor (*phēmē*). The speaker of Lysias 31 (*Against Philon*) explains that because he is not personally acquainted with the accused, he will substitute knowledge drawn from the public sphere.

> I would have spoken inadequately because of my ignorance of all he has done, but adequately because of his criminal nature. I ask those of you

who are more skilled at speaking than I am to show that his crimes are even greater. Let them subsequently accuse Philon on the basis of what they know about any topic that I may omit.[69]

Because he has denied enmity, the speaker cannot claim to have information drawn from personal experience but rather must appeal to common knowledge.

In some cases the rhetorical realities of the case forced the speaker to abandon extensive appeals to personal enmity. Hence, the deliverers of many speeches for public prosecutions must appeal to common knowledge to attack the accused. For the speakers of Lysias 12 and 13, both of whom deemphasize their personal enmity with their opponents, information about the defendant lay ready at hand. In both cases the defendant was a member of The Thirty, with whom the public was well acquainted, and in both cases the speaker had specific knowledge about the circumstances of the offense in question because of his involvement as a kinsman and friend of the victim. Accordingly, the narratives of these speeches provide a history, not of the defendant's enmity with the prosecutor but rather of the defendant's enmity "with the city." They develop character arguments about the opponents by drawing attention to their public actions that have proven hostile to the state as a whole. Following a cursory admission of enmity, the rest of their narratives focus on the defendant's detrimental influence on public policy or on the welfare of the state.[70]

Although many prosecutors who deemphasize enmity find another way to launch an attack on their opponents' character, Aeschines faced an especially acute problem in Aeschines 1 (*Against Timarchus*). The illicit acts of which he accused Timarchus (hiring himself out as a prostitute and squandering his inheritance) are not visible to the public at all because they would have been committed behind closed doors.[71] Without a narrative of enmity and without knowledge of the particular events of Timarchus' lewd behavior, he could not regale his audience with anecdotes about Timarchus' depravity drawn from personal experience or from his activities in the public limelight.[72] Yet the necessity of finding an alternative avenue for discussing his opponent's aberrant behavior was pressing because in a public scrutiny (*dokimasia*) the defendant's character is in a very real sense on trial. Aeschines consequently chose the tactic of exploiting what "everybody knows," that is, rumor and common opinion. When personal experience is lacking, second-hand knowledge will do. Aeschines' counterargument to Timarchus' anticipated objection that Aeschines can produce no witnesses is that no one would ever come forward to admit being involved in such disreputable activities. In scandalous crimes such as these, the jury should not expect eyewitnesses but rather establish the truth on the basis of probability.⁷³ Timarchus' character, with which everyone is acquainted, should serve as the guide to a correct verdict: "Do not give credence to anything as much as what you yourselves know and are convinced of in regard to Timarchus here; consider the matter not from the perspective of the present but of the past."⁷⁴ This rhetorical stratagem follows logically from Aeschines' choice to deemphasize enmity, which deprived him of an opportunity to include a narrative to speak to the defendant's past behavior. Several other litigants employ similar techniques.⁷⁵

While prosecutors sometimes found appeals to common knowledge useful substitutes for narratives of enmity, defendants who chose to deemphasize enmity tended to employ another device, the rhetoric of sycophancy. Rumor could prove a valuable source of information about an opponent's wrongdoing in general terms, but accusing the opponent of acting as a sycophant fit more precisely with a defendant's goal of showing that his opponent is the type of person to abuse the court system for his own ends. The defendant would point not only to his prosecutor's wickedness but more specifically to his vexatious litigating. The readily available stereotypes associated with sycophants made it very easy for speakers to appeal to this commonplace theme, especially when arguments about a vexatious enemy's personal attacks were not ready to hand. Ultimately, however, sycophancy and enmity served the same rhetorical purpose: questioning the prosecutor's motivations based on his past behavior.

The substitution of an accusation of sycophancy where we might expect a narrative of enmity can be seen in Lysias 25 (*On a Charge of Overthrowing the Democracy*). Part of the speaker's defense is his emphasis on his opponents' greed and political opportunism, which call their credibility into question. The speaker explicitly denies enmity, but he conspicuously ignores the issue, focusing instead on his opponents' sordid intentions in extorting money from vulnerable men of wealth. Interestingly, however, he has almost nothing specific to say in regard to the prosecutors' motives. For all his bluster about the "sycophancy" of his opponents, he can marshal no evidence to support his charge that they have engaged in frivolous litigation in the past or are doing so at present.⁷⁶ His accusations are limited to generalizations about vexatious busybodies who bring innocent men to trial. Perhaps because of the difficulty of attacking his accusers' credibility, the speaker adopts a "collective persona," focusing on broad issues of Athenian policy instead of portraying the issue as essentially an individual matter.⁷⁷ This reflection on Athens' future as a democracy led T. M. Murphy to call Lysias 25 "a deliberation on Athenian public policy."⁷⁸ Whatever the merits of this observation, the speaker's emphasis on policy may have resulted at least partially from the simple fact that he did not have much to say about his opponents' lives, and the only way to attack their credibility was to typecast them as sycophants.[79] This readily available stereotype allowed the speaker to portray the trial as merely a legal trick for the prosecutors to make money. His reasons for avoiding mention of his personal relationship with his accusers are not obvious,[80] but it is clear that he has declined the use of enmity to attack his opponents' credibility and substituted the device of sycophancy.

The interchangeability of sycophancy and enmity as rhetorical devices, both of which could function to attack the credibility of the opponent, might easily lead to the conclusion that they are mutually exclusive categories: being an enemy means not being a sycophant and being a sycophant means not being an enemy. Indeed, it has often been assumed that this is essentially the case. The reality is that the categories of "enemies" and "sycophants" tend to overlap. A speaker can juxtapose the two concepts and complain of being the victim of his enemies' sycophancy: ὑπὸ τῶν ἐχθρῶν ἀδίκως συκοφαντεῖσθαι.[81] Enmity and sycophancy serve similar rhetorical purposes and so are often used as bolstering arguments that lead to the same conclusion. Sometimes it was easier to accuse the opponent of enmity and at other times of sycophancy, but when circumstances allowed, a litigant could accuse him of both.[82]

The use of sycophancy and enmity in supporting roles is evident in Demosthenes 57 (*Against Eubulides*). The subject of the trial is an "appeal" (*ephesis*)[83] against the decision of the deme of the speaker (Euxitheus)[84] to remove him from the citizenship rolls.[85] In one of the most vigorous assertions of personal enmity in the corpus of Attic oratory, Euxitheus accuses Eubulides, his fellow demesman, of attempting every form of intrigue he could think of, including manipulating an entire deme assembly meeting, to satisfy his private vendetta by having Euxitheus disfranchised. Euxitheus narrates Eubulides' hostile actions against him at length and also explains that the reason for his hostility was a long-standing enmity that had roots in a feud between their fathers.[86] Although the immediate cause of Eubulides' plan to disfranchise Euxitheus was the latter's testimony against Eubulides in a previous trial (8), they have evidently been at each other's throats for quite some time.

The malicious-enemy motif is not the only one that Euxitheus employs in the service of his character attacks on Eubulides. He also labels Eubulides a sycophant and employs the stereotypes associated with blackmailers to drive home his point about the falsity of the accusations.[87] The key mark of a sycophant for Euxitheus is that he brings a charge that is false from an ulterior motive: "This is what a sycophant is: making all sorts of charges but proving nothing."[88] Eubulides has a history of such actions. In a previous review of the citizenship rolls, he and his friends forced some of their fellow demesmen to pay a fee to be enrolled on the deme register and alternatively prosecuted or accepted bribes not to prosecute other innocent people.[89] In the present trial, Eubulides' sycophantic habits are compounded by his personal grudge against Euxitheus: "The present occasion is suitable for someone who is an enemy and wants to play the sycophant."[90] Eubulides is both enemy and sycophant.

Because the defining characteristic of a sycophant, like that of a malicious enemy, is the pursuit of groundless charges, Eubulides can allow the categories of enmity and sycophancy to overlap. He is not concerned with uncovering a single explanation of the prosecutor's motivation but rather with showing that the prosecutor is lying. Both enemies and sycophants tend to be willing to lie in court because they had other interests in the trial besides a desire to see justice done. It does not matter to Euxitheus whether the jurors view Eubulides as motivated chiefly by hatred or by a desire to remove an obstacle to his scheming. He attacks Eubulides for both, hoping that at least one of the charges will stick. Whether as sycophant or vexatious enemy, Eubulides cannot be trusted.[91]

Another rhetorical ploy that integrates closely with the rhetoric of enmity is the *topos* of the prosecutor's delay in bringing suit. Defendants often assert that their opponents have long been their enemies but have failed to prosecute them on previous occasions and instead delayed, usually for many years. Had the prosecutors believed their charges credible at the time when the offense had actually occurred, they would clearly have lodged a suit immediately. Their delay in prosecuting indicates that they do not believe their own accusations and are dredging up old grievances in furtherance of a vendetta. This *topos*, in tandem with an assertion of enmity, creates an implicit plausibility argument with the following components: major (unstated) premise: an Athenian citizen would attack his enemy in the courts, given any pretext; minor (stated) premise #1: my opponent is my enemy; minor (stated) premise #2: my opponent did not prosecute me for this offense until much later; conclusion: my opponent is making accusations he knows to be false. Because the two stated premises must work together for the argument to have persuasive force, the presence of a hostile relationship between prosecutor and defendant is crucial for executing this rhetorical ploy.

Andocides makes use of this commonplace in connection with the mysterious affair of the suppliant's bough illicitly placed on the altar in the Eleusinium (Andocides 1, *On the Mysteries*). To counter his opponents' assertion that he was responsible for this sacrilegious act in addition to all his other profanations, Andocides points out that no one had accused him of the crime, even though Cephisius, the main prosecutor in the present trial, was standing right next to him during the meeting in which the placement of the bough came to light. Cephisius, being Andocides' long-time enemy, surely would have accused him on the spot if he had suspected him of involvement. His failure to act proves by implication that there is no truth in this charge. Andocides pursues the same line of attack on the rest of the prosecution team later in the speech: "As for these men who have now joined with Callias against me and instituted and financed this trial, why did it never occur to them that I had committed impiety during the three years that I was in Athens after returning from Cyprus?"[92] Not only did they fail to accuse him during all that time, they even proposed him as a liturgist on multiple occasions. Athenians would have considered it sacrilegious for anyone guilty of impiety to perform public service for the state, especially at religious festivals like the Hephaestia.[93] By putting Andocides forward as a candidate for a liturgy, his accusers admitted that they did not believe him guilty. Although the prosecutors' words accuse Andocides, their previous actions acquit him.

This *topos* of an enemy's failure to prosecute in the past is a veritable leitmotif in Demosthenes 18 (*On the Crown*). Demosthenes accuses Aeschines of inconsistency in taking up the greater part of his speech with his attacks on Demosthenes' public record, although he never prosecuted Demosthenes at the time of his alleged wrongdoing. If Aeschines had really believed Demosthenes guilty of these offenses, he could have prosecuted him under the relevant laws: "If he saw me doing things that deserved *eisangelia*, he should have brought me to trial by *eisangelia*, and if he saw me proposing illegal decrees (*graphonta paranoma*), he should have indicted me by *graphē paranomōn*."[94] Demosthenes asks why Aeschines, if he disagreed with Demosthenes' attempts at negotiation with other Greek states, never made the slightest protest.[95] He returns to this theme repeatedly, pointing out that Aeschines never attempted to prosecute him at the appropriate time but rather waited until many years later.[96] Aeschines is merely dredging up his own stale rancor and ignoring the facts.[97]

Demosthenes' point about Aeschines' failure to prosecute him in the past depends entirely on the character portrait of Aeschines that Demosthenes has developed through the rhetoric of enmity. Once the jurors believe that Aeschines has been Demosthenes' enemy for decades and has attempted to thwart him in every way possible, they will be ready to listen to Demosthenes' rhetorical questions about why Aeschines never accused him of these crimes previously. If Aeschines believed that there was any truth in these charges, he surely would have taken advantage of them to harm his rival immediately, as enemies typically do. Demosthenes can thus claim that Aeschines has "admitted" that Demosthenes is a good citizen, since he surely would have taken advantage of any opportunity to attack his enemy but never did so.[98]

This defense tactic of adducing an enemy's delay in prosecuting as evidence for the falsity of the accusations is quite common in the extant orations.[99] It was in fact well known enough to prompt prosecutors to anticipate the argument in their speeches. When Euthycles in Demosthenes 23 (*Against Aristocrates*) attempts to preempt the suspicion that enmity motivated him to rake up an old charge with no basis in fact,[100] he anticipates the objection that he did not protest when other orators passed decrees concerning Charidemus but waited to bring suit against Aristocrates. To justify himself, Euthycles flatly denies that enmity had any role in his decision to appear in court.[101] He asserts that he has made it a policy not to lodge a *graphē paranomōn* unless the problem with the decree is serious enough to oppose the city's interests directly. Had Euthycles admitted that he had been Aristocrates' enemy for a long time, this argument would have been quite unconvincing. An Athenian who knew that his enemy was proposing a decree that did not benefit the state would be eager to satisfy his desire for vengeance and help the city at the same time. Euthycles' denial of enmity functions as a response to the anticipated argument that he should have prosecuted Aristocrates long ago.

Enmity's integration with other commonplaces shows how it functioned as part of an overall argumentative strategy. A speaker could deploy the rhetoric of enmity to cover potential weaknesses in his case and invoke other *topoi* to cover gaps. This method of substitution highlights why enmity could be such a flexible device: other argumentative techniques were available to fill in the missing pieces when the rhetorical strategy changed. A speaker's decision on how to approach enmity was thus intimately bound up with his decision about how to employ other rhetorical techniques and shape his argumentative goals. When employed effectively, commonplaces worked together so that each one strengthened the potentially weak points of the others.

CONCLUSION

The sophisticated ways in which litigants shaped the rhetoric of enmity to their own needs is a direct result of enmity's connection to the rhetorical aim of creating an overall plausible account that convinces the jury of the speaker's version and interpretation of events. Because enmity integrated with an overall rhetorical strategy, it was susceptible to modification for each particular case. To appreciate fully the rhetorical use of enmity in a speech requires that we take into account as many of the individual factors as possible and tie them to the litigant's argumentative strategies. Only in considering the interaction between enmity and the rest of the speech can the rhetorical purposes behind the orators' statements be understood.

Patterns in litigants' use of the rhetoric of enmity are detectable, but these patterns are tied to broad similarities in the types of claims being made and not to one or two particular criteria. Similarities in strategies resulted from desires to create similar arguments about the case. If patterns in the rhetoric of enmity are to be found, they will run parallel to patterns in argumentative goals. On the other hand, the patterns are not rigid and consistent enough to make it easy to predict exactly which strategy a prosecutor will choose.

When we move from generalizations to investigation of individual speeches, the picture becomes more complex. The need to establish particular claims was a driving concern, but many other factors played a part in rhetorical decisions. Incidental details that varied from speech to speech forced changes. The rhetoric of enmity was capable of being transformed based on the particular legal and rhetorical situation in which it was deployed. When litigants' decisions about how to approach their relationship with their opponents made the use of enmity for particular types of argumentation impossible, they invoked other commonplaces or took advantage of the particular circumstances of their cases to meet their rhetorical needs. As part of an overall argumentative strategy, the rhetoric of enmity had to be molded to fit the differing requirements of different cases and consequently became flexible enough to accommodate a range of situations. The orators' presentations of enmity were not clunky set pieces that fit awkwardly into speeches of differing rhetorical goals; they were elegant and malleable motifs that each speaker could shape in his own way.

The flexibility of the enmity commonplace reveals that the orators' rhetoric is not reducible to a code of behavior that provides straightforward information about Athenian ideology. These enmities are first and foremost rhetorical constructs that met a particular speaker's needs. The narratives should not be taken as conforming to a generalized code and cannot reasonably be invoked to discover what jurors "wanted to hear" and therefore what the average Athenian would have thought the correct way to behave. The evidence leads to contradictory conclusions on this score. Scholars have often treated enmity as though it were a rigid and straightforward device, readily explained in terms of a litigant's desire to legitimize himself, but the diversity and complexity of litigants' rhetorical decisions on how to engage in discussions of enmity run counter to this common perception. The rhetorical nature of speakers' presentations of enmity must be taken fully into account if we are to find a satisfactory methodology by which to analyze these sources as evidence for Athenian culture and for Athenian thinking about the role of enmity within the democracy.

4. ENMITY UNDER THE LAW
The Limits to Vengeance

The argument of chapter 1, that Athenians viewed enmity as a socially acceptable relationship that was a pervasive force in the city and was liable to spread like a virus through the web of kinship and friendship groups, invites an examination of the relationship between this feuding behavior and the public ideology of the *polis*. Athenians were apparently comfortable with the injunction to "harm enemies," but what were their beliefs about legitimate and illegitimate ways to harm an enemy? In fact, the key values of the democratic regime (liberty, freedom, and security for individual citizens) pushed back against the forces of enmity in several ways. This chapter will consider three important areas in which Athenians prevented enmity from running unchecked: (1) in the democratic governing process, (2) in daily legal practice, and (3) in society at large. It will be argued that Athens tolerated feuding as an acceptable practice and even allowed it to spill over into the public domain but at the same time put strong limitations on it. In the several areas in which enmity threatened important tenets of democratic ideology, enmity had to yield.

The first section ("Enmity in Participatory Government") demonstrates how the institutional framework of the democracy was designed to prevent private enmities from disrupting the day-to-day business of the public sphere. This provides the background against which we may investigate the area in which public and private interests collided with full force, the courts.

The next section ("Enmity in the Legal Sphere") shows how the balance between the private feuding ethic and public ideology was maintained in the legal sphere. It cannot be denied that Athenians permitted feuding to continue through lawsuits. The jurors did not seem to mind if the prosecutor himself admitted that he was seeking vengeance for a previous wrong, even if the original dispute had little to do with the offense that was presently on trial. Rather, the courts practically invited enemies by offering them an opportunity to gain a clear-cut victory in a high-profile venue. At the same time, Athenian juridical practice put important limitations on the ways that feuds could be pursued. Jurors did not compromise on their demand that prosecutors serve the interests of justice by putting a real, punishable offense on trial. Courtroom performers were expected to tell the truth and had to be careful about being caught in a lie. A prosecutor could not simply thunder away about his opponent's poor conduct as a citizen and wretched family life and demand that the jury vote against him because of his disagreeable character. At some point, the opponent's disagreeable character had to support a real charge. Jurors seem to have been comfortable with enemies pursuing and insulting each other through the courts, but once they entered this arena, they had to respect the boundaries of the game.

Leaving aside the limitations on enmity in the public sphere, the third section ("Enmity in Society") addresses the limitations on the behavior of enemies as a general rule. It was not as though enemies faced certain strictures in the courts, but outside the public eye, they could do whatever they wanted. The Athenian democracy's commitment to the equality, freedom, and security of each individual citizen prevented such a radical laissez-faire attitude that would have resulted in social chaos. Of course there were regulations prohibiting actions such as theft, cheating, and slander, offenses for which the victims would have legal recourse against their enemies, but what about protection of the citizen's body itself? The evidence suggests that violence against a citizen was never condoned and was rather specifically prohibited by Athenian law and accordingly proscribed in civic ideology. Enemies were no doubt savvy at finding inventive ways of doing each other harm, but at the bounds of the body of the citizen they had to stop.

The unacceptability of violence in classical Athens was not, however, part of a larger movement toward prohibiting feuds altogether. The native and perhaps atavistic impulse for vengeance exerted considerable influence on the mind of the Athenian, but vigorous public sanctions pushed back against it with equal intensity. In the friction at the border, we see the potency of the opposing forces of instinct and communal sanctions. Athens allowed plenty of scope for "harming enemies" but permitted neither abuse of city institutions nor violent attacks against citizens.

ENMITY IN PARTICIPATORY GOVERNMENT

It was well known in antiquity that strife in politics could engender enmity and that such enmity could disrupt the successful operation of *polis* institutions. Many Greeks had seen the factional warfare between opposing camps of politicians degenerate into civil war (*stasis*), a process poignantly dramatized by Thucydides.¹ On a more mundane level, private enmities threatened the harmony of the Athenian citizen body, as idealized in Pericles' Funeral Oration,² and also the standard of justice to which Athenians held themselves. The public oaths required of those exercising their share in the *polis* emphasized that citizens acting in public capacity must keep justice and the public welfare foremost in their minds. The social bond between citizens was in danger if jurors were simply voting for their friends and against their enemies, and magistrates were abusing their powers to punish whomever they disliked. However much "help friends and harm enemies" continued to be an honestly held value, it could not be allowed to factionalize public processes.

Modern states address this problem by depersonalizing the governing process through bureaucracies, whose mechanical operations ideally prevent individuals from manipulating the system for personal reasons. Athenian thinking was obviously far removed from this. Rather, their system prevented undue manipulation of the public sphere by diffusing the influence of individual relationships through the sheer numbers of those who participated. The Athenian system was impersonal in a different sense. There was no theoretical abstraction of the state—a "government"; there was a series of political practices that ensured that no one person could unduly influence the decision-making process and hence that no one person could be held responsible for it. The forces of enmity and friendship were allowed to play themselves out in public deliberations and debates, but the decision-making body always had to be a large cross-section of the citizenry, a group so large that it was impossible to influence by either threats or promises. This prevented personal relationships from determining public policy.

An example of the problems that private enmity presented to daily political practice and the enmity-limiting mechanisms for coping with them may be found in the institutional framework of magistracies (*archai*). The potential opportunities for enemies to harm each other through public office are obvious. No impersonal bureaucratic machinery provided a barrier between magistrates and the people over whose lives they had authority and in whose problems and disputes they would become involved.³ The extended discussion of Athenian magistrates in the *Athenian Constitution* gives only a rudimentary idea of what involvement in government entailed but is enough to illustrate the point.⁴ The duties that these officers carried out (such as inscribing the names of public debtors, overseeing various trials, arresting accused criminals, or policing the marketplace, among many others) provided ready avenues for harming one's enemies.⁵ To fulfill the responsibilities of the office without taking revenge on an enemy or showing favor to a friend, as Polyaenus claims to have done,[6] was an exceptional mark of personal uprightness. Aristides' conduct in this regard earned him the sobriquet of "the Just." His willingness to work with his rival Themistocles for the good of the city was considered outstanding dedication to the public good.[7] More often, enemies in private were enemies in public, and most Athenians would not have scrupled so much over the private/public dichotomy.

But such behavior was wholly inappropriate to the just working of the system. Polyaenus and Aristides were upholding the ideal, which was to fulfill one's obligations without reference to friendship or enmity. The importance of this ideal seems to have been reinforced by the oaths that magistrates took before assuming office, which, unfortunately, survive only in fragments, primarily of the Council members' oath.[8] It is clear, however, that this oath included the stipulation to discharge one's duties "in accordance with the laws."[9] The oath taken by the nine archons had an identical provision.[10] These magistrates were supposed to behave according to the ordinances established by the people (the demos) and not indulge in private prejudice when such prejudice contravened the law.[11]

Oaths, however, were not the only thing hindering the abuse of magistracies for the sake of private enmities; the entire institutional setup did this as well. In the case of the Council of Five Hundred, the sheer number of members prevented private relationships from exerting undue influence on the process. A speaker at the meeting may have had a few enemies in the crowd who would vote against him just because they hated him, but it was very unlikely that there would be enough to sway the entire debate one way or the other. Selection by lot, regular rotation (tenure was only one year), and term limits (two years maximum per person), also prevented the development of long-standing animosities within the Council and ensured that a fresh cross-section of citizens would be involved each year. Power blocs and established enmities were dispersed on a regular basis. To abuse one's position as Council member to take revenge on an enemy would have been an enterprise of the utmost difficulty.[12]

The system for other magistracies was similar, though on a smaller scale. Not every magistracy could have five hundred members, but, with the exception of the nine archons, magistrates were appointed to boards, usually of ten.[13] Selection by lot and strict term limits were also common, although concessions were made to offices that required specialized skill, such as that of the ten generals, who were elected. Yet this principle of collegiality and random appointment made most magistracies difficult to manipulate for private ends; the citizens provided checks on each other.

A similar process ensured the impartiality of jurors in the courts. The procedure for selecting the heliastic body and for allotting jurors to individual trials has been explained above,[14] but suffice it to say that the similarities to the Council are clear. The sheer number of jurors, their selection by lot, and their vote by secret ballot hindered the influence of private enmities. This was in all likelihood intentional, as we know that part of the jurors' oath include the provision to vote "without favor or enmity."[15] This pledge that jurors took individually was collectively safeguarded; even if a few jurors voted based on their private prejudices, the normalizing force exerted by the hundreds of others counteracted them.

No such expectation of strict impartiality and fairness attached to those who participated in the governing process without acting in public capacity. There were times when magistrates, jurors, or men at the assembly needed to hear different perspectives on an issue, and one of the best ways to allow this to happen was to permit friends and enemies to give full vent to their emotions and explain them. At entry- and exit-examinations (*dokimasiai* and *euthynai*), any citizen who desired to speak could do so. This was an open invitation to the candidate's friends and enemies to air their views about him. Their task was to present to the jury the information required to scrutinize the candidate's character. It was not their task to be fair and impartial; that was the duty of the jurors themselves. The process was designed to allow competing interpretations to come out so that those who sat in judgment could make a decision based on as much available evidence as possible. The litigants and the jurors were present in the court for different reasons entirely.

ENMITY IN THE LEGAL SPHERE

Before analysis of the norms and protocols governing the legal system, a question of method must be addressed. Because enmity in Attic oratory is a rhetorical device, its rhetorical nature must constantly be kept in mind when these texts are mined as sources for Athenian values. Lack of attention to speakers' rhetorical purposes has been the chief culprit behind faulty conclusions about the evidence. Discussions of enmity were not designed primarily to appeal to an objectively correct code of behavior but rather to make arguments about a case, and so it would be a hazardous undertaking to treat these passages as straightforward examples of normative behavior. We must investigate not so much these litigants' particular narratives and arguments but rather the beliefs underlying their rhetoric. The assumptions that govern these rhetorical devices, which constitute the common framework that all speakers presuppose, are the best available guides to Athenian beliefs and values. Because Athenian litigants introduced enmity to construct arguments of plausibility, their narratives provide glimpses into a matrix of assumptions about how enmities were likely to arise and enemies likely to act. A litigant had to ensure that his plausibility argument was appropriate to his audience and harmonized with their preconceptions. Verisimilitude was crucial. The narrative had to complement the jury's presuppositions about how people typically behave even if the speaker was embellishing or completely fabricating his account.

The Attic orators are famous for distorting the facts, but fortunately their trustworthiness in matters of detail is not of great concern. Even if all extant speeches exaggerate or distort the events they describe, they still provide evidence for what an Athenian jury would have been ready to accept as plausible. Patterns of behavior depicted repeatedly in speakers' narratives reflect how Athenian citizens presumed that feuds were likely to happen (although not necessarily how they should happen).[16] When several different litigants describe similar sets of circumstances, they are often invoking a common scenario that entailed certain typical responses and consequences. We are therefore not concerned to determine whether or not the stories in the orators are true examples of feuds and enmities; we are rather trying to get at the assumptions and beliefs that underlie those stories.[17]

Using the method just described, this section will consider the ways in which litigants exploited the courts in the furtherance of personal hostilities and the criteria that Athenians employed for judging whether such use of the courts was acceptable or unacceptable. The appropriate use of the courts will be considered first ("Personal Vengeance in the Courts"), and their inappropriate use second ("The Importance of Being Honest"). Understanding the distinction between use and abuse of the legal system allows us to see where the limits on enemies' conduct lay. Athenians allowed personal enemies to play out their feuds through the courts but at the same time insisted that they not bring frivolous suits. Enemies could have their day in court, but litigants' options were circumscribed by the rules of the legal sphere.

Personal Vengeance in the Courts

From the litigant's perspective, legal recourse against one's enemy was a satisfactory way to seek revenge. Lysias' comment that prosecutors often must "explain their enmity with the defendants"[18] indicates that such motivation could be expected. The great number of prosecutors who explicitly assert their desire for vengeance on their opponents confirms this.[19] These invocations of the revenge motif provide information on Athenian assumptions about enmity because of their frequency and their connection with other arguments. Because this rhetorical device integrated with a speaker's overall claims and especially with the characterization of the prosecutor himself, it had to have a basis in perceived reality. If the jurors did not believe that many Athenians were willing to lodge prosecutions against their enemies out of a desire to gain a satisfactory victory over them, the revenge motif would have been ineffective, and plaintiffs would not have invoked it with such frequency and vehemence.

An Athenian could view successful prosecution of an enemy as legitimate recompense even for grievances that were unrelated to the trial. In [Demosthenes] 53 (*Against Nicostratus*), for example, the first words out of Apollodorus' mouth proclaim his desire for "revenge" (*timōria*) against the man for whom the speech is named, even though the case only indirectly related to their ongoing quarrel. Apollodorus was in fact suing Arethusius, Nicostratus' brother; Nicostratus himself was not the defendant on trial. Nor do any of the events recounted in Apollodorus' catalogue of Nicostratus' misdeeds have much to do with the charges for which the suit was lodged. Yet Apollodorus believed that his attack on Nicostratus and his family satisfied some sort of generalized need for revenge. Whether or not Apollodorus was being truthful about Nicostratus' wicked behavior, his desire to gain vengeance against his enemy through his court action had to have at least some initial plausibility for the average listener, or he could not have employed it to create arguments. If the jurors were not willing to accept that prosecutions could serve as a method of taking revenge on an enemy even when the cases were not directly related to the prosecutors' real grievances, Apollodorus' narrative and implied character arguments would fall flat.

As was pointed out above, the affirmation of enmity in this speech protects Apollodorus from attacks on his credibility, but it would certainly fail to do so if the audience believed such motivation highly improbable.[20] To have persuasive force, the rhetorical device must be grounded in a commonly perceived reality. The speakers who admit that their motivations for appearing in court are not limited to irritation at the offence on trial point to the initial plausibility of such a claim.[21] These orations therefore indicate that mutual lawsuits between enemies did not follow a linear path along the track of a particular series of events but rather formed part of a wider feud whose history included a matrix of attacks and ripostes.

Prosecutors' admissions that they have resorted to the courts in pursuit of vengeance suggest that there was real reason to fear the legal machinations of one's adversaries. The worries expressed by the victims of such attacks dramatically confirm this conclusion. The defense tactic of accusing one's opponent of prosecuting without regard for the truth indicates that jurors would not find it difficult to believe that enemies would be spurred on by their passionate hatred to seek revenge in an unjust manner. The extant defense speeches open up to us the view of those on the receiving end of the reciprocity of enmity.

Andocides 1 (*On the Mysteries*) begins with a bald statement about the malicious motivations of the speaker's opponents: "Of course you all know about my enemies' plotting and eagerness to do me harm in any way possible both justly and unjustly."[22] The content and even the form of this opening complaint is, interestingly, parallel to a *prooemium* to a Lysianic speech: "You all see my enemies' plotting and eagerness."[23] Attacking an opponent's credibility by pointing to his malevolent plotting was, as has been seen, very common.[24] In fact, the similarities between Andocides 1 and Lysias 19, which are both verbal and substantive, may well suggest that these arguments originated from a collection of introductory passages on which orators drew freely. Even if no written source with these exact formulae existed, the oral transmission of such stock phrases and themes could have allowed generations of speechwriters to reproduce similar complaints about a prosecutor's motivation with significant verbal correspondence. This particular tactic of accusing a prosecutor of concerted and prolonged attempts to do the defendant harm is well attested,[25] and Joseph Roisman's study of the "rhetoric of conspiracy" reveals how clichéd it was.[26] Accusing a prosecutor of excessive exertions in bringing about the downfall of an enemy was a timeworn tactic.

Such a *topos* is a window into a commonly perceived reality. Defendants' propensity for attacking their prosecutors' motivations by accusing them of malicious pursuit of an enemy suggests that such hatred-inspired litigation was far from unusual. Prosecutors invoked their desire for vengeance, while defendants in turn accused them of disregarding the truth in pursuit of a vendetta, but all admitted that enemies engaged in litigation with each other and in certain cases had the right to do so.

The *topos* of the prosecutor delaying in bringing suit further indicates that an Athenian was expected to be eager to take his enemy to court.[27] The assumption governing this commonplace is that a true enemy would take his foe to court on the slightest pretext. Other evidence confirms that legal action was an especially favored means of retaliating against a foe.[28] So strong was the correlation between enmity and court cases that if a man failed to prosecute when his enemy had done something controversial, the legitimacy of the claim to enmity could be called into question.[29] In a vignette from Demosthenes 25 (*Against Aristogiton*), Demosthenes reminds the jury that whenever the issue of debt to the state treasury arises, everybody accuses his own personal enemy of being a debtor (91). Such behavior was characteristic. An Athenian would be ready to pounce if his enemy committed an offense punishable by law.

Defendants also had to worry about the possibility that several of their enemies would combine to form a coalition against them. When one Athenian prosecuted another, he could often count on the network of his opponent's enemies to support him. Sometimes these enemies offered their services to the opposition by providing information or even performing reconnaissance on likely court strategies.[30] At other times they could be tapped as witnesses and *synēgoroi*.[31] Whether or not they had any direct connection with the events or parties of the trial, enemies were easily persuaded to insult each other before a jury. Even the act of bearing witness against an enemy in court could be viewed as a genuine method of taking revenge.[32] The expectation that a prosecutor would seek out those with whom his opponent had previously quarreled was so strong that if he could not produce his opponent's enemies to testify or speak on his behalf, he could be suspected of having an exceedingly weak case.[33] Whether as cospeakers, witnesses, or informers, personal enemies seem to have taken any opportunity to harm each other through the court system.

Defendants' constant complaints that their opponents had initiated suit for the sake of slander confirm that the prosecutor's supporting cast often took advantage of a prime opportunity to defame and insult the man on trial.[34] Over and above the possibility of scoring a victory against an enemy, a trial offered the prosecutor and his backers the opportunity to engage in a coordinated assault of verbal abuse. Because the satisfaction derived from vitriol against an enemy seems to have been directly proportional to the number of third parties privy to the malicious talk, the law courts, whose juries numbered at least two hundred-and-one and thus represented a significant segment of the citizen body, offered an especially favorable venue for humiliating the target. With his lawsuit a prosecutor co-opted an audience for his attack on the defendant, an audience that would certainly also include the litigants' friends and family, before whom an Athenian would be most reluctant to show loss of face.

The trial for which Lysias 10 (*Against Theomnestus*) was composed illustrates how deeply ingrained in the legal process the verbal battle over status was. The speaker alleges that a certain Theomnestus accused him of killing his own father, a form of insult prohibited by law, and so he lodged a "suit for slander" (*dikē kakēgorias*) against him.[35] Although Theomnestus did not actually call the speaker an *androphonos* ("manslayer"), the only term that was technically proscribed in the law, the speaker argues that Theomnestus' accusation of patricide amounts to the same thing. The plausibility of the plaintiff's case thus depends on his ability to show that Theomnestus indeed leveled illegal insults at him. One might therefore expect that the speaker would avoid engaging in slander himself so as to put Theomnestus in as negative a light as possible by contrast with the speaker's restraint. This is hardly the case. The speaker alludes repeatedly to a rumor that Theomnestus fled a battlefield without his shield, another illegal insult.[36] Although he puts Theomnestus on trial for slander, the plaintiff does not refrain from slander himself.[37] Verbal abuse was simply part of the process.

The use of the courts for slander often formed part of a larger insult and criticism campaign between enemies.[38] Verbal abuse was considered an entirely natural component of enmity, but many Athenians were not satisfied with casual remarks about those against whom they held a grudge.[39] When litigants express worries about the slander that their enemies have spread about them, they frequently allude to malicious misinformation campaigns.[40] These insults appear to have been more than offhand rants in the company of a few sympathetic ears; they were part of deliberate strategies that aimed at the humiliation of the target. When a defendant speaks of "slander," he usually refers to a concerted effort to undermine his reputation. Such mockery by enemies was to be feared as "a worse evil than death."[41]

From the evidence presented in this section, two conclusions follow. The first has already been set forth: prosecutors' claims to be seeking vengeance by their court action are entirely believable. The assumptions governing the rhetoric of enmity in defense speeches confirm this picture of Athens as a revenge culture. Tension in social relationships centered on honor and loss of face, and enemies were keen to exploit any opportunity to inflict shame and exult in their triumph. Room should be allowed for defendants' exaggeration, but overall their worries harmonize with the rest of our information regarding the prevalence of enmity and the eagerness with which rivals undertook hatred-inspired litigation.

The second conclusion is that the courts were not terribly concerned to discourage such behavior. If litigants had known that the jury would look unfavorably on those who sought vengeance in the courtroom (as Herman suggests), surely they would not have launched into such lengthy narratives of enmity and attempted to make the trial appear to be the result of a long series of grievances against them. They would rather have attempted to downplay their own desire for vindication and pursuit of honor, emphasizing merely the positive benefits that would accrue to the state upon conviction of a malefactor. But this is not what one finds in Attic oratory.

Feuds were permitted to play themselves out in the courts because the feuds themselves were not what concerned the jury. Enmity was not the main issue but was rather a rhetorical motif that provided opportunities for making arguments about the case through plausibility and characterization. Speakers employed narratives of hostile relationships to develop arguments; there is no reason to assume that they expected the jury simply to collaborate in their desire for vengeance or believed that their rhetoric of enmity would legitimize their prosecutions on its own merits. Bringing up a feud was acceptable because it could be illuminating, but the jurors were not interested in passing judgment on whether or not feuds were legitimate. The nature of the feud was important insofar as it supported the speaker's arguments, but it was not a stand-alone plea for justification.

The argument advanced by Herman and others that feuding in the courts was frowned upon is vitiated by a pair of questionable assumptions.[42] First is the notion that the nonaggressive and controlled conduct that speakers emphasize is normative. Herman's claim that litigants appealed to a dominant code of behavior dictating restrained and unemotional responses to wrongdoing does not account for this argumentative nature of the orators' rhetoric.[43]

Three speeches will serve as examples of the problematic nature of Herman's model. In Demosthenes 54 (*Against Conon*), Ariston emphasizes his own passivity because he must deny that he provoked the attack by Conon and his hubristic bullies. It is quite true, as Herman (2006: 284) points out, that Ariston "thought that the dikasts would be inclined to take his side if he portrayed Conon as having attacked in the aggressive manner of a fighting cock and himself as a helpless victim."[44] An important aspect of Ariston's technique is to emphasize the egregious nature of the crime so that the jury will be angry at Conon. Herman goes too far, however, when he asserts that Ariston "believed that they [the jurors] would approve of a man who presented himself as frail and un-cock-like and disapprove of Conon's cock-like display of aggressive, upper-class masculinity."[45] The speaker does not emphasize his own passivity because he believes it the morally superior way of responding to injustice. Rather, Ariston's self-restraint supports his character portrayal of Conon, which in turn supports a plausibility argument about his main contention, that Conon committed *hubris* against him. The speaker does not address how one should react when wronged as a general rule of conduct.[46]

Neither can the denial of enmity in Lycurgus 1 (*Against Leocrates*) be taken as paradigmatic for Athenian morality. A variety of reasons could be posited to account for Lycurgus' rhetorical strategy in this speech, but Herman (2006: 276–277) cites the speech as evidence for the illegitimacy of private vengeance in the legal system. Explaining that other law court speeches always include apologies for suing enemies, Herman assumes that the hesitancy with which litigants portrayed themselves as feuding individuals can be attributed to their desire to appear as socially acceptable citizens who observe the city's prohibition on harming enemies. He does not take into account any other factors affecting Lycurgus' decision-making process. In fact, important rhetorical considerations influenced Lycurgus' approach to the topic of enmity.[47] *Against Leocrates* does not provide evidence for a nonfeuding ethic in Athenian society in the way that Herman uses the speech because there is no reason to suppose that Lycurgus' denial of enmity was motivated by the belief that the jurors disapproved of prosecuting enemies. Lycurgus rather attempts to meet the particular needs of his case, employing his rhetorical strategy to assert his credibility as a speaker and to create an implicit argument about his claims.

Another example of this problematic methodology is Herman's discussion of Lysias 1 (*On the Murder of Eratosthenes*). The speaker, Euphiletus, emphasizes his dispassionate execution of Eratosthenes after catching him *in flagrante delicto* to prevent the other motivations attributed to him by the prosecution from sticking. Despite Herman's argument that this speech demonstrates a commitment to a nonviolent, nonretaliatory code of behavior on the part of the Athenians, Euphiletus' rhetorical choice is legally motivated by the necessities of his argument and is not evidence for a normative requirement.[48] For Herman, Euphiletus presents himself as a detached executor of civic justice because the jury would sympathize with this kind of behavior and find it acceptable. He does not take into account how Euphiletus' denial of enmity and consequent deemphasizing of his hatred for Eratosthenes arise from the legal consideration of denying an ulterior motive for murder.[49]

Many litigants make much of their own passivity in the history of a hostile relationship, but to take the frequency of such rhetoric as representing a dominant code of morality is a mistake. Speakers' assertions that they have underreacted when wronged do not point to a general "tit for two tats" code of restraint.[50] It is to be expected that they exaggerate their opponents' unjust behavior and downplay their own responses. Speakers' habitual emphasis on their opponents' culpability in fighting the feud is a result of the legal setting. They want to portray themselves as restrained and their opponents as aggressive because this depiction carries with it intrinsic likelihoods about who would be more likely to be led by passion to commit a crime or to lie in court. Litigants make themselves appear passive because their passivity supports their other argumentative objectives.

The second problem with the view that the courts forbade feuds is the assumption that individual honor had to be abandoned when the dispute was transferred to a public venue. Fisher is correct that "to claim as Herman does that self-restraint and recourse to appropriate legal procedures constitute a surrender of one's claim to honour and revenge is a fundamental error."[51] In fact, the redirection of personal revenge from the private sphere into the court system provided ample opportunity for litigants to continue their battle for honor. The public venue intensified rather than alleviated the personal element of the feud by putting both parties in the spotlight and forcing the jury to reproach one of them.[52] Loss of face before hundreds of members of one's own community (the jury, not to mention friends, family, and other spectators) dealt a serious blow to the status and honor of the unsuccessful litigant and gave the winner the gratification of watching his enemy suffer at his hands.[53] In this way the courts made the legal option all the more attractive.[54] Defendants would have regarded the prospect of their public disgrace with abhorrence, prosecutors with relish.

This practice of using the courts for vengeance confirms that Athens was an enmity culture. Relationships of hostility were widespread, openly recognized, and followed a retaliatory logic that put important normative pressures on individuals to perform in accordance with the rules of the game. Enemies could exploit the state apparatus in pursuit of such vendettas by prosecuting, defeating, and humiliating their adversaries. If Athenians had serious qualms about this type of behavior as a general rule, we do not hear much about them. Nonetheless, the conduct and actions that enmity encouraged were not unequivocally endorsed. Important limitations imposed by democratic ideology curbed the ways in which one could pursue an enemy and prevented illegitimate abuse of one's fellow citizen.

The Importance of Being Honest

Although it is not difficult to hear the rhetoric of anger and vengeance coursing through Attic oratory, at the same time the limits on enmity are clear. However much evidence the extant speeches provide for a strong feuding impulse, they also point the way to the limitations on enemies' pursuit of each other.[55] Clearly the jurors saw something wrong with the way that the courts were exploited for pursuing vendettas, or defendants would not have accused their opponents of attempting to slander them with such striking frequency and vehemence. The problem was not that Athenians saw the prosecution of an enemy for the sake of inflicting shame and rehabilitating one's own honor as illegitimate—too much evidence suggests that this was normal and acceptable. When defendants complain about the attacks of their enemies, they are not implying that nobody should employ the legal system to punish a personal enemy but are claiming that hatred has led their opponents to lodge a suit on utterly frivolous charges. The point at issue is whether or not the prosecutor is lying, not the acceptability of enmity-based prosecution as a rule.

Athenian litigants were obsessed with proving that they were telling the truth, as can be seen from the sheer number of times that litigants make statements such as, "So that you might know that I am speaking the truth, call, please, my witnesses. . . ." Beyond the calling of witnesses, the speeches are replete with similar formulaic statements. Often a speaker will say something like, "To show that I am speaking the truth, I will offer you such-and-such evidence."[56] Litigants constantly assert that they are presenting the jury with the "truth" of the case.

Litigants were also expected to stick to the point, that is, address the actual charges rather than distract from them. The homicide courts' stipulation that litigants swear not to speak "off the point" (*exō tou pragmatos*)[57] is well known,[58] but there is reason to believe that other courts also restricted irrelevant speech. The *Athenian Constitution* attests that litigants in dicastic courts took an oath similar to the one required by the Areopagus, which included the provision that the litigant speak "to the point" (*eis auto to pragma*).[59] The jurors were also under oath to cast their vote based on the charges themselves, as litigants never wearied of reminding them.[60] The oaths taken by both litigant and juror therefore suggest that considerable importance was attached to the injunction to stay on topic.

Further evidence that both speaker and audience were conscious of the importance of speaking to the *pragma* can be found in the speeches themselves.[61] Anaximenes' statement that the *prooemium* (introduction) of a speech functions to set forth the *pragma* reflects a concern with the legal charges that is well attested in the orators.[62] Litigants often remind the jurors that they are supposed to cast their votes based on the *pragma*[63] or assert that they will prove their case based on the *pragma* itself[64] or that the *pragma* itself will convict the opponent.[65] Conversely, they accuse their opponents of "despising" or making light of the *pragma*, occasionally even using the technical formula from the Areopagus Council's oath.[66] Some assert that their opponents are aware that they have no argument based on the *pragma*.[67] Aeschines and Demosthenes even go so far as to accuse the other of planning to boast (after the trial) that he has won a victory at court by distracting the jurors from the *pragma*.[68] This attitude is consistently portrayed as despicable. Near the end of his speech, Aeschines instructs the jury to "force him to keep on the track of the *pragma*, just as in horse races."[69] From the number of times the *pragma* is invoked as a technical phrase,[70] it can be concluded that dicastic courts were quite concerned about it.

Defendants expect to have won a substantial blow against their opponents if they can show them to be lying, distorting the facts, or distracting the jury from the legal issue. They accuse them of slander, deception, and all manner of illegitimate legal finagling and, in short, strive by all possible means to establish that their prosecutors are not concerned with the actual charges. Defendants often accuse their opponents of pursuing an enmity because enmity, while not problematic in itself, can call into question the prosecutor's incentives for telling the truth. (Anaximenes also recommends that litigants attack their opponents' witnesses along similar lines; if a witness can be shown to be an enemy, he can be suspected of lying for the sake of revenge.)[71] This is a major restriction on the use of the courts for pursuit of feuds: the requirement that the accusation be grounded in a real, identifiable offense. The legitimacy of the charges was the guiding principle by which orators shaped their rhetoric of enmity.

Clearly, a prosecutor's affirmation of enmity would not in itself justify a prosecution, since defendants could affirm enmity just as prosecutors did. The rhetoric of enmity must function within a litigant's overall argument. The speaker of Lysias 9 (*For the Soldier*) can admit that his opponents have attacked him because of their desire for vengeance and even allow that they are in some sense legitimately angry: "I have been only moderately angry at my opponents' unjust behavior, because I believed that life was organized on a principle of hurting one's enemies and helping one's friends."[72] But he is not conceding his case nor admitting that the anger of his opponents makes the prosecution legitimate. The truth of the accusation is the matter of paramount importance, and, as Polyaenus has pointed out, the charges are false. Enmity-based prosecution is problematic when it results in disregard for justice.[73] A prosecutor might attempt to exploit his enmity with the opponent to gain credibility for himself, but he had to keep in mind that his enmity could be turned against him. The defendant could argue that the anger of his opponents, which the prosecutor intended to use as proof of his sincerity, actually pointed to his ulterior motivations and lack of concern for making a bona fide charge.

Against this background the manifold complaints by defendants about their prosecutors' "slander" against them may be understood. Such protests tap into a fear that some prosecutors, blinded by hatred, would attempt to deceive the jury with trumped up charges and false accusations in single-minded pursuit of vengeance.[74] These malicious attackers enter into libelous diatribes against the accused, hoping to arouse anger among the jurors and prevent them from even listening to a reasoned response from the defense. The deception made possible by such slander was the problem, not the abusive nature of the speech itself. The paramount issue was whether or not the jury was in possession of the truth.

The concept of "defamation" in contemporary English jurisprudence can serve as a point of reference. "Defamation" usually refers to speech that is false, harmful, and malicious. The English concept of defamation and the Athenian concept of slander are similar, although Athenians did not generally care as much about the harm and malice. Harmful and malicious speech was to be expected and was not particularly problematic. Someone under prosecution for slander (by *dikē kakēgorias*) could get off if he demonstrated that his charges were true and did not need to prove that he had not defamed his victim.[75] On the other hand, defamatory speech that entailed false accusations was a serious threat to the integrity of the legal system. When defendants level charges of slander against their opponents, they are accusing them primarily of lying.[76]

The effectiveness of attacking an enemy's trustworthiness by emphasizing his lack of concern for the truth is demonstrated by the response it elicited from wary plaintiffs. The jury's concern about the honest intentions of those who brought accusations before the court compelled many prosecutors to moderate their behavior. The courtroom was not a free-for-all in which prosecutors felt comfortable saying whatever they pleased. If they overstepped, they were always vulnerable to counter-attack. The speaker of Lysias 27 (*Against Epicrates*), for example, is well aware of this danger and attempts to preempt the "malicious enemy" motif. Although he suggests that the jurors would do well to ignore the defense speech and vote for conviction without further deliberation, he immediately anticipates and refutes the possible objection that he thereby is attempting to obscure the facts. Epicrates and his fellow defendants would not be "convicted without a hearing" (*akritoi*)[77] because the jurors already know the necessary facts.

> It is not these men who are denied a trial (*akritoi*)—because you will be voting about them in full knowledge of their actions—but rather those who are slandered by their enemies and do not receive a full hearing on matters that you do not know about.[78]

The explicit contrast here is between secure knowledge of the facts and the slander of enemies. In this case, the prosecutors are not guilty of slander because "the facts themselves accuse these men."[79] This prosecutor admits that the technique of slandering the accused on irrelevant matters is not legitimate. His concession is telling. If the prosecutor wants to stir up dicastic anger against his opponents (which is precisely what this speaker is doing), he must couch it in terms of the manifest truth of the charges.

Demosthenes' well-known speech *Against Meidias* (Dem. 21) provides another illustration of this limitation on prosecutors' rhetorical options, not least because it is often cited for exactly the opposite viewpoint, that the trial was primarily about sociological judgments between the two parties. Cohen and Herman, although their conclusions are diametrically opposed, both begin their analysis of this oration with the premise that Demosthenes' rhetoric is intended to make the jurors sympathetic to him because of who he is, without reference to the truth of the claims. Cohen states that *Against Meidias* shows that litigants "manipulate the normative expectations of the community to convince the public (the Athenian court) that they 'deserve,' as *persons* [emphasis in original], to prevail."[80] On the other hand, Herman argues that Demosthenes cites two exempla of violent stories "to demonstrate the objective superiority of his own behaviour according to the values of his society."[81] These statements both assume that questions of fact are secondary to the broader question of the litigant's conformity to Athenian norms of behavior; Demosthenes asks the jurors for a favorable vote based on his character, apart from the claims of his case. The analysis here will attempt to show that this is a superficial reading of the text.

Demosthenes shapes the narrative of his feud with Meidias to paint a portrait of his opponent's character that will support his allegations, but he is well aware of the dangers of such character arguments. He makes it clear that he expects the jury not simply to take sides in the feud but to vote based on the law and the facts.[82] He consistently underlines that Meidias' offenses are real and emphasizes that he hopes to win based on Meidias' actual act of *hubris*, rejecting the idea that this trial is in essence "Meidias versus Demosthenes" and nothing more. Several times Demosthenes backs off his rhetorical attack to address a possible misinterpretation of what he is trying to accomplish. In an anticipatory argument, he posits that Meidias will make the allegation that Demosthenes is putting their feud on trial: "Do not hand me over to Demosthenes; do not destroy me for Demosthenes' sake! Will you destroy me because I am at war with him?"[83] Demosthenes discards this objection, asserting that the grounds for the charge are not personal enmity, but Meidias' offense against a public servant,[84] which deserves "public anger and punishment."[85]

This is but one example of Demosthenes' frequent appeals to the truth of his claims and the city's legal obligation to punish Meidias. He continually emphasizes that Meidias has committed many wrongs, stressing that these acts, not an evaluation of the two litigants' characters, are the focus of the trial. When Demosthenes anticipates that Meidias will ask why all the people he supposedly wronged have not come forward, Demosthenes retorts to the imagined objection: "This man should not make these arguments, but either he should demonstrate to you that he has not committed any of the crimes that I have charged him with or, if he cannot, then this is all the more reason for putting him to death."[86] The deeds of Meidias are on trial, not the relative social standing of the two disputants.

A defendant in another case actually uses an objection parallel to the one that Demosthenes anticipates Meidias will make ("Do not hand me over to Demosthenes; do not destroy me for Demosthenes' sake"), thus confirming that Demosthenes knew very well the type of rhetorical response he might expect.[87] The speaker of Isocrates 16 (*On the Team of Horses*), complaining that his personal enemies have no regard for truth, pleads with the jury, "I ask you not to give me over to my enemies nor to cast me into deadly misfortunes."[88] This defendant attempts to portray his opponents as motivated by a feuding ethos with no thought to the truth of their claims and asks the jury not to tolerate such abuse of the court system.[89] This is no doubt the claim that Demosthenes was attempting to preclude by anticipating Meidias' supposed objection and tearing it down. Demosthenes knew that he could be accused of attempting to distract the jury from the point at issue by slandering Meidias with false charges and therefore took steps to prevent the jury from believing that this was his intent. He was not free to ignore the merits of his accusation nor to pretend as if the trial were a judgment between two personalities.

The model of feuding in Athens that Cohen presents must be significantly revised. Cohen is right that the verdict of the jury had important social implications beyond the point at issue, providing vindication for the successful litigant and inflicting shame on the loser. It is his subsequent inferences that are questionable. The idea that the social judgment between two parties was the foremost issue in the trial and that the jury sought to mediate social tensions by eschewing the idea of strict "justice" and passing judgment on the feud itself is based on a questionable assumption about the purposes behind the rhetoric of enmity. Like Herman's argument about speakers' emphasis on their own passivity, Cohen's model presupposes that litigants describe their behavior in the way they do to elicit favorable sentiments from the jury.

Lawsuits were a legitimate way for an enemy to seek revenge, but the jurors did not see the desire for revenge as legitimizing the lawsuit. The many assertions of personal enmity in the Attic orators show that litigation was a commonly accepted means of pursuing an enemy but do not prove that jurors looked to extralegal criteria for rendering their verdict. Contrary to Cohen's model, there is good reason to believe that justice and legality were omnipresent in Athenian thinking and that the jurors were expected to cast their votes based on the point at issue rather than the social implications of the feud. The litigant himself may have sought a referendum on his feud with his opponent, but this is not what the courts were offering. Prosecutors could admit bringing others to trial out of a desire for vengeance, but they had to be able to make a legal argument about a crime deserving punishment. They could use but not abuse *polis* institutions for pursuing each other. They could follow a vendetta into the courtroom but, once there, were compelled to play by the rules.

The importance of the prosecutor's honesty about his charges entailed real limitations on feuding behavior in the courts. Frivolous accusations with no basis in fact could be rewarded with defeat and consequent loss of face for the plaintiff. The courts were not the no-holds-barred locus for feuding that Cohen envisions but were rather an arena with its own set of rules. A prosecutor could of course attempt to abuse the system merely to slander his enemies and vent his power over the vulnerable, but he did so at his own peril.

Excursus: Enmity in Assembly Speeches

The discussions of private enmity in the deliberative speeches of Demosthenes (1–17) are an interesting counterpart to the extant legal speeches discussed in the previous section. Although Demosthenes sometimes acknowledges that his political opponents are his enemies, he portrays enmity as the motivating factor only for his opponents. The reason for this is obvious: it would never do to suggest that a public policy had been formulated on the basis of private disagreements within the *polis*. Orators were expected to keep the public good constantly in mind. When Demosthenes speaks of enmities, it is invariably for disparagement. True public servants should put aside their quarrels when serving the city: "Every speaker, men of Athens, ought to speak neither out of enmity nor to curry favor but to declare what he thinks is the best policy."[90] Orators who indulge their private passions should be pushed to one side, Demosthenes continues, since the interests of Athens, not their private quarrels, are at stake.

The rhetorical strategy in these Assembly speeches is reminiscent of the downplaying or even denial of enmity that we see in lawsuits of special public importance.[91] If an orator wanted to attack his enemies, he had to avoid the language of personal enmity and couch his hostility toward his opponents in the language of their "enmity with the city." Demosthenes admonishes the Athenians to remember who their *echthroi* are, those orators who had given bad advice or betrayed the city's interests for bribes, and to punish them.[92] Of course, these men were undoubtedly Demosthenes' political opponents, but he carefully avoids implying that his advice is motivated by party spirit. He is the suffering servant of the democracy who gets involved in quarrels only because he pursues the state's interests to a fault: "I was the first, indeed the only one to come forward and oppose it, and I was virtually torn apart by those who were trying to persuade you."[93] Enmity between citizens had no place in the Assembly.

The Demosthenic Assembly speeches underscore the unique situation of the legal sphere, where two individuals were directly at odds and the histories of their enmities were consequently of great importance. Litigants were free to admit enmity because they were acting as private individuals, while speakers in the Assembly were constrained by their quasi-official role as public *rhētores* to appear as public figures. The law courts stand precisely at the intersection between private and public interests: two private citizens performing before a publicly sanctioned jury. The courts were a public institution, but their purpose was to pass judgment on both public and private matters. The Assembly was concerned with the city as a whole, and individual speakers were present only to offer alternative proposals. When Demosthenes delivered *On the Crown* (Dem. 18), his past actions were on trial, but when he delivered *On the Peace* (Dem. 5), his policies were up for a vote. There is a clear difference between the two.

ENMITY IN SOCIETY

The Athenian Attitude toward Violence

The threat that personal enmity posed to the well-being of the Athenian community was clearly recognized. Athens' commitment to providing freedom and security for its citizens would have been mere façade had restrictions on enemies' right to harm each other been a dead letter. We have seen how feuds pursued in the courts were limited by the requirement that each party speak to particular offenses, but enmity presented another and potentially more dangerous threat to society, the possibility of physical violence. If the restraints on such behavior had been nonexistent, merely nominal, or simply lenient, wealthy elites could have exploited their access to large networks of friends (or thugs), while citizens of more moderate means would be forced to expect protection from a local "Mr. Big." Poorer citizens had to be able to look for protection from the attacks of hubristic elites, or the polity could easily have devolved into a de facto oligarchy. Thus the threat was not only to the individual but to the integrity of the political community as a whole.

The citizen's body had to be protected lest the ideology of equality and freedom be threatened. Hence, formal measures ensured that an Athenian citizen could not be sold into slavery for a debt, nor be subjected to judicial torture or corporal punishment.[94] Such attacks on a citizen's person were forbidden for a number of reasons, but Athenian ideas about manhood are particularly important in this regard. As David Halperin has shown, the inviolability of the citizen's body was linked to the overtones of sex and gender that Athenian citizenship brought with it.[95] Citizens, who were supposed to be paradigms of the masculine ethic, were not to be violated as passive victims; their integrity as persons had to be protected.[96] Acts of law, such as the decree passed during the archonship of Scamandrius that forbade torture of citizens,[97] were sensible outcroppings of this belief in the security and equality of all and had important consequences for the behavior of enemies.[98] The insistence that the citizen's body was sacrosanct meant that the pursuit of enemies would be limited to acts that did not entail physical violence.

More than once in recent years historians have asserted that the Athenian system countenanced a certain degree of violence.[99] The machismo of Athenian culture supposedly encouraged the belief that dishonor should be repaid with violence and that a man who responded to a violent act with a legal action was deficient in manhood. This argument relies on problematic use of the evidence. The sources rather suggest a very different picture: Athenians recognized violence as a problem and took steps to curb it. Casual acts of violence, such as those characteristic of blood-feuding societies, never gained sanction from the Athenian people.

The closest the Athenians came to permitting violent behavior was in granting a degree of indulgence to minor aggressive acts inspired by irrational impulses. Activities such as drinking, conflict between rival lovers, and competition for honor (*philotimia*) had a recognized propensity for causing a person to act foolishly for a short period of time. A "battle" like the one described by the speaker of Lysias 3 (*Against Simon*) was probably not a completely atypical outcome for a competition for the love of a woman or boy.[100] Scuffles such as this are well documented. The laws appear to have allowed some leeway for such thoughtless acts, not punishing them as harshly as violence inspired by a premeditated attempt to shame. For this reason, Aristotle in the *Politics* lists a particular law of Pittacus as a novelty since it punished drunken offenders more harshly than sober ones in order to curb such violence. Aristotle implies that the opposite practice (that is, treating drunken offenders more leniently) was the standard in Greek cities.[101] The evidence, however, is very far from suggesting that such activities legitimized violence. It rather implies that many would have seen the irrational mindset of the assaulter as an extenuating circumstance.

A few passages in the Attic orators that have been taken as expressions of approval of violence were actually intended to point to irrational activities as mitigating factors in evaluating the heinousness of a crime. Demosthenes narrates several such stories in his speech against Meidias. He describes how a certain person punched a thesmothete in a drunken quarrel over a prostitute and how another man, named Polyzelus, struck a judge in a similar dispute over a flute-girl.[102] He asserts that both men deserve some sympathy since the former had the excuses of drunkenness and love and the latter also was acting irrationally (*phthasas ton logismon*) and intended no insult. Later in the speech, Demosthenes reminds his listeners of the famous case when Alcibiades struck Taureas on the face during a competition between choruses.[103] The agonistic nature of liturgy production offered some excuse for Alcibiades' action in the heat of the moment. In these two episodes, Demosthenes does not condone violent behavior but rather cites drunkenness, love, and competitiveness as mitigating factors in assessing the severity of a hostile act. In contrast to these relatively minor offenses, Demosthenes argues that Meidias' crime was egregious since it was a deliberate and premeditated attempt to dishonor Demosthenes. *Against Meidias* indicates that crimes of passion could be treated more leniently than deliberate *hubris* but does not suggest that they were justifiable and unworthy of censure.[104]

The Athenians did not endorse violent behavior as a general rule. Enmity-based, casual violence was consistently liable to prosecution. Athenian law did sanction the use of physical force in a few exceptional circumstances, but these were clearly delimited by statute and had to do with legal wrongs, not simply fights between enemies. Physical aggression against other citizens outside the context dictated by the state was not considered legitimate.

The only claims that such behavior was common and acceptable come from arguments that litigants attribute to their opponents, arguments of which the careful reader will be extremely wary. The classic example of such an anticipatory argument (*prokatalēpsis*) comes from Demosthenes 54 (*Against Conon*). Ariston predicts that Conon will attempt to make light of his hubristic attack by pointing out that members of aristocratic clubs commonly engage in such fighting; the whole affair should be disregarded as an unremarkable instance of young men getting into scuffles (13–14). Although Cohen and others have pointed to this passage as evidence that such violence could be viewed as acceptable,[105] the opposite conclusion is more warranted. It is unlikely that Ariston desired to put a strong argument into the mouth of his opponent. He introduces his anticipatory argument by speculating that the jurors, after hearing Ariston's narrative of the brutality of Conon and his sons, may be wondering "what Conon will possibly dare say in answer to this."[106] Ariston answers his own question by positing that Conon will make the audacious and outrageous claim that the jury should simply overlook the whole affair.[107] He does not believe that the jurors will agree with Conon. Quite the contrary: "If Conon says, 'We are members of the club of the *Ithyphalloi*, and when we fall in love we beat up and throttle whomever we want to,' then will you all laugh and let him off? I don't think so."[108] Ariston intends Conon's supposed argument not to be persuasive but incendiary.

The argument that Ariston attributes to Conon need not accurately represent what Conon actually intended to say. There are alternative ways to make sense of the evidence.[109] Some incidental references in Ariston's speech indicate that he could be exaggerating and intentionally distorting Conon's much more reasonable argument. Ariston's defensive comments about his own behavior (for instance, "we have never been seen by anybody acting drunk or committing *hubris*")[110] may reflect a fear that Conon would claim that everybody involved was drunk and acting foolishly. If this were the case, then assigning blame to only one side would be inappropriate, and the penalty proposed would not fit the crime. Conon could argue that the event in question was a chance encounter on the street that may have led to a couple of bloody noses but was certainly not a clear-cut, one-sided act of aggression. Conon would then be claiming drunkenness and competitive feeling merely as mitigating rather than legitimizing factors in the dispute. He would not need to assert that he and his aristocratic friends should be able to perpetrate acts of *hubris* with impunity, despite what Ariston would have us believe.

Such an argument would tally with other arguments made by litigants in similar circumstances. Defense speeches in cases of assault and wounding are a more reliable guide to the types of claims that Conon was likely to make than what Conon's opponent said he would say. In two speeches of Lysias composed for a defendant charged with assault, Lysias 3 (*Against Simon*) and Lysias 4 (*On a Premeditated Wounding*), neither litigant attempts to justify an act of violence but rather argues that the excessive penalty proposed by his prosecutor is out of all proportion with the seriousness of the crime. Cohen's argument that these speeches show that violence was an expected characteristic of hostile relationships in Athens does not take into account this aspect of the litigants' claims.[111] In *Against Simon* the speaker does not admit that he assaulted Simon and attempt to pass it off as a trivial affair but rather denies emphatically that he was responsible for starting the fight.[112] In any case, his contention that exile is too severe a penalty for the crime is actually a back-up argument. He uses the disparity between the relative pettiness of the alleged offense and the gravity of the consequences as a reinforcing argument to shield himself in the event that his narrative does not find complete acceptance: "Clearly our lawgivers also did not think they should prescribe exile from the fatherland for people who happen to crack each other's heads while fighting."[113] Even if the jurors believe that he was at fault for starting the melee, it would be preposterous for them to sentence him to exile for fisticuffs resulting from a competition in love. The speaker's argument addresses the legal issue of the correspondence between crime and punishment; it does not assume that certain acts of violence should receive unqualified acceptance.

The speaker of Lysias 4 (*On a Premeditated Wounding*) voices a similar concern about the appropriateness of lifetime exile as punishment for a minor squabble over a prostitute. When he complains about being on trial simply because of a slave, he is not excusing violent behavior but attempting to downplay the severity of the offense. He asserts that his opponent exaggerated the whole affair, calling a black eye a premeditated attempt at murder. The penalty of exile is excessive, the speaker argues, even if he were guilty of being involved in a drunken brawl. Again, the issue is whether the punishment fits the alleged crime.[114] The speaker does not admit that he is at fault and then assert that he should not be held accountable.[115]

The only extant oration in which a speaker unequivocally admits committing an act of violence is Lysias 1 (*On the Murder of Eratosthenes*). Yet the exceptional nature of the circumstances surrounding the killing confirm that violence was normally viewed as illegitimate. If Athenians had accepted homicide as an authorized response to a variety of situations, Euphiletus could have asserted that Eratosthenes was his enemy and that when he caught him on top of his wife, he killed him in hot blood. Such a defense would harmonize well with Athenians' tendency to show more lenience toward acts committed in the heat of the moment than cold and calculated ones.[116] Furthermore, if Todd is correct, Euphiletus' claim that he did not know Eratosthenes is highly suspect. They were probably members of the same tribe and possibly of the same deme.[117] If an ethic of violent feuding permeated Athenian culture as Cohen's model suggests, we might expect Euphiletus to have chosen a defense that corresponded with such values. As it is, Euphiletus had to represent himself as a cuckold and a bit of a buffoon to maintain that he was not driven by wrath and personal vengeance when he executed Eratosthenes in accordance with the laws. He maintains that he acted as a dispassionate executor of public punishment to prevent the jury from viewing his act as a violent display of private vengeance.[118]

Another passage often cited to show Athenian approval of violent reprisal is the story of Evaeon narrated in Demosthenes 21 (*Against Meidias*). At a drinking party, Evaeon killed someone in retaliation for an unprovoked punch. Demosthenes implies that he has acted more acceptably than Evaeon by resorting to the courts but carefully avoids condemning

Evaeon's action: "I have much sympathy for Evaeon and everyone else who has helped himself when dishonored."[119] It may appear at first that Demosthenes is tacitly sanctioning Evaeon's act of homicide, but in fact he merely uses this extreme example to illustrate how serious a punch with the intent of dishonoring can be (72). He makes a concession to Evaeon's behavior because it supports his argument that *hubris*, even when manifested in an act that causes only minor physical harm, is a serious offense.[120] The Evaeon episode is not an example of normal and acceptable behavior but an exaggerated story that supports Demosthenes' *a fortiori* argument.

> Consider among yourselves how much more reason I had to be angry when I suffered at Meidias' hands than Evaeon when he killed Boeotus. For he was struck by an acquaintance who was drunk before six or seven other persons. [. . .] But I was outraged (*hubrizomēn*) in front of many people, both foreigners and citizens, by a man who was a personal enemy and who did this early in the morning while he was sober, not prompted by the influence of alcohol but by *hubris*.[121]

If almost half of the jury at Evaeon's trial thought that it was acceptable to punish someone who committed such an act of *hubris* by killing him immediately, surely the present jurors should be willing to convict a worse offender for his illegal and shameless assault.[122] Although Demosthenes has cleverly made it appear that he is making a grudging concession to Evaeon's behavior, he in fact has a vested interest in casting Evaeon in as positive a light as possible. His statements about Evaeon are therefore contentious, aimed at making his own response seem impeccable.

A further point merits consideration. The man who punched Evaeon had violated Athenian law. Demosthenes makes it clear that this story is an example of an act of *hubris*, which was prosecutable by a *graphē hubreōs*. Evaeon's response can therefore be classified as self-help (*hautōi beboēthēken*). According to Demosthenes, Evaeon did not commit an act of random violence but responded to a criminal offense on his own initiative. Evaeon lost the trial because in his reprisal he had gone farther than the law allowed. He would have been much better off had he taken the route that Demosthenes took: "One should not punish all those who commit *hubris* and act without restraint in the moment of anger but rather should bring them before you since you confirm and preserve the safeguards granted by the laws to those who suffer."[123] Although Demosthenes has sympathy for those who help themselves when they are harmed, recourse to the courts is the best way to stay within the bounds of the law.

One might object that *Against Meidias*, *Against Conon*, *Against Simon*, and *On a Premeditated Wounding*, as they are trials concerning violent acts, prove by their mere existence that violence was not uncommon: "For every Ariston or Demosthenes who resorted to litigation, there was a Conon or Meidias who preferred to settle affairs with his fists."[124] It is true that many acts of violence are described in the extant orations, but this is what one would expect from a body of legal speeches that preserve in all probability the most virulent of quarrels. It would be foolhardy to attempt any sort of statistical analysis based on the number of violent episodes in our sources. The mere existence of cases concerning physical abuse does not shed much light on how typical such abuse was. The survival of these speeches may in fact suggest the reverse of what is commonly asserted, that such acts were so exceptional that they were marked out as interesting stories to be preserved for posterity. In any case, given the gaps in our information, it is not really possible to speak to the violence level of ancient Athens. More important than the number of such legal cases for which evidence survives are the assumptions that underlie the rhetoric of the speakers.[125] An examination of their assumptions reveals that violence is never condoned and that on the contrary it was a serious problem with which the state was intimately concerned.

In Demosthenes 54 (*Against Conon*), Ariston suggests that the legal code's different options for the prosecution of gradated types of offenses were intended to stop escalation that could end in violence.

> People say that these suits come about for this reason, that men who verbally abuse each other will not be incited to physical violence. Also, there are suits for battery (*aikeias*), and I hear that they serve this purpose, that a man who is getting the worst of it won't defend himself with a stone or anything else of that type but instead will wait for the legal process. Also, there are public suits for wounding (*graphai traumatos*) to prevent homicides when men are wounded. In my view, there is a provision for the least important of these acts, verbal abuse, to avoid the final and worst, homicide, from happening and to prevent the escalation by small steps from verbal abuse to blows, from blows to wounds, and from wounds to death; instead the laws provide a legal action for each of these.[126]

This can be corroborated from other sources, including a sympathetic passage in Isocrates 20 (*Against Lochites*), which similarly depicts the body of laws as designed to prevent violence. The speaker asserts that the lawgivers created a procedure for slander to prevent people from eventually coming to blows because they were "especially concerned about the bodies" of citizens.[127]

In the plays produced for their civic festivals, the Athenians celebrated their conviction that the legal system provided a check on violence. The chorus of Euripides' *Suppliants* sounds a theme prevalent throughout Greek theater: "Justice encourages justice and murder encourages murder."[128] Aeschylus' *Oresteia* dramatizes this conflict between blood feud and justice in the person of Orestes. In the final play of the trilogy, the *Eumenides*, the Athenian court of the Areopagus breaks the cycle of feuding and bloodshed brought on by the curse of Atreus and restores harmony. Athenian tragedy is replete with such opposition between an out-of-control spiral of vendettas and the appropriate means of dispute resolution. Isocrates expresses a similar sentiment in the *Panathenaicus* (4.40), asserting that those who wanted to solve their disputes "by reason and not violence" came to the homicide courts at Athens.[129] The sources consistently report that Athenians believed that their laws, homicide laws in particular, put limitations on violence.[130]

It is true that Athens granted citizens the right to use physical and even lethal force in defending their persons and property, but the laws governing such acts highlight that they were the exception rather than the rule. Only in the cases of theft and adultery was violence authorized; in other instances, the man who used physical force ran the risk of prosecution.[131] A man could defend himself, his property, and his household,[132] but there is no provision for him simply to assault his enemies. This distinction is precisely what is at issue in Lysias 1 (*On the Murder of Eratosthenes*), when Euphiletus denies any previous acquaintance with Eratosthenes. He understands that admitting that Eratosthenes was his enemy would be tantamount to conceding his case, and so he is extremely careful to argue that he did not act out of personal pique. Enmity-inspired violence is nowhere in view in these provisions; these laws were designed to authorize self-defense and defense of the *oikos*.[133]

Two further cautions against taking these laws as evidence for a pattern of violent behavior at Athens are in order. First, although the authorization of lethal force has a deadly ring to it, cases of such self-help were not likely to involve knives or clubs for the simple reason that Athenians did not typically carry weapons.[134] In the days when medicine was rudimentary at best, even a well-placed blow to the nose or a tumble onto a hard surface could kill. Since even fistfights were potentially deadly in antiquity, the law's authorization of lethal force should be distinguished from modern provisions for homeowners to use firearms against robbers. Excessive attempts to ensure the death of the assailant could backfire, as we see in Lysias 1, where Euphiletus challenges the argument of his opponents that the affair was premeditated and that the necessary equipment for execution had been prepared beforehand. The second caution is against the assumption that because violent reprisal was authorized in particular instances, violence naturally spilled over into the rest of Athenian society. This hypothesis is suspect because it flies in the face of the strong evidence for the unacceptability of casual violence cited above.

Related to these laws about self-defense are the provisions for "self-help," that is, for private individuals to employ coercive force in the name of the state. Herman is right to point out that these provisions were not intended to allow individuals to assault each other at will but were rather designed to support individual initiative: "The common denominator of all forms of self-help was therefore the expectation that in case of need some higher form of state power would intervene to assist."[135] By the procedures of *apagogē* and *ephēgēsis*, a private citizen could detain certain criminals and hand them over to the Eleven (the board of magistrates in charge of Athens' prison).[136] In some circumstances, such as when a disfranchised citizen was spotted in a forbidden area and needed to be removed immediately,[137] it was necessary for individuals swiftly to carry out the duty of apprehending the offender since there was no public law enforcement to perform this task.[138] But they still had to be careful how they went about it.[139] There was an institutional safeguard against frivolous use of these procedures: a fine for the prosecutor who failed to gain at least one-fifth of the votes at the trial.[140] The arrester also had to carry out the mandate of delivering the criminal directly to the Eleven and could not carry him off elsewhere,[141] or he presumably risked prosecution for abuse of the procedure. We do not know exactly what detainment actually entailed, but it is unlikely that Athenian citizens were authorized to assault and subdue whomever they suspected of a crime. The same might be said for the *dikē exoulēs*, "suit of ejectment," which allowed the successful prosecutor to take by force what was owed to him. Because the man who carried out such an ejectment was acting on behalf of the *polis* rather than as an individual, he could not be interfered with as he confiscated the property. It is unthinkable that the law authorized him to handle his opponent violently without cause.[142] Fights may well have resulted from the *dikē exoulēs*,[143] but the laws did not sanction them. All of these procedures were supposed to be carried out without resorting to blows, and anyone who violated that prohibition was liable to prosecution.[144] Certainly the Athenian system was not one that limited potential conflict among citizens as much as possible, but acts of violence were never unanswerable: the victim always had recourse to the courts. The specific legal provisions concerning self-help illustrate that the state monopolized the use of force in Athens in the sense that it clearly defined the parameters in which it could take place.[145]

Because Athens relied heavily on its own citizenry for policing the state,[146] the system was bound to put individuals into conflicts where violence might well result. It does not follow that such acts of violence were sanctioned. The expectations of the community were an important means of social control in tense and potentially dangerous situations, as enemy confronted enemy. Of course, for the system to work, citizens need to internalize the law code and put ideology into practice.[147] We have seen that on the level of ideas, Athenians took a hard line against violent behavior, but it is another question how far the ordinary citizen absorbed and lived out this ideology.

Individuals Seeking Vengeance in Athens

Was the ideological proscription against violence a strong societal norm, or more like a speed-limit sign, which everybody knows about but few take seriously? It is impossible to determine exactly how often an Athenian would resort to violence in contravention of the ideological and institutional strictures on such behavior, but there is good reason to believe that the prohibition on violence was effective. Of course, particular individuals may have derived enough satisfaction in the pain of their enemies to make violence seem worthwhile, despite the city's sanctions. In most instances, however, the Athenians' principled rejection of physical assault as a valid means of retaliation can be expected to have exerted a direct influence on conventional behavior.

In a society driven by the pursuit of honor, communal ideas and communal sanctions have a real impact on how feuds play out. Honor games are ultimately about treating one's enemies in such a way as to score victories over them, and the nature of a "victory" is determined by one's peers, who judge the behavior of the parties in terms of an unwritten code of conduct. The content of that code will have an effect on the actions of enemies because to win esteem from the rest of the community, they must modify their actions in accordance with the rules. When the expectations of society at large change, the game of enmity changes as well.

Athenians involved in hostile relationships were not necessarily seeking the most extreme form of retribution imaginable, such as mass murder of the adversary's entire family. They were seeking to humiliate their enemies, to avoid loss of face themselves, and to gain vindication in the eyes of the community. In a blood-feuding culture in which violence is viewed as acceptable, violence of course would be an attractive option, as it is an obvious assertion of dominance. However, if the peer group views direct physical assault as illegitimate and excessive, it is a dangerous path to vengeance. A violent attack could have the reverse effect from that intended by bringing shame on the perpetrator for acting as an arrogant *hubristēs*, especially if the victim won a court case against him and humiliated him publicly. That which had promised vindication would prove to be disgrace. A clever pursuer of feuds would avoid risking long-term loss of face before the community for the sake of the momentary gratification of sinking his knuckles into his enemy's skin. Boasting about an act of violence was in all likelihood simply a bad idea in view of the communal and legal sanctions against such behavior.

Democratic thinking required its citizens to exercise more restraint than the heroes of myth who were constantly spoiling for a fight. Those who broke this taboo on violence would be immediately subject to censure not only in formal venues through the courts but in their standing among fellow citizens. Violence would have been a highly risky game, but fortunately the average Athenian seeking vengeance actually had better options. A savvy pursuer of vendettas would probably have preferred the courts, which were more public than the settings for most acts of violence and so provided more favorable opportunities for inflicting dishonor. The very important differences between trials at Athens and trials in modern Western societies are relevant here. Today, a dispute between two individuals will ordinarily become known only to the parties in the trial, a professional judge, a few lawyers, and perhaps a handful of interested spectators. When the proceedings are over, the parties depart. Perhaps one of them is angry about the verdict, but this will probably result in a decision to avoid rather than persecute the opponent. If we were to add a large audience that included extensive networks of friends, family, and other members of the community, the mood would change significantly. People are watching now; honor and shame are at stake. At the end of the trial, one party is vindicated, and the other, humiliated. Nobody will go home and forget about it.

The courts were not the only arenas in which honor games could find an outlet. Adele Scafuro draws attention to the "staginess" of pretrial procedures such as arbitration and reconciliation, which provided an audience for those who wished to rehabilitate their honor.[148] Far from seeking resolution and peace, two disputants who called upon mediators often wanted merely to create a battleground with distinct boundaries in which they could play out their disagreements. Sometimes harmony was restored and sometimes not, but the point is that these procedures provided avenues to pursue honor without resorting to blows, and hence without violating community sanctions.[149]

Another way to harm an enemy was to "bind" him with a curse tablet that invoked the aid of the divine.[150] These tablets probably had a recognized function within the matrix of attacks and retaliations inherent in these elaborate games of honor and provided an additional outlet for aggressive feeling that obviated the need to resort to violence. In view of their potential publicity, curses could be a more effective means of inflicting loss of face than physical assault.

The courts, arbitration, and curse tablets were a few of the alternatives to violence, but there were undoubtedly many more. The ideology prohibiting assault on a citizen's body created a situation in which violence simply was not a sensible course of action even (or rather especially) for the most honor-driven of men.

Such acts were also discouraged by ideological pressures on all Athenian citizens to intervene when violence threatened. If an assault occurred in a public location, the witnesses were not to stand idly by and judge the outcome but to mediate and restore order. The active participation of bystanders in stopping fights provided a check on those renegades who refused to pay homage to the social expectations and legal sanctions concerning such behavior.[151] We often read of crowds of men uninvolved in the dispute who intervene to give aid to the victim of an attack or to break up a scuffle between two belligerents.[152] To Athenians, this normalizing force was important for social stability. Ariston makes Conon's behavior seem particularly egregious by setting up a contrast between his encouragement of his sons to continue beating Ariston and the appropriate response of bystanders, who were expected to help the afflicted.[153] The good Athenian was to be ready to come to the aid of his fellow citizen. Implicitly invoking this idea, Demosthenes flatters his audience in *Against Timocrates* by assuring them that if imprisoned criminals escaped en masse, all of the jury members would run to help.[154] Bystander help seems to have been a part of civic ideology; it provided "security"[155] for the average citizen.[156]

The absence in Athens of the blood-feuding ethic found in other societies is confirmed by the fact that Athenians did not carry weapons, as Herman has pointed out.[157] Thucydides asserts that the Athenians were the first among the Greeks to give up the practice of carrying arms.[158] Aristotle confirms Thucydides' observation, calling the practice "uncivilized."[159] In the *Gorgias* Socrates talks about carrying a dagger into the marketplace as if the concept were a novelty. He asserts that he would have the power of a tyrant to kill whomever he wanted, thus assuming that no one else would have a weapon.[160] This scenario proposed by Socrates resembles the story about Pisistratus' first attempt at seizing power. Pisistratus secured a group of bodyguards armed with clubs and took control of the acropolis. The Athenians were apparently unable to resist this small force and therefore must not have been armed themselves.[161] A passage of Andocides 1 (*On the Mysteries*) is the exception that proves the rule. According to Andocides, the citizen body was so fearful after the mutilation of the Herms that many took to carrying arms for a period of time.[162] Andocides presents this as an extreme aberration of the normal state of affairs. The customary belief that others were not armed was so deeply ingrained that it was often assumed even where resort to weapons might be most expected. In his list of the measures that people can take to avoid being wronged by their enemies, Apollodorus mentions guarding household effects, staying at home at night, and taking preparations against plots; he does not include carrying a weapon for self-defense.[163]

Athenians did not carry weapons because they did not view their society as violent. They did not condone violent behavior as normal and acceptable and rather expected that respect for the sacrosanctity of the body of the citizen would put a severe brake on bloodshed. When ideological proscriptions failed to prevent such behavior, citizens were encouraged to intervene when a quarrel began to escalate, and recourse to the legal system was available to victims. These were significant deterrents. If an Athenian wanted to humiliate his adversary, he would have to find some outlet other than physical assault. The inviolability of the citizen's body was institutionally guaranteed by decree, upheld in public ideology, embodied in public injunctions to intervene, and proven effective by the absence of *sidērophoria* ("arm-bearing"). To all appearances, it was well ingrained in Athenian culture.

Virtually all Athenian citizens would have been familiar with combat, having served in the army or navy, and would not have had a problem with violence as such, but the distinction between public and private was fundamental. In the *Republic*, Socrates distinguishes between two types of *echthra*: *stasis* (enmity with one's kindred) and war (*polemos*; enmity with outsiders).[164] The Athenians generally made a similar distinction between personal enmity and war and believed that the rules governing them were different. It was not contradictory that the same man was encouraged to slay his enemies (*polemioi*) on the battlefield and refrain from punching his enemies (*echthroi*) in the city.[165] The spheres of combat and everyday life were distinct, and so were the principles governing them. Athenians were supposed "to be mild and considerate in the Assembly, since it is there that you discuss your rights and those of your allies, but to show yourselves fearsome and severe in your preparations for war."[166]

Whether or not this prohibition on violence extended to noncitizens is an open question. Josiah Ober has posited that many of the rights held by adult male citizens gradually spilled over as "quasi-rights" to other groups.[167] Indeed, Athenian law prohibited *hubris* against women, children, and slaves, yet it is unclear how effective this was. Apollodorus accused Nicostratus of attempting to entrap him by sending a young boy to pick flowers from his rose bed so that Apollodorus might strike him, thinking he was a slave. Nicostratus could then prosecute him for *hubris*.[168] On the one hand, this may indicate that the criteria for what constituted *hubris* against a slave were stricter than that for *hubris* against a citizen. On the other hand, Apollodorus may be implying simply that a slave who was assaulted would have had difficulty obtaining justice if no witnesses were present. In either case, this passage should cause us to be skeptical of the Old Oligarch's statement that one could not strike a slave in Athens.[169]

Hubris is a tricky term, and prosecution by *hubris* must have been a difficult proposition. Even if *hubris* had been committed against a woman or slave, only a male with citizen status could take legal action. In other words, the rights of these marginalized groups were tied to the rights of their *kurioi* (masters or guardians). Citizen and slave were not on equal footing: the law specifies that only for *hubris* against a free person can a man be imprisoned. Furthermore, it is not necessarily the case that the same act of violence would have been considered *hubris* regardless of whether it was committed against a citizen or a slave. Could Demosthenes have claimed that Meidias' slap to the face was *hubris* if the victim had been a slave and not an elite orator? These are murky waters.[170]

On occasion, however, one does get the sense from the Attic orators that Athenians viewed unwarranted violence as inherently wrong. When the speaker of Demosthenes 47 (*Against Evergus*) says that his enemy, Theophemus, struck and killed a slave woman of his, there is no sense that he is complaining about only a loss of property.[171] He feels a need to obtain not restitution but vengeance. This cannot be pressed too far, however, as the speech concerns a murder and not a casual smack. While it is clear that there were limits to violence against noncitizens, it is not clear exactly what they were.

The available evidence about violence is strongest in regard to violence between citizens, and it seems that there was a connection between citizen status and the right to security of one's person. Ideologies are necessarily complex, and it would be foolhardy to posit a direct causal relationship between one ideological tenet and another. The belief in the inviolability of the citizen's body was not the only, and may not even have been the most important, factor in the development of Athenians' views about violence. However, there is an inherent contradiction between unchecked violence among citizens and an egalitarianism augmented by the belief in the security of each citizen in his person. A strong belief in equality virtually prescribes limitations on violence. This is the link between democratic citizenship and nonviolence. Slaves had to fear violence to their persons; free men were free from precisely that.[172] There were no class distinctions among

Athenian citizens that allowed one group to abuse the subservient class at will; being an Athenian citizen meant "to rule and be ruled in turn."[173] A tyrant strikes whomever he will, while a slave suffers what he must, but Athenian citizens were neither tyrants nor slaves.

CONCLUSION

The prospect of being at the mercy of one's enemies was abhorrent to Athenians. They were free to lead their lives as they pleased, as Demosthenes reminds his audience in *Against Meidias*:

> As soon as this court rises, each one of you will go home, one rather quickly, another more leisurely, not worrying, or checking over his shoulder, or fearing whether he will happen upon a friend or an enemy, a big man or a small one, a strong man or a weak one, or any of these sorts of things. Why? Because he knows in his soul and is confident and has trusted the state (*politeia*), that no one will drag him off or commit *hubris* against him or beat him up.[174]

Athenians did not have to walk in fear because their *politeia*—the institutions and practices of the democracy—prevented society from devolving into a violent free-for-all that would end in the rule of the strong over the weak. Citizens could go about their daily lives, even after delivering a verdict against a wealthy elite bully like Meidias, without worrying about the security of their persons. The system of participatory government prevented those who served as jurors from becoming directly entangled in the feuds of the orators by allowing them to cast their votes by secret ballot. The nonviolent practices of the Athenian people provided a further guarantee.

Athenians put these limitations on feuding in place without abrogating the honor-driven enmity culture that was so deeply ingrained in their thinking. Rather, they organized their *politeia* in such a way as to limit enmity's negative effects and provide each citizen with a guarantee of security for his person and property. The Athenians struck a balance between feud and public harmony.

This tension between the pursuit of enemies and the limits imposed by law finds expression in other venues such as tragedy, although the issue is somewhat obscured by the transference of the setting from contemporary Athens to mythic times. In Sophocles' *Ajax* the problem is the same even if the parameters are different. Odysseus pleads with Agamemnon to allow the burial of their mutual enemy, Ajax, asserting that enmity cannot trump the established laws of the gods: "Do not let the violence of your hatred overcome you so much that you trample on justice."[175] When he learns of the madness Athena has inflicted on Ajax, Odysseus realizes that he must pity him and not carry his hatred too far. Denying Ajax burial would have been a religious offense because Ajax's innate nobility entitles him to certain basic rights, enemy or not.[176] Sophocles thus dramatizes this tension between private enmity and the dictates of justice, although he projects the contemporary issue onto the legendary past.

The continued existence of feuds despite state regulations can tend to mislead us into thinking of Athens as a feuding society in which violence was probably commonplace no matter what ideology was publicly espoused in venues like the courts. It is of course impossible to discuss violence levels in Athens with confidence, but we should be careful to reject the assumption that there exists a spectrum between feuding/violent societies and nonfeuding/nonviolent societies, onto which Athens can be plotted at one point or another. As Cohen has pointed out, no linear axis need be envisioned.[177]

Athenians could simultaneously believe that enmity was a prevalent phenomenon in the city, that enemies would constantly attempt to harm each other, and that enemies could be prevented by democratic institutions and practices from using violence or threatening the integrity of the state. Enemies were allowed to pursue each other and to fight for honor, but state regulations and the social expectations of the citizen's body put strong restraints on their behavior. Perhaps the widespread approval of taking vengeance on one's enemies shares more in common with "feuding" societies, while restraints on enmity resemble the ideology of a "nonfeuding" society, but both can be found in Athens, whether or not we see them as incongruous. Athens was a complex society with its own distinctive features. It does not fit into the models of feuding or nonfeuding societies since it lacked the characteristic privatization of vengeance of the former and the prohibition on feuding of the latter. Athens was unique and came up with its own unique solutions to the problems inherent in personal enmity.

This brings us to the question of whether or not this system worked. Were the courts, for instance, effective or dysfunctional? Did the Athenians pay lip service to the importance of litigants' honesty, while clever enemies exploited the courts in illegitimate ways? The possibility of a significant gap between ideology and reality is real[178] but difficult to assess. Probably many citizens would have boasted that their legal system worked efficiently and protected the downtrodden, while many others would have complained of injustices and inconsistencies. We are in no position to judge which of these two perspectives was closer to the truth. On the topic of violence, we are on somewhat firmer footing. There is good reason to believe that the sanctions against physical attacks on the citizen body were effective. Public ideology consistently upheld the inviolability of the citizen body and was buttressed by widely understood injunctions on average citizens to intervene in violent encounters. The absence of a weapon-carrying ethos in Athens is further strong evidence against the idea of a widespread violent culture.

The model of Athenian enmity culture offered in this study is drawn directly from our sources, but it is difficult to know if anyone ever actually lived in that culture. The actual life of the average Athenian proves ever elusive. However, while we may not be able to reach certainties, we can know a great deal about the world that they talked about and believed in, that came up for discussion in the courtroom each day. This world, based on the public's conceptualization of their own society, is no less valuable than models constructed through statistics and "hard" empirical data.

Comparison of Athens with Rome suggests that certain social values and ideological tenets could indeed have a positive effect on society. Millett notes the relatively low level of political violence in Athens compared with Rome and the lack of a strong impulse toward revolution.[179] In Rome, the political temperature rose along with the stakes of the game. Loss of influence could result in being locked out of government or even exile or death. In Athens, all had a share in ruling, and officers were selected randomly by lot, and so there would have been correspondingly less fear of an illegitimate takeover and therefore less incentive for going outside the law to satisfy grievances. Political violence was simply not good policy at Athens, because on the one hand it was extremely risky and on the other hand it would not normally accomplish a great deal. The intimidation or assassination of one person could not have nearly the influence on policy in Athens as in Rome.

The Athenian sources present us with a vivid picture of what a feuding culture in a democracy could look like. Democracy and internal violence are, of course, not incompatible, as many modern third-world countries have demonstrated so tragically, but Athens, the first democracy in the world for which sufficient evidence remains for a thoroughgoing analysis, provides a glimpse of the tendency for egalitarian ideology to modify the violent feuding impulse. A complete ban on the pursuit of personal honor was in all probability utterly outside the framework of the ancient Greeks, but the limitations on personal enemies' behavior that the Athenian *polis* established were nonetheless significant. They provided the social underpinning for the remarkable internal strength and resilience that Athens demonstrated throughout the classical period.

CONCLUSION. PERSONAL ENMITY AND PUBLIC POLICY

Personal enmity, as a social phenomenon, does not worry us as much today as it worried the ancient Greeks. It is true that we still make enemies and seek to harm them, but the intensely personal culture of honor that undergirds feuding systems of the old style has largely passed away in the West. Cities are too big and social networking too complex for the opinions of neighbors, friends and family, and the community at large, especially their evaluation of one's character, to exert the necessary pressure. Members of the network can easily be dropped and their opinions ignored. Winning or losing in a relationship of enmity is no longer necessarily in the public view. Perhaps just as importantly, several competing ideologies tell modern men and women neither to contract enmities nor to pursue them. Alongside mainstream Judeo-Christian ethics are various secular movements toward peace and understanding. It is hard to imagine an ancient Greek asking, "Can't we all just get along?"

In politics also, the shift away from a culture of honor and enmity has been decisive. In the United States, the sheer size of the country and the impersonal nature of the civil system have forced most politicians to rely on larger political groups rather than their own honor and standing with the electorate. The closest parallel to the rhetoric of enmity today are the predictable and endless accusations of "partisanship." Although the personal relationships of elite politicians no longer take center stage, Americans are willing to believe that some politicians would lie, cheat, and ignore the public good for the sake of party loyalty and personal advancement. This is the language of personal enmity repackaged to fit larger groups. An ideal politician will perhaps be loyal to her party and her constituents but will not allow this loyalty to override her sense of justice. If he lived today, Aristides would undoubtedly be "bi-partisan."

It was not always thus. Two centuries ago, the people of the American South still adhered to a traditional system of values, rooted in the Homeric epics and other classical texts.[1] By and large the North had replaced the honor/shame scheme with one of conscience/guilt, and of course after the Civil War these values became the values of the ruling class and would eventually win the day. Yet before the mid nineteenth century, political enmity operated much as it always had. Read about the lives of the Americans who served in office shortly after the Revolution, and one will soon get the sense of being in a familiar world, similar to ancient societies like Athens. Personal ties, likes and dislikes, reconciliations and duels had a profound impact on the shape of the United States' government and public policy.[2] The Founding Fathers performed as if they were actors on the stage of history, constantly worried about how history would view them,[3] but this is unsurprising for men whose assiduous reading included stories about the relentless pursuit of honor and fame by the likes of Achilles, Demosthenes, and Cicero. They were indeed putting on a performance, but they were also pushing each other around and jockeying for position. The same could be said for most medieval and early modern European societies, both monarchical and parliamentarian.

In Ancient Greece we have the earliest example of such enmity-driven politics for which significant sources are extant. Alongside their Roman counterparts, the men of Greece, and especially Athens, exerted a disproportionate influence on Western culture, serving as paradigms (both positive and negative) that were popularized through literature, such as Plutarch's *Lives*, that was widely read in the Middle Ages. More broadly speaking, the Greeks' ideas about citizenship, freedom and tyranny, and the distinction between public and private set the tone for later debates. In the same way that Greece is the starting point for the study of Western civilization, it is also the starting point for the study of politics. It is here that we should turn to understand the roots of the conflict between feud and state.

The threat that feuds posed to political communities was clearly understood. Thucydides vividly recounts nightmarish scenarios in which the disintegration of the bonds of civilization resulted in unchecked violence and complete societal chaos. He perhaps saw the dangers of man's brutal nature more keenly than most, but the fear of such civil discord was by no means unique to him. *Stasis* was a frightening prospect to all Greeks. Personal feuds that destabilized a *polis* were neither surprising nor new in the fifth century. Elite infighting that led to constitutional change was a common phenomenon. In predemocratic Athens, the major reforms of Solon and Cleisthenes and the tyranny of Pisistratus were all results of prolonged personal animosities that ended in settlement. Even the bizarre institution of ostracism, introduced in the wake of the upheavals of 508–507, can be seen as a safeguard against these quarrels getting out of control.[4]

The danger of *stasis* increased proportionally as the ruling elites were fewer in number and more powerful. A handful of first families could, by their inveterate hostilities, hamstring the whole government. Hence, it is in the context of his discussion of oligarchic regimes that Anaximenes says that "disputes between citizens ought to be resolved as quickly as possible."[5] Such disputes often led to the dissolution of oligarchies.[6] Pisistratus and Megacles, whose personal alliance allowed them to end the factional strife in Athens and ushered in a few years of peace, illustrate this dynamic. They also illustrate the fragility of such agreements; Pisistratus' insult to Megacles' daughter precipitated his second exile.[7] There was, in any case, more than one way to "resolve" disputes. When the tyrant Periander sent a messenger to the more experienced tyrant Thrasybulus to ask how to maintain his regime, Thrasybulus did not reply directly but took the herald to a wheat field and chopped off any stalks of exceptional height. The message was lost on the herald, but Periander understood the parable.[8] Yet, regardless of the path rulers took, whether they removed their opposition or reconciled with their enemies, they could never put a final stop to the personal disputes that subverted the system. There were always challengers. The exiles and murders of various tyrants and aristocrats, especially in the sixth century, are emblematic of this problem of stability that oligarchic states face. Parallels to Rome during the Late Republic are obvious.

For Athenians of the fourth century, the exemplar of a *politeia* that must be avoided was not a theoretical oligarchy but a real, historical regime—the rule of The Thirty in 404–3. Athens had tasted the bitter fruit of an unrestrained junta whose members abused their positions of authority to benefit themselves and their friends and punish their enemies. Many of those who were perceived to be hostile to the oligarchy were summarily executed; many others, even oligarchic sympathizers, were executed so that their property could be confiscated. Xenophon portrays Critias, the oligarchic mastermind, as unconcerned about these administrative murders.[9] Theramenes, a more moderate oligarch, criticized The Thirty for cavalierly making many enemies and thereby undermining the regime.[10] In return for his advice, Theramenes was executed. Critias and company continued to pursue their private interests to such an extreme that they made their own position untenable. Their brief rule became, for years afterward, the dystopia of Athenian thought. It was remembered as a time when lawlessness ruled and all recourse to public justice was blocked.[11]

Athens under the democracy was different. The restored democracy's response to The Thirty, the amnesty of 403, was an emphatic rejection of Critias' principles; feuds would once again be reined in by public proscriptions. Certainly, the agonistic culture of honor was still operative and still created problems of conflict between private and public, but Athens subjected feuding to restraints that had been abrogated under The Thirty. Power was once again diffused by mass participation, which limited the effects of these personal hostilities. The safeguards protecting a citizen's person from bullies and property from sycophants, nonexistent under The Thirty, were restored.

These regulations limited the purview of the honor culture without renouncing it. The evidence does not suggest a transition from honor/shame to conscience/guilt such as we see in the United States in the nineteenth century. Such an interpretation of the Athenian evidence would be anachronistic. Rather, law and political practice circumscribed personal relationships. Athenians expected the pursuit and harming of enemies but also expected it to stay within the parameters established by the *polis*. In contrast to other societies, Athens had no category for private enmity that fell outside the realm of public interest and law. In thirteenth-century France, for instance, the normal rules of law did not completely apply to cases involving enemies.[12] When enmity was made "manifest," the normal legal recourse available to victims changed considerably. There was nothing like this at Athens. While plenty of evidence indicates that Athenians considered enmity an openly recognized relationship, there is nothing to suggest that it was granted formal legal status. Enmity was always subordinated to the legal system of the city and consequently susceptible to governmental sanctions. Athenians did not countenance the private pursuit of feuds through acts that the laws declared illicit. Even in the notorious cases of "self-help," the state apparatus decided which actions of self-help were legitimate. No special category of "manifest enmity" allowed enemies to ignore restrictions on their behavior and do things that would otherwise be illegal. Enmity always had to be played out within the context of public regulation.[13]

A useful analogy can be made between this ideology of enmity and the athletic games of which the Greeks were so fond. Competitors were motivated to achieve victory and even to humiliate their opponents, but they had to know the rules of the game and play by them. The presence of referees who guaranteed that no one cheated did not deaden the athletes' desire to win; rather, it ensured that the game proceeded correctly. Similarly, in Athenian society, competitors were free to pursue their enemies, but they had to play the game in a certain way.[14] Athens had to make sure that its citizens were feuding with each other in the right ways and were not spurred on by passion to compromise the integrity of the state for their own personal interests. The pursuit of honor was not dulled; it was refocused.

This solution to the problem of personal enmity was in all probability an important factor in the Athenians' remarkable stability during the classical period. During the fifth and fourth centuries, other city-states suffered from debilitating *stasis* or were overthrown by other powers when exiled citizens or a dissatisfied faction betrayed the city to its enemies to gain power. Athens was relatively free from such strife.[15] Demosthenes and Aeschines hated each other as much as any two orators in Greece, but they kept their feud within the walls of the city and did not destroy society through their bitter enmity. As powerful as these men were, they did not have the kind of power that their fellow elites had in other cities: to coerce other citizens and wreak havoc on the state through their personal disputes. As Aeschines himself says,

> Dictatorships and oligarchies are governed by the temperament of those in power, but democratic cities are governed by the established laws. You are aware, men of Athens, that in a democracy the persons of citizens and the constitution are protected by the laws, while dictators and oligarchs are protected by distrust and armed guards.[16]

The rule of the laws, rather than of a ruling class, protected the persons of the citizens and preserved the *politeia* itself. Athens could not be managed by a single man; a mass of well-informed citizens, whose political rights were protected, could with a simple vote nullify the power of an orator in an instant, as Pericles discovered in 429.[17] Athenian politicians had to be careful.

The limitations on enmity must have had salutary effects on the harmony and stability of the *polis*, but this pragmatic concern with the welfare of the state as a whole was not the only factor encouraging the development of these restraints. Enmity also posed a threat to the rights and freedoms of individual citizens, especially nonelites. The core values of the Athenian *politeia*—the equality, freedom, and security of every citizen[18]—would have been compromised if poorer citizens were answerable to the whims of the elite. In an unrestrained feuding culture, the elite has the ability to dominate others by applying the coercive power of threat and force, thus robbing the poor of their security and consequently of their equality and freedom. The weaker the protection of these egalitarian principles, the more the state slips into oligarchy. Where the citizen cannot vote and participate without fear, there can be no democracy. The security of individual citizens from violent attack and political machination was fundamental to the successful functioning of the Athenian regime.

Was this system for controlling enmity uniquely democratic? In view of the dearth of information about other *poleis*, a comparison to oligarchies will necessarily be tenuous, but some evidence indicates that Athens was unusual. Of the three spheres discussed in chapter 4 (political, legal, and social) the restrictions on enmity in the first have a necessary and obvious connection with democracy. The specifically democratic form of the *politeia* depersonalized the governing process and made the personalities and personal relationships involved less important than they would have been in other city-states. (A caveat should be added that "democracy" here means ancient-style democracy, which necessarily included election by lot, strict term limits, mass participation, and collegiality in offices, all principles distinctly lacking in most modern "democracies.") When politicians are elected and serve for life on a board of only thirty men, as in the Gerousia at Sparta, their personal relationships take on a new importance. The Athenian system prevented a concentration of power in the hands of a few influential men and thereby limited the effects of personal politics on the state.

The restrictions on enemies pursuing each other are likewise difficult to imagine without that hallmark of ancient democratic constitutions, the courts. Mass juries voting by secret ballot could exert social pressure even on elite orators in a way that was virtually impossible for the small groups of powerful magistrates who arbitrated disputes in oligarchies. It is not unlikely that in oligarchies the legal system became merely another venue for elite feuds to play themselves out (much as Cohen postulated about Athens). Backroom dealing of the type that Sphodrias used to secure his acquittal at Sparta in 378[19] was not possible at Athens. Athenians could not have counted on personal ties to the jurors that would allow them to finagle their way out of a case.

The prohibition on violence also seems to have been distinctively Athenian and, probably, distinctively democratic. The absence of a weapon-carrying ethic was noted as an especially Athenian characteristic,[20] and the concern for the bodies of poor citizens makes the most sense in an egalitarian society where people can "live as they please." In Sparta, enemies of a young age were expected to fight when they happened upon one another.[21] There was no reason to put restrictions on the aristocratic code of honor if Homeric-style hierarchy and the submission of the weak to the strong were accepted as social facts. Sometimes a Thersites needs a good whack.[22] Plato's Socrates was likewise toeing the oligarchic party line when he suggested that the ideal *polis* would not have any lawsuits for assault (*aikeias dikai*) because the citizens would then have an incentive to stay physically fit.[23] A little casual violence kept men sharp.

From this evidence it would appear that there was a link between these restraints on enmity and the democratic habitus at Athens, even if it was not a direct link of cause and effect. Perhaps the same sorts of social pressures led to both egalitarian ideology and the limiting of private vengeance through public institutions and practices. To push any further would be to go beyond the reach of the evidence.

This raises the old question of the connection, or lack of connection, between ancient democracy and classic liberalism. Many have denied any connection at all, and many early modern thinkers (the Founding Fathers, for instance) emphatically rejected Athenian democracy as a model because of its unrestrained mob rule, which was an inherent threat to the individual's right to hold personal property.[24] In the wake of the disastrous consequences of the French Revolution, which contemporaries perceived to be a failed attempt to return to ancient-style democracy, Benjamin Constant delivered a speech in which he made a distinction between the ancient and modern concepts of liberty, a distinction that would become standard. He argued that in Athens there was no theoretical limit to the will of the masses: "Among the ancients the individual, almost always sovereign in public affairs, was a slave in all his private relations."[25]

The contrast, however, is overstated. The principles of equality and security, foundational underpinnings of democratic practice, necessarily entailed that negative liberties of sorts had to be guaranteed to protect the integrity of collective rule.[26] The restraints on enemies in the political sphere, the courts, and society are clear examples of such freedoms. These civic protections were not based on abstract theories about the natural state of man, the right of self-preservation, or the necessity of sacrificing some liberties to gain the greater benefits resulting from life in a community;[27] they were in all probability much more pragmatic than that. For the citizen to exercise his share in the *politeia*, he had to be free to do so without constraints. In Athens "positive" and "negative" liberties were fundamentally linked and so were never identified as discrete categories, but if modern terminology is to be applied to ancient Athens, it would be false to assert that Athenian citizens had no protections guaranteed to individuals.[28]

To adopt an Athenian (and perhaps better) manner of viewing political ideology, the life of the citizen is characterized by a multitude of relationships, all of which entail associated duties. Instead of worrying about the liberties or rights that individual citizens held, we can often explain Athenian values in terms of these crosscutting and competing moral obligations. Athenians were supposed to be fierce with *polemioi*, respectful toward fellow citizens, loving with friends, hostile (but restrained) toward *echthroi*, and so forth. Sometimes these relationships came into conflict. When one man took another to court, the two litigants shared a relationship of personal enmity but also of citizenship, and they both had a relationship with the city itself and a duty to follow its prescriptions. Ideally, they were both supposed to do their best to balance their various obligations, and failure to keep these tensions in mind was subject to strong censure. Meidias' slap on the face was egregious because Demosthenes was at the time acting in a public capacity: "Along with Demosthenes, your chorus producer too was the victim of the outrage; and this is a matter of concern for the *polis*."[29] It may have been the case that in other cities "the most powerful men are not willing even to appear to respect the authorities,"[30] but this was not so for Athens. Just as they had obligations to their friends, family, and enemies, Athenians also had obligations to the *polis*. To these enmity had to submit.

NOTES

INTRODUCTION

1. Dem. 22.3: τοῦτον δὲ μεθ' ὑμῶν πειράσομαι καὶ νῦν καὶ τὸν ἄλλον ἅπαντα ἀμύνεσθαι χρόνον. Translation from Harris 2008.
2. [Dem.] 59.12: παρακαλούντων δή με ἁπάντων, ἰδίᾳ προσιόντων <τε> μοι, ἐπὶ τιμωρίαν τρέπεσθαι ὧν ἐπάθομεν ὑπ' αὐτοῦ, καὶ ὀνειδιζόντων μοι ἀνανδρότατον ἀνθρώπων εἶναι, εἰ οὕτως οἰκείως ἔχων <τὰ> πρὸς τούτους μὴ λήψομαι δίκην. Translation from Bers 2003.
3. Cf. Lys. 10.13, 12.2–3, 13.1, 14.2; Dem. 21.1, 22.1–2, 24.7, 24.8; [Dem.] 45.1, 53.1, 58.2, 59.1; Aeschin. 1.2.
4. Dem. 54.7–9.
5. The construction and choice of verbs in this book (e.g., "The Athenians never attempted to stifle enmity outright, nor did they approve . . .") are for convenience and should not be taken to imply that the Athenians made a reasoned and deliberate decision at a particular moment in time. In reality, restrictions on social practices such as feuding were part of a complex process originating in a publicly accepted ideology and practice and therefore according with other deeply held values.
6. This phrase (ψηφιεῖσθαι γνώμῃ τῇ δικαιοτάτῃ καὶ οὔτε χάριτος ἕνεκ' οὔτ' ἔχθρας, Dem. 57.63) comes from a fragment of the Heliastic Oath, a sworn statement required of all Athenian jurors. Although Dem. 24.149–151 purports to be a copy of this oath, it is clearly a later interpolation since it omits many of the phrases that are cited elsewhere in Attic oratory. On attempts to reconstruct the oath, see Fränkel 1878; A. R. W. Harrison 1968–1971, ii: 48. Recent discussion has focused on interpretation of the clauses (e.g., Christ 1998b: 194–196; Johnstone 1999: 33–43; Harris 2006a; Mirhady 2007; E. Harris 2013: 101–137). For a list of allusions to the judicial oath, see E. Harris 2013: 353–356.
7. Arist. *Rh.* 2.21 (1395a18): νήπιος ὃς πατέρα κτείνας παῖδας καταλείπει.
8. Bartlett 2010.
9. On the definition of a "feuding society," see pp. 000–000.
10. On these ideological tenets, see especially Ober 1996 and 2005: 92–127, along with Hansen 1996; Raaflaub 1996; E. Wood 1996; Liddel 2007.
11. D. Cohen 1995: 82.

12. Herman 2006. See also the articles (Herman 1993, 1994, 1995, 1998, 2000) in which Herman laid the foundation for his monograph.

13. Christ 1998b: 191.

14. Allen 2000b: 127–128.

15. Allen's overall thesis (2000b), which asserts the great importance of male citizen anger in the legal process, perhaps favors Cohen's conclusions more than Herman's, while Christ seems to lean toward Herman's model: Cohen 1995; Herman 1993, 1994, 1995, 1998, 2000, 2006; Christ 1998b.

16. W. Harris 1997; Fisher 1998: 80–86; Schofield 1998: 39; W. Harris 2001: 183–184; Roisman 2003: 137–138; E. Harris 2005; Lanni 2006: 25–31; McHardy 2008: 94–99; Hunt 2010: 204–205.

17. Christ 2007; Herman 2007. Cf. E. Harris 2005 and the response by Christ in the same volume.

18. This issue will be covered in detail in chapters 2–3.

19. For examples, see discussion below, especially in chapters 2 and 4.

20. Herman 2006: 200. Herman (2000: 18) stresses that litigants "hope, quite consistently, to enlist the dikasts' support by parading themselves [. . .] as moderate citizens." Speakers therefore attribute "feuding characteristics to their opponents [. . .] and gentle characteristics [. . .] to themselves." (This passage is cited approvingly by E. Harris [2013: 71].) Cf. Herman's (2007) rebuttal to Christ: "Had the majority of Athenian law court speakers attempted to swing the dikasts in their favor by swaggering round demanding respect and breathing vengeance, I would have concluded that Athens should indeed be grouped together with feuding, 'primitive' or Mediterranean societies."

21. On how the parameters of a dispute change once it enters the courtroom, see Johnstone 1999.

22. Herman 1994: 117.

23. Dover 1974: 5–6.

24. Sinclair 1988: 211–218; Todd 1993: 77–78.

25. Hansen 1991: 178–224.

26. Ar. *Nub.* 207–208: τί σὺ λέγεις; οὐ πείθομαι, / ἐπεὶ δικαστὰς οὐχ ὁρῶ καθημένους.

27. The Athenians may have kept some records of judicial proceedings in the Metroon, but, as Sickinger (1999: 132) notes, "our knowledge of such judicial records is extremely poor, so this point cannot be pushed too far."

28. If a noncitizen, such as a woman or slave, was wronged, the *kurios* (the male citizen who had authority over the aggrieved party—a husband, father, owner, etc.) had to bring suit. (See Patterson 2007.)

29. Many other exceptional procedures, which functioned essentially as *graphai* except for their preliminary phase, were also available (e.g., *apagogē/endeixis* and *probolē*). Todd (1993: 112–121) has produced a useful, though not exhaustive, list of these procedures.

30. Dover 1968: 149–150; MacDowell 1978: 251; Todd 1993: 94–95; Christ 1998b: 37; Kapparis 1999: 195. Advocates often stress their connections to the persons they

are supporting to dispel suspicions that they have been hired. Rubinstein (2000: 128–147) points out that while *synēgoroi* in private speeches conform to this expectation, the pattern does not always hold true for public prosecutions.

31. Of the eleven Attic orators whose speeches are extant, three (Lysias, Isaeus, and Dinarchus) were metics (resident aliens) who had no citizen rights and therefore could not normally speak before a law court. These logographers participated in the system by writing speeches for Athenian citizens to deliver. Other orators also engaged extensively in "logography," notably Antiphon and Demosthenes. See Kennedy 1963: 57–58; Lavency 1964; Edwards 2000; Gagarin 2002: 2–4; Todd 2007: 3.

32. *Federalist Papers* 51.

33. This was usually either one of the forty appointed deme judges or one of the nine archons. The archon basileus ("king archon") had jurisdiction over religious matters, including trials for homicide. The eponymous archon was responsible for overseeing various social matters. The polemarch ("war archon"), although originally a leader in the Athenian army, was in charge of metics and other foreigners. The remaining six archons were called thesmothetai ("lawgivers") and had jurisdiction over many areas, especially those concerned directly with matters of law, such as cases of *graphai paranomōn*. See Lipsius 1905–1915: 339–451; A. R. W. Harrison 1968–1971, ii: 7–17; MacDowell 1978: 24–27.

34. If the *dikē* was valued at less than ten drachmas, the magistrate simply gave a verdict himself.

35. Scholars have arrived at these figures through calculations based on the waterclocks that have been discovered in Athenian archaeological digs (MacDowell 1978: 249–250).

36. Isae. 3.3–5, 5.22; Dem. 21.81, 30.31; 37.19, 40.34. See Lipsius 1905–1915: 664–674; Harrison 1968–1971, ii: 217–220; MacDowell 1978: 153–154.

37. Roman law is actually similar on this point, at least during the Republic, when the execution of the judgment was left up to the individual. By the imperial period, however, the praetor carried out duties that had previously been left to individual citizens. The modern state's direct coercive involvement in the dispute process is in part a legacy of Roman imperial practice.

38. Although many scholars have argued that the defining characteristic of a sycophant was pecuniary motivation, others have posited that a sycophant was primarily a vexatious litigant rather than necessarily one seeking dishonest gain. (For the debate, see MacDowell 1978: 62–66; Harvey 1990; Osborne 1990; Todd 1993: 92–94; Christ 1998b: 48–71; Allen 2000b: 156–167; Rubinstein 2000: 199–213.)

39. Lys. 6.31: καίτοι ὅταν τις τὸν αὑτοῦ βίον τοῖς ἐχθροῖς καὶ τοῖς συκοφάνταις διανέμῃ, τοῦτ' ἔστι τὸ ζῆν βίον ἀβίωτον.

40. The only texts from classical Athens even approximating a legal handbook are the critical works on oratory, such as Alcidamas' *On the Sophists*, Anaximenes' *Rhetoric to Alexander*, and Aristotle's *Rhetoric*. Whether or not many other handbooks existed is a matter of debate. (For a controversially skeptical view, see Schiappa 1999: 4–6, 45–47.)

41. After the restoration of democracy in 403, prosecutors were required to bring others to trial under an existing law, but the definitions of offenses were often vague and left open to interpretation.

42. See especially Ober 1989. Todd (1990a) shows how invoking a set of ideas that alienates the jury could be detrimental to a litigant's case.

43. Studies that have used the rhetoric of court speeches to draw conclusions about Athenian ideology include Dover 1974; Ober 1989; D. Cohen 1991, 1995; Christ 1998b; Johnstone 1999; Allen 2000b; Herman 2006; McHardy 2008; Worman 2008; Riess 2012; E. Harris 2013.

44. Of course, the use of these speeches is not without its own set of problems (see Todd 1990c). The Attic orators are notorious for distorting the truth when it serves their interests.

45. The twelve speeches of Isaeus are the only ones filling in the middle.

46. Isae. 1, 4, 7–10; Lys. 17; Dem. 42; [Dem.] 45.

47. Dem. 32–35, 56. All but one of these cases are actually *paragraphai* (barring actions) resulting from a *dikē emporikē* (Dem. 32–35). On these speeches see Lanni 2006: 149–174.

48. Lys. 16, 24–26, 31; Aeschin. 1. Aeschines 1 is, furthermore, a different type of *dokimasia* (*dokimasia rhētorōn*, for which see Gagliardi 2005; MacDowell 2005). The *dokimasia rhētorōn* was designed to provide a vetting process for *rhētores*, men who spoke in the Assembly and attempted to influence public policy. Unlike other *dokimasiai*, this procedure was initiated by a volunteer prosecutor, who had to prove the defendant guilty of misconduct severe enough to prohibit him from continuing to give advice in the Assembly. Regular *dokimasiai* were automatic, required entry examinations for each incoming magistrate after he was selected for the post. For the *dokimasia* procedure, see Lipsius 1905–1915: 270–278; A. R. W. Harrison 1968–1971, ii: 200–203; MacDowell 1978: 167–169; Adeleye 1983; Todd 1993: 115–116; Hunter 1994: 106–108. The Lysianic authorship of Lysias 24 has been doubted (Darkow 1917: 73–77; Roussel 1966; E. Wood 1983), but several scholars have ably defended it as a genuine work of the fourth century (Dover 1968: 189; Winter 1973; Edwards and Usher 1985: 263; Carey 1990: 50–51, n. 19; Dillon 1995; Usher 1999: 106–110).

49. For justification of viewing this period synchronically, see Ober 1989: 36–38; Hunter 1994: 6–7; Christ 1998b: 6; Liddel 2007: 89–94. Hansen (1989a, b) has argued vigorously against scholars who include the Periclean democracy in such an analysis but allows that fourth-century Athens may be examined synchronically. The law-code revision of the late fifth century undoubtedly affected the makeup of the Athenian legal code, but rhetorical practice and societal norms were likely to remain more or less consistent as the Athenians saw the restored democracy as direct successor to the fifth century.

50. On which see Carey 1994b.

51. On *basanos*, see Hunter 1994: 70–95; Gagarin 1996; Mirhady 1996; Thür 1996.

52. "Binding" was the common metaphor for the cursing process. The formula "I bind X" occurs *ad nauseam* in the tablets. See Eidinow 2007: 142–152.

53. Gager 1992: 20–21.
54. For this method of analyzing philosophical sources, see Herman's (2006: 129–133) useful discussion.
55. Arist. *Rh.* 2.2 (1379b17–19): [ὑπόκειται ἡ ὀργὴ] τοῖς ἐπιχαίρουσι ταῖς ἀτυχίαις καὶ ὅλως εὐθυμουμένοις ἐν ταῖς αὐτῶν ἀτυχίαις· ἢ γὰρ ἐχθροῦ ἢ ὀλιγωροῦντος σημεῖον.
56. On this passage, see pp. 000–000.
57. Eur. *Supp.* 399–462.
58. Aesch. *Supp.* 398–400: οὐκ ἄνευ δήμου τάδε / πράξαιμ' ἄν, οὐδέ περ κρατῶν, μὴ καί ποτε / εἴπῃ λεώς.
59. See the discussion of Kurihara et al. in chapter 3.

CHAPTER 1

1. Ps. 38:12. English Standard Version.
2. Arist. *Rh.* 1.12 (1372b31–33).
3. D. Cohen 1995.
4. Gluckman 1955; cf. Peristiany 1966; S. Wilson 1988.
5. On the rules of honor games, see D. Cohen 1995: 15–24.
6. See the seminal article by Gluckman (1955).
7. Despite Herman's (2006: 95–97) sensible criticism of this idea of "Mediterraneity," that all Mediterranean societies share similar codes of behavior, David Cohen's (1995) comparative evidence has moved scholarship on enmity and violence at Athens forward by providing new ways to frame the questions.
8. See also the discussion in Cheyette 2010 and Bagge, Gelting, and Lingkvist 2011: 1–2. A classic work that lays out the old model of "feudalism" is Bloch 1961.
9. Athens as meeting the criteria for being termed a state: Hansen 1998; E. Harris 2013: 21–59.
10. S. Wilson 1988.
11. For further discussion, see the next section below.
12. The underlying dynamics of enmity (chapter 1) and the rhetorical manipulation of enmity as a courtroom strategy (chapters 2–3) will be explored before considering the question of Athens' place in the scheme of "feuding" and "non-feuding" societies (chapter 4).
13. Winkler 1990: 55.
14. Dover 1974: 226. See, e.g., Dem. 34.40. Cf. Dover's observation that "where a modern speaker would probably make some reference to good and bad conscience, the Athenians tended instead to use expressions such as 'be seen to . . .', 'be regarded as. . . .'"
15. Latin maintains a similar distinction between *inimicus* and *hostis*. From the former are derived the English words "enemy" and "enmity."
16. Although this distinction between *echthros* and *polemios* generally holds true, semantic overlap does occur. Words of the root *polem-* are occasionally employed to refer to a private dispute, typically emphasizing the intense nature of the conflict (e.g., Dem. 21.29; cf. Arist. *Pol.* 6.8 [1322a]). See Blundell 1989: 39; Phillips

2008: 15. Likewise, *echthros* can be employed as a general unmarked term for any hostile persons. In the speeches with which we are concerned, however, it typically refers to a personal enemy.

17. Lys. 15.12: καὶ ᾽Αλκιβιάδην ἐχθρὸν ὄντα ἐμαυτοῦ τιμωρούμενος, δέομαι τὰ δίκαια ψηφίσασθαι· ὑμᾶς δὲ χρὴ τὴν αὐτὴν γνώμην ἔχοντας τὴν ψῆφον φέρειν, ἥνπερ ὅτε ᾤεσθε πρὸς τοὺς πολεμίους διακινδυνεύσειν. Cf. Lys. 4.13, 22.14–15.

18. On the emotions in ancient Greece, see Konstan 2006. Other studies include Walcot 1978, on the Greeks' ideas about envy; Allen 2000b, on anger in classical Athens; and W. Harris 2001, on anger in the ancient world.

19. Words related to the verb *diapheromai* ("to be at variance with; quarrel with" + dative) are also frequently employed to denote hostile relationships (e.g., the noun, *diaphora*, "quarrel").

20. D. Cohen 1995: 20.

21. Objections to the term "feud" on the grounds that it cannot be applied to strife between individuals (E. Harris 2013: 76–78) are weak because any feud between two Athenian men would typically include their *oikoi* and potentially also their friends and relatives.

22. Debate continues as to whether *philia* was primarily formal (see, e.g., Millett 1991; Peachin 2001) or affectational (see especially Konstan 1997), but the dichotomy may be overstated. Much of Konstan's argument for the voluntary and affective nature of friendship (of which enmity is a mirror image) is compelling, but this does not exclude the possibility of a highly formalized quality to these relationships. Konstan (1997: 14) points out that the concept of friendship is "overdetermined" and possesses a double identity "as a spontaneous and unconstrained sentiment and as a social institution with its particular code of behavior." Cf. the similarly slippery Latin word, *amicitia* ("friendship"), which can refer to an emotional bond or a highly formalized relationship of patronage.

23. Lloyd 1966. On the Greek tendency to divide all acquaintances into "friends and enemies," see Dover 1974: 181; Blundell 1989: 39–49; Konstan 1997: 56–59; Phillips 2008: 15–21.

24. As a matter of course, enemies hated and were angry with each other, just as friends loved each other. Aristotle's well-known discussion of the emotions at the beginning of the second book of the *Rhetoric* seems to attempt to distinguish relationship and simple emotion by employing nominalized infinitives (*to philein* and *to misein*) for the latter and reserving *philia* and *echthra* for the former. This, however, is Aristotle's scheme and does not reflect standard Greek usage.

25. Arist *Rh*. 2.4 (1381a1–3): φίλος δέ ἐστιν ὁ φιλῶν καὶ ἀντιφιλούμενος· οἴονται δὲ φίλοι εἶναι οἱ οὕτως ἔχειν οἰόμενοι πρὸς ἀλλήλους. Cf. Pl. *Ly*. 213a–b.

26. Aristotle (*Rh*. 2.4 [1382a1–2]) implies this correlation when he introduces enmity by saying that it must be understood on the basis of "opposites" (*tōn enantiōn*).

27. Arist. *Rh*. 1.12 (1372a30–31): οἱ δὲ λανθάνουσι διὰ τὸ μὴ δοκεῖν ἂν ἐπιχειρῆσαι φυλαττομένοις.

28. This motto is found in many places in Greek literature (see, e.g., Lys. 14.19; Arist. *Rh.* 1.6 [1363a19–21, 33–34]; Dover 1974: 181–184; Blundell 1989: 26–59). The principle was so deeply ingrained that it could be considered as part of the very definition of virtue (*aretē*, Pl. *Men.* 71e). A serious insult could be leveled at one's opponent by suggesting that he had inverted the code of "help friends/harm enemies," helping his enemies and harming his friends (e.g., Lys. 6.7, 5.10; cf. Lys. 8.1–6, 12.66–67).

29. D. Cohen 1995: 70–72; Phillips 2008: 15–21.

30. On this dynamic of friendship, see Konstan 2006: 169–184, esp. 173–177. On *charis*, see Ober 1989: 226–230; J. Harrison 2003; Konstan 2006: 156–168.

31. Arist. *Rh.* 1.9 (1367a20–22): καὶ τὸ τοὺς ἐχθροὺς τιμωρεῖσθαι καὶ μὴ καταλλάττεσθαι· τό τε γὰρ ἀνταποδιδόναι δίκαιον. Cf. [Arist.] *Rh. Al.* 1.15 (1422a36–38).

32. Hunt 2010: 185–186. In Book I of Plato's *Republic*, part of the discussion centers around the dictum of Simonides that justice consisted of giving everyone what he was "owed"—harm to those who harm us, help to those who help us.

33. Andoc. 1.117–136.

34. Isae. 1.31–32; cf. 7.11, 9.20–21. For the counter-argument, see Isae. 8.15–16.

35. Lys. 1.43–44.

36. Pl. *Chrm.* 161d: δοκεῖ οὖν σοι τὸ αὐτοῦ ὄνομα μόνον γράφειν ὁ γραμματιστὴς καὶ ἀναγιγνώσκειν ἢ ὑμᾶς τοὺς παῖδας διδάσκειν, ἢ οὐδὲν ἧττον τὰ τῶν ἐχθρῶν ἐγράφετε ἢ τὰ ὑμέτερα καὶ τὰ τῶν φίλων ὀνόματα.

37. For further discussion of curse tablets, see the Introduction.

38. Blumenfeld (2002) 346. For another modern view, cf. this comment by a character in one of Cormac McCarthy's novels, "What joins men together [. . .] is not the sharing of bread but the sharing of enemies" (2001: 307).

39. Antiph. 6.39–40: καὶ ἐγὼ πεισθεὶς ὑπὸ τῶν φίλων διηλλάγην τούτοις ἐν Διιπολείοις ἐναντίον μαρτύρων, οἵπερ διήλλαττον ἡμᾶς πρὸς τῷ νεῷ τῆς Ἀθηνᾶς· καὶ μετὰ τοῦτο συνῆσάν μοι καὶ διελέγοντο ἐν τοῖς ἱεροῖς, ἐν τῇ ἀγορᾷ, ἐν τῇ ἐμῇ οἰκίᾳ, ἐν τῇ σφετέρᾳ αὐτῶν καὶ ἑτέρωθι πανταχοῦ. τὸ τελευταῖον, ὦ Ζεῦ καὶ θεοὶ πάντες, Φιλοκράτης αὐτὸς οὑτοσὶ ἐν τῷ βουλευτηρίῳ ἐναντίον τῆς βουλῆς, ἑστὼς μετ' ἐμοῦ ἐπὶ τοῦ βήματος, ἁπτόμενος ἐμοῦ διελέγετο, ὀνόματι οὗτος ἐμὲ προσαγορεύων, καὶ ἐγὼ τοῦτον. Translation from Gagarin and MacDowell 1998.

40. Isae. 2.40: τῆς ἔχθρας διάλυσιν. The cognate verb (*dialuō*) is often used with *echthra* (e.g., Isae. 7.11) or *polemos* (e.g., Isocr. 5.7), while sometimes the implied object is omitted. It seems the very word for reconciliation, *dialusis*, means precisely a "loosing" of the hostile relationship.

41. There is semantic overlap in the Greek terms. Words of the stem *diait-* can refer either to arbitration or to reconciliation, whereas words with *dialu-* or *dialla-* roots refer only to reconciliation. For a detailed exposition of the vocabulary of arbitration and reconciliation, see Scafuro 1997: 117–141.

42. Arbitration could be threatened as a back-up plan if one of the parties failed to abide by a reconciliation (Isocr. 17.19–20).

43. Antiph. 6.39; Dem. 33.18, 40.11, 47.12; [Dem.] 59.46. See Scafuro 1997: 135.

44. Isae. 2.30; Dem. 55.32; Theophr. *Char.* 5.3.

45. Arbitrations/reconciliations often failed: Lys. 4.1–4; Isae. 2.28–35, 2.38; Dem. 41.1, 41.14; Hyp. 3.1–5; cf. Lys. 32.2; Isocr. 17.17–21; Isae. 1.35, 1.51.

46. Lys. 4.1–5.

47. Todd 2007: 349 n. 6.

48. [Dem.] 59.46; cf. Isae. 7.11; Dem. 40.46. Zeus puts similar injunctions upon Odysseus and the family members of the slaughtered suitors when he puts an end to the feud at the end of the *Odyssey* (24.484–486). This type of clause was also known in interstate treaties (Meiggs and Lewis 1969: 10). It was common enough that Thucydides (1.44.1) had to specify that the Athenian-Corcyraean treaty of 433 did not include this clause.

49. Stipulation: Hyp. 3.5. Stipulation with oath: Isae. 2.32.

50. [Dem.] 59.48; Hyp. 3.5.

51. The precise legal meaning of this oath is debated (Wolpert 2001; Carawan 2002; Joyce 2008).

52. The speaker of *Against Boeotus II* explicitly compares a private reconciliation agreement with the amnesty (Dem. 40.46).

53. The speaker of Isocrates 18 (*Against Callimachus*) also exploits for argumentative purposes the jurors' presumed belief in the efficacy of reconciliation. The reconciliation between his friend Patrocles and Callimachus explains the former's absence from the speaker's witnesses (Isocr. 18.6–8). Patrocles may be following through on his reconciliation agreement not to harm Callimachus.

54. The sharing of sacrifices and other ritual acts was evidently an important aspect of reconciliation and of Greek friendship in general (Isae. 8.15–16; Men. *Dys.* 561–562, 613–614). Two men who knew each other well but did not share sacrifices could be suspected of enmity (Isae. 1.31–32, 9.21).

55. Isae. 2.38, 7.44; cf. 1.31–32.

56. They were often the result of the intervention of friends (Antiph. 6.39; Lys. 32.2, 11; Isae. 5.31; Dem. 34.18, 34.21; [Dem.] 52.30–31, 59.45; Hyp. 3.5), and even when it is unclear who initiated the reconciliation, friends were almost invariably involved in the process (Lys. 4.2, fr. 279.2–3 (Carey); Isae. 2.29–33; Dem. 29.58, 33.14–17, 41.29; [Dem.] 52.21, 59.45–48).

57. Hyams 2003: 201.

58. Arist. *Rh.* 2.4 (1381a8–9, 15–17): καὶ οἱ τοῖς αὐτοῖς φίλοι καὶ οἱ τοῖς αὐτοῖς ἐχθροί [. . .] καὶ τοὺς τοῖς αὐτοῖς ἐχθροὺς καὶ μισοῦντας οὓς αὐτοὶ μισοῦσιν, καὶ τοὺς μισουμένους ὑπὸ τῶν αὐτοῖς μισουμένων. Aristotle asserts that, generally speaking, friends "desire the same things" and share in similar activities.

59. Xen. *Mem.* 2.6.4: πολλοὺς τοῖς φίλοις ἐχθροὺς παρέχειν.

60. Gager 1992: 20; cf. Riess 2012: 177–188.

61. Pl. *Leg.* 11.933b.

62. Gager 1992: 20–21.

63. Pl. *Ap.* 18b–20d. Hunter (1994: 118–119) provides a list of the most common topics of gossip attested in Attic oratory, with accompanying primary source citations.

64. The *Rhetoric to Alexander* (29.16 [1437a22–3]) calls it a "common" (*koinon*) problem, "responsible for many evils" (πολλῶν κακῶν αἴτιον).

65. Hunter 1994: 96–119.

66. Lys. 8.19: πρὸς ὑμᾶς αὐτοὺς τρέψεσθε, κἄπειτα καθ' ἕνα ἕκαστον ὑμῖν αὐτοῖς ἀπεχθήσεσθε, τὸ δὲ τελευταῖον εἰς ὁ λειπόμενος αὐτὸς αὑτὸν κακῶς ἐρεῖ.

67. There were no corporate entities that would mediate the tension as in the modern world. Today one can sue a company rather than the CEO. A physician convicted of malpractice will not pay; his insurance company will. Going to court in Athens was much more personal.

68. This use of the courts for honor games is discussed further on pp. 000–000.

69. Hunt 2010: 185–214.

70. Isocr. 18.28: τὰς ἰδίας ἔχθρας καὶ τοὺς κοινοὺς πολέμους διαλυόμεθα.

71. Cf. the reconciliation at Hdt. 1.22, which blurs the line between private and public.

72. This point has important implications for historical method. Because enmities were formed and sustained by hostile actions, evidence for hostile actions indicates that a relationship of enmity was likely lurking in the background.

73. Dover 1974: 181.

74. See pp. 000–000.

75. Dem. 21.220: μισεῖ Μειδίας ἴσως ἐμέ, ὑμῶν δέ γε ἕκαστον ἄλλος τις. ἆρ' οὖν συγχωρήσαιτ' ἂν τούτῳ, ὅστις ἐστὶν ἕκαστος ὁ μισῶν, κύριον γίγνεσθαι τοῦ ταῦθ' ἅπερ οὗτος ἐμὲ ὑμῶν ἕκαστον ποιῆσαι; ἐγὼ μὲν οὐκ οἶμαι. Translation from Harris 2008. Elsewhere in the speech, Demosthenes compares Meidias (unfavorably, of course) with "many others" who quarreled with each other (62–65).

76. Eur. *Bacch*. 877–880: ἢ τί τὸ κάλλιον / παρὰ θεῶν γέρας ἐν βροτοῖς / ἢ χεῖρ' ὑπὲρ κορυφᾶς / τῶν ἐχθρῶν κρείσσω κατέχειν.

77. Pl. *Phlb*. 49d; Arist. *Rh*. 2.2 (1379b17–19).

78. Xen. *Hier*. 1.34: παρὰ μὲν γὰρ πολεμίων ἀκόντων λαμβάνειν πάντων ἥδιστον ἔγωγε νομίζω εἶναι. Cf. *Mem*. 2.1.19.

79. Eur. *Heracl*. 939–940: ἐκ γὰρ εὐτυχοῦς / ἥδιστον ἐχθρὸν ἄνδρα δυστυχοῦνθ' ὁρᾶν. Cf. Athena's rhetorical question in Sophocles' *Ajax*, "Isn't the most pleasant mockery mocking at one's enemies?" (οὔκουν γέλως ἥδιστος εἰς ἐχθροὺς γελᾶν; 79). In the *Antigone* Creon asserts that the man who has children that will not be a help to him in his old age has actually brought about "much laughter for his enemies" (πολὺν δὲ τοῖσιν ἐχθροῖσιν γέλων, 647). Cf. Soph. *El*. 1153; Eur. *Bacch*. 854; Ar. fr. 597 (Kassel and Austin); Men. *Sam*. 706.

80. "There is nothing funny about laughter in Greek tragedy" (Dillon 1991: 345).

81. *Il*. 18.108–10: καὶ χόλος, ὅς τ' ἐφέηκε πολύφρονά περ χαλεπῆναι, / ὅς τε πολὺ γλυκίων μέλιτος καταλειβομένοιο / ἀνδρῶν ἐν στήθεσσιν ἀέξεται ἠΰτε καπνός. Quoted at Arist. *Rh*. 2.2 (1378b5–7); cf. Thuc. 7.68.1; Arist. *Eth. Nic*. 4.5 (1126a21–22).

82. [Arist.] *Rh. Al*. 7.4 (1428a28): τοὺς ἐχθροὺς ἀτυχεῖν.

83. Cf. Hom. *Il.* 8.147–150, 22.100.
84. Dillon 1991: 348.
85. Versnel 1999.
86. Pl. *Grg.* 480e–481b.
87. The funeral games celebrated to honor the death of Patroclus provide another outlet for competitive feeling, revealing more of this internal struggle for standing. Five of the best of the Achaeans race against each other in chariots, but the rivalry does not stop when the horses do (Hom. *Il.* 23.287–650). First, Antilochus criticizes Achilles' decision to award a prize to Admetus because he was supposedly recognized as the "best" of the competitors despite the fact that his chariot had crashed and so he had not placed (Hom. *Il.* 23.535–585). Then the audience learns that Menelaus is furious with Antilochus for passing him by guile rather than with the strength and swiftness of his horses. His failure to compete in accordance with the unwritten code of conduct demands that he cede his prize. Vergil (*Aen.* 5.348–349) softly mocks Achilles' Greek oversensitivity to status.
88. van Wees 1992: 89.
89. On the concern of Athenian men of the classical period to preserve their honor, see especially Roisman 2005: 64–83.
90. On athletics as a manifestation of ancient Greek competitiveness, see Dover 1974: 229–234; Poliakoff 1987: 104–112; Golden 1998: 28–33. Poliakoff (1987: 115) argues that the athletic *agōn* fulfilled an important societal need as an outlet for the extreme innate competitiveness of the Greeks.
91. Miller 2004: 84. Other religious festivals created events for all manner of things, including drama, music, sculpture, pottery, dancing, and beauty.
92. *De L'esprit des Lois*, IV.8.
93. Pind. *Pyth.* 8.83–87: τοῖς οὔτε νόστος ὁμῶς / ἔπαλπνος ἐν Πυθιάδι κρίθη, / οὐδὲ μολόντων πὰρ ματέρ' ἀμφὶ γέλως γλυκὺς / ὦρσεν χάριν· κατὰ λαύρας δ' ἐχθρῶν ἀπάοροι / πτώσσοντι, συμφορᾷ δεδαγμένοι. Translation from Race 1986.
94. Faraone 1991: 11–12; Gager 1992: 42–46.
95. Dover 1974: 231. Excluding someone from being honored was by implication dishonoring them (Lys. 20.13; cf. Xen. *Lac.* 4.3–4).
96. van Wees 1992: 109. Cf. Hom. *Il.* 23.450–498.
97. That public service could function as a competition for honor among the wealthy leaders is well recognized (Davies 1981: 26; Whitehead 1983; Sinclair 1988: 188–190; Whitehead 1993; Gabrielsen 1994: 48–49; P. Wilson 2000: 144–197; Christ 2006: 171–172).
98. Speakers in the Assembly competed not only for the standing they would gain by general recognition of their abilities but also for the right to have their names inscribed on public stelai (Liddel 2007: 242–243). If a decree passed the Assembly, the typical formula for its inscription would include the name of the proposer, to whom honor would accrue.
99. Aeschin. 3.177–191; cf. Dem. 20.
100. Whitehead (1983; cf. Liddel 2007: 165–167) points out that these decrees

provide evidence for a democratization of the Greek noun *philotimia*, "love of honor," exhorting citizens to show *philotimia* toward the city.

101. *De Cive* (English version—1651) 10.9.

102. Din. fr. 87.126 Sauppe: αἱ γὰρ ἀπὸ τῶν κοινῶν ἔχθραι καὶ πραγματεῖαι αἰτίαι τῶν ἰδίων διαφορῶν καθεστήκασι. Cf. Dem. 19.80. Public speakers who differed on state policy also insulted their opponents' private lives even in orations composed for the Assembly or the law courts (Lys. 14.41, 16.13, 25.10; Aeschin. 1.2; see Mitchell and Rhodes 1996: 21–29). It also worked the other way around: private disputes could become public (Andoc. 1.117–123).

103. The Athenian stranger of the *Laws* anticipates this problem, suggesting that his imaginary state remove the causes for quarrels by dividing up "honors (*timai*) and offices (*archai*)" equally, preempting the strife that results from competition to acquire them (5.744c).

104. On liturgies, see Davies 1981; Gabrielsen 1987; Christ 1990; Veyne 1990: 77–78; Whitehead 1993; Gabrielsen 1994; Johnstone 1999: 93–108; Christ 2006: 143.

105. These were the most prominent liturgies, but there were others, including *hestiasis* (providing a public dinner for one's tribe) and *arrēphoria* (providing for the girls who performed religious services for Athena Parthenos). In times of special need during wartime, the Athenians could also levy a war tax (*eisphora*).

106. Take the example of Nicias, who, using his great wealth, "tried to capture the people by *chorēgiai, gymnasiarchiai*, and other such *philotimiai*" (χορηγίαις ἀνελάμβανε καὶ γυμνασιαρχίαις ἑτέραις τε τοιαύταις φιλοτιμίαις τὸν δῆμον, Plut. *Nic.* 3.2; cf. Lys. 19.18, 21.8, 21.12). For a more negative assessment of the liturgical system, see [Xen.] *Ath. Pol.* 1.13.

107. Following Davies (1981: 91–97), many scholars (e.g., Ober 1989: 231–233; Millett 1991: 123–126; Christ 2006: 181–183; Engen 2010: 45) have asserted that the wealthy performed liturgies so that they could later ask for gratitude (*charis*) from the jury if they became entangled in a court case. Johnstone (1999: 93–108) takes a slightly different approach, pointing out that elite litigants cited the liturgies they had performed to establish their character before the jury. Johnstone's approach more satisfactorily accounts for the evidence, but, regardless of the exact motives behind elites' performance of liturgies or citation of them in court, wealthy citizens certainly seem to have used liturgies to establish their standing and to gain honor among the citizen body. (See, e.g., [Arist.] *Rh. Al.* 2.14 [1424a15–19].) Cf. E. Harris 2013: 129–131.

108. P. Wilson (2000: 109–262) discusses in detail the honor game involved in elite performance of the *chorēgia* and the rivalries that could develop. *Chorēgia* and *philotimia* were intimately linked (see, e.g., Men. *Sam.* 13–14).

109. Isae. 5.36. The similarity between elite rivalry and athletic competition made for readily available analogies from one to the other (e.g., Isocr. 16.32–33; Aeschin. 3.179–180). The stakes were the same: victory, defeat, honor, shame.

110. Dem. 51.1; cf. *IG* II² 1629.190–204, a similar honorary decree by the terms of which the first, second, and third fastest to prepare their ships were to receive crowns and be publicly acclaimed by the herald of the Council so that their *philo-*

timia (202–203) toward the demos might be demonstrated. Christ (2006: 180) asserts that the practice of granting honors to outstanding trierarchs "was not, as far as we know routine," but neither do we know that it was uncommon. What can be said for certain is that it did happen, and it happened more than once.

111. Liddel 2007: 188–191. Contrast the censorious effect of the inscriptions about debtors or those who failed to contribute (Isae. 5.38).

112. Aeschin. 1.2: αἱ γὰρ ἴδιαι ἔχθραι πολλὰ πάνυ τῶν κοινῶν ἐπανορθοῦσι.

113. Complaints: Lys. 16.3, 16.11; Dem. 21.111. Assumptions that enmity was a common motivation for speaking at a *dokimasia*: Lys. 26.15, 31.2. A famous example of enmity-inspired prosecution at a *dokimasia* is the Demosthenes vs. Aeschines trial on the embassy (Dem. 19; Aeschin. 2).

114. The more *philotimia* an Athenian exhibited in performing his liturgies, the more enemies he was likely to make. The speaker in Lysias 7 (*On the Olive Stump*) explains that his zeal in performing liturgies caused him to become a target of malicious prosecution, probably implying that he had made powerful and wealthy enemies, who have now employed a prosecutor-for-hire as he alleges (39–40); *pace* P. Wilson 2000: 361 n. 98; Todd 2007: 536.

115. Assumption that liturgists generally made enemies: Antiph. 6.11. See also P. Wilson's (2000: 118–119) observation based on this passage that "enemies could be expected to be made, fines levied and force brought to bear."

116. Christ 2006: 194–195. Gabrielsen (1994: 73–78, 81–84) argues that the selection of trierarchs was performed mechanically and therefore would not be subject to personal influence. Cf. Hamel (1998: 28–31), who maintains that generals had discretion over the allocation of particular ships and expeditions to individual trierarchs. Regardless of the technical details, Christ is surely right to conclude from the available sources that the procedure was subject to influence and manipulation in some manner.

117. Ar. *Eq.* 912–914: ἐγώ σε ποιήσω τριηραρχεῖν / ἀναλίσκοντα τῶν / σαυτοῦ, παλαιὰν ναῦν ἔχοντ'. Cf. the scholion *ad loc.*, which explains the typical politics of enmity: "because the generals would put up their enemy, if they had one, for a trierarchy so that his livelihood would be squandered on it" (ἐπειδὴ οἱ στρατηγοί, εἴ τινα εἶχον ἐχθρόν, εἰς τριηραρχίαν ἐνέβαλλον, ὅπως ἂν αὐτῷ ὁ βίος ἀναλίσκοιτο). Cf. also Lys. 29.3.

118. The fiscal burden of liturgies could be oppressive (Xen. *Oec.* 2.4–6; cf. Lys. 32.24; see Davies 1981: 82–83; Christ 2006: 172).

119. Andoc. 1.132. The archon would appoint *chorēgoi* (Arist. *Ath. Pol.* 56.3). There is, however, disagreement over what "appoint" means in this context (Hamel 1998: 14–23).

120. Lys. 28.4, 29.4; Davies 1981: 67; Millett 1991: 87.

121. Gabrielsen 1994: 99–101. The existence of the practice of hiring out trierarchies (*misthōsis trierarchias*) demonstrates that at least some Athenians actively desired to outfit and sail one of the city's ships. This is only one of the ways in which elites could benefit financially from their privileged position (Millett 1991: 85–86).

122. On *antidosis*, see A. R. W. Harrison 1968–1971, ii: 236–238; MacDowell 1978: 162–164; Gabrielsen 1987; Christ 1990; MacDowell 1990: 1–2; Christ 2006: 159–160, 197–198. Christ (1990: 163–164) concludes from the ancient testimonia that *antidosis* was frequently employed. Such attempts to dodge liturgies (Christ 2006: 143–204) were often at someone else's expense.

123. Gabrielsen 1994: 95; cf. Christ's (2006: 155) negative judgment that the liturgy system "was considerably less effective and more troubled than [. . .] others have allowed."

124. *Antidoseis* leading to enmity: Lys. 4; Dem. 21.77–82, 42.

125. For example, disputes between trierarchs arose in the annual exchange of ships (Dem. 47; [Dem.] 50). Service as trierarch lasted one year, at the end of which the trierarch would hand over his warship, which was public property, to the next trierarch. Another attested area of conflict was abuse of the system of symmories instituted in the fourth century. This institution was supposed to alleviate the financial burden of the trierarchy, but it may have caused even more problems. If we may believe Demosthenes, the less wealthy members of such groups often complained that the head of a symmory could extort his fellow contributors so that he had to pay little or nothing himself (Dem. 18.104, 21.155).

126. In addition to the prestige and influence that accompanied participation in politics was the allure of financial benefit from a role in leadership (Millett 1991: 85–86).

127. Andoc. 4.1.

128. The rhetoric could get nasty. In one passage Demosthenes argues that the state ought to execute publicly his political opponents who wanted to make peace with Philip (*phanerōs apotympanisai*, 10.63). Other politicians commissioned formal curses against each other (Faraone 1991: 16; Gager 1992: 119).

129. Such trials often took the form of *eisangelia* (impeachment), *apocheirotonia* (a vote in the Assembly to depose a public official from office), or *euthynai* (the automatic exit examinations that all public officials were required to undergo). See Roberts 1982: 55–83.

130. Another man who made enemies through his political activity was Ephialtes, who prosecuted individual members of the Areopagus to undermine its power during the democratic reforms of the 460s (Arist. *Ath. Pol.* 25.2; Plut. *Per.* 10.7). Unfortunately for Ephialtes, these men did not think litigation a sufficient remedy; they assassinated him.

131. Xen. *Mem.* 2.1.3: τί δέ; τὸ μαθεῖν, εἴ τι ἐπιτήδειόν ἐστι μάθημα πρὸς τὸ κρατεῖν τῶν ἀντιπάλων, ποτέρῳ ἂν προσθεῖναι μᾶλλον πρέποι; πολὺ νὴ Δί', ἔφη, τῷ ἄρχειν παιδευομένῳ· καὶ γὰρ τῶν ἄλλων οὐδὲν ὄφελος ἄνευ τῶν τοιούτων μαθημάτων.

132. Wünsch *Def. tab.* 34, 45. See Eidinow 2007: 156–164. That there was also virulent competition among the playwrights is obvious from Aristophanes' *parabaseis*.

133. Rubinstein 2000: 91–111.

134. On the distinction between private citizens (*idiōtai*) and the well-known

public speakers (*rhētores*), see Connor 1971: 116–117; Hansen 1983a, 1983b; Ober 1989: 104–127; Rubinstein 1998.

135. On deme liturgies, see Wyse 1967: 267; Whitehead 1986: 150–152. *Chorēgia, gymnasiarchia, hestiasis,* and women's liturgies are attested for the deme level.

136. Honorary decrees provided by the community or dedications set up by an individual were legion. Many magistrates dedicated inscriptions to celebrate their terms in office as a form of self-advertisement (Liddel 2007: 250–253).

137. See esp. Dem. 57.63 and the discussion in chapter 3; cf. Isae. 12.12; Ar. *Nub.* 37.

138. Aspiring orators may well have cut their teeth at the local level before attempting to move on to the big stage at Athens. On the other hand, some evidence points to two distinct groups of people being active at the deme level and at the city level. There is very little prosopographical evidence for leaders at the deme level continuing on to the more vigorous politics of the city (Osborne 1985a: 83–87; Whitehead 1986: 313–326; cf. Jones 1999: 46). In any case, local politics were important, and many more people than elite politicians were engaged in them.

139. *P. Oxy.* 1606 fr. 6 col. iv = fr. 151.256–258 (Carey); Isae. 5.40. Consider also the enemies that the banker Pasion made in his disagreements with lessees (Isocr. 17; Dem. 36; [Dem.] 49.6–32, 52.12–15). Aristotle (*Rh.* 2.4 [1381b14–16]) assumes such competition to be normal. On Pasion (d. 370/69), the most famous banker of classical Athens and father of the orator Apollodorus, see Schäfer 1949; Bogaert 1968; Trevett 1992: 1–11, 155–165.

140. The great volume of litigation generated by financial disputes is mentioned several times in Plato's *Republic*. Socrates proposes that the "guardian" class be prohibited from having private possessions lest they "become enemies of the other citizens and spend their entire lives hating and being hated, making plots and being plotted against" (ἐχθροὶ [. . .] τῶν ἄλλων πολιτῶν γενήσονται, μισοῦντες δὲ δὴ καὶ μισούμενοι καὶ ἐπιβουλεύοντες καὶ ἐπιβουλευόμενοι διάξουσι πάντα τὸν βίον, 3.417b; cf. 5.464d–e, 7.521a, 8.549d; *Leg.* 3.678e–679c, 5.737b, 11.915d–916a). Elsewhere he compares Athenian legislative attempts to stop cheating on contracts to "cutting off the heads of a Hydra" (*Resp.* 4.426e).

141. Faraone 1991: 11; Gager 1992: 151–154; Eidinow 2007: 191–205.

142. Workshops: Wünsch *Def. tab.* 68, 71, 74, 75, 84 (cf. 87); Audollent *Def. tab.* 71. Cf. Audollent *Def. tab.* 70, which curses two taverns by name (the "Olympus" and the "Agathon"). Profits: Wünsch *Def. tab.* 86; cf. Audollent *Def. tab.* 52 (*aphormē*, "capital"). Art: Wünsch *Def. tab.* 73; Audollent *Def. tab.* 52; *SEG* 47:274. Work: Wünsch *Def. tab.* 52, 68, 69, 71, 74, 86, 87, 89, 97, 109; Audollent *Def. tab.* 47, 52, 70, 71, 72, 73; Jordan 1985b: 164, no. 43; Oikonomidēs, Peek, and Vanderpool (Kerameikos III C 9).

143. Faraone (1991) points to the "agonistic context" of Greek curse tablets. Cf. Riess 2012: 164–234. These *katadesmoi* ("binding spells") often assume some sort of competition that has led to the inscribing of the curse. Cf. Eidinow 2007: 4, 154–155.

144. Roisman (2005: 50–51) points out that the ideology of *oikos* solidarity

was not always put into practice, citing disputes over inheritances that involved adopted children. Cox (1998: 68–129) discusses friction between every conceivable family connection, arguing that conflict permeated the family structure in ancient Greece. See also Knox 1979: 20–23; Golden 1990: 105–114; Millett 1991: 130–132, 136–139; Christ 1998b: 168–173; Roy 1999: 7–8.

145. Arist. *Ath. Pol.* 9.2; Pl. *Leg.* 11.928d–e. At Lys. 24.14 the phrase "disputing over an heiress" is treated as equivalent to bringing a frivolous charge (cf. Ar. *Vesp.* 583–586).

146. A. R. W. Harrison (1968–1971, i: 122–123) states succinctly, "The rules were in the fourth century both complicated and fluid, and this gave play to litigation and the skill of the logographer." Lipsius (1905–1915: 537) commented, "Kein Teil des attischen Privatrechts bereitet unserer Darstellung gröfsere Schwierigkeiten als das Erbrecht" ["No part of Attic private law presents greater difficulty to our exposition than testamentary law"]. Cf. W. Thompson 1981: 13; Cox 1998: 84–92, 109–114. Roman law seems to have suffered from a similar affliction. Eleven out of the fifty books of the *Digest* are devoted to the inheritance law. "One must admit that in will-making the idiosyncrasies of humanity are at their most abundant and generate a lot of law" (Crook 1984: 118). These disputes have a long history in ancient literature (cf. Hes. *Erga* 27–41).

147. Isae. 4.8–9, 7.1–2. Cf. the argument at Dem. 44.63.

148. For the law, see Isae. 2.1, 2.14, 2.19; Dem. 48.56; [Dem.] 46.14. The Aristotelian *Athenian Constitution* (35.2) cites this provision as a special incentive to vexatious litigators.

149. For the lengths to which some went to secure their wills, see Scafuro 1997: 42–50.

150. Even when claimants did not dispute the status of the will, questions could arise over who actually possessed the money and whether they held it rightfully (Lys. 19.24–27; Dem. 41.5–6; cf. Lys. 20.33, 24.6; see Cox 1998: 85). Another fertile source of enmity within the *oikos* was the practice of guardianship (Lys. fr. 174 [Carey]; Isae. 1, 5, 7, 11; Dem. 27–31, 36, 38; [Dem.] 45; cf. Pl. *Resp.* 8.554c).

151. Lys. 7.18; Dem. 55.1; cf. Lys. fr. 1.3–4 (Carey). See Humphreys 1985: 313–316.

152. Jones 2004: 57–59.

153. That the inscription (*IG* II² 1177.22) orders the *horistai* to set up the decree implies that they were responsible for overseeing certain physical monuments. Whether or not they were responsible for regulating private *horoi* is not clear.

154. Pl. *Leg.* 8.843b–c: τὸ δὲ μετὰ τοῦτο βλάβαι πολλαὶ καὶ σμικραὶ γειτόνων γιγνόμεναι, διὰ τὸ θαμίζειν ἔχθρας ὄγκον μέγαν ἐντίκτουσαι, χαλεπὴν καὶ σφόδρα πικρὰν γειτονίαν ἀπεργάζονται.

155. Some Athenians attempted to avoid such wrangling and keep out of court, but it apparently required a lot of effort. On such "quietism," see Carter 1986; Lanni 2010: 58–64.

156. Serious insults resulting from intoxication: Ar. *Eccl.* 663–664, *Vesp.* 1253–1255, 1444–1445; Antiph. 4; Dem. 54; Arist. *Pol.* 2.12 (1274b18–23). To preempt sus-

picions of enmity, some litigants felt compelled to deny specifically that they were involved in such activities with their opponents (Lys. 1.43–45; Dem. 47.19). For the comic exploitation of such motifs, see Men. *Dys.* 59–60, *Sam.* 340–341.

157. Lys. 3; Isae. 3.13; Dem. 21.38; [Dem.] 59.30–47. Cf. the lovers' quarrel's famous precedent, the story of Harmodius and Aristogiton (Thuc. 6.54–59).

158. Lys. 1; [Dem.] 59.65.

159. Jordan 1985a: no. 8.4–5: μὴ δυνηθῶσιν ὁμ[ο]ῦ λαλῆσαι, μὴ περιπα[τῆσαι,] / μὴ ἰς τὸ ἐργαστήριν τὸ Ἰουλιανῆς δυνηθοῖσιν καθ[ίζειν]. Cf. Audollent *Def. tab.* 68. On curses inspired by affairs of the heart, see Eidinow 2007: 206–224.

160. See p. 000.

161. Isocr. 1.33; cf. Isae. 1.9.

162. Xen. *Mem.* 3.13.1; Dem. 18.269; cf. Arist. *Rh.* 2.2 (1379a30–32); Theophr. *Char.* 15. The animosities resulting from insults in epic and tragedy hardly need comment (e.g., the Achilles-Agamemnon dispute in the *Iliad*, Ajax's insult of Athena in Sophocles' *Ajax* [770–777]).

163. Blundell 1989: 47.

164. On the centrality of the *oikos*, see Lacey 1968: 84–99; MacDowell 1978: 84–108; Patterson 1998: 83–91; Roy 1999; E. Cohen 2000: 32–38; cf. MacDowell 1989. Litigants could present their family to the jury to gain sympathy (Hall 1995) because punishment of a *kurios*, even if directed against him personally, was a de facto punishment of the entire household. On the duty to help one's kinsmen, see Dover 1974: 275–276; Millett 1991: 127–129.

165. Strauss 1993: 77; Cox 1998: 80–81. Conversely, reconciliations from the previous generation were also expected to hold good (Dem. 40.46).

166. On the close connection of the son's interests, character, and relationships with his father, see Golden 1990: 101–105; Strauss 1993: 21–99; Cox 1998: 78–84. Even guilt and religious pollution could be transmitted from father to son: if jurors broke their oath, a curse would fall upon them—but also upon their offspring (Andoc. 1.31; see Pomeroy 1997: 83–85).

167. Lys. 10.3, 14.2 and *passim*; Isocr. 16.2–3; Dem. 57.61; [Dem.] 58.2. Cf. Dem. 20.144, in which the speaker refers to "Apsephion here" (*toutoui*), implying that he is present as a co-speaker, and to Leptines' indictment of Apsephion's father, who is now dead. Apsephion is taking up the fight for the family honor. See also Libanius' *hypothesis* to Dem. 25.

168. Lys. 32.22. The speaker of *On the Estate of Dicaeogenes* is probably speaking of such inherited enemies when he accuses his opponent of betraying young orphans and handing over their wealth "to their enemies" (Isae. 5.10). This is also possibly the case with the passage from Plato's *Charmides* discussed above (pp. 000–000).

169. Andoc. 1.141; Lys. 14.40; Dem. 25.65–66; Aeschin. 3.169.

170. A. R. W. Harrison 1968–1971, ii: 124–130.

171. Lys. 17.1–3, 19.1, fr. 50 (Carey); Dem. 36.20, 38.6, 47.32, 49.1; [Dem.] 52. Cf. Dem. 55, in which the speaker has been sued because of his father's construc-

tion of a wall around his property. For prosecutions of other relatives in their capacity as heirs, see Isae. 10.15–16; Dem. 35.3–4.

172. Isae. 2.13, 3.68.

173. A son should pursue his father's enemies whether they owe him money or "have done anything else wrong" (Pl. *Resp.* 8549e: ἤ τι ἄλλο ἀδικοῦντα).

174. Lys. 13.42–43; cf. Antiph. 1.29–30.

175. Soph. *Ant.* 641–643: τούτου γὰρ οὕνεκ' ἄνδρες εὔχονται γονὰς / κατηκόους φύσαντες ἐν δόμοις ἔχειν, / ὡς καὶ τὸν ἐχθρὸν ἀνταμύνωνται κακοῖς.

176. Eur. *Med.* 920–921: ἴδοιμι δ' ὑμᾶς εὐτραφεῖς ἥβης τέλος / μολόντας, ἐχθρῶν τῶν ἐμῶν ὑπερτέρους. Cf. *Supp.* 544–546; *Heracl.* 1000–1003.

177. Arist. *Rh.* 2.21 (1395a18): νήπιος ὃς πατέρα κτείνας παῖδας καταλείπει. Cf. Lys. 12.36, 14.30.

178. Athenian homicide law reflects this ideology of family solidarity. Because the members of an *oikos* must avenge their own, only relatives of the deceased could bring charges for murder. This provision was no mere relic of a forgotten Draconian past; it was still in force in the fourth century.

179. Lys. 13.42–43; cf. 92. Lysias' description of Dionysodorus' last wishes draws upon what seems to have been a commonplace scene in which a dying man adjures his friends and family to avenge him (compare Antiph. 1.29).

180. The speaker refers to Dionysius as present, using an epideictic pronoun (*toutōii*, 41).

181. E.g., Lys. 32; Dem. 30; cf. Lys. 20, a *synēgoria* speech on behalf of the speaker's father, at least for the portion following § 11. It is possible that the transmitted text is actually two speeches (see Rubinstein 2000: 153–154).

182. Millett 1991: 130; Cox 1998: 109; Roisman 2005: 46–50.

183. Dem. 23.56. The most basic division among social relationships was between *echthroi* and *philoi*. Kinsmen were a special type of *philoi* because they were automatically friends (although cf. Konstan 1997, esp. pp. 53–56).

184. Men. *Sam.* 518: συναδικοῦ γνησίως ὡς ἂν φίλος. Cf. Arist. *Rh.* 1.12 (1372b37–1373a4).

185. Pl. *Resp.* 4.424a, *Leg.* 5.739c; cf. Arist. *Eth. Nic.* 9.2 (1165a).

186. See also the discussion on pp. 000–000.

187. Perhaps the most famous instance is the case of Timarchus, who prosecuted Aeschines on Demosthenes' behalf but was preempted by Aeschines' successful prosecution by *dokimasia rhētorōn* (Aeschin. 1). Demosthenes in turn accused Aeschines of sending hired attackers against him while failing ever to prosecute Demosthenes himself (Dem. 18.249–251). Demosthenes had previously accused Meidias of similar tactics. Meidias supposedly hired Euctemon to prosecute Demosthenes, then paid the relatives of a deceased man to put Demosthenes on trial for murder (Dem. 21.103–104). Cf. [Dem.] 53.1–2, in which Apollodorus cites his decision not to hire out the prosecution as an exceptional mark of his confidence in the truth of his claims. Defendants often complain that one of their enemies is attacking them through a proxy (Antiph. 6.34–36; Andoc. 1.118–123, 2.4; Lys. 7.39–

40; Isae. 8.3; cf. Antiph. 5.33; Isocr. 16.7; Isae. 9.24; Dem. 24.14, 39.2; [Dem.] 53.14, 59.10; Aeschin. 2.154; Xen. *Mem.* 2.9.5).

188. Dem. 55.34; [Dem.] 59.

189. For the "extreme adversariality" of Athenian law, see Todd 1993: 67–68. Modern legal scholars divide the institutional methods for administering justice into two types, adversarial and inquisitorial. In the former, the judge acts basically as an "umpire" between two litigants who are engaged in a set-piece battle, while in the latter the judge interrogates witnesses himself and generally attempts to find out the truth on his own.

190. Lavency (1964: 80) also recognized that "les impératifs de la vie sociale athénienne sont tels que le procès réalisera moins l'opposition de deux individus que la confrontation de deux groups" ["The necessary operations of Athenian social life made the process less a conflict between two individuals than a confrontation between two groups"]. For a fuller treatment of the communal aspects of litigation, see Rubinstein 2000: 24–75.

191. Rubinstein 2000: 58–59, 158. *Synēgoriai*: Lys. 5, 6, 13–15, 20, 27, 32; Isocr. 21; Isae. 2, 4, 6, 12; Dem. 18, 20, 22, 25, 26, 29, 34, 36, 43, 44; [Dem.] 59; Hyp. 1, 3, 4; Din. 1, 2, 3.

192. Lys. 5.1, 21.17, 27.12; Isocr. 21.1; Isae. 1.7, 4.1, 7.10; Dem. 20.1, 36.1; Lycurg. 1.138; cf. Andoc. 1.150 (fellow tribesmen); Lys. 14.20. Appearing as an advocate could be viewed as a relatively minor service to pay a friend (Isae. 6.2).

193. Lys. 15.5; Isae. 3.19–22, 5.8, 9.25, 12.1, 12.4; Dem. 29.22–24, 37.48; [Dem.] 52.17; Aeschin. 1.47. A litigant can land a damaging blow to his opponent's credibility if he can prove that his opponent's friends and family do not support him (Isae. 1.2, 2.33). On the function of witnesses in Athenian law, see Humphreys 1985; Todd 1990b; Carey 1994a, 1995; Hall 1995; Mirhady 2002; Rubinstein 2005; Thür 2005; Gagarin 2007. Much debate has centered on the legal purposes of witnesses since Humphreys (1985) argued that witnesses were not expected to be impartial but rather to support one of the two litigants.

194. Lys. 8.18, 18.24.

195. E.g., [Dem.] 52.17; Isae. 12.4; cf. [Arist.] *Rh. Al.* 15.5 (1431b37–41).

196. The speaker of *Against the Stepmother* goes so far as to accuse the defense team of being murderers themselves by opposing him (Antiph. 1.2, 4).

197. A prosecutor might accuse an opponent's advocates of complicity in his crimes (Lycurg. 1.138; cf. Lys. 14.22, 26.23–24, 27.13, 30.31–35; Aeschin. 3.257).

198. Dem. 25.44: ἵν' ὡς εἰς ἐλαχίστους τὴν βλασφημίαν ἀγάγω.

199. [Dem.] 58.59; cf. Dem. 19.221.

200. Din. 1 (*Against Demosthenes*).112: κακόνους ἐστὶ τῇ πολιτείᾳ; Din. 1 (*Against Demosthenes*).113: κοινοὺς ἐχθροὺς εἶναι τῶν νόμων καὶ τῆς πόλεως ἁπάσης.

201. The speaker of *Against Eubulides* shows that a litigant could consider any witness who appeared against him an enemy. He complains that Eubulides attacked him in a deme meeting and caused his disfranchisement because of the role he had played as witness in a previous trial against Eubulides (Dem. 57.8).

202. [Arist.] *Rh. Al.* 15.4 (1431b33–36).
203. Anyone providing testimony made himself *hypodikos*, "liable to be put on trial" (Isae. 12.8). The *diamartyria* procedure would have caused even more problems for witnesses since testimony became the centerpiece. This procedure consisted of a formal declaration of fact by a witness who was presumed to have intimate knowledge of the point at issue. If a litigant objected, he would have to bring a *dikē pseudomartyriōn* against this key witness.
204. Lys. 10.12, 22, 24–25; Isae. 3.3–4, 5.12–13; Dem. 29, 47; [Dem.] 45, 53.15.
205. Dem. 19.237–238.
206. Aeschin. 3.171–172.
207. Aeschin. 3.172: ἵνα μὴ πολλοῖς ἀπεχθάνωμαι. Attacks on an opponent's mother or wife such as this were common. Hunter (1994: 111–116) has illustrated how female relatives were especially susceptible to such abuse since "gossip" about them was nearly impossible to refute. See also Henderson 1987. Demosthenes, in his defense speech against Aeschines, voices a similar concern. He names Eubulus and Cephisophon as Aeschines' supporters in the peace talks with Philip but refuses to speculate on their motivations (18.21; cf. Dem. 25.43–46, 25.79; Aeschin. 1.193). Speaking against someone in such a public venue was tantamount to declaring enmity.
208. Cf. Isaeus 3, in which the speaker attempts to prove that his opponent's niece is a high-class prostitute (*hetaira*). He seems to revel in drawing attention to her occupation (11). Cf. Andoc. 1.47; Lys. 13.65–68; Isae. 6.50, 8.1.
209. The curse tablets cited here can all be dated to fourth-century Attica (Faraone 1991).
210. Wünsch *Def. tab.* 39, 66, 81, 88, 103, 106, 107, 129; Audollent *Def. tab.* 62, 63; *SEG* 40.265, 42.217; Jordan (1985b) 165.49, 51; Oikonomidēs et al. (Kerameikos III C 4); Ziebarth (1934) No 3. See Eidinow 2007: 165–190. The word *syndikos* was often used interchangeably with *synēgoros* (Rubinstein 2000: 42–45) but may also have had wider application to all of one's opponent's associates. Cf. Humphreys 2010.
211. Wünsch *Def. tab.* 39: ᾿Αρ]ιφράδης / [Κ]λεοφῶν / ᾿Αρχέδαμος / Πολύξενος / ᾿Αντικράτης / ᾿Αντιφάνης / Ζάκορος / ᾿Αντιχάρης / Σάτυρα / Μίκα / Σίμων / ἡ Σατίρας / μήτηρ / Φεοδώρα / θο ... s / ... λο[υ]μένη / ῎Ανταμις / Εὐκολίνη / ᾿Αμεινίας / καὶ τοὺς τούτων / συνδίκο(υ)s πάντας / καὶ φίλους.
212. *Synēgoroi*: Wünsch *Def. tab.* 38, 63, 65, 95; Audollent *Def. tab.* 60; *SEG* 44.226. Witnesses: Wünsch *Def. tab.* 25, 65, 68, 94; Audollent *Def. tab.* 49, 63. The *Rhetoric to Alexander* (15.5 [1431b37–41]) states that a witness might be motivated by the desire for revenge on the litigant.
213. Wünsch *Def. tab.* 38: Φιλιππίδης / Εὐθύκριτος / Κλεάγορος / Μενέτιμος / καὶ το(ὺ)s ἄλλο(υ)s πάντας / ἢ ὅσοι συν[ήγο]ροι αὐτο[ῖs].
214. Curses against family and households: Wünsch *Def. tab.* 59, 68, 69, 77, 84, 102; Audollent *Def. tab.* 46, 47, 50; H. Thompson 1936: 181.
215. Arist. *Rh.* 1.12 (1372b31–32): τοὺς ὑπὸ πολλῶν ἀδικηθέντας καὶ μὴ ἐπεξελθόντας.

216. Arist. *Rh.* 1.12 (1372b31–33). The Mysians lived in northwest Asia Minor and were notoriously cowardly.

217. Roisman 2006. Socrates assumes that his enemies could easily be persuaded to speak against him as witnesses (Pl. *Ap.* 33c–34b).

218. Dem. 57.2, 7, 17. The speaker repeatedly refers to his opponents as "those in league with Eubulides," or "those in Eubulides' group" (13, 16, 59, 60–61). Cf. Andoc. 2.4; Isocr. 21.8; Isae. 12.12. On the typical language of conspiracy, see Roisman 2006: 2–7. This tactic is recommended by Anaximenes ([Arist.] *Rh. Al.* 29.13 [1437a10–11]).

219. On such gangs, see Fisher 1999: 56–59.

220. Wünsch *Def. tab.* 37, 39, 57, 67, 75, 79, 83, 94, 103; Audollent *Def. tab.* 60, 61, 67.

221. Wünsch *Def. tab.* 107: [τ]ὰ πράττει καὶ τὰ περὶ ἐμο(ῦ) βο(υ)λε[ύ]εται.

222. D. Cohen (1995: 67) posits three main incentives that drove Athenians to participate in relationships of enmity: fear of shame and pursuit of honor, pleasure, and deterrence.

CHAPTER 2

1. As Lavency (1964: 175) puts it, "Les logographes ne pouvaient connaître d'autre règle déontologique que la recherché inconditionnelle du succès" ["Logographers could not countenance any rule of conduct other than unconditional pursuit of victory"]. Cf. Bateman 1958. The meticulousness of speechwriters in ancient Athens was proverbial (Arist. *Rh.* 3.12 [1413b13]).

2. Johnstone (1999: 1–8) shows how the decision to move the dispute from the private sphere to the courtroom has important consequences for how the parties deploy their strategies.

3. Herman 1993: 416–417; Carey 1994b: 40–41; Wolpert 2001: 418–420; Todd 2007: 51. Cf. Porter (1997), who argues that Lysias 1 has elements from the "comic adultery scenario" known from Attic playwrights. He goes too far in concluding that the speech must be a forgery because of its comic elements.

4. Lys. 1.6–7, 10; cf. fr. 443 (Carey).

5. Usher (1965) shows that Lysias commonly had his clients admit some venial blemishes to add verisimilitude to their narratives. Lysias was not the only speechwriter to take this tack. For example, the speaker of *Against Eubulides* acknowledges his low birth and his mother's servile occupation, both serious reproaches to an Athenian citizen (Dem. 57.25, 30–31, 36, 45; cf. Isocr. 17).

6. On the "rhetorical situation" as a technical term in rhetorical theory, see especially Bitzer (1968).

7. See pp. 000–000.

8. Lys. 1.43: πλὴν ταύτης.

9. Plut. *De Garrulitate* 5 (504C): οὐχ ἅπαξ μέλλεις λέγειν αὐτὸν ἐπὶ τῶν δικαστῶν;

10. Arist. *Rh.* 1.2 (1357a34–36): τὸ μὲν γὰρ εἰκός ἐστι τὸ ὡς ἐπὶ τὸ

πολὺ γινόμενον, οὐχ ἁπλῶς δὲ καθάπερ ὁρίζονταί τινες, ἀλλὰ τὸ περὶ τὰ ἐνδεχόμενα ἄλλως ἔχειν.

11. A syllogism in the modern, not Aristotelian, sense. Aristotle's terms are confusing because modern terminology has not maintained his distinctions between "enthymeme" and "syllogism." Aristotle uses "syllogism" to describe an argument whose premises are scientific, while an "enthymeme" has an element of uncertainty and therefore of probability, because it is based on what usually happens or is perceived to happen (Kennedy 1963: 97–98; cf. Walton 2001: 97–99; Kraus 2006: 146–148; on "enthymeme," see Kremmydas 2007). In modern parlance, "syllogism" covers both categories, simply describing the process of combining two statements to form a conclusion through deductive reasoning. The modern distinction between "objective" and "subjective" probability arguments (see Schmitz 2000: 47–50) is of little practical value when it comes to the study of classical rhetoric since the definition of a "scientific premise" depends on the subjective expectations of the listener. If a juror in classical Athens believed that someone who angered the gods was just as sure to suffer misfortune as a ball is sure to fall when dropped, then both probabilities are of similar value to a litigant at trial, regardless of the reservations that a philosopher or scientist may express about this line of reasoning.

12. Goebel 1989: 42; Schmitz 2000: 49–50.

13. [Arist.] *Rh. Al.* 7.4 (1428a25–34): εἰκὸς μὲν οὖν ἐστιν, οὗ λεγομένου παραδείγματα ἐν ταῖς διανοίαις ἔχουσιν οἱ ἀκούοντες. λέγω δ' οἷον εἴ τις φαίη τὴν πατρίδα βούλεσθαι μεγάλην εἶναι καὶ τοὺς οἰκείους εὖ πράττειν καὶ τοὺς ἐχθροὺς ἀτυχεῖν καὶ τὰ τούτοις ὅμοια, <τοιαῦτα> συλλήβδην εἰκότα δόξειεν <ἄν>. ἕκαστος γὰρ τῶν ἀκουόντων σύνοιδεν αὐτὸς αὑτῷ περὶ τούτων καὶ τῶν τούτοις ὁμοιοτρόπων ἔχοντι τοιαύτας ἐπιθυμίας. ὥστε τοῦτο δεῖ παρατηρεῖν ἡμᾶς ἐν τοῖς λόγοις ἀεί εἰ τοὺς ἀκούοντας συνειδότας ληψόμεθα περὶ τοῦ πράγματος οὗ λέγομεν· τούτοις γὰρ αὐτοὺς εἰκός ἐστι μάλιστα πιστεύειν. Translation from Mayhew and Mirhady 2011. Cf. Pl. *Phdr.* 271d–272c, 273b. Kraus (2006) argues that the idea of the audience's presuppositions is built into the very term *eikos*.

14. Gagarin 2007: 12–13.

15. Or even earlier: Gagarin (1994) contends that arguments from probability predated the early sophists and should not be ascribed to them.

16. The well-known story about the lawsuit between Corax and Tisias is a good example. Tisias, who had received rhetorical instruction from Corax, refused to pay and so found himself accused of defaulting before a court of law. Tisias argued that the situation admitted of only two possibilities. If he had received adequate instruction in rhetoric from Corax, then he would win the case. If he lost the case, then obviously Corax had not taught him well enough to deserve his fees. In either case, Tisias should not be forced to pay. Cf. Plato's anecdote about Tisias (*Phdr.* 273b–c) and Aristotle's (*Rh.* 2.24 [1402a17–24]) example of the malleability of Corax's "art."

17. Cole (1991) suggests that the stories about Tisias and Corax refer to a sin-

gle original individual, but the rays of light illuminating this episode in history are dim.

18. Soph. *OR* 583–591.
19. Kennedy 1963: 30–31.
20. Gagarin 1994: 50–51. Another notable practitioner of *eikos* arguments was Gorgias (*Defense of Helen* and *Palamedes*).
21. For example, "A speaker must always pursue probability and bid 'farewell' to truth" (πάντως λέγοντα τὸ δὴ εἰκὸς διωκτέον εἶναι, πολλὰ εἰπόντα χαίρειν τῷ ἀληθεῖ, Pl. *Phdr.* 272e).
22. Dem. 57.51. Another example of making a virtue out of a vice is Lys. 29.1. The speaker's lack of supporters is supposed to prove that the defendant, Philocrates, is guilty of withholding the money that the speaker alleges; Philocrates must have paid off all his accusers.
23. [Arist.] *Rh. Al.* 7.5–6 (1428a34–1428b16).
24. [Arist.] *Rh. Al.* 7.9 (1428b23–24): ἀπὸ τῶν ἀντιδίκων αὐτῶν τὸ εἰκὸς λαμβάνειν.
25. Discussions of character as a type of *eikos* argument: Russell 1990; Scafuro 1997: 56–66; Hoffman 2008. Cf. Wisse (1989: 33–35), who understands Aristotle's formulation of a "rational" *ēthos* along the same lines, and Bateman (1962), who points to arguments *e contrario* based on *ēthos*, which parallel and sometimes overlap with plausibility arguments from character.
26. See Pearson 1981: 99–102. Cf. Dem. 36 (and the discussion at Pearson 1981: 47–51).
27. In a *paragraphē* the litigants switch roles, the defendant prosecuting the original prosecutor for an unlawful prosecution. If the man who was originally the defendant won the *paragraphē* trial, then the first lawsuit was voided. It is unclear what happened if he lost. Either the original prosecutor automatically won the suit, or the jury delivered a separate verdict. See Lipsius 1905–1915: 846–858; A. R. W. Harrison 1968–1971, ii: 106–124; MacDowell 1978: 214–217, 219; Carawan 2011.
28. Dem. 37.2, 3, 8, 13, 17, 18, 24, 35, 41, 45, 49, 52, 53.
29. Dem. 37.48: καίτοι τὸν ἐκείνους ἐξηπατηκότα τοὺς δικαστάς, ἆρα ὀκνήσειν ὑμᾶς ἐξαπατᾶν οἴεσθε. Translation from MacDowell 2004.
30. Dem. 37.45: ἵν' εἰδῆθ' ὅτι καὶ νῦν οὐδὲν οὔτ' ἀναιδείας οὔτε τοῦ ψεύδεσθαι παραλείψει. Translation from MacDowell 2004.
31. [Arist.] *Rh. Al.* 7.8 (1428b19–20): ἐπιδείκνυε αὐτὸν τοῦτο τὸ πρᾶγμα πολλάκις πεποιηκότα πρότερον, εἰ δὲ μή, ὅμοια τούτῳ. For the converse, see the advice to defendants: [Arist.] *Rh. Al.* 7.10 (1428b33–36); cf. 36.32–33 (1443b33–37).
32. Speechwriters may even have avoided explicit use of formulaic *eikos* constructions because of their associations in contemporary thought with sophistic wrangling (Dover 1968: 57).
33. Romilly 2012: 43.
34. Cf. Dewald 1999, a narratological analysis of the opening passages of Herodotus and Thucydides.

35. In a technical sense, *ēthopoiia* usually refers to a speaker's characterization of himself, but the term can be extended to include the speaker's characterizations of his opponents as well.

36. Carey 1994b: 42.

37. Lys. 1, 3, 7, 16.

38. [Arist.] *Rh. Al.* 7.10 (1428b33–35): τοῖς δὲ ἀπολογουμένοις μάλιστα δεικτέον, ὡς οὐδεπώποτε τῶν κατηγορουμένων τι πρότερον οὔτε αὐτοὶ οὔτε τῶν φίλων οὐδεὶς οὔτε τῶν ὁμοίων αὐτοῖς ἔπραξέ τις.

39. [Arist.] *Rh. Al.* 3.11 (1426b5–7): ὅστις δὲ τῶν φίλων κήδεται τοῦτον εἰκὸς καὶ τοὺς αὑτοῦ γονέας τιμᾶν· ὅστις δὲ τοὺς γονέας τιμᾷ, οὗτος καὶ τὴν πατρίδα τὴν ἑαυτοῦ εὖ ποιεῖν βουλήσεται. On the connection between an individual's behavior in *oikos* and *polis*, see Winkler 1990: 65–66; Strauss 1993: 41–53; Roisman 2005: 146–147; Bers 2009: 69–70.

40. This connection may have motivated the legal provision that those who maltreated their parents (*kakōsis goneōn*) could be prosecuted under threat of a harsh penalty (Lys. 13.91; Dem. 24.103–109; Arist. *Ath. Pol.* 56.6).

41. Aeschin. 3.78: ὁ γὰρ μισότεκνος καὶ πατὴρ πονηρὸς οὐκ ἄν ποτε γένοιτο δημαγωγὸς χρηστός, οὐδὲ ὁ τὰ φίλτατα καὶ οἰκειότατα σώματα μὴ στέργων οὐδέποθ' ὑμᾶς περὶ πολλοῦ ποιήσεται τοὺς ἀλλοτρίους, οὐδέ γε ὁ ἰδίᾳ πονηρὸς οὐκ ποτε γένοιτο δημοσίᾳ χρηστός, οὐδ' ὅστις ἐστὶν οἴκοι φαῦλος, οὐδέποτ' ἦν ἐν Μακεδονίᾳ κατὰ τὴν πρέσβειαν καλὸς κἀγαθός· οὐ γὰρ τὸν τρόπον, ἀλλὰ τὸν τόπον μετήλλαξεν. Translation from Carey 2000. Cf. Aeschin. 1.28, 3.105, 3.158; Lys. 19.56.

42. Dem. 25.66: ἡδέως ἂν εἰδείην τίς ἐστιν ὁ τὴν πρὸς τοὺς γονέας εὔνοιαν ὁρῶν προδεδωκότα τοῦτον, ἣν πρὸς τὸν δῆμον νῦν ἕξειν ὑπισχνεῖται, πιστεύων. Cf. Lys. 31.23.

43. The Roman concept was similar (May 1988: 6).

44. Arist. *Rh.* 2.12–17 (1388b31–1391b7).

45. For example, Aeschines (3.175) observes that cowardice is a characteristic born of *physis*, so that indictments for cowardice (*graphai deilias*) are in fact indictments for natural disposition (*graphai physeōs*). For discussion of the relationship between the determinacy of character and free will in the thought of the ancient Greeks, see, e.g., Halliwell 1990.

46. Dover 1974: 74–160.

47. These character types are familiar from both oratory and drama. In addition to the *Rhetoric* passage cited above, see Theophrastus' *Characters*.

48. Dem. 24.14–31.

49. Dem. 24.41–64.

50. Cf. the argument at Dem. 41.24.

51. A *graphē paranomōn* was a procedure for prosecuting an Athenian citizen who had proposed a law or decree that was illegal (*paranomos*), that is, contrary to the existing laws. Extant speeches using this procedure: Dem. 18, 20, 22, 23, 24; Aeschin. 3; Hyp. 2. See Lipsius 1905–1915: 383–396; Hansen 1974; MacDowell 1978: 50–52.

52. Diodorus' accusations are not dissimilar to the appeals to an opponent's "record" in modern American political debates. The wicked acts that the member of the other party committed as a congressman, governor, or even private citizen demonstrate that he is likely to continue his destructive practices if elected.

53. Pearson 1981: 65–68. Cf. Pearson's (1981: 103) comment on *Against Conon*, that Ariston presents Conon in such a way that "specific remarks about character are unnecessary." See also Morford 1966.

54. Dem. 54.37: τοίχους τοίνυν διορύττοντες καὶ παίοντες τοὺς ἀπαντῶντας, ἆρ' ἂν ὑμῖν ὀκνῆσαι δοκοῦσιν ἐν γραμματειδίῳ τὰ ψευδῆ μαρτυρεῖν ἀλλήλοις οἱ κεκοινωνηκότες τοσαύτης καὶ τοιαύτης φιλαπεχθημοσύνης καὶ πονηρίας καὶ ἀναιδείας καὶ ὕβρεως. Translation from Bers 2003.

55. Eur. fr. 812.9: τοιοῦτός ἐστιν οἷσπερ ἥδεται ξυνών. This passage is quoted by Aeschines (1.152) and Demosthenes (19.245). It later becomes a commonplace in classical oratory (see TrGF *ad loc.*). Cf. Eur. *Or.* 804–806.

56. Bers 2009: 69. Cf. Schön 1918: 61, "Sage mir, mit wem du umgehst, und ich sage dir, wer du bist" ["Tell me with whom you associate, and I will tell you who you are"].

57. [Arist.] *Rh. Al.* 7.9 (1428b23–32). On countering such attacks, see [Arist.] *Rh. Al.* 7.12 (1428b40–1429a4).

58. This is part of the reason for Lysias' long digression attacking his opponent's alleged connection with Theramenes (12.50–79; cf. Lys. 26.21; Dem. 21.205–208).

59. Andoc. 1.141, 2.26; Lys. 14.17, 14.39–40, 20.28–29; Isocr. 16.25. Cf. Ar. *Eq.* 445–447.

60. Pomeroy 1997: 95–98.

61. On the debate over nature versus nurture as being determinative, see Dover 1974: 88–95. On characteristics that are inherited and easily recognized because they are part of one's nature, see Adkins 1970: 79–89.

62. Orators might encounter distrust from a jury because their skill enabled them to make lies seem more plausible than the truth. Speakers in this situation would naturally attempt to convince the jury that they were not the type of swindlers jurors rightly feared. Conversely, they typically accuse their opponents of "spinning" the truth (Hesk 2000: 202–241).

63. See Dover 1974: 5. Aristotle (*Rh.* 1.2 [1356a13]) regarded the development of character as "almost" (*schedon*) the most persuasive part of a speech. On the importance of the congruence of a speaker's character and his words, see Lys. 19.61; cf. Pl. *La.* 188c–189c.

64. *PCG* 362.7: τρόπος ἔσθ' ὁ πείθων τοῦ λέγοντος, οὐ λόγος.

65. Hence the section at the end of the *Rhetoric to Alexander* (38.2–4 [1445b29–1446a3]) dedicated to advice on how to live one's life so that one's character would prove an asset at the trial.

66. Foucault and Pearson 2001: 15.

67. Lys. fr. 423 (Carey): ψεύδεσθαι προχειρότατον τοῖς πολλάκις ἁμαρτάνουσιν. Cf. Ar. fr. 694 (Kassel and Austin).

68. [Arist.] *Rh. Al.* 17.2 (1432a39–1432b1): τῶν αὐτῶν ἐστιν ἀνθρώπων τὰ πονηρὰ πράττειν καὶ μὴ φροντίζειν ἐπιορκοῦντας.

69. Dion. Hal. *Lys.* 19: καὶ τὰς ἐκ τῶν ἠθῶν γε πίστεις ἀξιολόγως πάνυ κατασκευάζειν ἔμοιγε δοκεῖ.

70. The authenticity of this speech has been ably defended in recent years despite two common objections based on style and supposed inaccuracies. The first has the advantage at least of having its roots in antiquity, although Dionysius of Halicarnassus (*Dem.* 57; cf. Libanius' *hypothesis* to Dem. 25–26) is the only ancient commentator to dispute Demosthenic authorship. The accusations of inconsistencies first leveled systematically by Lipsius (1883; cf. Sealey 1993: 237–239) and other scholars' objections to the style received convincing refutation by Hansen (1976: 144–152; see also Rubinstein 2000: 30–32; Worman 2008: 230–232; MacDowell 2009: 298–313).

71. The main prosecutor, Lycurgus, had lodged suit through a procedure called *endeixis*. Before Hansen (1976), it was generally thought that *endeixis* differed from *apagogē* in that the plaintiff lodged a charge with the magistrate for an *endeixis*, while in *apagogē* he arrested the accused himself (Lipsius 1905–1915: 317–337; A. R. W. Harrison 1968–1971, ii: 221–231; MacDowell 1978: 75). Hansen has shown that *endeixis* and *apagogē* are part of the same process. The act of arrest is called *apagogē*, which is sometimes preceded by an *endeixis*, a written denunciation. See also Volonaki 2000.

72. Demosthenes states at the outset that his goal is to show that Aristogiton has led a terrible life (5; cf. 76–77), a claim that he substantiates by turning to Aristogiton's private affairs (8). Many anecdotes are adduced, including one about a scuffle in which Aristogiton bit off his adversary's nose (60–61). Through his life the jury can see what type of person he is (πρόδηλος ὢν ὅτι τοιοῦτός ἐστι τῷ βίῳ, 50).

73. Dem. 25.36–39.

74. Dem. 25.39. The repetition of *toioutos* (21, 39, 45, 47, 51, 64, 83) underscores the argument based on Aristogiton's character.

75. Dem. 25.95–96.

76. Dem. 25.13. For the reluctant prosecutor motif, cf. Lys. 22.2–4; Dem. 23.187–188; [Dem.] 59.12.

77. Aristogiton's disregard for the laws is a central emphasis of this speech (see esp. 25–28).

78. These are two of the potential prejudices (*diabolai*) against which Anaximenes warns ([Arist.] *Rh. Al.* 29.18 [1437a34–37]).

79. Christ (1998b: 154–157) points out that asserting a personal interest in the case was a legal strategy for avoiding suspicions of sycophancy. Cf. Allen 2000b: 156–160. Lysias 25 provides an example of how a defendant could accuse his opponent of *polupragmosunē* and sycophancy at the same time.

80. This latter motivation is parodied in Philocleon (Ar. *Vesp.* 106–108, 849–850) though from the juror's point of view rather than the litigant's.

81. Apollodorus figures prominently in this section because of his preference for narrative over formal proofs. As Usher (1999: 343) states, "He was happiest when regaling his audiences with stories which embarrassed his opponents and showed his own actions in the most favourable light." Trevett (1992: 84 n. 26) provides statistics: in a sample from Demosthenes' corpus (36, 37, 39, 45, 54), narrative accounts for 14.6 percent of the speech, whereas in the six speeches of Apollodorus it is 54.5 percent. The great number of references to enmity in Apollodorus' speeches results naturally from his emphasis on narrative as a persuasive device.

82. [Dem.] 59.1–10.

83. Theomnestus and Apollodorus accuse Neaera of "living with" (*sunoikein*) a citizen, although she is a foreigner. They must prove that Neaera is not a citizen but nonetheless has been cohabitating with Stephanus and claiming that they are lawfully married with legitimate offspring.

84. The two previous trials that Theomnestus mentions were both between Apollodorus and Stephanus ([Dem.] 59.3–10). Apollodorus states several times that he is the de facto prosecutor ([Dem.] 59.121, 124, 125, 126; see Carey 1992: 4–5; Kapparis 1999: 29–31).

85. *Against Neaera* is an unusual text in that it actually consists of two separate orations.

86. On the authenticity of the law, see Kapparis 1999: 198–199.

87. Although Apollodorus may not have benefited directly from a favorable verdict (see Rubinstein 2000: 98–100), he and Theomnestus could have planned to split the money.

88. For this reason, some speakers even deny private enmity to present themselves as disinterested and public spirited (see below). Defendants, in turn, can attack the motivations of the prosecutor by claiming that enmity is the driving force and that their opponents are maliciously attacking them on trumped-up charges (see the following section).

89. [Dem.] 59.1: πολλά με τὰ παρακαλοῦντα ἦν, ὦ ἄνδρες Ἀθηναῖοι, γράψασθαι Νέαιραν τὴν γραφὴν ταυτηνὶ καὶ εἰσελθεῖν εἰς ὑμᾶς. καὶ γὰρ ἠδικήμεθα ὑπὸ Στεφάνου μεγάλα, καὶ εἰς κινδύνους τοὺς ἐσχάτους κατέστημεν ὑπ' αὐτοῦ, ὅ τε κηδεστὴς καὶ ἐγὼ καὶ ἡ ἀδελφὴ καὶ ἡ γυνὴ ἡ ἐμή, ὥστε οὐχ ὑπάρχων ἀλλὰ τιμωρούμενος ἀγωνιοῦμαι τὸν ἀγῶνα τουτονί· τῆς γὰρ ἔχθρας πρότερος οὗτος ὑπῆρξεν, οὐδὲν ὑφ' ἡμῶν πώποτε οὔτε λόγῳ οὔτε ἔργῳ κακὸν παθών. βούλομαι δ' ὑμῖν προδιηγήσασθαι πρῶτον ἃ πεπόνθαμεν ὑπ' αὐτοῦ, ἵνα μᾶλλόν μοι συγγνώμην ἔχητε ἀμυνομένῳ, καὶ ὡς εἰς <τοὺς> ἐσχάτους κινδύνους κατέστημεν περί τε τῆς πατρίδος καὶ περὶ ἀτιμίας. Translation from Bers 2003.

90. The law against cohabitation between citizens and foreigners was intended to prevent smuggling of illegitimate offspring into the ranks of the citizens (Kapparis 1999: 203–206). This *graphē* therefore addresses the preservation of the integrity of the citizenry.

91. Apollodorus merely "thought that the people ought to be able to do with

their own money whatever they wanted" (κύριον δ' ἡγούμενος δεῖν τὸν δῆμον εἶναι περὶ τῶν αὑτοῦ ὅ τι ἂν βούληται πρᾶξαι, 4).

92. An accusation of murder required a formal proclamation that banned the suspected murderer from entering the agora and other holy places important to the city. This prevented possible *miasma* (religious pollution) from staining the city (*IG* I³ 104.20–23; [Dem.] 43.57). See MacDowell 1978: 17, 23–25; Gagarin 1981: 109–112; Parker 1983; Carawan 1998: 17–20; Phillips 2008: 62.

93. [Dem.] 59.12: παρακαλούντων δή με ἁπάντων, ἰδίᾳ προσιόντων <τε> μοι, ἐπὶ τιμωρίαν τρέπεσθαι ὧν ἐπάθομεν ὑπ' αὐτοῦ, καὶ ὀνειδιζόντων μοι ἀνανδρότατον ἀνθρώπων εἶναι, εἰ οὕτως οἰκείως ἔχων <τὰ> πρὸς τούτους μὴ λήψομαι δίκην ὑπὲρ ἀδελφῆς καὶ κηδεστοῦ καὶ ἀδελφιδῶν καὶ γυναικὸς ἐμαυτοῦ.

94. Neaera's advanced age would present a further problem for Apollodorus in this regard (Kapparis 1999: 214–215). His attack on a seemingly harmless old woman could have led the jurors to the conclusion that Apollodorus was pursuing a vendetta over a trivial affair. The restraint that Theomnestus attributes to Apollodorus helps to combat this problem.

95. [Dem.] 59.15: ἐξ αὐτῆς τῆς ἀληθείας.

96. See pp. 000–000.

97. Herman 2006: 193.

98. Herman's citations of Demosthenes 24 (*Against Timocrates*) and Lysias 14 (*Against Alcibiades*) in the same passage (2006: 191–193) are similarly problematic. Both speakers portray themselves as exercising restraint and paint their opponents as shameless and malicious but do not assert categorically that it was illegitimate to retaliate on one's enemies.

99. See pp. 000–000.

100. See A. R. W. Harrison 1968–1971, ii: 211–217; MacDowell 1978: 166; Osborne 1985b: 44–47, 54–55; Todd 1993: 118–119; Hunter 2000.

101. The opposition evidently claimed that the slaves belonged to Nicostratus not Arethusius.

102. [Dem.] 53.1: ὅτι μὲν οὐ συκοφαντῶν, ἀλλ' ἀδικούμενος καὶ ὑβριζόμενος ὑπὸ τούτων καὶ οἰόμενος δεῖν τιμωρεῖσθαι τὴν ἀπογραφὴν ἐποιησάμην, μέγιστον ὑμῖν ἔστω τεκμήριον, ὦ ἄνδρες δικασταί, τό τε μέγεθος τῆς ἀπογραφῆς, καὶ ὅτι αὐτὸς ἐγὼ ἀπέγραψα. Translation from Bers 2003.

103. The syntax of the sentence reflects this. The first participle (*sykophantōn*) is without an accompanying explanation of the grounds for prosecution, while Apollodorus' desire for revenge is connected with real offenses (*adikoumenos kai hubrizomenos*). Sycophantic charges are naturally baseless, but desire for retribution presupposes a real offense.

104. This "antithesis of sycophancy and revenge" (D. Cohen 1995: 102) supports an implicit plausibility argument and does not merely establish Apollodorus as a man of honor, worthy of deference from the jury.

105. [Dem.] 53.1–2. Two and a half minae amount to two hundred-fifty drach-

mas. On the penalty for frivolous prosecution, see E. Harris 2006b: 405–422; MacDowell 2008; E. Harris 2013: 72–76.

106. [Dem.] 53.2: ἀλλὰ τῶν ἐν ἀνθρώποις ἁπάντων ἡγησάμενος δεινότατον εἶναι ἀδικεῖσθαι μὲν αὐτός, ἕτερον δ' ὑπὲρ ἐμοῦ τοῦ ἀδικουμένου τοὔνομα παρέχειν, καὶ εἶναι ἄν τι τούτοις τοῦτο τεκμήριον, ὁπότε ἐγὼ λέγοιμι τὴν ἔχθραν πρὸς ὑμᾶς, ὡς ψεύδομαι (οὐ γὰρ ἄν ποτε ἕτερον ἀπογράψαι, εἴπερ ἐγὼ αὐτὸς ἠδικούμην), διὰ μὲν ταῦτα ἀπέγραψα.

107. Accusing the prosecutor of acting as a hired agent of a behind-the-scenes mastermind was a popular way to undercut his credibility (see above, pp. 000–000, esp. n. 000).

108. Cf. Lys. 23.5: "I was very concerned that I should not appear eager to behave with arrogance (*hubris*) rather than simply wanting to obtain satisfaction for the wrongs done to me" (περὶ πολλοῦ ποιούμενος μηδενὶ δόξαι ὑβρίζειν βούλεσθαι μᾶλλον ἢ δίκην λαβεῖν ὧν ἠδικήθην). Translation from Todd 2000. The speaker admits enmity with the defendant, but he emphasizes that his desire to take vengeance is based on actual wrongs that deserve punishment not on trumped-up charges.

109. [Dem.] 53.14–18. Because Apollodorus had been on the friendliest of terms with Nicostratus, his behavior appears so much the worse. Apollodorus was accustomed to trust Nicostratus with his personal affairs (4–5). He includes the apparently irrelevant comment that he had given two slaves to Nicostratus as a gift (6) and recounts how he lent three hundred drachmas to free Nicostratus from slavery in Aegina (6–7), which he later forgave in full (8–9), even providing an additional sum to pay Nicostratus' debts (10–11). Nicostratus considered him a better friend than his relatives (7) but repaid him with treachery (13).

110. On Nicostratus' use of "entrapment" against Apollodorus, see Scafuro 1997: 334–336; Roisman 2006: 63–64.

111. Cf. the explicitly formulated version of this argument at Isocr. 17.46.

112. This analysis of *Against Neaera* and *Against Nicostratus* has the incidental effect of defending Apollodorus' abilities as an orator. His deficiencies in style have been discussed (e.g., Pearson 1966, but cf. Trevett 1992: 77–110; Kapparis 1999: 52–56) and indeed were the basis for determining the spurious attribution of his speeches to Demosthenes, but his heavy use of narrative should be taken as a rational technique rather than as the sign of a bumbling speaker. He creates arguments with his stories; he does not simply content himself with contrasting the delinquency of his opponent with his own probity.

113. D. Cohen 1995: 103. Cf. Trevett 1992: 90–91; Roisman 2006: 64.

114. D. Cohen 1995: 102. Cf. Trevett 1992: 91.

115. Compare the argument that Nicostratus' failures as a friend are the central issue in the trial (Roisman 2005: 54–55). Roisman (2005: 55) asserts that "in essence, he [Apollodorus] was asking them to render their verdict less on the ownership of the slaves than on Nicostratus' disloyalty."

116. Fisher 2001: 119.

117. This is not to say that they ran no risk of appearing to be sycophants

but that the danger was less acute than in other procedures. Blackmailing knew no procedural bounds since extortion artists could threaten to bring any type of court action if they planned to receive a monetary settlement prior to the actual trial. Procedures without financial rewards, however, had no structural advantage for a sycophant and were less susceptible to suspicion. On frivolous litigation, see E. Harris 2006b: 405–422; MacDowell 2008; E. Harris 2013: 72–76.

118. Cf. Cic. *Red. Pop.*, in which Cicero plays a similar game of denying a personal interest in the trial in order to appear magnanimous (Morstein-Marx 2004: 217).

119. Probably for these reasons, most prosecutors who deny enmity initiated public suits (Lys. 22, 27, 31; Dem. 20, 23; Din. 1 [*Against Demosthenes*]; Lycurg. 1; cf. Lys. 26).

120. He attacks the defendant for his panicked abandonment of Athens following the city's defeat at the hands of Philip of Macedonia in the battle of Chaeronea in 338 BC. Leocrates, an Athenian citizen, allegedly fled the city with his family and as many of his possessions as he could carry with him, sailed to Rhodes, and later went to Megara (17–21). For reasons that are unclear, he returned to Athens and found himself under prosecution by Lycurgus in 330.

121. Lycurg. 1.1–2.

122. Lycurg. 1.5: ἐγὼ δ', ὦ Ἀθηναῖοι, εἰδὼς Λεωκράτην φυγόντα μὲν τοὺς ὑπὲρ τῆς πατρίδος κινδύνους, ἐγκαταλιπόντα δὲ τοὺς αὐτοῦ πολίτας, προδεδωκότα δὲ πᾶσαν τὴν ὑμετέραν δύναμιν, ἅπασι δὲ τοῖς γεγραμμένοις ἔνοχον ὄντα, ταύτην τὴν εἰσαγγελίαν ἐποιησάμην, οὔτε δι' ἔχθραν οὐδεμίαν οὔτε διὰ φιλονικίαν οὐδ' ἡντινοῦν τοῦτον τὸν ἀγῶνα προελόμενος, ἀλλ' αἰσχρὸν εἶναι νομίσας τοῦτον περιορᾶν εἰς τὴν ἀγορὰν ἐμβάλλοντα καὶ τῶν κοινῶν ἱερῶν μετέχοντα, τῆς τε πατρίδος ὄνειδος καὶ πάντων ὑμῶν γεγενημένον. Cf. Lys. 14.22.

123. Cf. Lys. 31.2, where the speaker similarly denies that he is either an enemy or a busybody.

124. Lycurg. 1.6: πολίτου γάρ ἐστι δικαίου, μὴ διὰ τὰς ἰδίας ἔχθρας εἰς τὰς κοινὰς κρίσεις καθιστάναι τοὺς τὴν πόλιν μηδὲν ἀδικοῦντας, ἀλλὰ τοὺς εἰς τὴν πατρίδα τι παρανομοῦντας ἰδίους ἐχθροὺς εἶναι νομίζειν, καὶ τὰ κοινὰ τῶν ἀδικημάτων κοινὰς καὶ τὰς προφάσεις ἔχειν τῆς πρὸς αὐτοὺς διαφορᾶς.

125. Leocrates' enmity with the city prepares the way for Lycurgus' impassioned narrative about his offenses against Athens (39).

126. Similar denials of enmity in prosecution speeches: Lys. 22, 27, 31; Dem. 20, 23; Din. 1 (*Against Demosthenes*); cf. Lys. 26. These speeches tend to have a heavy deliberative component that would have made focusing on private enmity inappropriate. See Papillon 1998: 14–18 on Dem. 23 and Kremmydas 2007 on Dem. 20.

127. E.g., Andoc. 1.6; Lys. 7.2–3; cf. Dem. 18.1–2; Plut. *Arist.* 4.1.

128. Johnstone (1999: 54–60) calls these "counternarratives" and "antinarratives." In a "counternarrative" the defendant challenges key elements of his oppo-

nent's story to give it a new interpretation. In an "antinarrative" the defendant argues that the story is a complete fabrication.

129. A significant number do not address enmity: Lys. 18, 20; Isae. 2, 11; Dem. 29; [Dem.] 52; Hyp. 2.

130. This speech has been subject to scholarly doubts about its authenticity, but the objections are weak. One issue, raised long ago about the date of the speech, has been resolved (see MacDowell 1994: 154). Todd (2007: 582–584) discusses objections to allegedly non-Attic words and objections based on stylometry. Todd (2007: 584–585) himself concludes that the speech is probably a genuine fourth-century oration but not by Lysias because of "a certain lack of structural and narrative clarity." This judgment has flaws. Todd asserts that the speaker does not fulfill "the promise at §3 to discuss his general character," but this is not quite what Polyaenus says. The speaker objects to his opponents' slander of his character and says that he has "to make my defense about everything" (περὶ πάντων <τὴν> ἀπολογίαν ποιήσασθαι). By denying that he harmed anyone while in office (14), denying that the generals had any pretext for hating him (15), and simply omitting any disreputable actions of his own in his narrative, Polyaenus essentially fulfills this promise. Nor is editorial confusion on the name of the speaker any proof against authenticity. The "cryptic" remark of §5 may puzzle later readers of the speech, but the original hearers would surely have already known Polyaenus' name and not have been confused.

131. It is far from clear who these prosecutors were. Scholars had interpreted the phrase of §6 (οἱ δὲ μετὰ Κτησικλέους τοῦ ἄρχοντος ["those with Ctesicles when he was in office"]) as referring to Ctesicles and his fellow generals, but MacDowell (1994: 157) raised objections to this on several grounds: "It is not credible that ten men who happened to have been elected as *stratēgoi* in the same year would remain a coherent group taking joint action long after their year of office had ended" (158). He also pointed out that the speaker asserts that these men did not undergo their *euthynai* (Lys. 9.11), something that seems impossible for an entire board of generals. MacDowell proposed that these men be identified as the secretaries associated with Ctesicles. The objections of Dreher (1994) and Todd (2007: 587–589) to MacDowell's hypothesis have some merit, but, although they cast doubt on MacDowell's identification of the prosecutors, they fail to provide a convincing account of their own. We may never know who these men were, but MacDowell was probably correct to argue that it was not the entire board of generals.

132. MacDowell 1994: 163. The procedure was *apographē* (see pp. 000–000), whereby the prosecutors listed certain of the soldier's possessions that were liable to confiscation to defray his debt to the state (pp. 000–000).

133. Cf. [Dem.] 53.1, in which Apollodorus, prosecuting in an *apographē*, anticipates a possible objection to his motivations.

134. Polyaenus uses words for slander (*diaballō, diabolē*) three times in his first short paragraph (1–3).

135. Polyaenus chastises the plaintiffs for "despising" (*kataphronēsantes*) the point at issue (*tou pragmatos*).

136. It is not certain to which officials Polyaenus refers when speaking of the *tamiai* (MacDowell 1994: 161).

137. Following §7, "enmity" and "enemy" recur often (nine times in sixteen sections). Although enmity is an important focus of the speech, the first instance of the word is delayed because Polyaenus wants to establish the prosecutors' terrible character first and then attribute the enmity to their vicious combativeness. He implies that the prosecutors are at enmity with the speaker because they are evil, not that they act abusively because they are enemies.

138. Lys. 9.8–12. The defendant argues he had never spoken ill of the generals in a venue prohibited by law.

139. Lys. 9.13: δεῖ δ' ὑμᾶς μὴ μόνον τοῦ ἐγκλήματος τὴν αἰτίαν ἀλλὰ καὶ τῆς ἔχθρας τὴν πρόφασιν εἰδέναι.

140. Discussion of prosecutor's character: Lys. 9.13–18. No *prophasis* for enmity: Lys. 9.15.

141. Lys. 9.16, 19. At this point the defendant may be speaking at cross-purposes. It is hard to see how they would "benefit" from Polyaenus' travails if what he says is true, that they have no real reason to be angry with him. Compare this character portrait to that of Eratosthenes in Lysias 12, in which Lysias, in a bid to make Eratosthenes seem completely depraved, avoids attributing any motive to him for his wrongdoing except "gratifying his own lawless passions" (23).

142. Lys. 9.16: καταλιγωρήσαντες δὲ τοῦ δικαίου, βιαζόμενοι βλάπτειν ἐξ ἅπαντος {τοῦ} λόγου. Translation from Todd 2000.

143. E. Harris 2005: 127 (also E. Harris 2013: 66) on Lys. 9.14. In fact, in §20 Polyaenus accepts the legitimacy of the help/harm motto. Furthermore, Polyaenus' statement at §14 addresses a very specific situation: his role as a public figure. Magistrates commonly took oaths not to abuse their offices to help friends or harm enemies because this sort of behavior would compromise the egalitarian nature of democratic government. These oaths say much about how the Athenians thought their government should be run, not how they thought lives should be ordered as a general rule.

144. The legal issue gets a bit muddied in the two enemies' vitriolic attacks on each other's characters, but Aeschines' argument is essentially that the decree proposed in honor of Demosthenes is illegal for two reasons. First, it contravenes the law that a public official must undergo his *euthynai* before receiving such an honor; Demosthenes had not yet undergone his *euthynai* for being *teichopoios* ("wall-builder") for that year (Aeschin. 3.9–31). Second, the decree included the provision that the award be announced in the theater of Dionysius, in contravention of another law that stipulated such awards be announced only in the Assembly and the Council (Aeschin. 3.32–48). Demosthenes responds to the first charge that, although he was indeed a public official who had not undergone his *euthynai*, the crown was proposed for a previous office that he had held several years previous. E. Harris (1994: 141–148) argues that Demosthenes was technically correct that the law stated that he must undergo his *euthynai* for the office for which the crown was proposed. On the second point, Demosthenes defends Ctesiphon's de-

cree by citing a law that authorized announcing such honors in the theater of Dionysus if the Assembly voted for it (Dem. 18.120–121). Aeschines also adds a third accusation, that the decree is misguided since Demosthenes' career has harmed rather than benefited Athens. (On this issue and its relevance to the legal charges, see Gagarin 2012.)

145. Yunis 2000–2001.

146. Dem. 18.278: οὔτε γὰρ τὴν ὀργὴν οὔτε τὴν ἔχθραν οὔτ' ἄλλο οὐδὲν τῶν τοιούτων τὸν καλὸν κἀγαθὸν πολίτην δεῖ τοὺς ὑπὲρ τῶν κοινῶν εἰσεληλυθότας δικαστὰς ἀξιοῦν αὑτῷ βεβαιοῦν. Translation from Yunis 2005.

147. Accusations of Aeschines' enmity or spite: 18.9–16, 31, 50, 121–125, 138, 143, 189, 243, 249, 257, 277–279, 285, 293–294, 307. Demosthenes does not, however, leave this as a private matter. He accuses Aeschines of enmity with the city (18.31, 40–41, 82, 109, 124–125, 131–138, 163, 198, 217, 227–228, 265, 277, 286), appropriating the role of public-minded servant for himself. On Lycurgus 1, see the previous section.

148. If Aeschines had had any decency, he would have fought it out with Demosthenes one-on-one (15–16). For the motif of the illegitimacy of the attacks of *rhētores* on private persons, cf. Aeschin. 1.173.

149. Dem. 18.17: πάντα μὲν τοίνυν τὰ κατηγορημένα ὁμοίως ἐκ τούτων ἄν τις ἴδοι, οὔτε δικαίως οὔτ' ἐπ' ἀληθείας οὐδεμιᾶς εἰρημένα. Translation from Yunis 2005.

150. Dem. 18.277: εἰ δ' οὖν ἐστι καὶ παρ' ἐμοί τις ἐμπειρία τοιαύτη, ταύτην μὲν εὑρήσετε πάντες ἐν τοῖς κοινοῖς ἐξεταζομένην ὑπὲρ ὑμῶν ἀεὶ καὶ οὐδαμοῦ καθ' ὑμῶν οὐδ' ἰδίᾳ, τὴν δὲ τούτου τοὐναντίον οὐ μόνον {τῷ λέγειν} ὑπὲρ τῶν ἐχθρῶν, ἀλλὰ καὶ εἴ τις ἐλύπησέ τι τοῦτον ἢ προσέκρουσέ που, κατὰ τούτων. Translation from Yunis 2005.

151. D. Cohen 1995: 78.

152. E. Harris 2005: 129 and 2013: 69.

153. Dem. 18.283: ἀλλ' ἐμὲ τὴν αἰτίαν σοι ταύτην ἐπάγειν τῆς ἰδίας ἕνεκ' ἔχθρας, οὐκ οὖσαν ἀληθῆ. Cf. 141, 143.

154. As an example, words of the *echthr-* root occur only four times in Aeschines' speech as against 46 times in Demosthenes'.

155. Aeschin. 3.119, 125, 164.

156. Aeschin. 3.215–225.

157. The trial took place shortly following the restoration of the democracy, in either 400 or 399.

158. Andocides narrates the history of the supposed religious offenses of which he is accused (11–70), discusses the applicability of the amnesty of 401 to his case (71–91), briefly attacks three of his prosecutors and addresses the political implications of his trial (92–109), and rebuts a secondary accusation of the prosecution about a suppliant branch illicitly placed on the altar at Eleusis (110–116).

159. On the theme of Callias' overarching conspiracy against Andocides, see Roisman 2006: 51–54. Roisman (2006: 54) shows how Andocides uses his conspiracy theory to "convert the prosecution of serious offenses against Athens's religious

beliefs and practices into a scandalous attack on an individual in a private matter." This calculated rhetoric is, however, "relevant" (*pace* Roisman 2006: 53) because of its use in the service of plausibility arguments.

160. Andoc. 1.118–123. It is unclear why this heiress was so desirable (see Scafuro 1997: 70). If Andocides is to be believed, she had inherited a huge debt from her father, Epilycus, which would be passed down to her husband upon her marriage (118). Epilycus had two talents' worth of property but also five talents of debt, which would presumably have been split between his two daughters. Andocides and his brother, Leagrus, wed the two women (their cousins) out of sympathy for the plight of the *oikos*. Andocides' wife died, and Leagrus had decided to put his wife away. The dispute between Callias and Andocides was over the fate of Leagrus' wife.

161. Andoc. 1.133–136.

162. "Tax farming" refers to a collection of fixed rents through a contract with a third party (the collector). In Athens the right to collect taxes was regularly auctioned off to the highest bidder. The individual who won the auction had to pay the state a determined sum and could keep anything he collected above that sum as profit. Andocides explains that several men (including his prosecutors) had formed a cartel to keep bidding artificially low until he outbid them and broke their monopoly.

163. Andocides points to his own patriotic motivations as opposed to his opponents' greed. The most natural interpretation of the dispute over the tax collection is that Andocides was trying to horn in on Agyrrhius' profitable operations. Andocides cautiously does not allow this possibility but rather links their conspiracy on the collection of taxes to their conspiracy against himself in the present trial (Roisman 2006: 87).

164. Darkow (1917: 28–34) provides a history of the debate over the authenticity of this speech up to her own time, while Todd (2007: 403–408) offers more recent discussion. Dover (1968: 82–83) accepts the authenticity of the speech. MacDowell (1962: 14–15) believes that the speech was not written by Lysias but rather by another of the prosecutors. Furley (1996: 8) states that "there is no way of knowing," but points out that the speech raises issues that Andocides addresses in his speech. Therefore, even if the extant speech was a literary pamphlet, the speech "contained much the same material as one speech for the prosecution contained" (8). Rubinstein (2000: 140–142) also defends the speech's authenticity.

165. Lys. 6.41: οὐ γὰρ τοῦτο λύειν ἐστὶ τὰ συγκείμενα, εἰ 'Ανδοκίδης ἕνεκα τῶν ἰδίων ἁμαρτημάτων δίδωσι δίκην, ἀλλ' ἐάν τις ἕνεκα τῶν δημοσίων συμφορῶν ἰδίᾳ τινὰ τιμωρῆται. Translation from Todd 2000.

166. The case would have taken place at the Delphinium. This court was staffed by the *ephetai*, a body of fifty-one jurors chosen by lot, probably from the members of the Areopagus. The *ephetai* oversaw trials at the Delphinium in cases of alleged justifiable homicide and at the Palladion in cases of alleged unintentional homicide. See MacDowell 1963: 48–57; Gagarin 1981: 134–136; Rhodes 1981: 647–648; Carawan 1998: 8–15.

167. For an account of Euphiletus' attempts to avoid possible charges of plotting, see Roisman 2006: 16–18.

168. As Todd (2007: 92) points out, Euphiletus was concerned to rebut the charge of preexisting enmity that would have led him to be on the lookout for an opportunity to kill Eratosthenes. Of course, once Euphiletus found out about Eratosthenes' affair with his wife, he considered Eratosthenes an enemy. Euphiletus implies this with his concession: "There was no enmity between me and him *except for this* [the adultery]" (οὔτε ἔχθρα ἐμοὶ καὶ ἐκείνῳ οὐδεμία ἦν πλὴν ταύτης, 4).

169. Todd 1998: 165.

170. Lys. 1.43: σκέψασθε δὲ παρ' ὑμῖν αὐτοῖς οὕτως περὶ τούτου τοῦ πράγματος, ζητοῦντες εἴ τις ἐμοὶ καὶ Ἐρατοσθένει ἔχθρα πώποτε γεγένηται πλὴν ταύτης. οὐδεμίαν γὰρ εὑρήσετε. Translation from Todd 2000.

171. Lys. 1.44: οὔτε γὰρ συκοφαντῶν γραφάς με ἐγράψατο, οὔτε ἐκβάλλειν ἐκ τῆς πόλεως ἐπεχείρησεν, οὔτε ἰδίας δίκας ἐδικάζετο, οὔτε συνῄδει κακὸν οὐδὲν ὃ ἐγὼ δεδιὼς μή τις πύθηται ἐπεθύμουν αὐτὸν ἀπολέσαι, οὔτε εἰ ταῦτα διαπραξαίμην, ἤλπιζόν ποθεν χρήματα λήψεσθαι· ἔνιοι γὰρ τοιούτων πραγμάτων ἕνεκα θάνατον ἀλλήλοις ἐπιβουλεύουσι. Translation from Todd 2000.

172. Lys. 1.45: οὐδὲ ἑωρακὼς ἦν τὸν ἄνθρωπον πώποτε πλὴν ἐν ἐκείνῃ τῇ νυκτί. τί ἂν οὖν βουλόμενος ἐγὼ τοιοῦτον κίνδυνον ἐκινδύνευον, εἰ μὴ τὸ μέγιστον τῶν ἀδικημάτων ἦν ὑπ' αὐτοῦ ἠδικημένος. Translation from Todd 2000.

173. Cf. the very similar probability argument at Antiph. 5.57.

174. Quint. *Inst.* 4.2.21: *neque enim narratio in hoc reperta est, ut tantum cognoscat iudex, sed aliquanto magis ut consentiat* ["The purpose narrative is not simply that the judge will understand, but that he will agree"].

175. The use of character argument for probabilities has not been recognized to the extent that it deserves (but cf. Johnstone 1999: 93–108). Hence this comment on an implicit argument in Demosthenes 45: "An implied probability argument and an implied argument from character are rolled into one. The argument has no near parallel in extant oratory" (Hesk 2000: 226).

176. The Simpson trial: Shapiro 1996; Feldman 2002. The Anthony trial: Alvarez and Carter 2011; Hightower 2011.

177. See Gagarin 2003.

178. Some litigants explicitly connect their characterization of themselves or others to arguments about *to pragma* itself (Isocr. 18.58; Dem. 36.55; Aeschin. 1.93). Others criticize the use of character discussion as a means to distract from *to pragma* (Lys. 9.1–3, 30.7. Cf. Dem. 21.128).

179. P. Wilson 1991: 166. Cf. Todd 1990c: 172: "The jury are not there to find out the truth, but to decide which of two theses they find preferable"; D. Cohen 1995: 180: "Given the structural impediments to establishing with certainty the most basic facts [. . .] it is not surprising that the judges [. . .] looked to other cri-

teria." See also Humphreys 1985. This line of thinking has been widely influential (e.g., Riess 2012: 31–32).

180. For the idea, see Arist. *Eth. Nic.* 15.4 (1322a2–6).

181. This is not to say that sociological judgments based on extralegal arguments have absolutely no role in Athenian oratory. Such a claim would be untenable for any court system; humans tend to allow many more considerations to creep into their judgment than those of which they are conscious.

182. See Dover 1974: 292–293.

CHAPTER 3

1. See below for further discussion.
2. Christ 1998b: 133–159; Johnstone 1999; Rubinstein 2004; Lanni 2006.
3. Scholars have to some extent neglected to investigate this dynamic (Rubinstein 2004: 187), but in the case of enmity it has not gone unnoticed (Christ 1998b: 157–159; Kurihara 2003; Scheid-Tissinier 2007). Rubinstein is well aware of the need for taking into account individual features of the cases to qualify overall patterns.
4. Kurihara 2003; Rubinstein 2004; Christ 1998b: 157–159; Scheid-Tissinier 2007.
5. Christ (1998b: 157–159) comes to similar conclusions, though he only mentions two speeches (Lycurg. 1; Dem. 23) and does not attempt as thoroughgoing an analysis as Kurihara. Cf. Hunter 1994: 125–129.
6. Kurihara 2003: 466 n. 11. Lys. 12, 13, 14, 15, 22, 26, 31; Aeschin. 1, 3; Dem. 19–24, 53, 58, 59; Lycurg. 1. Exceptions: Lys. 12, 13, 14, 15; Aeschin. 1; Dem. 21, 22, 24, 53, 58, 59.
7. Obvious enmity: Dem. 24; Aeschin. 1. Unimportant speakers: [Dem.] 53, 58, 59.
8. Theomnestus in [Dem.] 59.
9. Cf. scholars' conflicting conclusions about *Against Leocrates*. Herman (2006: 276–277) cites the denial of enmity in *Against Leocrates* to cap his argument for Athenian intolerance of the use of the courts for private vengeance, while Allen (2000a) asserts that the speech is an anomaly, even going so far as to classify the denial of enmity as "heterodox." No single impulse such as an appeal to the ideology of restraint or the politics of anger governs Athenian litigants' decisions on how to present their relationships with their opponents. For a more balanced assessment of these dynamics, see Kucharski 2012.
10. Lys. 32; Isocr. 17, 21; Isae. 5; Dem. 40, 48; [Dem.] 49, 50; but cf. Dem. 39, 47.
11. Lys. 22, 27, 31; Dem. 20, 23; Din. 1 (*Against Demosthenes*); Lycurg. 1; but cf. Lys. 12, 13; Dem. 19, 21, 22, 24, 25; [Dem.] 53, 59; Aeschin. 1, 3.
12. In other words, substantive similarities are more important than procedural. Procedure follows substance (see E. Harris 2013: 138–174).

13. Lys. 12, 13, 22, 27, 31; Dem. 20, 23; Aeschin. 1, 3; Din. 1 (*Against Demosthenes*); Lycurg. 1.

14. But not always: [Dem.] 50 (see p. 000).

15. For this reason, terms like "norms" or "protocols" when applied to differences in procedure (Kremmydas 2013) are misleading.

16. Physical assault: Lys. 3, 4; Isocr. 20; Dem. 21, 54. Homicide: Antiph. 1, 5, 6; Lys. 1, 12, 13.

17. "Motive" in this context refers to the perpetrator's reasons for assaulting the target, not to the technical distinctions in homicide law between unintentional murder and "malice aforethought" (*pronoia*).

18. Presumably, the second stage of the *probolē* resembled a *graphē* trial. Cf. E. Harris (2008: 79–81), who argues that the first phase of the trial (the *probolē*) was distinct from the second phase, which, in Demosthenes' case, was a *graphē hubreōs* lodged two years later.

19. The best discussion of the *probolē* can be found in MacDowell 1990: 13–17; see also E. Harris 1989: 130–131 and 1992: 73–74; Rowe 1994. It has been debated whether or not this speech was actually delivered. Aeschines (3.52) says that Demosthenes dropped the suit in return for thirty minae. On the basis of this statement, many scholars, noting inconsistencies and defects in its style, argued that the speech is incomplete and was never delivered. Others, however, have cast doubt on both Aeschines' reliability and the idea that the speech is unfinished (Erbse 1956; E. Harris 1989; cf. Ober 1994: 90–92). MacDowell (1990: 26–28), by contrast, accepts Erbse's argument that the stylistic difficulties have been exaggerated, but he argues that the speech was not delivered in the form that has been transmitted. Thus, the extant oration may represent a draft of the speech, which may or may not have been delivered. For the history of scholarship on this problem, see E. Harris 1989: 118–121; MacDowell 1990: 24–25.

20. Dem. 21.77–82. Demosthenes was involved in an *antidosis*, on which see pp. 000–000.

21. Dem. 21.114: εἰ δ' ἀληθὲς ἢ ψεῦδος.

22. Dionysius of Halicarnassus (*Dem.* 13) cites *Against Conon* as an outstanding example of Demosthenes' rhetorical skill and compares it to Lysias' stylistic excellence. Today it is one of the most frequently read and discussed orations of Demosthenes.

23. In *Against Meidias* Demosthenes attempts to cast himself in the role of the defenseless common man pitted against the arrogant elite in what Ober (1989: 221–226) calls the dramatic fiction of the "poor little rich man." He alternates between this self-representation and the assertion of his own elite status.

24. Dem. 54.8: ὡς δ' ἀνεμείχθημεν, εἰς μὲν αὐτῶν, ἀγνώς τις, τῷ Φανοστράτῳ προσπίπτει καὶ κατεῖχεν ἐκεῖνον, Κόνων δ' οὑτοσὶ καὶ ὁ υἱὸς αὐτοῦ καὶ ὁ 'Ανδρομένους υἱὸς ἐμοὶ προσπεσόντες τὸ μὲν πρῶτον ἐξέδυσαν, εἶθ' ὑποσκελίσαντες καὶ ῥάξαντες εἰς τὸν βόρβορον οὕτω διέθηκαν ἐναλλόμενοι καὶ ὑβρίζοντες, ὥστε τὸ μὲν χεῖλος διακόψαι, τοὺς δ' ὀφθαλμοὺς συγκλεῖσαι. Translation from Bers 2003.

25. Dem. 54.41: ἦ μὴν παθὼν ὑπὸ Κόνωνος ταῦτα ὧν δικάζομαι, καὶ λαβὼν πληγάς, καὶ τὸ χεῖλος διακοπεὶς οὕτως ὥστε καὶ ῥαφῆναι, καὶ ὑβρισθείς. Translation from Bers 2003.

26. Gagarin (2005: 366) posits that Ariston probably did defend himself and so may be distorting the facts to appear restrained.

27. He narrates the incident from the perspective of his group of messmates (οἱ σύσσιτοι, 4) and makes frequent use of first-person plural constructions (ἦμεν, 3; ἡμεῖς [. . .] εἰώθειμεν, 3; διηγομεν, 3; εἰς ἡμᾶς αὐτούς, 4; ἡμεῖς [. . .] ἀπεπεμψάμεθα, 4; ἡμᾶς, 4).

28. Dem. 54.4: τῷ στρατηγῷ τὸ πρᾶγμα εἴπομεν κοινῇ πάντες οἱ σύσσιτοι προσελθόντες, οὐκ ἐγὼ τῶν ἄλλων ἔξω. Translation from Bers 2003.

29. Pearson 1981: 60.

30. On the argument Conon may have attempted to make, see pp. 000.

31. The same shift in rhetorical situation occurs in inheritance cases, in which the relationship between the disputants is not as important as the relationships between the disputants and the deceased testator.

32. Alleged murderers could also be prosecuted by *apagōgē*, which came before the *dikastēria*. On this use of *apagōgē*, see Volonaki 2000. See also p. 000, n. 00.

33. On the tragic elements of Antiphon 1, see Bers 2009: 32–34. To make the whole affair look like a well-conceived conspiracy, the speaker also asserts that the stepmother had made previous attempts on his father's life (Roisman 2006: 11–13).

34. Lysias 4 is a *graphē* (MacDowell 1978: 123–124; Phillips 2007); Antiphon 5 is an *endeixis/apagōgē* (see Hansen 1976: 14, 124–125).

35. Antiph. 6.7, 34–36.

36. The involvement of various third parties in their dispute may also have made denying enmity difficult.

37. Lys. 3.20, 39. It had been four years.

38. On the narrative's function to create a probability argument about the accusation, see Scafuro 1997: 58–60; cf. Griffith-Williams 2013.

39. The defendant was accused of destroying the stump of an olive tree on his property, a capital offense in fourth-century Athens that fell within the purview of the Areopagus. It was illegal to cut down a sacred olive tree (*moria*) or violate its enclosure (*sēkos*). The Areopagus had jurisdiction over the sacred olives as well as some other religious matters. See Arist. *Ath. Pol.* 60.2; Smith 1927; MacDowell 1978: 135; Carey 1989: 114–115; Wallace 1989: 106–112; Hansen 1991: 288–295; Todd 2007: 482–485.

40. He starts his speech with a complaint about being harassed by sycophants (Lys. 7.1).

41. Invention of charges: Lys. 7.3. Desire for money: Lys. 7.20, 39.

42. When the speaker says, "You would have taken vengeance on me if you were my enemy" (αὐτὸς δέ, εἰ μέν σοι ἐχθρὸς ἦν, ἐν τούτῳ τῷ τρόπῳ ἦσθα ἄν με τετιμωρημένος, 20), the comment "if you had been my enemy" (in a past contra-factual condition) is a sneering allusion to Nicomachus not being an enemy and concerned only for money.

43. Lys. 7.39–40. According to the speaker, this is not their first experiment with such tactics against him (cf. Andoc. 1.132; Isae. 8.3).

44. In addition to Lys. 12 and Aeschin. 1 (discussed below), see Lys. 13; Dem. 22, 24. Private suits concerning disputed ownership also illustrate how enmity could be affirmed but not emphasized. Prosecutors in such cases typically limit their narrative to the dispute at hand (Lys. 32; Isocr. 17, 21; Isae. 5; Dem. 40, 48; [Dem.] 49, 50). Only occasionally did a speaker find it beneficial to provide the jury with the full background (Dem. 39, 47).

45. Wolpert 2002: 120–129.

46. Lys. 12.2: ἀλλ' ὡς ἅπασι πολλῆς ἀφθονίας οὔσης ὑπὲρ τῶν ἰδίων ἢ ὑπὲρ τῶν δημοσίων ὀργίζεσθαι.

47. On the subordination of private interests to public in this speech, see also Schön 1918: 52–53; Scheid-Tissinier 2007; Phillips 2008: 157.

48. Similarly, in Lysias 13 (*Against Agoratus*), the speaker arraigns a participant in The Thirty's regime for murdering one of the speaker's relatives. This leads to a similar tactic of affirming enmity but then subsuming private motivation into the public issues at stake: "I have the same enmity toward the defendant Agoratus as does your democracy" (τυγχάνει οὖν ἐμοὶ ἡ αὐτὴ ἔχθρα πρὸς Ἀγόρατον τουτονὶ καὶ τῷ πλήθει τῷ ὑμετέρῳ ὑπάρχουσα, Lys. 13.1). Translation from Todd 2000.

49. Aeschines was evidently successful since Demosthenes (19.283–286) mentions in a later speech that Timarchus was disfranchised.

50. Aeschines says very little about the history of the political wrangling between himself, Timarchus, and Demosthenes. Fisher (2001: 54–55, 121) notes that although Aeschines promises to tell the jury about the background of the dispute, his discussion of the broader political context is strikingly sparse.

51. Aeschin. 1.1–2: οὐδένα πώποτε τῶν πολιτῶν, ὦ ἄνδρες Ἀθηναῖοι, οὔτε γραφὴν γραψάμενος οὔτ' ἐν εὐθύναις λυπήσας, ἀλλ' ὡς ἔγωγε νομίζω μέτριον ἐμαυτὸν πρὸς ἕκαστα τούτων παρεσχηκώς, ὁρῶν δὲ τήν τε πόλιν μεγάλα βλαπτομένην ὑπὸ Τιμάρχου τουτουὶ δημηγοροῦντος παρὰ τοὺς νόμους, καὶ αὐτὸς ἰδίᾳ συκοφαντούμενος (ὃν δὲ τρόπον, προϊόντος ἐπιδείξω τοῦ λόγου) ἔν τι τῶν αἰσχίστων ἡγησάμην εἶναι μὴ βοηθῆσαι τῇ τε πόλει πάσῃ καὶ τοῖς νόμοις καὶ ὑμῖν καὶ ἐμαυτῷ· εἰδὼς δ' αὐτὸν ἔνοχον ὄντα οἷς ὀλίγῳ πρότερον ἠκούσατε ἀναγιγνώσκοντος τοῦ γραμματέως, ἐπήγγειλα αὐτῷ τὴν δοκιμασίαν ταυτηνί. καὶ ὡς ἔοικεν, ὦ ἄνδρες Ἀθηναῖοι, οἱ εἰωθότες λόγοι λέγεσθαι ἐπὶ τοῖς δημοσίοις ἀγῶσιν οὐκ εἰσὶ ψευδεῖς. αἱ γὰρ ἴδιαι ἔχθραι πολλὰ πάνυ τῶν κοινῶν ἐπανορθοῦσι. Translation from Carey 2000.

52. Even this admission (αὐτὸς ἰδίᾳ συκοφαντούμενος) has been carefully tied to public advantage. Aeschines labels Timarchus a sycophant and therefore a public menace.

53. There was no dispute about whether or not Timarchus had exercised the privileges of citizenship. Aeschines must prove only that he was disqualified from doing so. On the prostitution law, see Halperin 1990: 98–99; Winkler 1990: 56–59; D. Cohen 1991: 221–223; E. Cohen 2007; Lanni 2010.

54. Cf. Lycurg. 1.5. Aeschines does not attempt simply to "win the judges' good will" (E. Harris 2005: 130) with his character portrayal of himself but rather to make an argument about his case.

55. This tactic could also be used in a "private" procedure (*dikē*) if the trial had enough public interest. In *Against Polycles*, Apollodorus emphasizes the public nature of the trial and recounts his hostile relationship with the defendant only insofar as is necessary to provide the outline of the history of the dispute. This is in keeping with his assertion that the trial is not private (*idios*) but common (*koinos*) to the whole city ([Dem.] 50.1). The substance of the trial rather than the procedure was what counted.

56. Lycurg. 1.5: ταύτην τὴν εἰσαγγελίαν ἐποιησάμην, οὔτε δι' ἔχθραν οὐδεμίαν.

57. Cf. the fragmentary passage from Lysias (*P. Oxy.* 1606 fr. 6 col. iv = fr. 151 [Carey]) in which the speaker argues that he was previously a friend to the defendant to make it seem more likely that he actually did loan money to him, which was the point at dispute.

58. On this point, see pp. 58–67.

59. Lys. 3.28–39.

60. This is the argument about a weak man being unlikely to assault a stronger one that Aristotle mentions (*Rh.* 1402a17–24).

61. In contrast to this speaker's confidence in his arguments about the series of events leading to the supposed crime, Euphiletus, the speaker of *On the Murder of Eratosthenes*, faces a much more serious problem. The circumstances surrounding his killing of Eratosthenes are quite suspicious. Euphiletus' emphatic denial of enmity covers the weak nature of his other arguments. Cf. Lysias 4, in which the speaker apparently does not have much confidence that his denial of enmity will stick (4) and so, much like the speaker of *Against Simon*, launches into a rebuttal of any credible reason to have attacked his opponent in the manner alleged (6–7).

62. See pp. 000–000.

63. Hansen 1991: 195.

64. May (1988: 7–12) notes that the speaker's standing in the community was more influential for Roman than for Greek law court speeches, but public persona was still important in high-profile trials at Athens.

65. Lycurg. 1.3–4. He asserts that it is not fair to classify as interferers those who benefit the state, as Lycurgus himself does (5–6). The parody of this type of argument in Aristophanes' *Wealth* (911–919) may indicate that this was a common line of defense.

66. Usher 1999: 325.

67. For studies on Lycurgus' role in fourth-century Athenian government, see Faraguna 1992; Habicht 1997: 6–35; Hintzen-Bohlen 1997.

68. The absence of a monetary reward in the procedure Lycurgus employed helped protect him from the suspicion of avarice.

69. Lys. 31.4: ἐνδεῶς μὲν γὰρ διὰ τὴν ἀπειρίαν πάντων τῶν τούτῳ πεπραγμένων, ἱκανῶς δὲ διὰ τὴν περὶ αὐτὸν κακίαν εἰρηκὼς ἂν εἴην. ἀξιῶ

δὲ καὶ ὑμῶν οἵτινες δυνατώτεροι ἐμοῦ εἰσι λέγειν, ἀποφῆναι μείζω ὄντα αὐτοῦ τὰ ἁμαρτήματα, καὶ ἐξ ὧν ἂν ἐγὼ ὑπολίπω, πάλιν αὐτοὺς περὶ ὧν ἵ σασι κατηγορῆσαι Φίλωνος. Translation from Todd 2000.

70. Cf. Lys. 22, 27; Dem. 24; Lycurg. 1.
71. On the case, see pp. 000–000.
72. Another reason that Aeschines denies enmity with Timarchus could be that he wants to distance himself as much as possible from Timarchus' alleged conduct. If Timarchus was as bad as Aeschines says he is, Aeschines would do well to stay clear of him.
73. Aeschin. 1.91: ἐκ τῶν εἰκότων.
74. Aeschin. 1.93: πρῶτον μὲν μηδὲν ὑμῖν ἔστω πιστότερον ὧν αὐτοὶ σύνιστε καὶ πέπεισθε περὶ Τιμάρχου τουτουί, ἔπειτα τὸ πρᾶγμα θεωρεῖτε μὴ ἐκ τοῦ παρόντος, ἀλλ' ἐκ τοῦ παρεληλυθότος χρόνου. Cf. D. Cohen 1995: 110–111.
75. Cf. Lys. 22.22, 27.8, 31.2–4; Dem. 25.4.
76. Sycophancy of the opponents: §§1–6, 30–32. At §§25–26 the speaker mentions three sycophants by name, but it is unclear whether these three men were the prosecutors in this trial (see Murphy 1992: 546 n. 11).
77. Murphy 1992: 555–558. The speaker accuses his opponents of helping produce the factionalism that led to civil war, asserting that the city's demagogues created a class warfare of sorts by prosecuting the elites for extortion (Wolpert 2002: 123).
78. Murphy 1992: 544.
79. The language of enmity is reserved for the enemies of the democracy. Of the seven uses of *echthros* in the speech, all but one (§16) refer to the enemies of the state (§§6, 18, 20, 21, 22, 23), that is, the oligarchical partisans.
80. The denial of enmity probably has to do with the nature of the charge. The speech seems to have been composed for some type of *dokimasia*, at which several men charged the speaker with staying in Athens during the rule of The Thirty Tyrants and colluding in some way with the regime. To support his contention that his conduct while serving in office under The Thirty was exemplary, the speaker must avoid an admission that he is an agonistic individual involved in many quarrels. Had he acknowledged that he made enemies during the regime of The Thirty, he would have put himself under suspicion of misconduct under the oligarchs' rule.
81. "I have been the object of an unjust and sycophantic attack by my enemies" (Lys. 21.17).
82. See also Kucharski 2012.
83. Contrary to normal practice at Athens, the person who lodged the appeal apparently spoke second at trial, and so it is justifiable to refer to Demosthenes 57 as a "defense" speech, even though the speaker initiated the procedure. On *ephesis*, see Just 1965; A. R. W. Harrison 1968–1971, ii: 190–192. In the only other extant *ephesis*, Isaeus' *On Behalf of Euphiletus*, the speaker also accuses his prosecutors of acting out of enmity (Isae. 12.8).

84. This, at any rate, is the name ascribed to him in Libanius' hypothesis to the speech. This may or may not be correct, but it provides a convenient label.

85. Athenian citizenship was granted at the deme level. The local government, comprised of demesmen, decided who would be enrolled on the *lēxiarchikon grammateion* and therefore who would have a share in the polis (Arist. *Ath. Pol.* 42.1).

86. Dem. 57.61; cf. 48. Eubulides' co-conspirators had also squabbled with the speaker. Euxitheus had served as demarch and became involved in quarrels when he attempted to collect rents due from public properties let out to certain demesmen (63).

87. Dem. 57.32; cf. §8, where Euxitheus recounts that Eubulides previously lost a case and failed to receive even one-fifth of the votes. As Christ (1998b: 64) points out, "Arguably, a prosecutor's conspicuous loss of a suit, especially if he won less than one fifth of the votes cast in a public suit and therefore incurred the normal statutory penalties, might make him more susceptible to the claim in later suits that he was a sykophant."

88. Dem. 57.34: τοῦτο γάρ ἐστιν ὁ συκοφάντης, αἰτιᾶσθαι μὲν πάντα, ἐξελέγξαι δὲ μηδέν.

89. Dem. 57.59–60.

90. Dem. 57.49: ὁ δὲ νυνὶ παρὼν ἐχθροῦ καὶ συκοφαντεῖν βουλομένου.

91. In the debate on "sycophancy," scholars often focus on the goals and motivations that drive the "sycophant": was the sycophant actuated by desire for financial gain or was he simply a vexatious litigant? The Attic orators, on the other hand, tend to be more concerned with the sycophant's methods than his goals. Motivation and aims are important only insofar as they imply something about the credibility of the person to whom they are attributed. The sycophant is a liar par excellence because he is willing to use rhetorical tricks and legal technicalities to gain a verdict that he knows to be unjust.

92. Andoc. 1.132: διὰ τί ποτε τοῖς ἐμοὶ νυνὶ ἐπιτιθεμένοις μετὰ Καλλίου καὶ συμπαρασκευάσασι τὸν ἀγῶνα καὶ χρήματα εἰσενεγκοῦσιν ἐπ' ἐμοὶ τρία μὲν ἔτη ἐπιδημῶν καὶ ἥκων ἐκ Κύπρου οὐκ ἀσεβεῖν ἐδόκουν αὐτοῖς.

93. MacDowell 1962: 156–157.

94. Dem. 18.13: εἰ μὲν εἰσαγγελίας ἄξια πράττοντα ἑώρα, εἰσαγγέλλοντα [. . .] εἰς κρίσιν καθιστάντα παρ' ὑμῖν, εἰ δὲ γράφοντα παράνομα, παρανόμων γραφόμενον.

95. Dem. 18.22–23.

96. Dem. 18.83, 117, 124, 189–191, 222–225, 243, 251. Aeschines (3.215–225) defends himself against this criticism.

97. Dem. 18.15, 191.

98. Dem. 18.251. Interestingly, Aeschines made a very similar argument against Demosthenes in a trial thirteen years earlier (343 BC) when their roles were reversed: "You dare to claim that I went on it [the embassy] without having been elected, yet though my personal enemy you have not seen fit even to this day to impeach me for misconduct as an envoy?" (ἐφ' ἣν [πρεσβείαν] τολμᾷς με λέγειν ὡς οὐ χειροτονηθεὶς ᾠχόμην, ἐχθρὸς δ' ὢν οὐδέπω καὶ τήμερον ἠθέληκάς με

εἰσαγγεῖλαι παραπρεσβεύσασθαι, Aeschin. 2.139). Translation from Carey 2000. The use of this type of argument by several different orators shows that it was a well-known *topos*.

99. In addition to the examples discussed above, see Antiph. 6.9; Lys. 7.20–21, 7.42, 19.60; Isae. 3.9, 8.25–27; Dem. 37.2, 55.4–5; Aeschin. 2.139; cf. Lys. 7.18; Dem. 25.38. Sycophancy could substitute for enmity in the delay *topos* (Lys. 7.20).

100. Dem. 23.187–189. See also Lys. 13.83–84; Isae. 10.18–20.

101. Dem. 23.1; cf. 190.

CHAPTER 4

1. The Corcyraean civil war: Thuc. 3.70–85. On *stasis* and the ancient Greeks' fear of it, see Ruschenbusch 1978; Ste. Croix 1981; D. Cohen 1995: 25–33; Ober 1998: 66–72; Raaflaub 2009.

2. Thuc. 2.37.

3. Magistrates who in the performance of their duties came into conflict with other citizens: Antiph. 6.43; Dem. 21.13, 25.50, 39.3. Aristotle recognizes the tendency of magistrates to fall into enmity and suggests that the officials who impose penalties be different from those who exact payment, because if the same people were responsible for both, they would become "everybody's enemies" (*Pol.* 6.8 [1322a16–19]; cf. Pl. *Resp.* 1.343e). Cf. the extensive regulations in Plato's *Laws* about government officials who become involved in quarrels. The Athenian process of tax collection is a notorious example. Because the tax collectors paid the state a fixed sum and kept the overages for themselves, they profited directly from their activities. It is no surprise that tax collectors made enemies (Andoc. 1.133–136; Lys. 22.8, 63; cf. Dem. 21.153, 166; Lycurg. 1.19, 58). On public finances in ancient Athens, see Hansen 1991: 260–264.

4. Arist. *Ath. Pol.* 43–61.

5. The absence of professionals and bureaucrats, a hallmark of Athenian democracy, was characteristic of administrations at the deme level as well. Demes had leaders, demarchs, and many other types of magistrates. Attested officials for the demes include herald (*kēryx*), examiner (*euthynos*), religious officials (*hieropoioi*), and treasurers (*tamiai*). Probably there were many more magistracies. Several more are attested for only a single deme: secretary (*grammateus*), advocate (*syndikos*), *merarchai, meritai, antigrapheus, logistēs*, and *horistai*. See Osborne 1985a: 74–79; Whitehead 1986: 139–148.

6. Lys. 9.14: οὔτ' ἐχθρὸν ἐτιμωρησάμην οὔτε φίλον ηὐεργέτησα.

7. Hdt. 8.79–81; Plut. *Arist.* 8.1–4, 25.7.

8. On the oath, see Hansen 1991: 227–228.

9. Xen. *Mem.* 1.1.18: κατὰ τοὺς νόμους βουλεύσειν. Cf. Lys. 31.1, "to recommend the course of action most advantageous for the city" (τὰ βέλτιστα βουλεύσειν τῇ πόλει), which also emphasizes the necessary public mindedness of the Council member.

10. Arist. *Ath. Pol.* 55.5: δικαίως ἄρξειν καὶ κατὰ τοὺς νόμους.

11. The significant limits on magistrates' activities (see A. R. W. Harrison 1968–1971, ii: 4–7) also mitigated the temptation to abuse one's power to pursue enemies.

12. A member of the Council could bring charges against his enemy before the Council, but, as in the jury courts, he had to secure a conviction from a mass jury.

13. On the principle of collegiality in magistracies, see Hansen 1991: 237–239.

14. See pp. 000–000.

15. See p. 000.

16. The extant speeches of course mirror the values of the society in which they were delivered, and so correspondences between the way enmity is depicted in the speeches and the jury's ideological expectations of proper behavior are inevitable, but it is not always obvious where these correspondences are.

17. For an explanation of how this method differs from previous scholarly writing on the subject, see pp. 00–00.

18. Lys. 12.2: πρότερον μὲν γὰρ ἔδει τὴν ἔχθραν τοὺς κατηγοροῦντας ἐπιδεῖξαι, ἥτις εἴη πρὸς τοὺς φεύγοντας.

19. Lys. 10.13, 12.2–3, 13.1, 14.2; Dem. 21.1; 24.8; [Dem.] 45.1, 53.1, 58.2, 59.1; Aeschin. 1.2. Cf. Dem. 22.1–2, 24.7.

20. On this speaker's affirmation of enmity, see pp. 000. He affirms enmity with Nicostratus to attack the latter's credibility as a speaker.

21. Lys. 14.2; Aeschin. 1.2; see also Rhodes 1998.

22. Andoc. 1.1: τὴν μὲν παρασκευήν ὦ ἄνδρες, καὶ τὴν προθυμίαν τῶν ἐχθρῶν τῶν ἐμῶν, ὥστ' ἐμὲ κακῶς ποιεῖν ἐκ παντὸς τρόπου καὶ δικαίως καὶ ἀδίκως [. . .] σχεδόν τι πάντες ἐπίστασθε.

23. Lys. 19.2: τὴν μὲν οὖν παρασκευὴν καὶ τὴν προθυμίαν τῶν ἐχθρῶν ὁρᾶτε. This speaker also accuses his enemies of attacking him on false charges (11).

24. In addition to Andocides 1 and Lysias 19, cf. Lys. 3.15, 24.27; Isocr. 16; Dem. 37.23, 40.32, 43.10, 55.33–34, 57.1–17.

25. MacDowell 1962: 62; cf. Lavency 1964: 155–157.

26. Accusations of "conspiracy" had the advantage of not needing supporting evidence. Roisman (2006: 13) draws attention to this "perverse logic of conspiracism, in which lack of knowledge suggests the existence of a plot rather than being a reason to doubt it."

27. On the delay *topos*, see pp. 000–000.

28. Christ (1998b: 154–156) illustrates this point well. See also Dover 1974: 182; D. Cohen 1995: 101–115; Rhodes 1998.

29. [Dem.] 58.39–44.

30. Lys. 8.18, 29.1; Isae. 12.10; Dem. 21.23; [Dem.] 53.14; cf. Lys. 9.6; Aeschin. 3.173. Another source seems to have been the opponent's disaffected slaves, who were often more than happy to share inside information with their masters' foes (Lys. 7.16; Dem. 25.80; cf. Lys. 5.5).

31. Witnesses: Lys. 23.4, 23.7–8; Dem. 25.58, 25.60–62, 40.58; [Dem.] 58.4;

Lycurg. 1.19; Xen. *Mem.* 2.9.5. *Synēgoroi*: Lys. 13.3, 29.1. Cf. *Against Boeotus I* in which the speaker asserts that his father avoided the courts because he knew that his enemies would appear against him (Dem. 39.3).

32. [Arist.] *Rh. Al.* 15.5 (1431b37–41).

33. Lys. 7.19. Cf. Lys. 24.7 and the worries the prosecutor expresses at Lys. 29.1; [Dem.] 58.59.

34. E.g., Antiph. 6.7; Andoc. 1.30, 1.54; Lys. 9.1–3, 16.1, 19.1–3, 19.53, 20.30, 25.5; Isocr. 16.2; Isae. 11.4; Dem. 18.7–8, 29.22, 29.27, 57.30, 57.53; Aeschin. 2.2. Cf. Lys. 18.9; Dem. 21.103.

35. Certain "unspeakable" words (*aporrhēta*) such as *androphonos, patraloias, mētraloias*, and *apobeblēkenai* were forbidden (see Lipsius 1905–1915: 646–651; MacDowell 1978: 126–129; Todd 1993: 268–269; Todd 2007: 631–635). A separate law also governed insults against magistrates (Lys. 9.6–10; Dem. 21.32–33). It may also have been possible to prosecute someone for slander under the law for *hubris* (MacDowell 1978: 129–132).

36. Lys. 10.3, 5, 9, 12, 21, 22, 25.

37. In a previous suit, Theomnestus had been accused of throwing away his shield and the speaker of Lysias 10 served as a witness against Theomnestus. It was during that trial that Theomnestus allegedly slandered the speaker as a parricide.

38. Disparagement of those whom one dislikes seems to be a natural human response. As Freud (1960: 102–103) observed, "Since our individual childhood [. . .] hostile impulses against our fellow men have been subject to the same restrictions, the same progressive repression, as our sexual urges [. . .] By making our enemy small, inferior, despicable or comic, we achieve in a roundabout way the enjoyment of overcoming—to which the third person, who has made no efforts, bears witness by his laughter."

39. Lys. 19.60; Isocr. 11.38; Dem. 18.123; [Dem.] 58.40.

40. Andoc. 1.4, 1.54, 4.2; Lys. 8.14–17, 9.1–3, 16.11, 19.2–6, 20.11, 20.30; Isae. 12.12; Dem. 21.104. Cf. Andoc. 4.25–28; Isae. 5.39, 8.40–42.

41. Eur. *HF* 286; cf. *Supp.* 343; Aeschin. 2.182. If Bers (2009: 51–54) is correct, such verbal abuse may have been even more common than these restrained and formal orations would lead us to believe (cf. Carey 1999). The curse tablets also provide evidence for Athenians' fears about their enemies' mockery.

42. For instance, Herman (2006: 196) draws a distinction between "vengeance" and "punishment" (for which the same Greek word is used, *timōria*). The Athenian system, he contends, is designed for the latter, the "ultimate aim" of which "is not to inflict harm in retribution for past wrongdoings, but [. . .] to protect the community against future ones by means of education."

43. Cf. Gagarin's (2005) remarks about violence in the orators. Out of all the violent acts described in the corpus, none is portrayed as legitimate and acceptable. Furthermore, if a speaker narrates a violent encounter, he always tries to reduce his own participation to a minimum. Gagarin's observations are correct, but these patterns are not necessarily representative of Athenian morality; litigants portray themselves as passive to meet their legal argumentative needs.

44. Cf. Herman 2006: 157–158.

45. Herman 2006: 284–285. Cf. E. Harris (2005: 130) who cites Demosthenes 54 to show that "Athenian values discouraged men from using the courts to pursue feuds with each other."

46. Other than Demosthenes 21 and 54, only one other prosecution case alleging violent *hubris* as the crime on trial has survived, Isocrates 20 (*Against Lochites*). This speech unfortunately is fragmentary and so of little use in speaking to rhetorical strategies since important arguments about the speaker's opponent may have been lost.

47. See pp. 000–000.

48. Herman 1993, 1994, 1995, 2006. See pp. 000–000.

49. Euphiletus presents himself as dispassionate because he believes that it will help him counter an important part of the prosecution's case, the charge of entrapment. On the other hand, Allen (2000b: 126–127) argues that the jury would have sympathized with Euphiletus if he had portrayed the whole affair as a crime of passion. According to Allen, Euphiletus' main problem was that he had not obeyed the norm of "hot blood" (i.e., he did not kill Eratosthenes in a moment of anger). Although her conclusion differs markedly from Herman's, Allen's analysis suffers from the same assumptions. Her argument implicitly accepts the premise that Euphiletus portrays his relationship with Eratosthenes in a way that will win him favor with the jury because he has behaved in accordance with social norms apart from the legal considerations at stake.

50. Herman 2006: 402–414. "The crucial point [. . .] is that in attempting to ingratiate themselves with the dikasts they chose to represent themselves as preferring Tit for two tats and their opponents as preferring Tit for tat or Two tits for a tat" (409).

51. Fisher 1998: 8. The assumption that these are exclusive categories has persisted. For example, "When an Aristophanic character is attacked or mistreated, he or she is more likely to call upon witnesses and threaten a lawsuit than to take personal revenge to repair their honor" (Hunt 2010: 216). Calling witnesses and threatening lawsuits was a means of taking revenge and rehabilitating honor, not a surrendering of it.

52. Loss of the case meant loss of face. See Lys. 16.3, 19.1, 21.12, 27.16; Isocr. 17.1; cf. Dem. 25.6.

53. Loss was especially difficult to bear if it was inflicted by an enemy (Dem. 18.5).

54. D. Cohen 1995: 89–90; Johnstone 1999: 6–7.

55. For the institutional limitations on the abuse of the courts for private ends, see Harris 2006b: 406–410.

56. E.g. Isae. 5.26: ἡμεῖς δ' ὡς λέγομεν ἀληθῆ, καὶ ἄλλο τι τεκμήριον παρεξόμεθα.

57. Antiph. 5.11; Lys. 3.45–46; Lycurg. 1.11–13; Arist. *Rh.* 1.1 (1354a21–24).

58. Lanni (2006) argues that these restrictions on extralegal argumentation were limited to the Areopagus and mercantile cases (*dikai emporikai*). The dicastic

courts, on the other hand, tended to allow for all sorts of extralegal argumentation, and Athenians consciously endorsed the broad-ranging nature of the jury's discretionary power. For criticism of this position, see Gagarin 2012.

59. Arist. *Ath. Pol.* 67.1. Lanni (2006: 100) brushes the passage aside as "problematic," but there is no good reason to reject it (see Rhodes 1981: 718–719; Gagarin 2012: 295). The oath is introduced in the context of *dikai*, which has led some to believe that it was only employed for that type of lawsuit.

60. E.g. Aeschin. 1.154; [Dem. 45.50, 58.41]; cf. [Arist.] *Rh. Al.* 36.21 (1443a16–18). On the oath, see E. Harris 2006a; Mirhady 2007; E. Harris 2013: 101–137.

61. Johnstone 1999: 60–62. See Aeschines' (3.197–200) distinction between those who speak to the point and those who "ask for a vote" (E. Harris 2006a: 175–176).

62. [Arist.] *Rh. Al.* 36.2 (1441b32–34); cf. 29.1 (1436a33–35). P. J. Rhodes (2004: 156) was quite correct when he observed that "Athenian litigants were much better than we have allowed at keeping to the point." Thür (2008) has shown that the legal charges were clearly stated and known before the trial (cf. Gagarin 2012: 295–296; E. Harris 2013: 114–126).

63. Lys. 26.9; Isocr. 20.18; Isae. 1.41, 2.47; Dem. 22.47, 24.5, 25.4, 32.3, 32.13, 34.22, 48.3, 56.48; [Dem.] 58.41; Aeschin. 1.186. Cf. Dem. 21.224, 36.3, 47.46.

64. Lys. 23.1, 26.15; Isae. 3.72, 10.18; Isocr. 21.6; Dem. 19.117, 34.4, 35.5, 47.3, 57.7, 57.60; Dem. 44.31; [Dem.] 45.2; Aeschin. 1.45, 3.163; Lycurg. 1.91.

65. Dem. 27.41, 37.25. Cf. Dem. 38.11.

66. Lys. 9.1–2; Isocr. 20.5; Isae. 1.49, 3.72; Dem. 21.192, 29.39, 38.14, 40.61, 51.2, 54.13, 54.26; [Dem.] 45.13, 45.17–18; Aeschin. 1.166, 2.10, 3.193; Hyp. in Dem. fr. 3; Lycurg. 1.63. Cf. Aeschin. 1.113. With *exōlexōthen*: Dem. 57.33, 57.63, 57.66; Aeschin. 1.170. Cf. Lycurg. 1.149, where slander and speaking *exō tou pragmatos* are closely connected. The accusations of slander (on which see pp. 000–000) may have served the same purpose as accusations of speaking off the point. (See also Plut. *Arist.* 25.3.)

67. Lys. 13.88, 14.16; Isae. 4.5, 8.27; Dem. 25.5.

68. Dem. 19.242; Aeschin. 1.175.

69. Aeschin. 1.176: ὥσπερ ἐν ταῖς ἱπποδρομίαις εἰς τὸν τοῦ πράγματος αὐτὸν δρόμον εἰσελαύνετε.

70. Of the passages cited above, many invoke the specific phrase of the oath, including a form of *auto* in predicate position (e.g., *eis auto to pragma*): Lys. 14.16, 26.15; Isae. 3.72; Dem. 25.5, 27.41, 34.4, 34.22, 37.25, 38.11, 57.7, 57.59; [Dem.] 58.41; cf. Aeschin. 1.178. The plural of this construction (*auta ta pragmata*/*autōn tōn pragmatōn*) is sometimes used with similar force: Dem. 18.15, 18.226, 37.21, 38.19, 55.2; [Dem.] 45.16, 45.51; cf. Dem. 27.58. Discussions of the *pragma* in the *Rhetoric to Alexander*: 4.3 (1426b39–1427a1), 7.8 (1428b16–20), 29.23–25 (1437b18–27), 36.17 (1442b32–35), and 36.21–23 (1443a15–28).

71. [Arist.] *Rh. Al.* 15.5 (1431b37–41).

72. Lys. 9.20: τούτων μὲν οὖν ἀδικούντων μετρίως {ἄν} ἠγανάκτουν,

ἡγούμενος τετάχθαι τοὺς μὲν ἐχθροὺς κακῶς ποιεῖν, τοὺς δὲ φίλους εὖ. Translation from Todd 2000. Furthermore, Polyaenus' statement addresses a very specific situation: his role as a public figure. Magistrates commonly took oaths not to use their offices to help friends or harm enemies because this sort of behavior would compromise the egalitarian nature of democratic government. These oaths say much about how the Athenians thought their government should be run, not how lives should be ordered as a general rule.

73. "Do not look on while those who have done nothing wrong fall into the greatest misfortunes because of personal enmities" (τοὺς μηδὲν ἀδικήσαντας διὰ τὰς ἔχθρας μὴ περιίδητε ἀδίκως τοῖς μεγίστοις ἀτυχήμασι περιπεσόντας, Lys. 9.22).

74. Mayhew and Mirhady's edition of the *Rhetoric to Alexander* (2011) often translates *diabolē* as "prejudice." This draws attention to Athenians' concern that *diabolē* could prevent the object of slander from receiving a fair hearing.

75. MacDowell 1978: 128, but cf. Todd 2007: 634–635, who posits that *aporrhēta* could not be spoken even if true.

76. Connection of slander and distorting truth: Lys. 19.53, 25.5; Isocr. 16.2, 17.1; Isae. 11.4; Dem. 18.225, 29.22, 29.27; Aeschin. 2.2.

77. This adjective *akritos* in a legal context usually refers to persons who fail to receive a trial at all (see LSJ *ad loc.*). Here it is used in a somewhat strained sense of persons who fail to get a proper hearing during a trial.

78. Lys. 27.8: οὐ γὰρ οὗτοι ἄκριτοί εἰσι, περὶ ὧν ἂν ὑμεῖς εἰδότες τὰ πραχθέντα ψηφίσησθε, ἀλλ' οἵτινες ἂν ὑπὸ τῶν ἐχθρῶν διαβληθέντες περὶ ὧν ὑμεῖς μὴ ἴστε, ἀκροάσεως μὴ τύχωσι. Translation from Todd 2000.

79. Lys. 27.8: τούτων δὲ τὰ μὲν πράγματα κατηγορεῖ.

80. D. Cohen 1995: 92.

81. Herman 2006: 169.

82. Dem. 21.136. Cf. Dem. 41.13.

83. Dem. 21.29: μή με Δημοσθένει παραδῶτε, μηδὲ διὰ Δημοσθένην με ἀνέλητε. ὅτι ἐκείνῳ πολεμῶ, διὰ τοῦτό με ἀναιρήσετε.

84. Dem. 21.31–35.

85. Dem. 21.34: δημοσίας ὀργῆς καὶ τιμωρίας. Demosthenes' defense against Meidias' supposed objection that he should have initiated a private case is in the same vein (25–28). Cf. Dem. 47.41 for the argument that an act against a public official constitutes a crime against the state.

86. Dem. 21.142: προσήκειν μέντοι τούτῳ μὴ ταῦτα λέγειν ἡγοῦμαι νυνί, ἀλλ' ὡς οὐ πεποίηκέν τι τούτων ὧν αὐτοῦ κατηγόρηκα διδάσκειν, ἐὰν δὲ μὴ δύνηται, διὰ ταῦτ' ἀπολωλέναι πολὺ μᾶλλον. Translation from Harris 2008. Cf. Dem. 21.7.

87. Interestingly, having denied the legitimacy of this plea in Meidias' case, Demosthenes actually uses it himself (in accordance with his argument that he is the true defendant in the case): "Do not hand me over to any one of these men, men of Athens" (τούτων μηδενί με, ὦ ἄνδρες Ἀθηναῖοι, προῆσθε, 213; cf. 220).

88. Isocr. 16.45: ὑμᾶς δ' ἀξιῶ μὴ προέσθαι με τοῖς ἐχθροῖς μηδ' ἀνηκέστοις συμφοραῖς περιβαλεῖν. Cf. Lys. 9.1–3; Dem. 19.296–297.

89. Compare also the closing plea of the speaker of Lysias 19 (*On the Property of Aristophanes*): "I beg you not to sit by and watch us be annihilated by our personal enemies" (δέομαι οὖν ὑμῶν [. . .] μὴ περιιδεῖν ὑπὸ τῶν ἐχθρῶν ἀναιρεθέντας, 64). Like the speaker of Isocrates 16, this defendant attempts to portray his enemies as maliciously attacking him on false charges (2). Cf. Lys. 9.22.

90. Dem. 8.1: ἔδει μέν, ὦ ἄνδρες Ἀθηναῖοι, τοὺς λέγοντας ἅπαντας μήτε πρὸς ἔχθραν ποιεῖσθαι λόγον μηδένα μήτε πρὸς χάριν, ἀλλ' ὃ βέλτιστον ἕκαστος ἡγεῖτο, τοῦτ' ἀποφαίνεσθαι. Translation from Trevett 2011. Cf. Dem. 2.29, 4.44, 9.2, 9.29, 14.5, 16.1. Denials of enmity: 3.21, 5.6, 16.32.

91. Downplaying: Lys. 12, 13, 14; Dem. 22, 24; Aeschin. 1. Denying: Lys. 22, 26, 27, 31; Dem. 20, 23; Din. 1 (*Against Demosthenes*); Lycurg. 1. See pp. 000–000.

92. Dem. 9.53, 10.63.

93. Dem. 5.5: πρῶτος καὶ μόνος παρελθὼν ἀντεῖπον, καὶ μόνον οὐ διεσπάσθην ὑπὸ τῶν ἐπὶ μικροῖς λήμμασιν πολλὰ καὶ μεγάλα ὑμᾶς ἁμαρτάνειν πεισάντων. Translation from Trevett 2011.

94. Dem. 10.27, 22.54–55, 24.166–167. To be liable for punishment on the body was considered the hallmark of slavery (cf. Hunter 1994: 173–185). See also Fisher's (1990: 131) discussion of the public's interest in limiting *hubris* by law. Oligarchies were often accused of treating poorer citizens as slaves (e.g., Lys. 20.3; see Raaflaub 1983).

95. Halperin 1990: 88–112.

96. If a citizen prostituted himself, that is, willingly took pay to have his manhood violated, he forfeited certain civic privileges. The democracy's concern for the body of citizens may have been behind the anxiety that the institution of pederasty provoked in the fifth century (on which see Lanni 2010: 50–54).

97. Andoc. 1.43; see MacDowell 1962: 92–93. The date of this law is not secure, but it goes back at least to the early democracy (between 510 and 490) and possibly even to the reign of Pisistratus.

98. On the "expressive effect" of laws in Athens, their power to influence social norms, see Lanni 2010. On the shift in scholarship toward viewing Athenian citizenship not just in terms of institutions and regulations but as an organic and diffuse concept based upon shared values, see, for example, Manville 1994; Patterson 2007.

99. E.g., Winkler 1990: 49; D. Cohen 1995: 119–130; Roisman 2005: 73; McHardy 2008: 99; Phillips 2008: 19; Riess 2012.

100. Lys. 3.18.

101. Arist. *Pol.* 2.12 (1274b18–23). The law itself may not have "recognize[d] intoxication as a mitigating factor" (Phillips 2007: 89), but the jurors may have.

102. Dem. 21.36.

103. Dem. 21.147. This seems to have been a well-known incident (Andoc. 4.20; Plut. *Alc.* 16.4).

104. Athenian indulgence for violence committed under the influence of alco-

hol, love, or competitiveness was not unequivocal. Several litigants condemn such behavior (Lys. 3.6; Dem. 54.4–5, 54.7–9; Aeschin. 1.58–59).

105. D. Cohen 1995: 119–130; Roisman 2005: 73; McHardy 2008: 99; Phillips 2008: 19; Riess 2012: 37; cf. Winkler 1990: 49.

106. Dem. 54.13: τί ποτ' ἐστὶν ἃ πρὸς ταῦτα τολμήσει Κόνων λέγειν. Translation from Bers 2003.

107. Conon thus makes light of the *pragma*, the legal point at issue (13).

108. Dem. 54.20: ἂν δ' εἴπῃ Κόνων "ἰθύφαλλοί τινές ἐσμεν ἡμεῖς συνειλεγμένοι, καὶ ἐρῶντες οὓς ἂν ἡμῖν δόξῃ παίομεν καὶ ἄγχομεν," εἶτα γελάσαντες ὑμεῖς ἀφήσετε; οὐκ οἴομαί γε.

109. Cohen recognizes that Ariston is probably distorting what Conon will say, but Cohen's (1995: 128) reconstruction of Conon's real argument is surprisingly similar to the one Ariston attributes to him: "that in young men's drunken revelry and sexual rivalry such brawls are part of the fun and should be tolerated and regarded with amusement."

110. Dem. 54.16: ἡμεῖς γὰρ οὔτε παροινοῦντες οὔθ' ὑβρίζοντες ὑπ' οὐδενὸς ἀνθρώπων ἑωράμεθα.

111. D. Cohen 1995: 131–137; cf. Roisman 2005: 73; McHardy 2008: 99; Phillips 2008: 19; Riess 2012: 37.

112. Lys. 3.4: "If I have done anything wrong, members of the Council, I do not expect any mercy" (ἀξιῶ δέ, ὦ βουλή, εἰ μὲν ἀδικῶ, μηδεμιᾶς συγγνώμης τυγχάνειν). Translation from Todd 2000.

113. Lys. 3.4: ἀλλὰ δῆλον ὅτι καὶ οἱ τοὺς νόμους ἐνθάδε θέντες, οὐκ εἴ τινες μαχεσάμενοι ἔτυχον ἀλλήλων κατάξαντες τὰς κεφαλάς, ἐπὶ τούτοις ἠξίωσαν τῆς πατρίδος φυγὴν ποιήσασθαι. Translation from Todd 2000.

114. Cf. Dem. 55.24–25.

115. It would be uncharitable to fault the speaker for never explicitly denying the charge of attack (Phillips 2007: 90), given the fragmentary nature of the speech.

116. Allen 2000b: 153–156.

117. Todd 1998: 165. Euphiletus reveals in passing that his wife had gone with Eratosthenes' mother to the Thesmophoria (20).

118. Cf. Herman 2006: 175–183. W. Harris (1997), responding to one of Herman's earlier articles, rightfully critiqued his interpretation of Lysias 1 by showing that Euphiletus was not categorically denying the right to revenge but in his own situation felt that it was advantageous to portray himself as the agent of public justice (cf. Fisher 1998: 80–82).

119. Dem. 21.74: τῷ δ' Εὐαίωνι καὶ πᾶσιν, εἴ τις αὐτῷ βεβοήθηκεν ἀτιμαζομένος, πολλὴν συγγνώμην ἔχω. Herman (2006: 169–170) argues that Demosthenes is providing an example of what not to do in response to an injury. This may be true, but it proves little. We could conclude perhaps that murder was an unacceptable response to a minor physical injury (see Dem. 21.75) but not that one was always expected to resort to the courts.

120. Demosthenes' trial was part of the *probolē* procedure (see p. 000), but be-

cause his main accusation against Meidias was that he committed *hubris* against him, he focuses throughout the speech on proving that Meidias' act was indeed *hubris* and deserves to be punished severely.

121. Dem. 21.73–74: λογίσασθε παρ' ὑμῖν αὐτοῖς, ὅσῳ πλείονα ὀργὴν ἐμοὶ προσῆκε παραστῆναι πάσχοντι τοιαῦτα ὑπὸ Μειδίου ἢ τότ' ἐκείνῳ τῷ Εὐαίωνι τῷ τὸν Βοιωτὸν ἀποκτείναντι. ὁ μέν γ' ὑπὸ γνωρίμου, καὶ τούτου μεθύοντος, ἐναντίον ἓξ ἢ ἑπτὰ ἀνθρώπων ἐπλήγη [. . .] ἐγὼ δ' ὑπ' ἐχθροῦ, νήφοντος, ἕωθεν, ὕβρει καὶ οὐκ οἴνῳ τοῦτο ποιοῦντος, ἐναντίον πολλῶν καὶ ξένων καὶ πολιτῶν.

122. Compare the implicit *a fortiori* argument in Lysias 12 (*Against Eratosthenes*). Lysias asserts that Eratosthenes put Polemarchus to death "not having suffered any private wrong from him" (οὔτε αὐτὸς ἰδίᾳ ἀδικούμενος, 23). Lysias does not imply that Eratosthenes would have been justified in murdering Lysias' brother if he did have a private pretext. He denies that Eratosthenes had this motivation so that his acts will appear all the more heinous.

123. Dem. 21.76: τοὺς ὑβρίζοντας ἅπαντας καὶ τοὺς ἀσελγεῖς οὐκ αὐτὸν ἀμύνεσθαι μετὰ τῆς ὀργῆς, ἀλλ' ἐφ' ὑμᾶς ἄγειν δεῖ, ὡς βεβαιούντων ὑμῶν καὶ φυλαττόντων τὰς ἐν τοῖς νόμοις τοῖς παθοῦσι βοηθείας.

124. Phillips 2008: 23. Cf. the Lysianic fragment, *Against Tisias* (frr. 278–279 [Carey]), and the interpretations in D. Cohen 1995: 137–138; Phillips 2008: 18.

125. It would be even more dangerous to use drama to such an end. Theatrical works make use of embellishment and exaggeration intended to shock the audience. Hence, Odysseus in Euripides' satyr play *Cyclops* exclaims, "O Zeus, what will I say, now that I have seen things inside the cave that are not believable, like events in myths and not real life?" (ὦ Ζεῦ, τί λέξω, δείν' ἰδὼν ἄντρων ἔσω / κοὐ πιστά, μύθοις εἰκότ' οὐδ' ἔργοις βροτῶν; 375–376). There was a gap between the stories of myth, with which tragedy was concerned, and the reality at Athens. See also Dover 1974: 17–18; Blundell 1989: 10.

126. Dem. 54.18–19: φασὶ τοίνυν ταύτας διὰ τοῦτο γίγνεσθαι, ἵνα μὴ λοιδορούμενοι τύπτειν ἀλλήλους προάγωνται. πάλιν αἰκείας εἰσί· καὶ ταύτας ἀκούω διὰ τοῦτ' εἶναι τὰς δίκας, ἵνα μηδείς, ὅταν ἥττων ᾖ, λίθῳ μηδὲ τῶν τοιούτων ἀμύνηται μηδενί, ἀλλὰ τὴν ἐκ τοῦ νόμου δίκην ἀναμένῃ. τραύματος πάλιν εἰσὶν γραφαὶ τοῦ μὴ τιτρωσκομένων τινῶν φόνους γίγνεσθαι. τὸ φαυλότατον, οἶμαι, τὸ τῆς λοιδορίας, πρὸ τοῦ τελευταίου καὶ δεινοτάτου προεώραται, τοῦ μὴ φόνον γίγνεσθαι, μηδὲ κατὰ μικρὸν ὑπάγεσθαι ἐκ μὲν λοιδορίας εἰς πληγάς, ἐκ δὲ πληγῶν εἰς τραύματα, ἐκ δὲ τραυμάτων εἰς θάνατον, ἀλλ' ἐν τοῖς νόμοις εἶναι τούτων ἑκάστου τὴν δίκην. Translation from Bers 2003.

127. Isocr. 20.2; cf. Dem. 23.39.

128. Eur. *Supp.* 614: δίκα δίκαν δ' ἐκάλεσε καὶ φόνος φόνον.

129. Cf. Lys. 2.19; Thuc. 2.37.

130. Phillips 2008: 56–57.

131. Christ 1998a: 522–523.

132. On the connection between "self-help" and the defense of the *oikos*, see Christ 1998a.

133. To claim justifiable homicide, the defendant had to show that the death was the victim's fault (Carawan 1998: 282–284). Hence, Demosthenes (23.54) links the slaying of an adulterer with other examples of accidental deaths. Note that Demosthenes refers to men who commit adultery with another man's wife not as *echthroi* but as *polemioi* (enemies of the state).

134. See pp. 000–000.

135. Herman 2006: 236.

136. These actions were designed primarily for the detainment of "evildoers" (*kakourgoi*), a particular class of criminals who violated someone's property, and of those who had lost citizen rights (*atimoi*). (Murderers could be arrested, but these fit into the category of *atimoi*.) See Hansen 1976.

137. The original purposes behind these procedures are unclear, and there is debate over how *apagōgē* in particular developed (see Hansen 1976; Carawan 1998; Volonaki 2000). On the applicability of the clause stipulating that the culprit be caught "in the act" (*ep' autophōrōi*), see Hansen 1976: 48–53; Carawan 1998: 352–353; Volonaki 2000: 167–170. It does seem clear, however, that these procedures were intended to be remedies for offenses that occurred in exceptional circumstances.

138. The Scythian archers are sometimes described as a police force, as they seem to have been in charge of keeping order in certain public areas, such as the Assembly, the Council, and the Agora. They did not, however, patrol the streets to prevent crime like a modern police force. It also seems clear that they acted upon orders from others (magistrates—possibly the Eleven) and not on their own authority. In any case, the Scythian archers were primarily a fifth-century phenomenon and did not continue long into the fourth. (See discussion in Hunter 1994: 145–149).

139. The scholion to Ar. *Nub.* 498–499 states that in the case of privatized search and seizure, it was the custom (*ethos*) for the individual who claimed that his property had been stolen to enter the house of the accused naked to preempt suspicion that he planted an item out of enmity (*hupo echthras*). This practice provides evidence for Athenians' attempt to limit the abuse of self-help by malicious enemies. Cf. Harris (2013: 54–55), who takes this passage along with Isae. 6.42 as evidence for a formal legal regulation about such searches.

140. Andoc. 4.18; Dem. 22.27, 23.80. See Harris 2006b: 405–422.

141. Dem. 23.80: ἀπάγειν ἔξεστιν εἰς τὸ δεσμωτήριον, οὐκ οἴκαδε οὐδ' ὅποι βούλεται.

142. Todd 1993: 145.

143. Dem. 21.81–92; cf. 47.38–39.

144. Dem. 47.33–40. The speaker had obtained a decree from the Council that authorized him to take certain property from Theophemus "in whatever way we could" (*tropōi hōi an dunōmetha*, 33). He entered Theophemus' house forcibly, and

a fight ensued. The speaker had to prove, however, that he did not start it (38–40). The decree did not authorize him to assault Theophemus.

145. See also E. Harris 2013: 21–59.

146. E. Harris (2013: 28–50) argues that magistrates in fact performed many functions (levying fines, using public slaves for coercion, and intervening to enforce the law) analogous to a police force. The argument has merit, but Harris minimalizes the role of private citizens in informing against offenders, prosecuting them, and joining in as bystanders against blatant abuses.

147. Ober 2008: 256.

148. Scafuro 1997.

149. On arbitration and its agonistic context, see pp. 000–000.

150. See pp. 000–000.

151. Hunter 1994: 138–139. See also Sternberg 2006: 76–103. Christ (2010: 269–280; cf. 2012: 28–41) has recently argued that bystander intervention was not normal behavior or a normative requirement, but many of his points are problematic. For instance, when a litigant fails to mention bystander intervention in his description of a physical confrontation, it is not safe to assume that the neighbors, who must have heard the hustle and bustle, chose to do nothing. This is a precarious *e silentio* argument. Christ also points out that bystanders would not normally intervene physically unless there was minimal risk to their persons, but, as Christ (2010: 273) himself notes, the mere presence of witnesses could force the disputants to end their quarrel. In any case, we should expect that the disputes that ended up in the courts would have been the worst disputes and hence least likely to have been resolved by the intervention of bystanders. A count of the number of bystanders who intervened physically versus those who stayed aloof is not very informative.

152. Lys. 3.16; Isocr. 18.6; [Dem.] 53.17. Cf. the similar incident narrated in *Against Evergus*, in which the speaker's neighbors saw that his house was being invaded and so rushed to the rescue (Dem. 47.60–61). This was seemingly the ancient equivalent of the "hue and cry" (Hyams 2003: 97). In many medieval societies, a witness to a crime was expected to blow a horn and announce the wrongdoing with a shout.

153. Dem. 54.25.

154. Dem. 24.208.

155. Dem. 54.25: σωτηρία.

156. Cf. Lys. 7.18; Men. *Epitrep.* 234–235, *Peric.* 384–385. The *astynomoi* may have had a similar function in keeping order in the streets (Scafuro 2007). Pericles may be referring to this ideology in the Funeral Oration when he says that Athenians carefully observe the laws and customs, "especially those concerning giving aid to those being wronged" (μάλιστα αὐτῶν ὅσοι τε ἐπ' ὠφελίᾳ τῶν ἀδικουμένων κεῖνται, Thuc. 2.37.3).

157. Herman 1994: 99–105; cf. Fisher 1998: 86–87.

158. Thuc. 1.6.3; cf. 6.56.2.

159. Arist. *Pol.* 2.8 (1268b40): βαρβαρικούς.

160. Pl. *Grg.* 469d.

161. Hdt. 1.59.3–5. Cf. Arist. *Ath. Pol.* 18.4.
162. Andoc. 1.45; cf. 66.
163. [Dem.] 58.65.
164. Pl. *Resp.* 5.470b.
165. The principles Socrates lays out for the Guardian class in the *Republic* are similar.
166. Dem. 8.33: ἐν μὲν ταῖς ἐκκλησίαις πράους καὶ φιλανθρώπους ὑμᾶς ἐθίζειν εἶναι (πρὸς γὰρ ὑμᾶς αὐτοὺς καὶ τοὺς συμμάχους ἐν ταύταις ἐστὶ τὰ δίκαια), ἐν δὲ ταῖς παρασκευαῖς ταῖς τοῦ πολέμου φοβεροὺς καὶ χαλεποὺς ἐπιδεικνύναι.
167. Ober 2005: 92–127 = Ober 2000.
168. [Dem.] 53.16.
169. [Xen.] *Ath. Pol.* 1.10. Cf. Pl. *Resp.* 8.562d–563a; Aeschin. 1.17.
170. For discussion of this issue, see Ober 2005: 114–116.
171. Cf. Aeschin. 1.58–62.
172. Dem. 10.27, 22.54–55, 24.166–167.
173. Arist. *Pol.* 6.2 (1317b3): τὸ ἐν μέρει ἄρχεσθαι καὶ ἄρχειν.
174. Dem. 21.221: αὐτίκα δὴ μάλα, ἐπειδὰν ἀναστῇ τὸ δικαστήριον, εἷς ἕκαστος ὑμῶν, ὁ μὲν θᾶττον ἴσως, ὁ δὲ σχολαίτερον, οἴκαδ' ἄπεισιν οὐδὲν φροντίζων οὐδὲ μεταστρεφόμενος οὐδὲ φοβούμενος, οὔτ' εἰ φίλος οὔτ' εἰ μὴ φίλος αὐτῷ συντεύξεταί τις, οὐδέ γ' εἰ μέγας ἢ μικρός, ἢ ἰσχυρὸς ἢ ἀσθενής, οὐδὲ τῶν τοιούτων οὐδέν. τί δήποτε; ὅτι τῇ ψυχῇ τοῦτ' οἶδε καὶ θαρρεῖ καὶ πεπίστευκε τῇ πολιτείᾳ, μηδέν' ἕλξειν μηδ' ὑβριεῖν μηδὲ τυπτήσειν.
175. Soph. *Aj.* 1334–1335: μηδ' ἡ βία σε μηδαμῶς νικησάτω / τοσόνδε μισεῖν ὥστε τὴν δίκην πατεῖν.
176. The same could be said for Polyneices in the *Antigone*.
177. D. Cohen 1995: 5–6.
178. On ideology and reality in Athenian culture, see D. Cohen 1989.
179. Millett 1991: 89–90.

CONCLUSION

1. Wyatt-Brown 1982.
2. As an example, the duel between Alexander Hamilton and Aaron Burr, arising out of both personal and political disputes, effectively ended the life of one man and the political career of the other. The fate of the Federalist Party would surely have been different had Hamilton, its vigorous and brilliant advocate, lived. Another example is a dinner party at Thomas Jefferson's home that provided the setting for a reconciliation and compromise between Jefferson's friend, James Madison, and his colleague, Alexander Hamilton. (Jefferson was Secretary of State; Hamilton was Secretary of Treasury.) Through Jefferson's personal mediation on this evening in 1790, Hamilton's plan for the recovery of public credit was rescued from Madison's roadblock, and Madison's desire for a U.S. capital on the Potomac was realized. (Both of these episodes are described in Ellis 2001.)

3. On the Founders' obsession with personal honor, see G. Wood 2006.

4. Ostwald 1988: 344–346. Against objections to this view, Forsdyke (2005: 149–165) argues that the institution had an important symbolic function, whether or not it could actually diffuse elite enmity.

5. [Arist.] *Rh. Al.* 2.19 (1424b6–7): χρὴ δὲ καὶ τὰς διαφορὰς τῶν πολιτῶν ὅτι τάχιστα διαλύειν.

6. [Arist.] *Rh. Al.* 2.19 (1424b8–10).

7. Hdt. 1.60.2, 61.1.

8. Hdt. 5.92. The tallest stalks represented powerful citizens who could pose a threat to the tyranny. Cf. Polycrates' tactics (Hdt. 3.44).

9. Xen. *Hell.* 2.3.

10. Xen. *Hell.* 2.3.38–44.

11. Wolpert 2002: 126–129.

12. Bartlett 2010.

13. The regulations on enemies within the city of Athens can be contrasted with the anarchic world of *polis* diplomacy. City-states were essentially autonomous and so could pursue their enemies as they pleased.

14. The sport analogy can also give substance to the language of two competing "codes of behavior" that has become popular. (For a recent and more nuanced use of this concept, see Riess 2012: 131–140.) The dichotomy between a code of restraint on the one hand and an agonistic code on the other is overly simplistic since the two "codes" (if we can call them that) were not really in tension in the sense of being ultimately irreconcilable. They could be said to be contradictory only when someone decided that pursuit of the agonistic code trumped the rules of the game. In any sport, some players will respect the rules and internalize them, spending most of their careers trying to win the game without cheating, while others will break or "bend" the rules at any opportunity if they believe they will not be caught. The difference between these two outlooks is explained not by competing ideas of what the game is really about but rather by competing ideas about how important the regulations of players' behavior are.

15. No revolutions occurred in Athens under the restored democracy (403–322 BC). In the preceding century, there had been only one, in 411–410. The rule of The Thirty (404–403) was imposed from without after a defeat in war and does not have much to say about the internal stability of Athens. On the success of the democracy, see Ober 2008.

16. Aeschin. 1.4–5: διοικοῦνται δ' αἱ μὲν τυραννίδες καὶ ὀλιγαρχίαι τοῖς τρόποις τῶν ἐφεστηκότων, αἱ δὲ πόλεις αἱ δημοκρατούμεναι τοῖς νόμοις τοῖς κειμένοις. εὖ δ' ἴστε, ὦ ἄνδρες Ἀθηναῖοι, ὅτι τὰ μὲν τῶν δημοκρατουμένων σώματα καὶ τὴν πολιτείαν οἱ νόμοι σῴζουσι.

17. Pericles' reputation as the most powerful statesman in Athens for the past couple decades did not protect him from being deposed from the generalship and fined in 429. Xenophon could explain Spartan policy in the final decade of the fifth century primarily in reference to Lysander's friendships and enmities with

other Spartan elites, but any attempt to make sense of Athenian policy as a story about the interactions within a small clique of men is bound to fail.

18. See p. 000, n. 000.

19. Xen. *Hell.* 5.4.24–33. Sphodrias, the Spartan harmost at Thespiae, made an unsuccessful attack on the Athenian harbor (the Piraeus) during peacetime. The Athenians demanded the Spartans punish him for his crime, but Sphodrias exploited a political connection to the Spartan king, Agesilaus, who campaigned for him and secured his (manifestly unjust) acquittal.

20. Thuc. 1.6.3.

21. Xen. *Lac.* 4.5–6.

22. In the *Iliad* (2.211–277), Thersites, apparently a commoner, speaks against the leaders of the Greek army. Odysseus reprimands him with harsh words and a cane.

23. Pl. *Resp.* 5.464e.

24. The Enlightenment thinkers who admired Athens generally admired its commercialism, freedom of thought and expression, and cultural productivity, not its political arrangement (Morris 2004). Approval of Athenian democracy did not become widespread until the seminal work of George Grote (*A History of Greece*, 1846–1856). See also Roberts 1994.

25. Constant 1988: 311. The speech was delivered in 1819.

26. See Ober's (2005: 93–97) thesis that Athenian participatory democracy gave rise to some values that resemble modern liberal values.

27. Although cf. Pl. *Resp.* 2.358e–359b. It is difficult to tell whether the theory of political justice described by Glaucon here actually represents common democratic thinking in Athens.

28. Ober's (2012) argument for citizen "dignity" as a core value of democracy is another way to conceive of the ideological underpinnings of such liberties. Citizens ought to be able to participate on a free and equal basis, but also without systematic humiliation. Bullying, whether physical, legal, or political, is an obvious threat to this value.

29. Dem. 21.34: ἅμα γὰρ τῷ Δημοσθένει καὶ ὁ χορηγὸς ὑβρίζετο, τοῦτο δ' ἐστὶ τῆς πόλεως.

30. Xen. *Lac.* 8.2: ὅτι ἐν μὲν ταῖς ἄλλαις πόλεσιν οἱ δυνατώτεροι οὐδὲ βούλονται δοκεῖν τὰς ἀρχὰς φοβεῖσθαι.

WORKS CITED

Adeleye, Gabriel. 1983. "The Purpose of the '*Dokimasia*.'" *GRBS* 24: 295–306.
Adkins, A. W. H. 1970. *From the Many to the One: A Study of Personality and Views of Human Nature in the Context of Ancient Greek Society, Values, and Beliefs.* Ithaca, NY: Cornell University Press.
Allen, Danielle. 2000a. "Changing the Authoritative Voice: Lycurgus' 'Against Leocrates.'" *ClAnt* 19: 5–33.
———. 2000b. *The World of Prometheus: The Politics of Punishing in Democratic Athens.* Princeton: Princeton University Press.
Alvarez, Lizette, and Bill Carter. 2011. "Juror in Anthony Case Says Acquittals Took an Emotional Toll." *New York Times*, July 6. http://www.nytimes.com/2011/07/07/us/07casey.html.
Bagge, Sverre, Michael Gelting, and Thomas Lindkvist, eds. 2011. *Feudalism: New Landscapes of Debate.* Turnhout: Brepols.
Bartlett, Robert. 2010. "'Mortal Enmities': The Legal Aspect of Hostility in the Middle Ages." In *Feud, Violence and Practice: Essays in Medieval Studies in Honor of Stephen D. White*, edited by B. Tuten, 197–212. Farnham: Ashgate.
Bateman, John. 1958. "Lysias and the Law." *TAPA* 89: 276–285.
———. 1962. "Some Aspects of Lysias' Argumentation." *Phoenix* 16: 157–177.
Bers, Victor. 2003. *Demosthenes: Speeches 50–59.* Austin: University of Texas Press.
———. 2009. *Genos Dikanikon: Amateur and Professional Speech in the Courtrooms of Classical Athens.* Washington: Center for Hellenic Studies.
Bitzer, Lloyd. 1968. "The Rhetorical Situation." *Ph&Rh* 1: 1–14.
Bleicken, Jochen. 1985. *Die Athenische Demokratie.* Paderborn: Wolfgang Schuller.
Bloch, Marc. 1961 (original 1949). *Feudal Society*, translated by L. A. Manyon. Chicago: University of Chicago Press.
Blumenfeld, Laura. 2002. *Revenge: A Story of Hope.* New York: Simon & Schuster.
Blundell, Mary. 1989. *Helping Friends and Harming Enemies: A Study in Sophocles and Greek Ethics.* Cambridge: Cambridge University Press.
Bogaert, Raymond. 1968. *Banques et Banquiers dans les Cités Grecques.* Leiden: A. W. Sijthoff.
Brown, Elizabeth. 1974. "The Tyranny of a Construct: Feudalism and Historians of Medieval Europe." *AHR* 79: 1063–1088.

Carawan, Edwin. 1998. *Rhetoric and the Law of Draco*. Oxford: Clarendon Press.
———. 2002. "The Athenian Amnesty and the 'Scrutiny of the Laws.'" *JHS* 122: 1–23.
———. 2011. "*Paragraphē* and the Merits." *GRBS* 51: 254–295.
Carey, Christopher. 1989. *Lysias: Selected Speeches*. Cambridge: Cambridge University Press.
———. 1990. "Structure and Strategy in Lysias 24." *G&R* 37: 44–51.
———. 1992. *Apollodoros against Neaira: (Demosthenes) 59*. Warminster: Aris & Phillips.
———. 1994a. "'Artless' Proofs in Aristotle and the Orators." *BICS* 39: 95–106.
———. 1994b. "Rhetorical Means of Persuasion." In *Persuasion: Greek Rhetoric in Action*, edited by I. Worthington, 26–45. London: Routledge.
———. 1995. "The Witness's *Exomosia* in the Athenian Courts." *CQ* 45: 114–119.
———. 1999. "Propriety in the Attic Orators." In *Studi sull' Eufemismo*, edited by F. de Martino and A. Sommerstein, 369–391. Bari: Lavante.
———. 2000. *Aeschines*. Austin: University of Texas Press.
———. 2007. *Lysiae Orationes cum Fragmentis*. Oxford: Oxford University Press.
Carter, L. B. 1986. *The Quiet Athenian*. Oxford: Clarendon Press.
Cheyette, Frederic. 2010. "'Feudalism': A Memoir and an Assessment." In *Feud, Violence and Practice: Essays in Medieval Studies in Honor of Stephen D. White*, edited by B. Tuten, 119–134. Farnham: Ashgate.
Christ, Matthew. 1990. "Liturgy Avoidance and Antidosis in Classical Athens." *TAPA* 120: 147–169.
———. 1998a. "Legal Self-Help on Private Property in Classical Athens." *AJP* 119: 521–545.
———. 1998b. *The Litigious Athenian*. Baltimore: Johns Hopkins University Press.
———. 2005. "Response to M. Harris." In *Symposion 2001: Vorträge zur Griechischen und Hellenistischen Rechtsgeschichte*, edited by R. Wallace and M. Gagarin, 143–146. Vienna: Austrian Academy of Sciences.
———. 2006. *The Bad Citizen in Classical Athens*. Cambridge: Cambridge University Press.
———. 2007. Review of Herman 2006. *Bryn Mawr Classical Review* 07.37: http://ccat.sas.upenn.edu/bmcr/2007/2007-07-37.html.
———. 2010. "Helping Behavior in Classical Athens." *Phoenix* 64: 254–290.
———. 2012. *The Limits of Altruism in Democratic Athens*. Cambridge: Cambridge University Press.
Cohen, David. 1989. "Seclusion, Separation, and the Status of Women in Classical Athens." *G&R* 36: 3–15.
———. 1991. *Law, Sexuality, and Society: Enforcement of Morals in Classical Athens*. Cambridge: Cambridge University Press.
———. 1995. *Law, Violence, and Community in Classical Athens*. Cambridge: Cambridge University Press.
Cohen, Edward. 2000. *The Athenian Nation*. Princeton: Princeton University Press.

———. 2007. "Laws Affecting Prostitution at Athens." In *Symposion 2005: Vorträge zur Griechischen und Hellenistischen Rechtsgeschichte*, edited by E. Canterella, 201–224. Vienna: Austrian Academy of Sciences.
Cole, Thomas. 1991. "Who Was Corax?" *ICS* 16: 65–84.
Connor, Robert. 1971. *The New Politicians of Fifth-Century Athens*. Princeton: Princeton University Press.
Constant, Benjamin. 1988. *Political Writings*, translated by Biancamaria Fontana. Cambridge: Cambridge University Press.
Cox, Cheryle. 1998. *Household Interests: Property, Marriage Strategies, and Family Dynamics in Ancient Athens*. Princeton: Princeton University Press.
Crook, John. 1984. *Law and Life of Rome: 90 B.C–A.D. 212*. Ithaca, NY: Cornell University Press.
Darkow, Angela. 1917. *The Spurious Speeches in the Lysianic Corpus*. Bryn Mawr, PA: Lord Baltimore Press.
Davies, John. 1981. *Wealth and the Power of Wealth in Classical Athens*. New York: Arno Press.
Dewald, Carolyn. 1999. "The Figured Stage: Focalizing the Initial Narratives of Herodotus and Thucydides." In *Contextualizing Classics: Ideology, Performance, Dialogue (Essays in Honor of John J. Peradotto)*, edited by T. Falkner, N. Felson, and D. Konstan, 221–252. Lanham, MD: Rowman & Littlefield.
Dillon, Matthew. 1991. "Tragic Laughter." *CW* 84: 345–355.
———. 1995. "Payments for the Disabled at Athens: Social Justice or Fear of Aristocratic Patronage?" *AncSoc* 26: 27–57.
Dover, Kenneth. 1968. *Lysias and the Corpus Lysiacum*. Berkeley: University of California Press.
———. 1974. *Greek Popular Morality in the Time of Plato and Aristotle*. Berkeley: University of California.
Dreher, Martin. 1994. "Diskussionsbeitrag zum Referat von Douglas M. MacDowell." In *Symposion 1993: Vorträge zur Griechischen und Hellenistischen Rechtsgeschichte*, edited by G. Thür, 165–168. Cologne: Böhlau.
Edwards, Michael. 2000. "Antiphon and the Beginnings of Athenian Literary Oratory." *Rhetorica* 18: 227–243.
Edwards, Michael, and Stephen Usher. 1985. *Antiphon and Lysias*. Warminster: Aris & Phillips.
Eidinow, Esther. 2007. *Oracles, Curses, and Risk among the Ancient Greeks*. Oxford: Oxford University Press.
Ellis, Joseph. 2001. *Founding Brothers: The Revolutionary Generation*. Alfred A. Knopf: New York.
Engen, Darel. 2010. *Honor and Profit: Athenian Trade Policy and the Economy and Society of Greece, 415–307 B.C.E.* Ann Arbor: University of Michigan Press.
Erbse, Hatmut. 1956. "Über die Midiana des Demosthenes." *Hermes* 84: 135–151.
Faraguna, Michele. 1992. *Atene nell'eta di Alessandro: Problemi Politici, Economici, Finanziari*. Rome: Accademia Nazionale dei Lincei.
Faraone, Christopher. 1991. "The Agonistic Context of Early Greek Binding

Spells." In *Magika Hiera: Ancient Greek Magic and Religion*, edited by C. Faraone and D. Obbink, 3–32. Oxford: Oxford University Press.
Feldman, Shosana. 2002. *The Juridical Unconscious: Trials and Traumas in the Twentieth Century*. Cambridge, MA: Harvard University Press.
Fisher, Nicolas. 1990. "The Law of *Hubris* in Athens." In *Nomos*, edited by P. Cartledge, P. Millett, and S. Todd, 123–138. Cambridge: Cambridge University Press.
———. 1998. "Masculinity, Violence and the Law in Classical Athens." In *When Men Were Men*, edited by L. Foxhall and J. Salmon, 68–97. London: Routledge.
———. 1999. "Workshops of Villains." In *Organized Crime in Antiquity*, edited by K. Hopwood, 53–96. London: Duckworth.
———. 2001. *Aeschines*: Against Timarchos. Oxford: Clarendon Press.
Forsdyke, Sara. 2005. *Exile, Ostracism, and Democracy: The Politics of Expulsion in Ancient Greece*. Princeton: Princeton University Press.
Foucault, Michel, and Joseph Pearson. 2001. *Fearless Speech*. Los Angeles: Semiotext(e).
Fränkel, Max. 1878. "Der Attische Heliasteneid." *Hermes* 13: 452–466.
Freud, Sigmund. 1960 (original 1905). *Jokes and Their Relation to the Unconscious*, translated by James Strachey. London: The Hogarth Press and the Institute of Psycho-Analysis.
Furley, William. 1996. *Andokides and the Herms: A Study of Crisis in Fifth-Century Athenian Religion*. London: London Institute of Classical Studies.
Gabrielsen, Vincent. 1987. "The *Antidosis* Procedure in Classical Athens." *C&M* 38: 7–38.
———. 1994. *Financing the Athenian Fleet: Public Taxation and Social Relations*. Baltimore: Johns Hopkins University Press.
Gagarin, Michael. 1981. *Drakon and Early Athenian Homicide Law*. New Haven: Yale University Press.
———. 1994. "Probability and Persuasion: Plato and Early Greek Rhetoric." In *Persuasion: Greek Rhetoric in Action*, edited by I. Worthington, 46–68. London: Routledge.
———. 1996. "The Torture of Slaves in Athenian Law." *CP* 91: 1–18.
———. 2002. *Antiphon the Athenian: Oratory, Law, and Justice in the Age of the Sophists*. Austin: University of Texas Press.
———. 2003. "Telling Stories in Athenian Law." *TAPA* 133: 197–207.
———. 2005. "La Violence dans les Plaidoyers Attiques." In *La Violence dans les Mondes Grec et Romain*, edited by J.-M. Bertrand, 365–376. Paris: Publications de la Sorbonne.
———. 2007. "Rational Argument in Early Athenian Oratory." In *Logos: Rational Argument in Classical Rhetoric*, edited by J. Powell, 9–18. London: London Institute of Classical Studies.
———. 2012. "Law, Politics, and the Question of Relevance in the Case On the Crown." *ClAnt* 31: 293–314.
Gagarin, Michael, and Douglas MacDowell. 1998. *Antiphon and Andocides*. Austin: University of Texas Press.

Gager, John. 1992. *Curse Tablets and Binding Spells from the Ancient World*. Oxford: Oxford University Press.
Gagliardi, Lorenzo. 2005. "The Athenian Procedure of *Dokimasia* of Orators: A Response to Douglas M. MacDowell." In *Symposion 2001: Vorträge zur Griechischen und Hellenistischen Rechtsgeschichte*, edited by R. Wallace and M. Gagarin, 89–98. Vienna: Austrian Academy of Sciences.
Gluckman, Max. 1955. "The Peace in the Feud." *Past and Present* 8: 1–14.
Goebel, George. 1989. "Probability in the Earliest Rhetorical Theory." *Mnemosyne* 42: 41–53.
Golden, Mark. 1990. *Children and Childhood in Classical Athens*. Baltimore: Johns Hopkins University Press.
———. 1998. *Sport and Society in Ancient Greece*. Cambridge: Cambridge University Press.
Griffith-Williams, Brenda. 2013. "Violence in Court: Law and Rhetoric in Athenian and English Assault Cases." *G&R* 60: 89–100.
Habicht, Christian. 1997. *Athens from Alexander to Antony*. Cambridge, MA: Harvard University Press.
Hall, Edith. 1995. "Lawcourt Dramas: The Power of Performance in Greek Forensic Oratory." *BICS* 40: 39–58.
Halliwell, Stephen. 1990. "Traditional Greek Conceptions of Character." In *Characterization and Individuality in Greek Literature*, edited by C. Pelling, 32–59. Oxford: Oxford University Press.
Halperin, David. 1990. *One Hundred Years of Homosexuality and Other Essays on Greek Love*. New York: Routledge.
Hamel, Debra. 1998. *Athenian Generals: Military Authority in the Classical Period*. Leiden: Brill.
Hansen, Mogens. 1974. *The Sovereignty of the People's Court in Athens in the Fourth Century BC and the Public Action against Unconstitutional Proposals*. Odense: Odense Universitetsforlag.
———. 1976. *Apagoge, Endeixis and Ephegesis against Kakourgoi, Atimoi and Pheugontes: A Study in Athenian Administration of Justice in the Fourth Century B.C.* Odense: Odense University Press.
———. 1983a. "The Athenian 'Politicians,' 403–322 B.C." *GRBS* 24: 33–55.
———. 1983b. "*Rhetores* and *Strategoi* in Fourth-Century Athens." *GRBS* 24: 151–180.
———. 1989a. Review of Bleicken 1985. *CP* 39: 137–148.
———. 1989b. Review of Sinclair 1988. *CR* 84: 69–76.
———. 1991. *The Athenian Democracy in the Age of Demosthenes: Structure, Principles, and Ideology*. Oxford: Blackwell.
———. 1996. "The Ancient Athenian and the Modern Liberal View of Liberty as a Democratic Ideal." In *Demokratia: A Conversation on Democracies, Ancient and Modern*, edited by J. Ober and C. Hedrick, 91–104. Princeton: Princeton University Press.
———. 1998. *Polis and City-State: An Ancient Concept and Its Modern Equivalent*. Copenhagen: Munksgaard.

Harris, Edward. 1989. "Demosthenes' Speech against Meidias." *HSCP* 92: 117–136.
———. 1992. Review of MacDowell 1990. *CP* 87: 71–80.
———. 1994. "Law and Oratory." In *Persuasion: Greek Rhetoric in Action*, edited by I. Morris, 130–152. London: Routledge.
———. 2005. "Feuding or the Rule of Law? The Nature of Litigation in Classical Athens: An Essay in Legal Sociology." In *Symposion 2001: Vorträge zur Griechischen und Hellenistischen Rechtsgeschichte*, edited by R. Wallace and M. Gagarin, 125–141. Vienna: Austrian Academy of Sciences.
———. 2006a. "The Rule of Law in Athenian Democracy: Reflections on the Judicial Oath." *Dike* 9: 157–181.
———. 2006b. *Democracy and the Rule of Law in Classical Athens: Essays on Law, Society, and Politics*. Cambridge: Cambridge University Press.
———. 2008. *Demosthenes: Speeches 20–22*. Austin: University of Texas Press.
———. 2013. *The Rule of Law in Action in Democratic Athens*. Oxford: Oxford University Press.
Harris, William. 1997. "Lysias III and Athenian Beliefs about Revenge." *CQ* 47: 363–366.
———. 2001. *Restraining Rage: The Ideology of Anger Control in Classical Antiquity*. Cambridge, MA: Harvard University Press.
Harrison, A. R. W. 1968–1971. *The Law of Athens*. 2 vols. Oxford: Clarendon Press.
Harrison, James. 2003. *Paul's Language of Grace in Its Graeco-Roman Context*. Tübingen: Mohr Siebeck.
Harvey, David. 1990. "The Sykophant and Sykophancy: Vexatious Redefinition?" In *Nomos*, edited by P. Cartledge, P. Millett, and S. Todd, 103–122. Cambridge: Cambridge University Press.
Henderson, Jeffrey. 1987. "Older Women in Attic Comedy." *TAPA* 117: 105–129.
Herman, Gabriel. 1993. "Tribal and Civic Codes of Behaviour in Lysias 1." *CQ* 43: 406–419.
———. 1994. "How Violent Was Athenian Society?" In *Ritual, Finance, Politics: Athenian Democratic Accounts Presented to David Lewis*, edited by R. Osborne and S. Hornblower, 99–117. Oxford: Oxford University Press.
———. 1995. "Honour, Revenge and the State in Fourth-Century Athens." In *Die Athenische Demokratie im 4. Jahrhundert v. Chr.: Vollendung oder Verfall einer Verfassungsform?*, edited by W. Eder, 43–66. Stuttgart: Steiner.
———. 1998. "Reciprocity, Altruism, and the Prisoner's Dilemma: The Special Case of Classical Athens." In *Reciprocity in Ancient Greece*, edited by C. Gill, N. Postlethwaite, and R. Seaford, 199–225. Oxford: Oxford University Press.
———. 2000. "Athenian Beliefs about Revenge: Problems and Methods." *PCPS* 46: 7–27.
———. 2006. *Morality and Behaviour in Democratic Athens: A Social History*. Cambridge: Cambridge University Press.
———. 2007. Review of Christ 2007. *Bryn Mawr Classical Review* 09.21.
Hesk, Jon. 2000. *Deception and Democracy in Classical Athens*. Cambridge: Cambridge University Press.

Hightower, Kyle. 2011. "Shock and Outrage Greet Casey Anthony's Not Guilty Verdict." July 6. http://www.cnsnews.com/news/article/shock-and-outrage-greet-casey-anthony-s-not-guilty-verdict.
Hintzen-Bohlen, Brigitte. 1997. *Die Kulturpolitik des Eubolos und des Lykurg: Die Denkmäler- und Bauprojekte in Athen zwischen 355 und 322 v. Chr.* Berlin: Akademie Verlag.
Hoffman, David. 2008. "Concerning *Eikos*: Social Expectation and Verisimilitude in Early Attic Rhetoric." *Rhetorica* 26: 1–29.
Humphreys, Sally. 1985. "Social Relations on Stage: Witnesses in Classical Athens." *History and Anthropology* 1: 313–369.
———. 2010. "A Paranoiac Sycophant? The Curse Tablet NM 14470 (D. R. Jordan and J. Curbera, *ZPE* 166, 2008, 135–150)." *ZPE* 172: 85–86.
Hunt, Peter. 2010. *War, Peace, and Alliance in Demosthenes' Athens*. Cambridge: Cambridge University Press.
Hunter, Virginia. 1994. *Policing Athens: Social Control in the Attic Lawsuits, 420–320 B.C.* Princeton: Princeton University Press.
———. 2000. "Policing Public Debtors in Classical Athens." *Phoenix* 54: 21–38.
Hyams, Paul. 2003. *Rancor and Reconciliation in Medieval England*. Ithaca, NY: Cornell University Press.
Johnstone, Steven. 1999. *Disputes and Democracy: The Consequences of Litigation in Ancient Athens*. Austin: University of Texas Press.
Jones, Nicholas. 1999. *The Associations of Classical Athens*. Oxford: Oxford University Press.
———. 2004. *Rural Athens under the Democracy*. Philadelphia: University of Pennsylvania Press.
Jordan, David. 1985a. "Defixiones from a Well near the Southwest Corner of the Athenian Agora." *Hesperia* 54: 205–255.
———. 1985b. "A Survey of Greek Defixiones Not Included in the Special Corpora." *GRBS* 26: 151–197.
Joyce, Christopher. 2008. "The Athenian Amnesty and Scrutiny of 403." *CQ* 58: 507–518.
Just, Manfred. 1965. *Die Ephesis in der Geschichte des Attischen Prozesses: Ein Versuch zur Deutung der Rechtsnatur der Ephesis.* Würzburg.
Kapparis, Konstantinos. 1999. *Apollodoros: Against Neaira*. Berlin: Walter de Gruyter.
Kennedy, George. 1963. *The Art of Persuasion in Greece*. Princeton: Princeton University Press.
Knox, Bernard. 1979. *Word and Action: Essays on the Ancient Theater*. Baltimore: Johns Hopkins University Press.
Konstan, David. 1997. *Friendship in the Classical World*. Cambridge: Cambridge University Press.
———. 2006. *The Emotions of the Ancient Greeks: Studies in Aristotle and Classical Literature*. Toronto: University of Toronto Press.
Kraus, Manfred. 2006. "Nothing to Do with Truth? Εἰκός in Early Greek Rhet-

oric and Philosophy." In *Papers on Rhetoric VII*, edited by L. Montefusco, 129–150. Rome: Herder.

Kremmydas, Christos. 2007. "Logical Argumentation in Demosthenes, *Against Leptines*." In *Logos: Rational Argument in Classical Rhetoric*, edited by J. Powell, 19–34. London: London Institute of Classical Studies.

———. 2013. "The Discourse of Deception and Characterization in Attic Oratory." *GRBS* 53: 51–89.

Kucharski, Janek. 2012. "Vindictive Prosecution in Classical Athens: On Some Recent Theories." *GRBS* 52: 167–197.

Kurihara, Asako. 2003. "Personal Enmity as a Motivation in Forensic Speeches." *CQ* 53: 464–477.

Lacey, Walter. 1968. *The Family in Classical Greece*. Ithaca, NY: Cornell University Press.

Lanni, Adriaan. 2006. *Law and Justice in the Courts of Classical Athens*. Cambridge: Cambridge University Press.

———. 2010. "The Expressive Effect of the Athenian Prostitution Laws." *ClAnt* 29: 45–67.

Lavency, Marius. 1964. *Aspects de la Logographie Judicaire Attique*. Louvain: Bureaux de Recueil, Bibliothèque de l'Université.

Liddel, Peter. 2007. *Civic Obligation and Individual Liberty in Ancient Athens*. Oxford: Oxford University Press.

Lipsius, Justus. 1883. "Über die Unechtheit der Ersten Rede gegen Aristogeiton." *Leipziger Studien zur Classichen Philologie* 6: 317–331.

———. 1905–1915. *Das Attische Recht und Rechtsverfahren*. 3 vols. Leipzig: O. R. Reisland.

Lloyd, G. E. R. 1966. *Polarity and Analogy: Two Types of Argumentation in Early Greek Thought*. Cambridge: Cambridge University Press.

MacDowell, Douglas. 1962. *Andokides: On the Mysteries*. Oxford: Clarendon Press.

———. 1963. *Athenian Homicide Law in the Age of the Orators*. Manchester: Manchester University Press.

———. 1978. *The Law in Classical Athens*. Ithaca, NY: Cornell University Press.

———. 1989. "The Oikos in Athenian Law." *CQ* 39: 10–21.

———. 1990. *Demosthenes: Against Meidias*. Bristol: Bristol Classical Press.

———. 1994. "The Case of the Rude Soldier (Lysias 9)." In *Symposion 1993: Vorträge zur Griechischen und Hellenistischen Rechtsgeschichte*, edited by G. Thür, 153–164. Cologne: Böhlau.

———. 2004. *Demosthenes: Speeches 27–38*. Austin: University of Texas Press.

———. 2005. "The Athenian Procedure of Dokimasia of Orators." In *Symposion 2001: Vorträge zur Griechischen und Hellenistischen Rechtsgeschichte*, edited by R. Wallace and M. Gagarin, 79–88. Vienna: Austrian Academy of Sciences.

———. 2008. "The Athenian Penalty of *Ephobelia*." In *Symposion 2007: Akten der Gesellschaft für Griechischen und Hellenistischen Rechtsgeschichte*, edited by E. Harris and G. Thür, 87–94. Vienna: Austrian Academy of Sciences.

———. 2009. *Demosthenes the Orator*. Oxford: Oxford University Press.

Manville, Philip. 1994. "Toward a New Paradigm of Athenian Citizenship." In *Athenian Identity and Civic Ideology*, edited by A. Boegehold and A. Scafuro, 21–33. Baltimore: Johns Hopkins University Press.
May, James. 1988. *Trials of Character: The Eloquence of Ciceronian Ethos*. Chapel Hill: University of North Carolina Press.
Mayhew, Robert, and David Mirhady. 2011. *Aristotle: Problems; Rhetoric to Alexander*. Cambridge, MA: Harvard University Press.
McCarthy, Cormac. 2001 (reprint; original 1985). *Blood Meridian, or, The Evening Redness in the West*. New York: The Modern Library.
McHardy, Fiona. 2008. *Revenge in Athenian Culture*. London: Duckworth.
Meiggs, Russell, and David Lewis. 1969. *A Selection of Greek Historical Inscriptions to the End of the Fifth Century B.C.* Oxford: Clarendon Press.
Miller, Stephen. 2004. *Ancient Greek Athletics*. New Haven: Yale University Press.
Millett, Paul. 1991. *Lending and Borrowing in Ancient Athens*. Cambridge: Cambridge University Press.
Mirhady, David. 1996. "Torture and Rhetoric in Athens." *JHS* 116: 119–131.
———. 2002. "Athens' Democratic Witnesses." *Phoenix* 56: 255–274.
———. 2007. "The Dikast's Oath and the Question of Fact." In *Horkos: The Oath in Greek Society*, edited by A. Sommerstein and J. Fletcher, 48–59. Bristol: Bristol Phoenix Press.
Mitchell, Lynette, and P. J. Rhodes. 1996. "Friends and Enemies in Athenian Politics." *G&R* 43: 11–30.
Morford, Mark. 1966. "*Ethopoiia* and Character-Assassination in the Conon of Demosthenes." *Mnemosyne* 19: 241–248.
Morris, Ian. 2004. "The Paradigm of Democracy: Sparta in Enlightenment Thought." In *Spartan Society*, edited by T. Figueira, 339–362. Swansea: Classical Press of Wales.
Morstein-Marx, Robert. 2004. *Mass Oratory and Political Power in the Late Roman Republic*. Cambridge: Cambridge University Press.
Murphy, T. M. 1992. "Lysias 25 and the Intractable Democratic Athens." *AJP* 113: 543–558.
Ober, Josiah. 1989. *Mass and Elite in Democratic Athens: Rhetoric, Ideology, and the Power of the People*. Princeton: Princeton University Press.
———. 1994. "Power and Oratory in Democratic Athens: Demosthenes 21, against Meidias." In *Persuasion: Greek Rhetoric in Action*, edited by I. Worthington, 85–108. London: Routledge.
———. 1996. *The Athenian Revolution: Essays on Ancient Greek Democracy and Political Theory*. Princeton: Princeton University Press.
———. 1998. *Political Dissent in Democratic Athens: Intellectual Critics of Popular Rule*. Princeton: Princeton University Press.
———. 2000. "Quasi-Rights: Participatory Citizenship and Negative Liberties in Democratic Athens." *Social Philosophy and Policy* 17: 27–61. Reprinted in Ober 2005: 92–127.
———. 2005. *Athenian Legacies: Essays on the Politics of Going on Together*. Princeton: Princeton University Press.

———. 2008. *Democracy and Knowledge: Innovating and Learning in Classical Athens*. Princeton: Princeton University Press.
———. 2012. "Democracy's Dignity." *American Political Science Review* 106: 827–846.
Oikonomidēs, Al, Werner Peek, and Eugene Vanderpool. 1984. *Inscriptiones Atticae: Svpplementvm Inscriptionvm Atticarvm 5*. Chicago: Ares Publishers.
Osborne, Robin. 1985a. *Demos: The Discovery of Classical Attika*. Cambridge: Cambridge University Press.
———. 1985b. "Law in Action in Classical Athens." *JHS* 105: 40–58.
———. 1990. "Vexatious Litigation in Classical Athens: Sycophancy and the Sycophant." In *Nomos*, edited by P. Cartledge, P. Millett, and S. Todd, 83–102. Cambridge: Cambridge University Press.
Ostwald, Martin. 1988. "The Reform of the Athenian State by Cleisthenes." In *The Cambridge Ancient History, Volume 4: Persia, Greece and the Western Mediterranean, c. 525 to 479 B.C.*, edited by J. Boardman, N. G. L. Hammond, D. Lewis, and M. Ostwald, 303–346. Cambridge: Cambridge University Press.
Papillon, Terry. 1998. *Rhetorical Studies in the Aristocratea of Demosthenes*. New York: P. Lang.
Parker, Robert. 1983. *Miasma: Pollution and Purification in Early Greek Religion*. Oxford: Clarendon Press.
Patterson, Cynthia. 1998. *The Family in Greek History*. Cambridge, MA: Harvard University Press.
———. 2007. "Other Sorts: Slaves, Foreigners, and Women in Periclean Athens." In *The Cambridge Companion to the Age of Pericles*, edited by L. J. Samons, II, 153–178. Cambridge: Cambridge University Press.
Peachin, Michael, ed. 2001. *Aspects of Friendship in the Graeco-Roman World: Proceedings of a Conference Held at the Seminar für Alte Geschichte, Heidelberg, on 10–11 June, 2000*. Portsmouth, RI: *Journal of Roman Archaeology*.
Pearson, Lionel. 1966. "Apollodorus, the Eleventh Attic Orator." In *The Classical Tradition: Literary and Historical Studies in Honor of Harry Caplan*, edited by L. Wallach, 347–359. Ithaca, NY: Cornell University Press.
———. 1981. *The Art of Demosthenes*. Chico, CA: Scholars Press.
Peristiany, John. 1966. *Honour and Shame: The Values of Mediterranean Society*. Chicago: University of Chicago Press.
Phillips, David. 2007. "*Trauma ek Pronoias* in Athenian Law." *JHS* 127: 74–105.
———. 2008. *Avengers of Blood: Homicide in Athenian Law and Custom from Draco to Demosthenes*. Stuttgart: Steiner.
Poliakoff, Michael. 1987. *Combat Sports in the Ancient World: Competition, Violence, and Culture*. New Haven: Yale University Press.
Pomeroy, Sarah. 1997. *Families in Classical and Hellenistic Greece: Representations and Realities*. Oxford: Clarendon Press.
Porter, John. 1997. "Adultery by the Book: Lysias I (on the Murder of Eratosthenes) and Comic Diegesis." *EMC* 16: 421–453.
Raaflaub, Kurt. 1983. "Democracy, Oligarchy, and the Concept of the 'Free Citizen' in Late Fifth-Century Athens." *Political Theory* 11: 517–544.

———. 1996. "Equalities and Inequalities in Athenian Democracy." In *Demokratia: A Conversation on Democracies, Ancient and Modern*, edited by J. Ober and C. Hedrick, 139–174. Princeton: Princeton University Press.

———. 2009. "Conceptualizing and Theorizing Peace in Ancient Greece." *TAPA* 139: 225–250.

Race, William. 1986. *Pindar: Olympian Odes, Pythian Odes*. Cambridge, MA: Harvard University Press.

Rhodes, P. J. 1981. *A Commentary on the Aristotelian Athenaion Politeia*. Oxford: Clarendon Press.

———. 1998. "Enmity in Fourth-Century Athens." In *Kosmos: Essays in Order, Conflict and Community in Classical Athens*, edited by P. Cartledge, P. Millett, and S. von Reden, 144–161. Cambridge: Cambridge University Press.

———. 2004. "Keeping to the Point." In *The Law and the Courts in Ancient Greece*, edited by E. Harris and L. Rubinstein, 137–158. London: Duckworth.

Riess, Werner. 2012. *Performing Interpersonal Violence: Court, Curse, and Comedy in Fourth-Century BCE Athens*. Berlin: de Gruyter.

Roberts, Jennifer. 1982. *Accountability in Athenian Government*. Madison: University of Wisconsin Press.

Roberts, Jennifer. 1994. *Athens on Trial: The Antidemocratic Tradition in Western Thought*. Princeton: Princeton University Press.

Roisman, Joseph. 2003. "The Rhetoric of Courage in the Attic Orators." In *Andreia: Studies in Manliness and Courage in Classical Antiquity*, edited by R. Rosen and I. Sluiter, 127–143. Leiden: Brill.

———. 2005. *The Rhetoric of Manhood*. Berkeley: University of California Press.

———. 2006. *The Rhetoric of Conspiracy in Ancient Athens*. Berkeley: University of California Press.

de Romilly, Jacqueline. 2012 (original 1967). *The Mind of Thucydides*, translated by Elizabeth Trapnell Rawlings. Ithaca, NY: Cornell University Press.

Roussel, Louis. 1966. *(Pseudo-) Lysias: L'invalide*. Paris: Presses Universitaire de France.

Rowe, Galen. 1994. "The Charge against Meidias." *Hermes* 122: 55–63.

Roy, J. 1999. "'Polis' and 'Oikos' in Classical Athens." *G&R* 46: 1–18.

Rubinstein, Lene. 1998. "The Athenian Political Perception of the *Idiotes*." In *Kosmos: Essays in Order, Conflict, and Community in Classical Athens*, edited by P. Cartledge, P. Millett, and S. von Reden, 125–143. Cambridge: Cambridge University Press.

———. 2000. *Litigation and Cooperation: Supporting Speakers in the Courts of Classical Athens*. Stuttgart: Steiner.

———. 2004. "Stirring up Dicastic Anger." In *Law, Rhetoric, and Comedy in Classical Athens: Essays in Honour of Douglas M. MacDowell*, edited by D. Cairns, R. Knox, D. MacDowell, and I. Arnaoutoglou, 187–203. Swansea: Classical Press of Wales.

———. 2005. "Main Litigants and Witnesses in the Athenian Courts: Procedural Variations." In *Symposion 2001: Vorträge zur Griechischen und Hellenistischen*

Rechtsgeschichte, edited by R. Wallace and M. Gagarin, 99–120. Vienna: Austrian Academy of Sciences.

Ruschenbusch, Eberhard. 1978. *Untersuchungen zu Staat und Politik in Griechenland vom 7.–4. Jh. v. Chr.* Bamberg: Aku.

Russell, D. A. 1990. "*Ēthos* in Oratory and Rhetoric." In *Characterization and Individuality in Greek Literature*, edited by C. Pelling, 197–212. Oxford: Oxford University Press.

de Ste. Croix, G. E. M. 1981. *The Class Struggle in the Ancient Greek World: From the Archaic Age to the Arab Conquests.* Ithaca, NY: Cornell University Press.

Scafuro, Adele. 1997. *The Forensic Stage: Settling Disputes in Greco-Roman New Comedy.* Cambridge: Cambridge University Press.

———. 2007. "The *Astynomoi*, Private Wills and Street Activity." *CQ* 57: 769–775.

Schäfer, H. 1949. "Pasion." *Real-Encyclopädie der klassischen Alterumswissenschaft* 28: 2064–2068.

Scheid-Tissinier, Évelyne. 2007. "Le Rôle de la Colère dans les Tribunaux Athéniens." In *Athènes et le Politique: Dans le Sillage de Claude Mossé*, edited by P. Pantel and F. de Polignac, 179–198. Paris: Albin Michel.

Schiappa, Edward. 1999. *The Beginnings of Rhetorical Theory in Classical Greece.* New Haven: Yale University Press.

Schmitz, Thomas. 2000. "Plausibility in the Greek Orators." *AJP* 121: 47–77.

Schofield, Malcolm. 1998. "Political Friendship and the Ideology of Reciprocity." In *Kosmos: Essays in Order, Conflict and Community in Classical Athens*, edited by P. Cartledge, P. Millett, and S. von Reden, 37–51. Cambridge: Cambridge University Press.

Schön, Karl. 1918. *Die Scheinargumente bei Lysias.* Paderborn: Ferdinand Schöningh.

Sealey, Raphael. 1993. *Demosthenes and His Time: A Study in Defeat.* New York: Oxford University Press.

Shapiro, Robert L. 1996. *The Search for Justice: A Defense Attorney's Brief on the O. J. Simpson Case.* New York: Warner Books.

Sickinger, James. 1999. *Public Records and Archives in Classical Athens.* Chapel Hill: University of North Carolina Press.

Sinclair, Robert. 1988. *Democracy and Participation in Athens.* Cambridge: Cambridge University Press.

Smith, Gertrude. 1927. "The Jurisdiction of the Areopagus." *CP* 22: 61–79.

Sternberg, Rachel. 2006. *Tragedy Offstage: Suffering and Sympathy in Ancient Athens.* Austin: University of Texas Press.

Strauss, Barry. 1993. *Fathers and Sons in Athens: Ideology and Society in the Era of the Peloponnesian War.* Princeton: Princeton University Press.

Thompson, Homer. 1936. "Pnyx and Thesmophorion." *Hesperia* 5: 151–200.

Thompson, Wesley. 1981. "Athenian Attitudes toward Wills." *Prudentia* 13: 13–23.

Thür, Gerhard. 1996. "Reply to D. C. Mirhady: Torture and Rhetoric in Athens." *JHS* 116: 132–134.

———. 2005. "The Role of Witnesses in Athenian Law." In *The Cambridge Com-*

panion to Ancient Greek Law, edited by M. Gagarin and D. Cohen, 146–169. New York: Cambridge University Press.

———. 2008. "The Principle of Fairness in Athenian Legal Procedure: Thoughts on the Echinos and Enklema." *Dike* 11: 51–73.

Todd, Stephen. 1990a. "*Lady Chatterley's Lover* and the Attic Orators: The Social Composition of the Athenian Jury." *JHS* 110: 146–172.

———. 1990b. "The Purpose of Evidence in Athenian Courts." In *Nomos*, edited by P. Cartledge, P. Millett, and S. Todd, 19–38. Cambridge: Cambridge University Press.

———. 1990c. "The Use and Abuse of the Attic Orators." *G&R* 37: 159–178.

———. 1993. *The Shape of Athenian Law*. Oxford: Oxford University Press.

———. 1998. "The Rhetoric of Enmity in the Attic Orators." In *Kosmos: Essays in Order, Conflict and Community in Classical Athens*, edited by P. Cartledge, P. Millett, and S. Todd, 162–169. Cambridge: Cambridge University Press.

———. 2000. *Lysias*. Austin: University of Texas Press.

———. 2007. *A Commentary on Lysias, Speeches 1–11*. Cambridge: Cambridge University Press.

Trevett, Jeremy. 1992. *Apollodorus, Son of Pasion*. Oxford: Clarendon Press.

———. 2011. *Demosthenes: Speeches 1–17*. Austin: University of Texas Press.

Usher, Stephen. 1965. "Individual Characterization in Lysias." *Eranos* 63: 99–119.

———. 1999. *Greek Oratory: Tradition and Originality*. Oxford: Oxford University Press.

van Wees, Hans. 1992. *Status Warriors: War, Violence and Society in Homer and History*. Amsterdam: J.C. Gieben.

Versnel, Hendrik S. 1999. "Κόλασαι Τοὺς Ἡμᾶς Τοιούτους Ἡδέως Βλέποντας 'Punish Those Who Rejoice in Our Misery': On Curse Texts and *Schadenfreude*." In *The World of Ancient Magic: Papers from the First International Samson Eitem Seminar at the Norwegian Institute at Athens, 4–8 May 1997*, edited by D. Jordan, H. Montgomery, and E. Thomassen, 125–162. Bergen: Norwegian Institute at Athens.

Veyne, Paul. 1990. *Bread and Circuses: Historical Sociology and Political Pluralism*. London: Penguin Books.

Volonaki, Eleni. 2000. "'Apagoge' in Homicide Cases." *Dike* 3: 147–176.

Walcot, Peter. 1978. *Envy and the Greeks*. Warminster: Aris & Phillips.

Wallace, Robert. 1989. *The Areopagus Council to 307 B.C.* Baltimore: Johns Hopkins University Press.

Walton, Douglas. 2001. "Enthymemes, Common Knowledge, and Plausible Inference." *Ph&Rh* 34: 93–112.

Whitehead, David. 1983. "Competitive Outlay and Community Profit: Φιλοτιμία in Democratic Athens." *C&M* 34: 55–74.

———. 1986. *The Demes of Attica, 508/7–ca. 250 B.C.: A Political and Social Study*. Princeton: Princeton University Press.

———. 1993. "Cardinal Virtues: The Language of Public Approbation in Democratic Athens." *C&M* 44: 37–75.

Wilson, Peter. 1991. "Demosthenes 21 (*against Meidias*): Democratic Abuse." *PCPS* 37: 164–195.

———. 2000. *The Athenian Institution of the Khoregia: The Chorus, the City and the Stage*. Cambridge: Cambridge University Press.

Wilson, Stephen. 1988. *Feuding, Conflict and Banditry in Nineteenth-Century Corsica*. Cambridge: Cambridge University Press.

Winkler, John. 1990. *The Constraints of Desire: The Anthropology of Sex and Gender in Ancient Greece*. New York: Routledge.

Winter, Thomas. 1973. "On the Corpus of Lysias." *CJ* 69: 34–40.

Wisse, Jakob. 1989. *Ethos and Pathos from Aristotle to Cicero*. Amsterdam: Hakkert.

Wolpert, Andrew. 2001. "Lysias 1 and the Politics of the Oikos." *CJ* 96: 415–424.

———. 2002. *Remembering Defeat: Civil War and Civic Memory in Ancient Athens*. Baltimore: Johns Hopkins University Press.

Wood, Ellen. 1983. "Agricultural Slavery in Classical Athens." *AJAH* 8: 1–47.

———. 1996. "Demos Versus 'We, the People': Freedom and Democracy Ancient and Modern." In *Demokratia: A Conversation on Democracies, Ancient and Modern*, edited by J. Ober and C. Hedrick, 121–139. Princeton: Princeton University Press.

Wood, Gordon. 2006. *Revolutionary Characters: What Made the Founders Different*. New York: Penguin.

Worman, Nancy. 2008. *Abusive Mouths in Classical Athens*. Cambridge: Cambridge University Press.

Wyatt-Brown, Bertram. 1982. *Southern Honor: Ethics and Behavior in the Old South*. New York: Oxford University Press.

Wyse, William. 1967. *The Speeches of Isaeus*. Hildesheim: Olms.

Yunis, Harvey. 2000–2001. "Politics as Literature: Demosthenes and the Burden of the Past." *Arion* 8: 97–118.

———. 2005. *Demosthenes: Speeches 18–19*. Austin: University of Texas Press.

Ziebarth, Erich. 1934. *Neue Verfluchungstafeln aus Attika, Boiotien und Euboia*. Berlin: Preussische Akademie der Wissenschafte.

INDEX

abuse, verbal. *See* slander
Achilles, 3, 38–39, 170n87
Admetus, 170n87
Aeschines, 15–16, 85–87, 157; *Against Ctesiphon*, 40, 53, 85, 87, 183n45, 191–192n144, 201n96, 202n98; *Against Timarchus*, 42–43, 78, 106–107, 110–111, 130, 164n48, 177n187
Aeschylus: *Eumenides*, 143; *Suppliants*, 19
Agamemnon, 38–39, 150
aggression, 126–129
Alcidamas, *On the Sophists*, 163n40
Allen, Danielle, 6, 162n15, 205n49
"amnesia clause," 32–33
amnesty of 401 BC, 32–33, 155
Anaximenes of Lampsacus, 58. *See also Rhetoric to Alexander*
Andocides, 15, 29–30; *On the Mysteries*, 87–89, 113–114, 124, 147–148
anger (*orgē*), 28, 132, 162n15, 205n49
Anthony, Casey, 92
antidosis, 44, 173n122, 196n20
Antiphon, 15; *Against the Stepmother*, 98, 102; *First Tetralogy*, 59; *On the Chorus Boy*, 31, 103–104; *On the Murder of Herodes*, 102, 197n34
apagōgē, 144, 185n71, 197n32, 211n137
apographē ("inventory"), 76–77, 82, 190n132
Apollodorus (pseudo-Demosthenes), 15, 188n112; *Against Neaera*, 71–75, 76;

Against Nicostratus, 75–78, 123, 148–149; *Against Polycles*, 199n55
aporrhēta (unspeakable words), 204n35
appeal (*ephesis*), 112, 201n83
arbitration (*diaita*), 13, 31–32, 107, 146, 167n42, 168n45
arbitrators, 32
archers, Scythian, 211n138
archons, 99, 120, 163n33, 172n119
Areopagus Court, 101, 130, 143, 173n130, 193n166, 197n39
arguments: *a fortiori*, 64, 141; anticipatory (*prokatalēpsis*), 87, 110–111, 115, 132, 133–134, 138–139; character (*ēthos*) 7, 60–67, 68–71, 73–80, 83, 86–87, 91, 92–93, 99, 110–111, 133, 171n107, 194n175; extralegal (limitations on), 130–131; offensive and defensive, 68, 74; probability/plausibility (*eikos*), 17, 57, 58–62, 78, 86–87, 89–90, 108–109, 110–111, 113, 122, 182n25, 187n104, 197n38. *See also* rhetorical strategy
Aristides "the Just," 120
Aristophanes, 19; *Clouds*, 11, 60, 211n139; *Knights*, 43; *Wasps*, 11, 185n80, *Wealth*, 199n65
Aristotle, 18, 181n111; *Athenian Constitution*, 119, 130, 175n148; *Politics*, 137, 147, 202n3; *Rhetoric*, 28–29, 34, 48, 58, 59, 63–64, 80, 163n40, 166n24

assault, 37, 97–104, 108–109. *See also* violence
Assembly, Athenian, 40, 44, 45, 98, 135–136, 170n98
Athena, 150–151, 169n79
Athenian-Corcyraean treaty of 433, 168n48
Athens: compared to other *poleis*, 157–158; as "enmity culture," 26–27, 54, 129, 152; not a "feuding society," 5–6, 24–26, 134–135, 140, 150–151; societal structure of, 24–26, 48–51, 54
athletic games, 39–40, 156, 170n90
auctoritas, 109

Bacchylides, 39
benefactors, civic, 40–41, 109
binding spells (*katadesmoi*), 18, 30, 34, 38, 39–40, 42, 45, 46, 47, 53, 54, 146–147, 173n128, 204n41
blackmail. *See* sycophancy
blood feud, 24, 26, 28, 145, 147
Blumenfeld, Laura, 31
Briseis, 38–39
Brown, Elizabeth, 25
bullying, 101, 215n28
bureaucracy: medieval, 25–26; modern, 119
Burr, Aaron, 213n2

Callias, 88, 192n159
Carey, Christopher, 63
Chaeronea, Battle of, 85, 189n120
character: hereditary nature of, 65; as persuasive element, 66, 184n63; types of, 63–64. *See also under* arguments
charis, 29, 171n107
Charmides, 30. *See also under* Plato
chorus production (*chorēgia*), 36, 41, 43, 99
Christ, Matthew, 6, 162n15, 172n110, 173nn122,123, 185n79, 195n5, 201n87, 212n151
citizen, Athenian: and democratic ideology, 5, 11; the "just citizen," 79–80; physical body, 4, 118, 136–137, 142, 148, 208n94; representing non-citizens, 162n28
citizenship, 60, 71, 74, 112, 137, 163n31
Civil War (American), 154
civil war (*stasis*), 118–119, 148, 154–155, 157, 202n1
Clytemnestra, 102
cohabitation, law against, 186n90
Cohen, David, 5–6, 8–9, 24, 26, 28, 78, 86, 133–135, 138–139, 151, 180n222, 187n104, 195n79
competitiveness, 38–41, 46, 137–140, 170nn87,90
"competitive outlay," 40
Conon. *See under* Demosthenes
"conspiracism," 54
conspiracy, 87–88, 124, 180n218, 197n33
Constant, Benjamin, 159
contracts (*sunthēkai*), 36, 174n140
Corsica, 26
Council of Five Hundred, 45, 98, 120
court proceedings, 13–14; as arena for honor games, 146; as forum for enmity, 35, 51–53, 121–129; and modern standards, 91; third-party litigation, 51; witnesses, 51–52, 125, 130, 131, 178n193; women, 71
cowardice (*deilia*), 183n45f
credibility. *See under* rhetorical strategy
Critias, 155
Ctesiphon. *See under* Aeschines
curse tablets. *See* binding spells
cursing ceremonies, 18, 34

Danaus, 19
debtors, 69, 124–125, 172n111
defamation, 132
defense speeches, 80–90, 102, 103, 108–109, 111–115
delay *topos*. *See under* rhetorical strategy
Delphinium, 193n166
Demades, 15
demes, 45–46, 202n5

democracy, 3, 11, 19, 47, 111, 152, 155–156, 157–159, 164n49, 200n79, 214n15
Demosthenes, 15, 28, 29, 36, 44, 135–136, 157, 173n125; *Against Aristocrates*, 115; *Against Aristogiton*, 52, 68–70, 124–125, 185nn70–72,74; *Against Boeotus I*, 204n31; *Against Boeotus II*, 168n52; *Against Conon*, 3, 64, 65, 98, 99–102, 127, 138–139, 142, 147, 184n53, 196n22; *Against Eubulides*, 45, 54, 112–113, 178n201, 180n5; *Against Evergus*, 149, 212n152; *Against Meidias*, 37, 98–99, 105, 132–134, 138, 140–141, 150, 160, 169n75, 196n23; *Against Pantaenetus*, 61; *Against Spudias*, 107; *Against Timocrates*, 64, 147; *On the Crown*, 85–87, 114–115, 136; *On the Embassy*, 53. See also Apollodorus
deterrence (of crime), 37, 148
diadikasia, 15–16, 44
diapheromai ("quarrel"), 166n19
dikē (private legal suit), 12, 13, 86, 199n55; *dikē aikeias*, 99–100; *dikē emporikē*, 16, 164n47; *dikē exoulēs*, 14, 99, 144; *dikē kakēgorias*, 125–126, 132; *dikē phthonou*, 86; *dikē pseudomartyriōn*, 52, 179n203; and private enmity, 95–96. See also *graphē*
Dinarchus, 15, 40; *Against Demosthenes*, 52
Dionysia, 33, 99
Dionysius of Halicarnassus, 67, 196n22
Dionysodorus, 49–50
dokimasia, 16, 43, 99, 106, 110, 121, 164n48
Dover, Kenneth, 36, 64
drunkenness, 47, 137–138, 140–141, 175n156

echthra. See enmity
echthros. See under enemies
eisangelia, 114
Eleusinian Mysteries, 88, 113–114
Eleven, the, 144
elite bias, 46
embezzlement, 103
emotions, 28, 32, 121, 166n18
endeixis, 185n71
enemies: Athenian definition of, dangers of, 23–24; 30; *echthros* and *polemios*, 26–27, 35, 165–166n16, 200n79, 211n133; fear of, 37, 38, 123–124, 125; harming one's, 2, 119–120; humiliation of, 145–146; mockery of, 204n41; shared among friends, 32, 48, 50–51; as *synēgoroi* and witnesses, 54, 125, 131, 180n217
England, medieval, 25, 33
enmity (*echthra*): affirmation or denial of, 57, 72, 79–80, 89, 95–97, 104–105, 189n26; against Athens, 110, 135; Athenian attitudes toward, 2, 3, 5, 10, 20, 22, 27, 30, 36–37, 48, 80, 126–129, 161n5; and Athenian democracy, 3, 158; in Athenian government, 118–121; in contemporary United States, 153; in defense speeches, 81–82; defining characteristics, 31–32, 42; distinct from anger and hatred, 28; downplaying, 105–107; establishing pretext for, 70–73, 77, 83–84, 191n140; formation of, 43–48, 52–53; vs. friendship, 28–29, 166n22; in Greek literature, 37–39; Greek terminology, 26, 27–28; Homeric models, 2–3; 38–39; and honor, 2–3, 35, 38–41; Latin terminology, 165n15; and liturgies, 41, 43, 97; narratives of, 9, 61–62, 66–67, 189–190n128; non-oratorical sources for, 18; and *oikos*, 48–49; policing function, 42; and politics, 40–41, 42–43, 44; in prosecution speeches, 68–80, 120–129; proving, 29–30; public context of, 33–34; reciprocity of, 26–27; reconciliation (*diallagē, dialusis*), 31–34, 36, 167n41, 168nn45,54; regulation of, 129, 151, 205n55, 214n13; as rela-

enmity (*echthra*) (*continued*)
    tionship, 28–29, 156; rhetorical function of, 2, 7–8, 20–21, 56, 78–79, 84, 86–87, 97, 108–116; role of in litigation, 86–87, 99–104, 121–128, 130–135 196n17; spread of, 48–53; and sycophancy, 112–113; *synēgoroi*, 96; in theater productions, 45, 99; transgenerational, 48–50; and violence, 4–5, 138; as war, 35–36. See also enemies; revenge; violence
Ephialtes, 173n130
epimeletai, 41
Eratosthenes. See under Lysias
Eris ("Strife"), 43
Euphiletus, 30, 55–56, 57, 89–90, 102, 128, 140, 143
Euripides: *Bacchae*, 37; *Cyclops*, 210n125; *Heraclidae*, 37–38; *Medea*, 50; *Suppliants*, 19, 143
euthynai, 43, 69, 106, 121, 190n131, 191n144
Evaeon, 140–141
executions, 155

family: enmity within, 46; shared character traits, 65; shared debt, 49; shared enemies, 48–50; supporting each other at trial, 33, 51–53
Federalist Party, 213n2
feudalism, 24–25, 165n8
feuding societies, 5–6, 22, 24–26, 151
feuds, role of in court, 122–129. See also enmity; revenge
finances, public, 202n3
Fisher, Nicolas, 78, 128–129
Foucault, Michel, 66
Founding Fathers (American), 154
France, medieval, 4, 156
freedom, 5, 85, 136, 159
French Revolution, 159
Freud, Sigmund, 204n38
friendship (*philia*), 27, 28–29, 33–34, 35, 166nn22,24; sharing moral values,
63–65, 75–76; termination of, 47–48; transgenerational, 48–50

Gabrielsen, Vincent, 43, 44
Gagarin, Michael, 59, 181n15, 197n26, 204n43
gender, 137
generals, 36, 43, 83, 101, 120
Gerousia (Sparta), 158
Gorgias, 182n20
gossip, 35
government, Athenian: controlling enmity within, 118–121; preservation of public welfare, 119
graphē (public legal suit), 12, 13, 71, 106, 196n18; *graphē hubreōs*, 141; *graphē paranomōn*, 64, 72, 73–74, 85, 114, 115, 183n51. See also *dikē*
greed, 56. See also sycophancy
gymnasiarchia, 41

Halperin, David, 137
Hamilton, Alexander, 13, 213n2
Hansen, Mogens, 109
Harmodius and Aristogiton, 176n157
hatred (*misos*), 28, 63
Herman, Gabriel, 5–6, 8, 9, 75, 126–129, 133, 144, 147, 162n20, 165nn7,54, 187n98, 195n9, 209n119
Hobbes, Thomas, 40
homicide, 4, 15, 50, 55–56, 73, 98, 128, 142; Athenian attitudes toward, 140–141; laws concerning, 89, 143, 177n178, 187n92, 193n166, 211n133; in trials, 101–103
honor, 35, 38–41, 128–129, 156, 170n87
honorary decrees, 40, 41
honor games, 2–3, 145–147
hubris, 77, 101, 127, 138, 140–141, 148–149, 150, 204n35, 208n94
Hunt, Peter, 36
Hyams, Paul, 33
Hyperides, 15

Iliad, 38–39, 170n87, 215n22
infidelity, 55–56
inheritance, 15, 33, 46, 49, 96–97
Isaeus, 15–16, 33; *On Behalf of Euphiletus*, 201n83
Isocrates, 15, 47; *Against Callimachus*, 36, 168n53; *Against Lochites*, 142; *On the Team of Horses*, 134; *Panathenaicus*, 143

Jefferson, Thomas, 213n2
juries, Athenian: beliefs and expectations of, 59, 122, 203n16; impartiality of, 120–121, 134–135; selection of, 11–12; self-interest of, 37
justice, 131, 134, 143; adversarial, 178n189; inquisitorial, 178n189
Justinian, law code of, 12

Kurihara, Asako, 95–96

laughter, 38
law: Modern European, 11; Roman, 11, 12, 163n37, 175n146
law, Athenian, 11–14; enforcement of, 14, 144; publishing of, 12–13; sources for, 14–17
Leocrates. *See under* Lycurgus
liturgies, 41–45, 97, 138, 171n105, 172n118
living well, 37
logographers, 12, 58
lovers, 47, 137–140
Lycurgus, 15, 109, 200n67; *Against Leocrates*, 79–80, 85, 107, 127–128, 195n9
Lysias, 15, 16, 28, 58, 63, 67, 180n5; *Against Agoratus*, 110, 198n48; *Against Andocides*, 89, 193n164; *Against Epicrates*, 132; *Against Eratosthenes*, 105–106, 110, 210n122; *Against Eubulides*, 180n5; *Against the Members of a Sunousia*, 35, 47; *Against Simon*, 103–104, 108–109, 137, 139–140; *Against Theomnestus*, 125–126; *For the Soldier*, 82–84, 131, 190n130; *On a Charge of Overthrowing the Democracy*, 111–112; *On the Murder of Eratosthenes*, 30, 55–56, 57, 89–90, 102, 104, 128, 140, 143, 191n141; *On the Olive Stump*, 104–105, 185n79; *On a Premeditated Wounding*, 32, 33, 102, 139, 140, 199n61; *On the Property of Aristophanes*, 124, 208n89

magistracies (*archai*), 13, 43, 119–120, 202nn3,5, 204n35, 212n146
manhood, 137
manslayer (*androphonos*), 125
McCarthy, Cormac, 167n38
medieval Europe, 24–25
"Mediterraneity," 165n7
Megacles, 155
Meidias, 29, 36, 169n75. *See also under* Demosthenes
Menelaus, 170n87
methodology, 6–10, 24–25, 121–122, 169n72
metics, 163nn31,33
miasma (religious pollution), 176n166, 187n92
Montesquieu, Charles, 39
morality, Athenian, 8–9, 63, 64, 126–129, 159–160
motive: denial of, 108–109; establishment of, 97–98, 101–102, 103–104, 196n17
murder. *See* homicide
Murphy, T. M, 111
"Mysian booty," 54
mythology, 19, 150–151, 210n125

narrative. *See under* rhetorical strategy
nature vs nurture, 65, 184n61
Neaera. *See under* Apollodorus
Nicomachus (of Lys. 7), 104–105
Nixon, Richard, 36

236　INDEX

oaths, public, 119, 120, 130, 206n70; Heliastic Oath, 121, 161n6
Ober, Josiah, 148
obligations, filial, 49
Odysseus, 150–151, 168n48, 210n125, 215n22
oligarchy, 155
olive tree, sacred (*moria*), 197n39
Olympic games, 39
orations. *See* speeches, assembly; speeches, legal; defense speeches; prosecutors
orators, Attic: citizenship, 163n31; goals, 55, 180n1; and "public good," 135–136; specialization, 15. *See also* individual orators
ostracism, 154

Panactum, 101
paragraphē (barring action), 61, 182n27
paranoia, 38
parents: love of, 63; mistreatment of, 63, 183n40
Pasion (banker), 174n139
Passage to India, A, 60
patricide, 125–126
patriotism, 40, 79, 80, 109
Patroclus, funeral games of, 170n87
peace treaties, 36
pederasty, 208n96
peer pressure, 33, 145
Peloponnesian War, 105
Periander, 155
Pericles, 44, 157, 214n17; Funeral oration of, 5, 119, 212n156
perjury, 73, 84
Philip of Macedonia, 85, 106, 189n120
Philocrates: of Antiphon 6, 31; of Demosthenes 25, 52; of Lysias 29, 182n22
philotimia, 43, 137, 171n100
Pindar, 39
Pisistratus, 147, 154, 155

Pittacus, law of, 137
Plato, 18, 60; *Apology*, 35; *Charmides*, 30, 37; *Gorgias*, 38, 147; *Laws*, 34, 47, 171n103; *Republic*, 148, 158, 167n32, 174n140
Plutarch, 58, 62
polemios. *See under* enemies
police force, 211n138, 212n146
politeia, Athenian, 150, 155–160
pollution, religious. *See* miasma
Polyaenus, 82–84, 120, 131
pragma, 130–131, 194n178, 206n70, 209n107
prejudices (*diabolai*), 185n78, 207n74
premise, major (stated) and minor (unstated), 59, 61, 113
probability. *See under* arguments
probolē, 98, 196nn18,19, 210n120
procedure, legal, 95–97. *See also* court proceedings
proofs: *atechnoi*, 17; *entechnoi*, 17; *pisteis*, 16, 62; *sēmeia*, 30
property, 46–47
prosecutors, 67–80, 81; acting in public interest, 105, 106–107, 198n52; financial rewards, 56, 71; "reluctant prosecutor," 69, 185n76; volunteer, 42–43
prostitutes, 47, 110, 137–140, 179n208, 198n53, 208n96
prytaneis, 98
punishment: corporal, 136; of criminals, 37, 140

Quintilian, *Institutio Oratoria*, 90–91

reciprocity, 23, 28–29, 49
reconciliation. *See under* enmity
relationships, 28–34; and personal character, 67; reciprocal nature of, 28–29
revenge (timōria), 1, 6, 23, 29, 31, 38, 50, 75, 76, 78, 86, 122–123; limitations on, 118–121, 129–135, 136–150, 205n55; manifestations of, 145–147

rhetorical strategy, 55–56, 60; appeals to rumor, 109–111; based on procedure, 96–98; credibility, 65–66, 68–69, 70–71, 73–74, 81–82, 103, 111, 112, 130–135, 188n107; "delay" *topos*, 113–115, 124–125, 202n102; narrative, 61–67, 189–190n128; and public persona, use of, 109; revenge motif, 122–123; sycophancy, 111–113. *See also* arguments
Rhetoric to Alexander, 16, 18–19, 52, 58, 59, 60–61, 66, 155, 163n40, 169n64, 179n211, 184n65, 206n70
robbery, 211n139
Roisman, Joseph, 54, 124, 192n159
Romilly, Jacqueline de, 62
rumor (*phēmē*), 109–111

Scafuro, Adele, 146
Scamandrius, archonship of, 137
Schadenfreude, 38
self-defense, 101, 141, 143–144, 148
self-portrayal, negative, 55–56
self-promotion, 41
Senate Watergate Committee, proceedings of, 36
sex, 47, 137
Sicilian Expedition, 62
Simonides, 39
Simpson, O. J., 92
slander, 35, 47–48, 125–126, 131–132, 142, 190n134, 204nn35,41
slavery, 136, 208n94
slaves, 56, 76, 140, 148–149, 162n28, 204n30
Socrates, 13, 30, 34, 35–36, 38, 44–45
Solon, 154
sophists, 19, 60, 181n15, 182n32
Sophocles, 19; *Ajax*, 150–151, 169n79; *Antigone*, 19, 49, 169n79; *Oedipus Rex*, 60
sōphrosynē (prudence), 30
speeches, assembly, 135–136
speeches, legal: argumentative goals of, 55–56, 96–97; "descriptive" vs "prescriptive" use of, 9–10; formulaic content of, 16–17; interpretive approaches to, 6–10; limitations of evidence, 55, 65–66; patterns in affirmation/denial of enmity, 95–104; preservation of, 15, 142; as sources for Athenian values, 6–7, 10, 164n43; stock phrases in, 124; structural division of, 16. *See also* defense speeches
speechwriters. *See* orators
spending, conspicuous, 41
Sphodrias, 158, 215n19
Spudias. *See under* Demosthenes
sycophancy, 14, 61, 69, 70–71, 78, 88, 99, 104, 109, 111–113, 185n79, 187n104, 189n117, 198n52; ancient definition of, 14, 113, 163n38, 201n91
syllogism, 58–59, 181n11
synēgoroi (co-speakers), 12, 13, 45, 51, 52, 53, 69, 71, 88, 96, 125

tax farming, 88, 193n162
testamentary law, 46, 175n146
Themistocles, 120
Theomnestus, 71–75. *See also under* Lysias
Theophrastus, *Characters*, 183n47
Theramenes, 155, 184n58
Theseus, 19
Thirty, The, 105, 110, 155–156, 198n48, 200n80
Thucydides, 62, 118–119, 147, 154, 168n48
Timarchus. *See under* Aeschines
Tisias and Corax, 59–60, 181n16, 181–182n17
"tit for tat," 128, 205n50
Todd, Stephen, 32, 89, 140, 190n130
topoi, 16
torture, 16, 137
trials, Athenian. *See* court proceedings
trierarchy, 41, 43, 173n125

vengeance. *See* revenge
victory odes, 39–40
violence, 4–5, 97–104; alternatives to, 145–147; Athenian views on, 136–145; and irrationality, 137–138, 209n104; and noncitizens, 148–149; prevalence of, 141–142; prevention of, 142–143, 147; in Rome, 152; and "self-help," 143–144, 156, 211n132
virtue (*aretē*), 167n28

war, 148
water clock (*klepsydra*), 13, 163n35

weapons, 143, 147–148
Whitehead, David, 40
Wilson, Stephen, 26
witnesses. *See under* court proceedings
women: in court, 71; slandering of, 179nn207,208

Xenophon: *Hellenica*, 155; *Hiero*, 37; *Memorabilia*, 34, 35–36, 44–45

Zeus, 168n48

INDEX LOCORUM

Aeschines
1: 106–107, 110–111, 164n48, 177n187, 195n6, 195n7, 196n11, 196n13; 208n91
1.1–2: 106, 198n51
1.2: 42, 161n3, 171n102, 203n19, 203n21
1.4–5: 157, 214n16
1.17: 213n169
1.28: 183n41
1.45: 206n64
1.47: 178n193
1.58–59: 209n104
1.58–62: 213n171
1.91: 200n73
1.93: 111, 194–195n178, 200n74
1.113: 206n66
1.152: 184n55
1.154: 206n60
1.166: 206n66
1.170: 206n66
1.173: 192n148
1.175: 206n68
1.176: 130, 206n69
1.178: 206n70
1.186: 206n63
1.193: 179n207
2: 172n113
2.2: 204n34, 207n76
2.10: 206n66
2.139: 202n98
2.154: 177n187
2.182: 204n41
3: 85, 87, 183n51, 191n144, 195n6, 196n11, 196n13
3.9–31: 191n144
3.32–48: 191n144
3.52: 196n19
3.78: 63
3.105: 183n41
3.119: 192n155
3.125: 192n155
3.158: 183n41
3.163: 206n64
3.164: 192n155
3.169: 176n169
3.171–172: 53, 179n206
3.172: 53, 179n207
3.173: 204n30
3.175: 183n45
3.177–191: 40
3.179–180: 171n109
3.193: 206n66
3.197–200: 206n61
3.215–225: 192n156, 201n96
3.257: 178n197

Aeschylus
Suppliants
398–400: 19, 165n58

Andocides
1: 87–89, 113–114, 124
1.1: 124, 203n22

Andocides (*continued*)
    1.4: 204n40
    1.6: 189n127
    1.11–70: 192n158
    1.30: 204n34
    1.31: 176n166
    1.43: 137, 208n97
    1.45: 147–148, 213n162
    1.47: 179n208
    1.54: 204n34, 204n40
    1.66: 213n162
    1.71–91: 192n158
    1.92–109: 192n158
    1.117: 88
    1.117–123: 171n102
    1.117–136: 29–30
    1.118–123: 88, 177n187, 193n160
    1.132: 114, 172n119, 198n43, 201n92
    1.133–136: 88, 193n161, 202n3
    1.141: 176n169, 184n59
    1.150: 178n192
    2.4: 177n187, 180n218
    2.26: 184n59
    4.1: 173n127
    4.2: 204n40
    4.18: 211n140
    4.20: 209n103
    4.25–28: 204n40

Antiphon
    1: 98, 102, 196n16, 197n33
    1.2: 178n196
    1.4: 178n196
    1.15: 102
    1.17: 102
    1.29: 177n179
    1.29–30: 177n174
    4: 175n156
    5: 102, 196n16
    5.11: 206n57
    5.33: 177n187
    5.57: 194n173
    6: 103, 196n16
    6.7: 103, 197n35, 204n34
    6.9: 202n99
    6.11: 172n115
    6.34–36: 103, 177n187, 197n35
    6.39: 167n43, 168n56
    6.39–40: 31
    6.43: 202n3

Aristophanes
Clouds
    37: 174n137
    207–208: 11, 162n26
    498–499: 211n139
Knights
    445–447: 184n59
    912–914: 43
Wasps
    106–108: 185n80
    583–586: 175n145
    849–850: 185n80
    1253–1255: 175n156
    1444–1445: 175n156
Wealth
    911–919: 199n65
Women of the Assembly
    663–664: 175n156
Fragments
    597: 169n79
    694: 184n67

Aristotle
Athenian Constitution
    9.2: 175n145
    18.4: 213n161
    25.2: 173n130
    35.2: 175n148
    42.1: 201n85
    43–61: 202n4
    55.5: 203n10
    56.3: 172n119
    56.6: 183n40
    60.2: 197n39
    67.1: 130, 206n59
Nicomachean Ethics
    4.5 (1126a21–22): 169n81

INDEX LOCORUM 241

9.2 (1165a): 177n185
15.4 (1132a2–6): 195n180
Politics
  2.8 (1268b40): 147, 212n159
  2.12 (1274b18–23): 137, 175n156, 208n101
  6.2 (1317b3): 150, 213n173
  6.8 (1322a): 165n16
  6.8 (1322a16–19): 202n3
Rhetoric
  1.1 (1354a21–24): 206n57
  1.2 (1356a13): 184n63
  1.2 (1357a34–36): 58
  1.6 (1363a19–21, 33–34): 167n28
  1.9 (1367a20–22): 29
  1.12 (1372a30–31): 29
  1.12 (1372b31–33): 54, 165n2, 180n216
  1.12 (1372b37–1373a4): 177n184
  2: 166n24
  2.2 (1379a30–32): 176n162
  2.2 (1379b17–19): 18, 165n55, 169n77
  2.4: 48
  2.4 (1382a1–2): 166n26
  2.4 (1381a1–3): 29, 166n25
  2.4 (1381a9–9, 15–17): 34, 168n58
  2.4 (1381b14–16): 174n139
  2.12–17 (1388b31–1391b7): 63, 183n44
  2.21 (1395a18): 4, 50, 161n7, 177n177
  2.24 (1402a17–24): 181n16, 199n60
  3.12 (1413b13): 180n1

Aristotle, Pseudo-
Rhetoric to Alexander
  1.15 (1422a36–38): 167n31
  2.14 (1424a15–19): 171n107
  2.19 (1424b6–7): 155, 214n5
  2.19 (1424b8–10): 214n6
  3.11 (1426b5–7): 63, 183n39
  4.3 (1426b39–1427a1): 206–207n70
  7.4 (1428a25–34): 59, 181n13
  7.4 (1428a28): 38
  7.5–6 (1428a34–1428b16): 60, 182n23
  7.8 (1428b16–20): 61, 206n70
  7.8 (1428b19–20): 182n31
  7.9 (1428b23–24): 61, 182n24
  7.9 (1428b23–32): 65, 184n57
  7.10 (1428b33–36): 63, 182n31
  7.12 (1428b40–1429a4): 184n57
  15.4 (1431b33–36): 52
  15.5 (1431b37–41): 131, 178n195, 179n211, 204n32, 207n71
  17.2 (1432a39–1432b1): 66, 185n68
  29–37: 16
  29.1 (1436a33–35): 206n62
  29.13 (1437a10–11): 180n218
  29.16 (1437a22–23): 169n64
  29.18 (1437a34–37): 185n78
  29.23–25 (1437b18–27): 206n70
  36.2 (1441b32–34): 206n62
  36.17 (1442b32–35): 206n70
  36.21 (1443a16–18): 206n60
  36.21–23 (1443a15–28): 206n70
  36.32–33 (1443b33–37): 182n31
  38.2–4 (1445b29–1446a3): 184n65

A. Audollent, *Defixionum Tabellae*
  46: 179n214
  47: 174n142, 179n214
  49: 179n211
  50: 179n214
  52: 174n142
  60: 179n211, 179n214, 180n220
  61: 180n220
  62: 179n209
  63: 179n209, 179n211
  67: 180n220
  68: 176n159
  70: 174n142
  71: 174n142
  72: 174n142
  73: 174n142

Cicero
Post Reditum ad Populum: 189n118

Demosthenes
  2.29: 208n90
  3.21: 208n90

Demosthenes (*continued*)
4.44: 208n90
5.5: 136, 208n93
  5.6: 208n90
8.1: 135, 208n90
  8.33: 148, 213n166
9.2: 208n90
  9.29: 208n90
  9.53: 135, 208n92
10.27: 208n94, 213n172
  10.63: 135, 173n128, 208n92
14.5: 208n90
16.1: 208n90
  16.32: 208n90
18: 85–87, 114–115, 178n191, 183n51
  18.1–2: 189n127
  18.5: 205n53
  18.7–8: 204n34
  18.9–16: 192n147
  18.13: 114, 201n94
  18.15: 201n97, 206n70
  18.15–16: 192n148
  18.17: 86, 192n149
  18.21: 179n207
  18.22–23: 114, 201n95
  18.31: 192n147
  18.40–41: 192n147
  18.50: 192n147
  18.82: 192n147
  18.83: 201n96
  18.104: 173n125
  18.109: 192n147
  18.117: 201n96
  18.120–121: 191n144
  18.121–125: 192n147
  18.123: 204n39
  18.124: 201n96
  18.124–125: 192n147
  18.131–138: 192n147
  18.138: 192n147
  18.143: 192n147
  18.163: 192n147
  18.189: 192n147
  18.189–191: 201n96

  18.191: 201n97
  18.198: 192n147
  18.217: 192n147
  18.222–225: 201n96
  18.225: 207n76
  18.226: 206n70
  18.227–228: 192n147
  18.243: 192n147, 201n96
  18.249: 192n147
  18.249–251: 177n187
  18.251: 114, 201n96, 202n98
  18.257: 192n147
  18.265: 192n147
  18.269: 176n162
  18.277: 86, 192n150
  18.277–279: 192n147
  18.278: 85, 192n146
  18.278–279: 86–87
  18.283: 87, 192n153
  18.285: 192n147
  18.286: 192n147
  18.293–294: 192n147
  18.307: 192n147
19: 172n113, 195n6, 196n11
  19.80: 171n102
  19.117: 206n64
  19.221: 178n199
  19.237–238: 53, 179n205
  19.242: 206n67
  19.245: 184n55
  19.296–297: 208n88
20: 170n99, 178n191, 183n51, 189n119, 189n126, 195n6, 196n11, 196n13, 208n91
  20.1: 178n192
  20.144: 176n167
21: 98–99, 132–134, 140–141, 195n6, 196n11, 196n16, 196n23
  21.1: 161n3, 203n19
  21.7: 207n86
  21.13: 202n3
  21.14–18: 99
  21.23: 204n30
  21.29: 133, 165n16, 207n83

INDEX LOCORUM   243

21.31–35: 133, 207n84
21.32–33: 204n35
21.34: 133, 160, 207n85, 215n29
21.36: 138, 208n102
21.38: 176n157
21.62–65: 169n75
21.72: 141
21.73–74: 141, 210n121
21.74: 209n119
21.75: 209n119
21.76: 141, 210n123
21.77–82: 99, 173n124, 196n20
21.81: 163n36
21.81–92: 211n143
21.103: 204n34
21.103–104: 177n187
21.104: 204n40
21.111: 172n113
21.114: 196n21
21.128: 194n178
21.136: 207n82
21.142: 133, 207n86
21.147: 138, 141, 209n103, 209n119
21.153: 202n3
21.155: 173n125
21.166: 202n3
21.175–180: 98
21.192: 206n66
21.205–208: 184n58
21.213: 207–208n87
21.220: 37
21.221: 150, 213n174
22: 178n191, 183n51, 195n6, 196n11, 198n44, 208n91
22.1: 161n3
22.3: 1, 161n1
22.27: 211n140
22.47: 206n63
22.54–55: 208n94, 213n172
23: 115, 183n51, 189n119, 189n126, 195n5, 195n6, 196n11, 196n13, 208n91
23.1: 115, 202n101
23.39: 210n127
23.54: 211n133

23.56: 177n183
23.80: 211n140, 211n141
23.187–188: 185n76
23.187–189: 115, 202n100
23.190: 202n101
24: 183n51, 195n6, 195n7, 196n11, 198n44, 200n70, 208n91
24.5: 206n63, 206n67
24.7: 161n3
24.8: 161n3, 203n19
24.14: 177n187
24.14–31: 64, 183n48
24.41–64: 64, 183n49
24.103–109: 183n40
24.149–151: 161n6
24.166–167: 208n94, 213n172
24.208: 212n154
24.224: 206n63
25: 68–69, 178n191, 196n11
25.4: 200n75, 206n63
25.5: 185n72, 206n70
25.6: 205n52
25.8: 185n72
25.13: 185n76
25.21: 185n74
25.36–39: 185n73
25.38: 202n99
25.39: 185n74
25.43–46: 179n207
25.44: 52
25.45: 185n74
25.47: 185n74
25.50: 185n72, 202n3
25.51: 185n74
25.58: 204n31
25.60–61: 185n72
25.60–62: 204n31
25.64: 185n74
25.65–66: 176n169
25.66: 63
25.76–77: 185n72
25.79: 179n207
25.80: 204n30
25.83: 185n74

Demosthenes (*continued*)
  25.91: 124–125
  25.95–96: 185n75
  26: 178n191
  27: 175n150
    27.41: 206n65, 206n70
    27.58: 206n70
  28: 175n150
  29: 175n150, 178n191, 179n204, 190n129
    29.22: 204n34, 207n76
    29.22–24: 178n193
    29.27: 204n34, 207n76
    29.39: 206n66
    29.58: 168n56
  30: 163n36, 175n150, 177n181
  31: 163n36, 175n150
  32: 164n47
    32.3: 206n63
    32.13: 206n63
  33: 164n47
    33.14–17: 168n56
    33.18: 167n43
  34: 164n47, 178n191
    34.4: 206n64, 206n70
    34.18: 168n56
    34.21: 168n56
    34.22: 206n63, 206n70
    34.40: 165n14
  35: 164n47
    35.3–4: 176n171
    35.5: 206n64
  36: 174n139, 175n150, 178n191, 182n26
    36.1: 178n192
    36.3: 206n63
    36.20: 176n171
    36.55: 194n78
  37: 61
    37.2: 182n28, 202n99
    37.3: 182n28
    37.8: 182n28
    37.13: 182n28
    37.17: 182n28
    37.18: 182n28
    37.19: 163n36
    37.21: 206n70
    37.23: 203n24
    37.24: 182n28
    37.25: 206n65, 206n70
    37.35: 182n28
    37.41: 182n28
    37.45: 61, 182n28
    37.48: 61, 178n193
    37.49: 182n28
    37.52: 182n28
    37.53: 182n28
  38: 175n150
    38.6: 176n171
    38.11: 206n65, 206n70
    38.14: 206n66
    38.19: 206n70
  39: 195n10, 198n44
    39.2: 177n187
    39.3: 202n3, 204n31
  40: 195n10, 198n44
    40.11: 167n43
    40.32: 203n24
    40.34: 163n36
    40.46: 168n48, 168n52, 176n165
    40.58: 204n31
    40.61: 206n66
  41: 107
    41.1: 168n45
    41.5–6: 175n150
    41.13: 207n82
    41.14: 168n45
    41.24: 183n50
    41.29: 168n56
  42: 164n46
  43: 173n124, 178n191
    43.10: 203n24
  44: 178n191
    44.31: 206n64
    44.63: 175n147
  47: 173n125, 179n204, 195n10, 198n44
    47.3: 206n64
    47.12: 167n43
    47.19: 175n156
    47.32: 176n171
    47.33–40: 211n144
    47.38: 211n143

INDEX LOCORUM   245

47.38–40: 211n144
47.41: 207n85
47.46: 206n63
47.60–61: 212n152
48: 195n10, 198n44
  48.3: 206n63
  48.56: 175n148
49.1: 176n171
51.1: 171n110
52.2: 206n66
54: 98, 99–102, 127, 138–139, 175n156, 196n16
  54.3–4: 197n27
  54.4: 101, 197n28
  54.4–5: 209n104
  54.7–9: 3, 100, 209n104
  54.8: 100, 196n24
  54.13: 206n66, 209n106
  54.13–14: 138
  54.16: 139, 209n110
  54.18–19: 142, 210n126
  54.20: 209n108
  54.25: 212n153, 212n155
  54.26: 206n66
  54.37: 65
  54.41: 101, 197n25
55: 176n171
  55.1: 175n151
  55.2: 206n70
  55.4–5: 202n99
  55.24–25: 209n114
  55.32: 168n44
  55.33–34: 203n24
  55.34: 178n188
56: 164n47
  56.48: 206n63
57: 54, 112–113
  57.1–17: 203n24
  57.2: 180n218
  57.7: 180n218, 206n64, 206n70
  57.8: 178n201, 201n87
  57.13: 180n218
  57.16: 180n218
  57.17: 180n218
  57.25: 180n5

57.30: 204n34
57.30–31: 180n5
57.32: 112, 201n87
57.33: 206n66
57.34: 112, 201n88
57.36: 180n5
57.45: 180n5
57.48: 201n86
57.49: 113, 201n90
57.51: 60, 182n22
57.53: 204n34
57.59: 180n218, 206n70
57.59–60: 113, 201n89
57.60: 206n64
57.60–61: 180n218
57.61: 112, 176n167, 201n86
57.63: 4, 45, 161n6, 174n137, 201n86, 206n66
57.66: 206n66

Demosthenes, Pseudo-
43.57: 187n92
45: 164n46, 175n150, 179n204
  45.1: 161n3, 203n19
  45.2: 206n64
  45.13: 206n66
  45.16: 206n70
  45.17–18: 206n66
  45.50: 206n60
  45.51: 206n70
46.14: 175n148
49: 195n10, 198n44
  49.6–32: 174n139
50: 173n125, 195n10, 196n14, 198n44, 199n55
  50.1: 199n55
52: 176n171, 190n129
  52.12–15: 174n139
  52.17: 178n193, 178n195
  52.21: 168n56
  52.30–31: 168n56
53: 71, 75–78, 123, 195n6, 195n7, 196n11
  53.1: 76, 161n3, 187n102, 190n133, 203n19
  53.1–2: 177n187, 187n105

Demosthenes, Pseudo- (*continued*)
53.2: 77, 188n106
53.4–13: 188n109
53.14: 177n187, 204n30
53.14–18: 77, 188n109
53.15: 179n204
53.16: 148–149, 213n168
53.17: 212n152
58: 195n6, 195n7
58.2: 161n3, 176n167, 203n19
58.4: 204n31
58.39–44: 124, 203n29
58.40: 204n39
58.41: 206n60, 206n63, 206n70
58.59: 178n199, 204n33
58.65: 148, 213n163
59: 71–75, 178n188, 178n191, 195n6, 195n7, 196n11
59.1: 72, 161n3, 203n19
59.1–10: 186n82
59.4: 72, 186n91
59.10: 177n187
59.12: 1, 73, 185n76, 187n93
59.15: 74, 187n95
59.16: 71
59.30–47: 176n157
59.46: 167n43, 168n48
59.45: 168n56
59.45–48: 168n56
59.48: 168n50
59.65: 176n158

Dinarchus
1: 178n191, 189n119, 189n126, 196n11, 196n13, 208n91
1.112: 52
1.113: 52
2: 178n191
3: 178n191
fr. 87.126 (Sauppe): 40, 171n102

Dionysius of Halicarnassus
On Demosthenes
13: 196n22

57: 185n70
On Lysias
19: 67, 185n69

Euripides
Bacchae
854: 169n79
877–880: 37
Cyclops
375–376: 210n125
Heracles Furens
286: 204n41
Heraclidae
939–940: 38
1000–1003: 177n176
Medea
920–921: 50
Orestes
804–806: 184n55
Suppliants
286: 204n41
343: 204n41
399–462: 19, 165n57
544–546: 177n176
614: 143, 210n128
Fragments
812.9: 184n55

Herodotus
1.59.3–5: 147, 213n161
1.60.2: 155, 214n7
1.61.1: 155, 214n7
3.44: 214n8
5.92: 214n8
8.79–81: 120, 203n7

Hesiod
Works and Days
27–41: 175n146

Homer
Iliad
2.211–277: 215n22
8.147–150: 170n83

18.108–110: 38
22.100: 170n83
23.287–650: 170n87
23.450–498: 170n96
23.535–585: 170n87

Hyperides
1: 178n191
2: 183n51, 190n129
3: 178n191
   3.1–5: 168n45
   3.5: 168n49, 168n50, 168n56
in Dem. fr. 3: 206n66

Inscriptiones Graecae
   I³ 104.20–23: 187n92
   II² 1177.22: 175n153
   II² 1629.190–204: 171n110

Isaeus
1: 164n46, 175n150
   1.2: 178n193
   1.7: 178n192
   1.9: 176n161
   1.31–32: 30, 167n34, 168n54, 168n55
   1.35: 168n45
   1.41: 206n63
   1.49: 206n66
   1.51: 168n45
2: 178n191, 190n129
   2.1: 175n148
   2.13: 177n172
   2.14: 175n148
   2.19: 175n148
   2.28–35: 168n45
   2.29–33: 168n56
   2.30: 168n44
   2.32: 168n49
   2.33: 178n193
   2.38: 168n45, 168n55
   2.40: 31
   2.47: 206n63
   3.3–4: 179n204
   3.3–5: 163n36

3.9: 202n99
3.11: 179n208
3.13: 176n157
3.19–22: 178n193
3.68: 177n172
3.72: 206n64, 206n70
4: 164n46, 178n191
   4.1: 178n192
   4.5: 206n67
   4.8–9: 175n147
5: 175n150, 195n10, 198n44
   5.8: 178n193
   5.10: 176n168
   5.12–13: 179n204
   5.22: 163n36
   5.26: 206n56
   5.31: 168n56
   5.36: 41, 171n109
   5.38: 172n111
   5.39: 204n40
   5.40: 174n139
6: 178n191
   6.2: 178n192
   6.50: 179n208
7: 164n46, 175n150
   7.1–2: 175n147
   7.10: 178n192
   7.11: 167n34, 167n40, 168n48
   7.44: 168n55
8: 164n46
   8.1: 179n208
   8.3: 177n187, 198n43
   8.7: 206n67
   8.15–16: 167n34, 168n54
   8.25–27: 202n99
   8.40–42: 204n40
9: 164n46
   9.20–21: 167n34
   9.21: 168n54
   9.24: 177n187
   9.25: 178n193
10: 164n46
   10.15–16: 176n171
   10.18: 206n64

Isaeus (continued)
    10.18–20: 202n100
11: 175n150, 190n129
    11.4: 204n34, 207n76
12: 178n191
    12.1: 178n193
    12.4: 178n193, 178n195
    12.8: 179n203, 201n83
    12.10: 204n30
    12.12: 174n137, 180n218, 204n40

Isocrates
1.33: 47
4.40: 143
5.7: 167n40
11.38: 204n39
16: 203n24
    16.2: 204n34, 207n76
    16.2–3: 176n167
    16.7: 177n187
    16.25: 184n59
    16.32–33: 171n109
    16.45: 134, 208n88
17: 174n139, 180n5, 195n10, 198n44
    17.1: 205n52, 207n76
    17.17–21: 168n45
    17.19–20: 167n42
    17.46: 188n111
18.6: 212n152
    18.6–8: 168n53
    18.28: 36
    18.58: 194n178
20: 196n16, 205n46
    20.2: 142, 210n127
    20.5: 206n65
    20.18: 206n63
21: 178n191, 195n10, 198n44
    21.1: 178n192
    21.6: 206n64
    21.8: 180n218

Lycurgus
1: 79–80, 85, 107, 109, 127–128, 189n119, 195n5, 195n6, 196n11, 196n13, 200n70, 208n91
    1.1–2: 189n121
    1.3–4: 199n65
    1.5: 79, 189n122, 199n54, 199n56
    1.5–6: 199n65
    1.6: 79, 189n124
    1.11–13: 206n57
    1.19: 202n3, 204n31
    1.39: 189n125
    1.58: 202n3
    1.63: 206n66
    1.91: 206n64
    1.138: 178n192, 178n197
    1.149: 206n66

Lysias
1: 55–57, 89–90, 102, 128, 140, 143, 176n158, 183n37, 196n16
    1.4: 194n168
    1.6–7: 56
    1.10: 56
    1.11–14: 56
    1.20: 209n117
    1.43: 57, 90, 180n8, 194n170
    1.43–44: 30, 167n35
    1.43–45: 175n156
    1.44: 90, 194n171
    1.44–46: 56
    1.45: 90, 194n172
2.19: 210n129
3: 103, 108–109, 176n157, 183n37, 196n16
    3.4: 139–140, 209n112, 209n113
    3.6: 209n104
    3.15: 203n24
    3.16: 212n152
    3.18: 137, 208n100
    3.20: 197n37
    3.28–39: 199n59
    3.39: 197n37
    3.45–46: 206n57
4: 102, 140, 173n124, 196n16, 197n34, 199n61
    4.1–4: 168n45
    4.1–5: 32
    4.2: 168n56
    4.4: 199n61

4.6–7: 199n61
4.13: 166n17
5: 178n191
　5.1: 178n192
　5.5: 204n30
6: 89, 178n191
　6.7: 167n28
　6.31: 14
　6.41: 89, 193n165
7: 104–105, 183n37
　7.1: 197n40
　7.2–3: 189n127
　7.3: 104, 197n41
　7.8: 202n99
　7.16: 204n30
　7.18: 175n151, 212n156
　7.19: 204n33
　7.20: 104, 197n41, 197n42, 202n102
　7.20–21: 202n99
　7.39: 104, 197n41
　7.39–40: 105, 172n114, 177n187, 198n43
　7.42: 202n99
8: 47–48
　8.1–6: 167n28
　8.14–17: 204n40
　8.18: 178n194, 204n30
　8.19: 35
9: 82–84
　9.1–2: 206n66
　9.1–3: 190n134, 194n178, 204n34, 204n40, 208n88
　9.3: 190n130
　9.4–7: 83
　9.5: 190n130
　9.6: 190n131, 204n30
　9.6–10: 204n35
　9.8–12: 83, 191n138
　9.11: 190n131
　9.13: 83–84, 191n139
　9.13–18: 191n140
　9.14: 120, 190n130, 191n143, 202n6
　9.15: 190n130, 191n140
　9.16: 84, 191n141, 191n142
　9.19: 191n141

9.20: 131, 191n143, 207n72
9.22: 131, 207n73, 208n89
10: 125–126
　10.3: 126, 176n167, 204n36
　10.5: 204n36
　10.9: 204n36
　10.12: 179n204, 204n36
　10.13: 161n3, 203n19
　10.21: 204n36
　10.22: 179n204, 204n36
　10.24–25: 179n204, 204n36
12: 105–106, 110, 195n6, 196n11, 196n13, 196n16
　12.2: 105, 122, 198n46, 203n18
　12.2–3: 161n3, 203n19
　12.23: 191n141, 210n122
　12.36: 177n177
　12.50–79: 184n58
　12.66–67: 167n28
13: 110, 178n191, 195n6, 196n11, 196n13, 196n16, 198n48
　13.1: 161n3, 198n48, 203n19
　13.3: 204n31
　13.42–43: 49, 50, 177n174, 177n179
　13.65–68: 179n208
　13.83–84: 202n100
　13.88: 206n67
　13.91: 183n40
　13.92: 177n179
14: 178n191, 195n6
　14.2: 161n3, 176n167, 203n19, 203n21
　14.16: 206n67, 206n70
　14.17: 184n59
　14.19: 167n28
　14.20: 178n192
　14.22: 178n197, 189n122
　14.30: 177n177
　14.39–40: 184n59
　14.40: 176n169
　14.41: 171n102
15: 178n191, 195n6
　15.5: 178n193
　15.10: 167n28
　15.12: 28
16: 164n48, 183n37

Lysias (*continued*)
  16.1: 204n34
  16.3: 172n113, 205n52
  16.11: 172n113, 204n40
  16.13: 171n102
17: 164n46
  17.1–3: 176n171
18.9: 204n34
  18.24: 178n194, 190n129
19.1: 176n171, 205n52
  19.1–3: 204n34
  19.2: 124, 203.23
  19.2–6: 204n40
  19.11: 203n23
  19.18: 171n106
  19.24–27: 175n150
  19.53: 204n34, 207n76
  19.56: 183n41
  19.60: 202n99, 204n39
  19.61: 184n63
  19.64: 208n89
20: 177n181, 178n191, 190n129
  20.3: 208n94
  20.11: 204n40
  20.13: 170n95
  20.28–29: 184n59
  20.30: 204n34, 204n40
  20.33: 175n150
21.8: 171n106, 189n126
  21.12: 171n106, 205n52
  21.17: 112, 178n192, 200n81
22: 189n119, 195n6, 196n11, 196n13, 200n70, 208n91
  22.2–4: 185n76
  22.8: 202n3
  22.14–15: 166n17
  22.22: 200n75
  22.63: 202n3
23.1: 206n64
  23.4: 204n31
  23.5: 188n108
  23.7–8: 204n31
24: 164n48
  24.6: 175n150
  24.7: 204n33
  24.14: 175n145
  24.27: 203n24
25: 111–112, 164n48, 185n79
  25.1–6: 200n76
  25.5: 204n34, 207n76
  25.10: 171n102
  25.25–26: 200n76
  25.30–32: 200n76
26: 164n48, 189n119, 189n126, 195n6, 208n91
  26.9: 206n63
  26.15: 172n113, 206n64, 206n70
  26.21: 184n58
  26.23–24: 178n197
27: 178n191, 189n119, 189n126, 196n11, 196n13, 200n70, 208n91
  27.8: 132, 200n75, 207n78, 207n79
  27.12: 178n192
  27.13: 178n197
  27.16: 205n52
28.4: 172n120
29.1: 182n22, 204n30, 204n31, 204n32
  29.3: 172n117
  29.4: 172n120
30.7: 194n178
  30.31–35: 178n197
31: 109–110, 164n48, 189n119, 189n126, 195n6, 196n11, 196n13, 208n91
  31.1: 203n9
  31.2: 172n113, 189n123
  31.2–4: 200n75
  31.4: 109–110, 200n69
  31.23: 183n42
32: 177n181, 178n191, 195n10, 198n44
  32.2: 168n45, 168n56
  32.11: 168n56
  32.22: 176n168
  32.24: 172n118
fr. 1.3–4 (Carey): 175n151
fr. 50 (Carey): 176n171
fr. 151 (Carey): 199n57
fr. 174 (Carey): 175n150
fr. 279.2–3 (Carey): 168n56

fr. 423 (Carey): 66, 184n67
fr. 443 (Carey): 180n4

Menander
Dyscolus
  59–60: 175n156
  561–562: 168n54
  613–614: 168n54
Samia
  13–14: 171n108
  340–341: 175n156
  518: 50, 177n184
  706: 169n79

Pindar
Pythian Odes
  8.83–87: 39, 170n93

Plato
Apology
  18b–20d: 35
  33c–34b: 180n217
Charmides
  161d: 30, 167n36
Gorgias
  469d: 147
  480e–481b: 38
Laches
  188c–189c: 184n63
Laws
  3.678e–679c: 174n140
  5.737b: 174n140
  5.739c: 177n185
  5.744c: 171n103
  8.843b–c: 47
  11.915d–916a: 174n140
  11.928d–e: 175n145
  11.933b: 34, 168n61
Lysis
  213a–b: 166n25
Meno
  71e: 167n28
Phaedrus
  271d–272c: 181n13

  272e: 182n21
  273b: 181n13
  273b–c: 181n16
Philebus
  49d: 169n77
Republic
  1.343e: 202n3
  2.358e–359b: 215n27
  3.417b: 174n140
  4.424a: 177n185
  4.426e: 174n140
  5.464d–e: 158, 174n140, 215n23
  5.470b: 148, 213n164
  7.521a: 174n140
  8.549d: 174n140
  8.549e: 177n173
  8.554c: 175n150
  8.562d–563a: 213n169

Plutarch
Concerning Talkativeness
  5 (504c): 58
Life of Alcibiades
  16.4: 209n103
Life of Aristides
  4.1: 189n127
  8.1–4: 120, 203n7
  25.3: 206n66
  25.7: 120, 203n7
Life of Nicias
  3.2: 171n106
Life of Pericles
  10.7: 62, 173n130

Poetae Comici Graeci
  362.7: 184n64

Quintilian
Institutio Oratoria
  194n174

Sophocles
Ajax
  79: 169n79

Sophocles (*continued*)
   770–777: 176n162
   1334–1335: 150–151, 213n175
Antigone
   641–643: 49
   647: 169n79
Electra
   1153: 169n79
Oedipus Rex
   583–591: 60

Supplementum Epigraphicum Graecum
   40.265: 179n209
   42.217: 179n209
   44.226: 179n211
   47.274: 172n142

Theophrastus
Characters
   5.3: 168n44
   15: 176n162

Thucydides
   1.6.3: 212n158, 215n20
     1.44.1: 168n48
   2.37: 202n2, 210n129, 212n156
   3.70–85: 202n1
   6.54–59: 176n157
     6.56.2: 147, 212n158
   7: 62
     7.68.1: 169n81

Vergil
Aeneid
   5.348–349: 170n87

Wünsch, *Defixionum Tabellae*
   25: 179n211
   34: 173n132
   35: 30
   37: 180n220
   38: 53, 179n211, 179n212
   39: 53, 179n209, 179n210, 180n220
   45: 173n132
   52: 174n142
   57: 180n220
   59: 179n214
   63: 179n211
   65: 179n211
   66: 179n209
   67: 180n220
   68: 174n142, 179n211, 179n214
   69: 174n142, 179n214
   71: 174n142
   73: 174n142
   74: 174n142
   75: 174n142, 180n220
   77: 179n214
   79: 180n220
   81: 179n209
   83: 180n220
   84: 174n142, 179n214
   86: 174n142
   87: 174n142
   88: 179n209
   94: 174n142, 179n211, 180n220
   95: 179n211
   97: 174n142
   102: 179n214
   103: 179n209, 180n220
   106: 179n209
   107: 54, 179n209, 180n221
   109: 174n142
   129: 179n209

Xenophon
Constitution of the Spartans
   4.3–4: 170n95
   4.5–6: 215n21
   8.2: 160, 215n30
Hellenika
   2.3: 155, 214n9
   2.3.38–44: 155, 214n10
   5.4.24–33: 215n19
Hieron
   1.34: 37
Memorabilia
   1.1.18: 120, 203n9
   2.1.3: 45

2.1.19: 169n78
2.6.4: 34
2.9.5: 177n187, 204n31
3.4: 35–36
3.13.1: 176n162
Oeconomicus
  2.4–6: 172n118

Xenophon, Pseudo-
Constitution of the Athenians
  1.10: 149, 213n169
  1.13: 171n106

www.ingramcontent.com/pod-product-compliance
Lightning Source LLC
Chambersburg PA
CBHW021852230426
43671CB00006B/365